Enhancing Health Services Management

Health Services Management

Series Editors:

Chris Ham, Health Services Management Centre, University of Birmingham
Chris Heginbotham, Chief Executive, East and North Hertfordshire Health Authority

The British National Health Service is one of the biggest and most complex organizations in the developed world. Employing around one million people and accounting for £36 billion of public expenditure, the service is of major concern to both the public and politicians. Management within the NHS faces a series of challenges in ensuring that resources are deployed efficiently and effectively. The challenges include the planning and management of human resources, the integration of professionals into the management process, and making sure that services meet the needs of patients and the public.

Against this background, the Health Services Management series addresses the many issues and practical problems faced by people in managerial roles in health services.

Current and forthcoming titles

Judith Allsop and Linda Mulcahy: *Regulating Medical Work: Formal and Informal Controls*
Steve Cropper and Paul Forte (eds): *Enhancing Health Services Management: The Role of Decision Support Systems*
Steve Harrison: *Managing Health Services: A Basic Text*
Valerie Iles: *Really Managing Health Care*
Richard Joss and Maurice Kogan: *Advancing Quality: Total Quality Management in the National Health Service*
Justin Keen (ed.): *Information Management in Health Services*
Maurice Kogan, Sally Redfern *et al.*: *Making Use of Clinical Audit: A Guide to Practice in the Health Professions*
Gordon Marnoch: *Doctors and Management in the National Health Service*
John Øvretveit: *Purchasing for Health*

Enhancing Health Services Management

The role of decision support systems

Edited by
Steve Cropper and Paul Forte

Open University Press
Buckingham · Philadelphia

Open University Press
Celtic Court
22 Ballmoor
Buckingham
MK18 1XW

and
1900 Frost Road, Suite 101
Bristol, PA 19007, USA

First Published 1997

A catalogue record of this book is available from the British Library

ISBN 0 335 19634 9 (pb) 0 335 19635 7 (hb)

Library of Congress Cataloging-in-Publication Data
Enhancing decision making in the National Health Service: the role of decision support systems / edited by Steve Cropper, Paul Forte.
p. cm. – (Health services management series)
Includes bibliographical references and index.
ISBN 0-335-19635-7 (hc). – ISBN 0-335-19634-9 (pbk.)
1. Health services administration – Great Britain – Decision making.
2. National Health Service (Great Britain) – Administration.
3. Decision support systems. I. Cropper, Steve, 1957–
II. Forte, Paul, 1957– . III. Series.
RA395.G6E54 1997
362.1'0941–dc21 96-51488
CIP

Copy-editing and typesetting by The Running Head Limited, London and Cambridge
Printed in Great Britain by Biddles Ltd, Guildford and King's Lynn

Contents

Notes on contributors ix
Foreword by Professor Alan Wilson xv
Acknowledgements xvii
Permissions xviii
Preface xix

Part 1 Context and definition 1

1 **The context of decision making in the NHS** 3
Steve Cropper and Paul Forte
Introduction: NHS management and decision making complexity 3
The changing context of NHS decision making 4
Theories of decision making 7
Decision making domains: investments in the NHS 11
Concluding remarks 16

2 **The nature of decision support systems** 19
Steve Cropper and Paul Forte
Introduction 19
Defining 'decision support systems' 19
The definition of DSS expanded 22
Evaluating the contribution of DSS 29
DSS design 30
Concluding remarks 33

Part 2 Strategic service planning 37
Introduction 39

3 **Spatial decision support systems for health care planning** 43
Graham Clarke and Martin Clarke
Introduction 43
The geography of health care reforms 44
Geographical information systems in the NHS 46
Linking models with geographical information systems 54
Conclusions: towards a research agenda in applied medical geography 65

4 **Improving the balance of elderly care services** 71
Paul Forte and Tom Bowen
Introduction 71
Planning long-term care for elderly people 71
The Balance of Care approach and system 75
Applications of the Balance of Care approach 78
Concluding remarks 82

5 **Activity and capacity planning in an acute hospital** 86
Tom Bowen and Paul Forte
Introduction 86
Developing a business planning capacity 88
The Business Planning Model 89
Application of the Business Planning Model 93
The business planning game 100
Concluding remarks 102

6 **Capital investment appraisal in the NHS** 103
Tim Keenan
Introduction 103
Decision support for capital investment appraisal 105
Stage 1: the case for change 107
Stage 2: option appraisal 113
Stage 3: identify the optimal method of financing the project 118
Concluding remarks 121

Part 3 Operational service planning and management 123
Introduction 125

7 **Decision support in primary care** 128
Paul Bradley
Introduction 128
Decision support in the consultation 133
Decision support in practice management 138
Decision support beyond the practice 141
Concluding remarks 143

8 **The MatS maternity staffing model** 145
Patricia Meldrum, Sara Twaddle, Patricia Purton and Barbara MacLennan
Introduction 145
The management problem: planning maternity care services 145
Benefits of a modelling approach 147
Developing a maternity staffing model 148
Applying the model 152
Implications of the results 161
Conclusions 162
Appendix: Royal College of Midwives definitions 164

9 **A decision support system for planning continuity of midwifery services** 165
Roger Beech, Alicia Mejia and Rabia Shirazi
Introduction 165
The management task: planning for continuity of care 166
Alternative responses to guidelines on continuity 166
The development of a DSS for planning continuity of maternity care 167
Model inputs 168
Model analysis and outputs 170
Validation of the model 170
Using the model to plan and test service changes 170
Concluding remarks 175

10 **Queue management: what has a DSS approach to offer to improve the running of outpatient clinics?** 177
Dave Worthington
Introduction 177
Queue management problems 178
DSS approaches 180
Applications of DSS approaches to health service queues 181
Case study 1: plaster check clinics 184
Case study 2: ophthalmology clinics 189
Discussion 194
Conclusions 195

11 **Decision support systems in neurosciences: measurement and analysis of clinical activity** 199
Peter D. Lees and Lisa Macfarlane
Introduction 199
Resource management issues in a clinical directorate 200
Methodology 201
Using the DSS for resource management 203
Discussion and conclusions 208

Part 4 Policy and organizational learning 213
Introduction 215

12 **A management flight simulator for community care** 217
Eric Wolstenholme and John Crook
Introduction 217
Community care – the management task 218
System dynamics modelling – the rationale 219
System dynamics – the method 221
System dynamics and community care 224
Conclusions 243

13 **Decision support in objective-setting, monitoring and review** 245
Steve Cropper
Introduction 245
A DSS approach to objective-setting, monitoring and review 247
A personal DSS for project management 249
A group DSS: preparing for a review of Trust strategic direction 256
A DSS for IPR objective-setting, monitoring and review 260
Conclusions 265

Part 5 Future prospects 269
Introduction 271

14 **Future prospects: issues, informatics and methodologies** 272
David Clayden and Martyn Croft
Introduction 272
The use of information 273
The use of technology 276
Implementing information support 278
Future prospects 280

15 **Conclusions** 287
Paul Forte and Steve Cropper
Introduction 287
Variety in DSS 287
Who uses DSS? 293
The experience of using DSS 294
Future agenda 296

Index 299

Notes on contributors

Roger Beech is Senior Research Fellow in Operational Research at the Department of Public Health Medicine, United Medical and Dental Schools, St Thomas' Campus (University of London). Much of his published research concerns health service planning and management, costing and resource allocation. His doctoral research concerned the information needs of health planners.

Tom Bowen is an independent consultant in Healthcare Planning and Information Systems. He has degrees in both mathematics and operational research and, for several years, worked in the Department of Health Operational Research Service. There he was closely involved with the development of decision support systems, including an expert system for performance monitoring.

This interest led to a move to Brighton Health Care NHS Trust, where, as Assistant Director of Information and Contracting, he was responsible for all analytical and IT services, and for contract management.

His current consultancy interests include both information strategy and business analysis, with a particular focus on the use of decision support systems both for management development, and to drive the development of management information systems.

Paul Bradley qualified from Leeds University Medical School in 1978 and, after vocational training, became a principal in general practice in Chester. As a general practitioner he has had a long-term interest in the application of information management and technology in supporting the delivery of high quality and effective primary health care through the development of management information systems. He has previously held the post of Chairman of the Primary Health Care Specialist Group of the British Computer Society and was Associate Adviser in

Information Technology in the Department of Postgraduate General Practice at the University of Liverpool. He has recently taken up a post as Senior Lecturer in the Department of Healthcare Education at the University of Liverpool.

Graham Clarke is a senior lecturer in geography at the School of Geography, University of Leeds, specializing in urban services, GIS and spatial modelling. He is co-author of *Modelling the City* (Routledge, London, 1994); *GIS for Business and Service Planning* (Geoinformation, Cambridge, 1995); *Intelligent GIS: Location Decisions and Strategic Planning* (Geoinformation, Cambridge, 1996); and *Microsimulation for Urban and Regional Policy Analysis* (Pion, London, 1996).

Martin Clarke is Professor of Spatial Decision Support Systems at the School of Geography, University of Leeds. He is also Managing Director of GMAP Ltd, a company specializing in the application of geographical modelling methods. He has worked on applications of systems modelling health care in London, East Midlands and West Yorkshire in the UK, and the Piemonte region of north-west Italy. He is author of *Planning and Analysis in Health Care Systems* (Pion, London, 1984); and co-author of *Intelligent GIS: Location Decisions and Strategic Planning* (Geoinformation, Cambridge, 1996).

David Clayden was educated at London University and the University of East Anglia. For his PhD he carried out original research on the North Atlantic codfish, producing what would now be called a DSS to enable better understanding of international fish stock management.

He then first worked for a local authority on the planning of transportation networks, and subsequently researched and lectured in universities for more than 20 years on the application of medical statistics and personal computers to health and health care. A strong belief in the use of simulation exercises to integrate quantitative and qualitative aspects of problems led to the development and application in health services internationally of a number of operational research models.

With the restructuring of the NHS, he became the Director of Information Services for a large NHS Trust hospital, and now acts as an information consultant to organizations, within and outside health care, which are undergoing IT-associated organizational change. His major focus is to improve information management through education and training and the understanding and effective application of better business processes.

He is author of many research papers and contributor to a number of books, and is the current chairman of the European Working Group on Operations Research applied to Health Services.

Martyn Croft has worked in a variety of posts in the business, academic and service worlds. He cut his software 'teeth' on SPSS, and has researched and published papers on, among others, the use of expert systems to support statistical advisers.

He has worked in hospitals both as a medical laboratory scientist and as an information services specialist. His overall focus has been to ensure that information systems provide efficient management of data to aid the organization as well as the individual.

He has been responsible for the design and implementation of a number of health care information systems. Projects as staff member and as a consultant have included executive information systems, relational database design, migration to client server architecture and the effective use of corporate intranets.

John Crook graduated from Birmingham University with a degree in Economics and initially worked as a Research Officer in Lancashire Children's Department. He has a Masters degree from the LSE and a professional social work qualification. He practised social work and became Director of Social Services in Bradford in 1977, remaining there until December 1994. For two years, 1988–90, he was Director of a combined Department of Social Services, Housing and Environmental Health. In January 1995 he founded a consultancy service – Planning and Care Management Services (PCMS) – and has undertaken consultancies in strategic planning, management and information, and community care for national organizations and government departments.

Steve Cropper is Senior Lecturer in Management at the Centre for Health Planning and Management, Keele University. He has a degree and PhD in town and regional planning. Between 1983 and 1991, he worked at Sussex and Strathclyde universities developing and applying problem structuring, decision support and group decision support methods. His current research and consultancy work is mainly in the field of health services organization and management, and includes inter-agency collaborative working, strategic management and decision support.

Paul Forte holds a part-time appointment as Lecturer in the Centre for Health Planning and Management, Keele University, and is an independent health planning and management consultant. His PhD was on the development of a specialty costing model. He worked four years in health services research at the University of Leeds, followed by six years with the Department of Health Operational Research Service. Throughout this time his research and consultancy interests have been on decision support systems development, with a particular focus on their application.

Tim Keenan is a Director of Secta, a specialist health care management consultancy. He has a BComm degree from the University of Liverpool and is also a qualified accountant. With Secta, and previously with Coopers and Lybrand, Tim provides consultancy support to health authorities and Trusts in the fields of strategic planning, economic investment appraisal and, more recently, private finance.

Peter D. Lees graduated at Manchester (1975), completed his surgical training at Leicester and Nottingham (FRCS 1981) and his neurosurgical training at Derby and Southampton (MS 1990). Currently he is Senior Lecturer and Honorary Consultant Neurosurgeon, Southampton (1989) and was Clinical Director of Neurosciences (1993–5). He has a major clinical interest in pituitary disease and provides the pituitary surgery service to the former Wessex region.

Peter has much operational medical management experience and a wide-ranging management research interest. He became Trust Director of Research and Development in 1995 and is the Chairman elect of the British Association of Medical Managers (BAAM). The book *Navigating the NHS – Core Issues for Clinicians*, which he edited, has just been published.

His other roles include Director of Healthcare Analysis Research Unit (resource profiling), Specialty Working Group Leader (development of HRGs in neurosurgery), Honorary Senior Research Fellow (National Casemix), member of Culyer Information Working Group (1995), and a member of the Efficiency Scrutiny Team, which presented a report on the burdens of paperwork in the NHS, Trust and health authorities to the Cabinet Office in 1996.

Lisa Macfarlane MBA, BA Hons, Cert. Health Econ. is currently Projects Manager for the Healthcare Analysis Research Centre, a collaborative research group set up between Southampton University Hospitals Trust, Southampton University and Wessex Institute of Public Health Medicine.

Lisa joined the NHS in 1984. In a range of information-related roles she developed expertise in managing change, systems implementation, data management, analysis and interpretation. As Director of Information and IT at Parkside Health Authority, Lisa was responsible for developing and implementing operational information systems for purchasing implementation of the national IM&T strategy.

Further roles have included Acting Head of Purchasing Development at Wessex RHA in 1993, and Community Care Coordinator at Southampton Health Commission.

Barbara MacLennan has experience in managing midwifery services at operational and strategic levels through her current post as Midwifery Adviser to Greater Glasgow Health Board and previously as Unit Nurse with overall responsibility for all five Glasgow maternity units. Her vision of the future service is to enable stakeholders to work together to make best use of resources. Barbara believes the profession will develop by empowering young midwives and developing their keen minds to continue to seek new models of care, which will give a quality service to women.

Alicia Mejia holds an MSc in operational research and a PhD in simulation. She lectured in electronics engineering for over 12 years and has been involved in research in the health area since 1993: research topics have included follow-up of patients with ankylosing spondylitis, sicklecell modelling, midwifery planning and, more recently, stroke care modelling.

Patricia Meldrum has been involved in health services research for eight years, both in academic departments and in a service department. She has been employed by Greater Glasgow Health Board for over four years, most recently as Research and Development Officer. Patricia's background is in health economics, but she has worked on a variety of projects, many in women's health. Her current research is in the area of community care.

Patricia Purton has been Director of the Royal College of Midwives Scottish Board since May 1992. For the previous five years she held the post of Midwifery Services Manager for the Raigmore Maternity Unit and was Supervisor of Midwives for the Local Supervising Authority of Highland Health Board. Since commencing work with the RCM Patricia has sought to focus on supporting midwives in all spheres of College activity. The issues which her work covers are those of professional activity; the enhancement of midwifery practice; the development of educational programmes accessible and appropriate to the profession; and industrial relations matters, which may be on an individual or collective basis. She is also active in research projects and maintains close link with other professional, governmental and statutory bodies.

Rabia Shirazi holds an MSc in operational research from the LSE and undertook project work in the area of maternity services and continuity of care. She is currently undertaking research at Cambridge University towards a PhD in scheduling.

Sara Twaddle has worked in the NHS for eight years, initially as a health economist and latterly as a purchasing commissioner for women's acute services. Sara's research interests lie mainly in the field of women's health, and she has recently completed a PhD on the economic implications of alternative forms of care in obstetrics.

Eric Wolstenholme is Professor of 21st Century Business Learning at Leeds Metropolitan University Business School and is a director of COGNITUS, a consultancy company specializing in system dynamics training and consultancy. He holds a Bachelors degree and a Doctorate in engineering from Nottingham University, and a Masters degree in operational research from Brunel University. He has headed management science departments at Bradford and Stirling universities and worked for British Coal in Operational Research and Purchasing Management. He is a past president of the Systems Dynamics Society and has a national and international reputation in the application of systems thinking and dynamic modelling, including consultancy experience with government and private industry. His publications include two books, *A System Dynamics Approach* and *The Evaluation of Management Information Systems – a Dynamic and Holistic Approach*, both published by Wiley.

Dr Dave Worthington trained as a mathematician and then as an operational researcher/statistician specializing in health and social services. After working for three years in the UK's National Health Service he took up his present post on the faculty of the Department of Management Science, Lancaster University. Research interests include the application of management science methods to health service problems and the development and application of 'useful' queueing models, particularly for queues which exhibit time-dependent behaviour. In a health system in which queues abound these two interests often combine!

Foreword

I very much welcome this book. Perhaps I can be allowed to offer a personal perspective? My own career in the social sciences began in the 1960s in a research team which was working on cost-benefits analysis in the transport sector. This was clearly a powerful tool for public sector planning and decision making in transport – and indeed any other sector involving major investment. It became clear at the outset, however, that the analytical requirements were stringent: it was necessary to have a capability to predict the consequences of alternative investments (and the 'do nothing' scenario) and this, to say the least, was a non-trivial task. This need fuelled the development of predictive models in a variety of social science disciplines, including those like health services' studies, which were essentially interdisciplinary.

As a complement to what was basically a strategic perspective, there was another more operational strand of work which thrived in the 1960s (which had its roots in the Second World War): *operational research*. Again, the focus was the application of appropriate and powerful analytical techniques to problems in both industry and the public services.

The promise of 30 years ago has not been fully delivered – and yet the need is more urgent than ever. The ideas have not been incorporated sufficiently deeply into education and training. The health services in the UK – and indeed their equivalents in all other countries – involve enormous expenditure and investment. A small percentage improvement in the benefits which can be achieved from improved planning and decision making could generate many millions of pounds of 'value' for patients. The researchers and practitioners who continue to carry this banner, under the heading of decision support systems, deserve support, both in resource terms and from policy makers and politicians at the highest levels.

Researchers and practitioners from diverse backgrounds are represented here, each with extensive experience of developing and applying management decision support systems. They point the way forward – showing how the developments of the past 30 years provide secure platforms for future work. They demonstrate this through a case study approach at both strategic and operational levels; they also draw on the full variety of kinds of practice in the health service. In addition to pointing up the role of decision support as a means of policy and organizational learning, they are also right to focus – throughout the book – on organizational development, because change will be needed to take full advantage of the power of decision support systems which is now available. The presentations in this book should influence both practitioners and students – the future generation of practitioners.

Health services research is coming of age. The Calman Report on Cancer Care illustrates the implementation of research-led policy. It should help to reduce the present considerable inequities in the provision of cancer treatment and demonstrates the feasibility of more developments of this kind. It is significant that this initiative has been led personally by the Chief Medical Officer. The examples of this book, coupled with the ongoing teaching and training programmes which are needed, will help to drive this process forward.

Alan Wilson
Vice-Chancellor's Office
University of Leeds

Acknowledgements

The support and encouragement given to us by our friends and family in the preparation of this book has been very important to us. Special thanks are due to Professor Kenneth Lee, our colleagues at the Centre for Health Planning and Management, Keele University and to participants on the MBA Health Executive programme. Over the years, they have inspired (and occasionally frustrated) our attempts to explain what decision support systems are and why they matter: their contributions have helped to shape the perspectives presented here.

The European Working Group on Operational Research Applied to Health Services, a group of researchers and practitioners from across Europe (and beyond!) has also provided a useful – and convivial – forum for ideas. Geoff Royston, Mårten Lagergren, Duncan Boldy and Jan Vissers all deserve special mention for this.

Finally, a special thank you to Liz Cropper, whose forbearance of the whole exercise was above and beyond the call of duty.

Permissions

Figures 10.6, 10.7, and 10.8 are reproduced by kind permission of the International Journal of Health Care Quality Assurance and are taken from Worthington, D. and Brahimi, M. (1993) Improving out-patient appointment systems, *IJHCQA*, 6: 18–23.

The Appendix to Chapter 8 is included with the kind permission of Churchill Livingstone, Edinburgh, and is taken from P. Meldrum, P. Purton, B. MacLennan and S. Twaddle (1994) Moving to-wards a common definition for maternity services; standard definitions for common terms, *Midwifery*, 10: 165–70.

Preface

This book explores and illustrates how planning and decision making in health services can be enhanced through the use of decision support systems (DSS). It draws specifically on DSS experience in the UK National Health Service (NHS), but we believe the approaches used and the lessons learned have wider applicability.

The idea for this book arose from our experience of teaching operations management and management science to health service managers and professionals on the MBA (Health Executive) and other programmes at the Centre for Health Planning and Management, Keele University. A general frustration was a lack of any recent book bringing together examples of DSS in health service management. It had been 15 years since Duncan Boldy edited a collection of applications of operational research techniques in health services. We knew that contemporary DSS existed, but pressures of time on practitioners to write up accounts of how or why they used particular methods and what made them work (or not) meant that their use often went unrecorded.

Several of the book's contributors have presented on the programmes and we have drawn extensively on this resource. All have experience of developing and using decision support systems in planning and management applications in the health service.

A second reason for the book is to highlight DSS as an item for debate. It is timely to reassess the place and potential of these systems, particularly as technological capacity and the management agenda are increasingly closely linked. So, why are management decision support systems not more widely recognized or used? They may be in all but name. First, the mass availability of powerful software and computers means that many health service managers will have access to the basic resources needed for a DSS approach. Second, there is no lack of crucial management issues. Two of the conditions in which DSS should flourish are therefore in place. The third condition is a management awareness of the DSS way of thinking and an organizational environment which supports such thinking – it may be that this is what is lacking. Our aim, then, is to provide insight into the DSS approach, illustrated, warts and all, in ways which should give the idea immediacy and life.

A focus for the book

Reference to 'decision support systems' is often rather wide-ranging. In the health services field, clinical decision support is the predominant field of development and application. A literature search on Medline (an on-line health bibliography) using the search words 'decision support' produced a list of over 7,300 papers covering such varied topics as evidence-based medicine, consensus conferences, clinical protocols and pathways, and informatics (including clinical support systems and computer-based networks). A search on the key words 'management decision support', however, reduced this to 940; a further refinement, 'health services management decision support', reduced this still further to barely 100. While clinical decision support is clearly an important domain for DSS, nevertheless it is only one potential application field, so here we try to redress the balance by concentrating on ways in which they can contribute to decision making in non-clinical areas of health service management.

To help sharpen our focus still further, we concentrate on computer-based DSS. Computers are now on virtually every manager's desk. They enable more varied forms of support and offer greater speed, power and flexibility of analysis than were found even five years ago. In short, technological and economic barriers preventing take-up of DSS have been so dismantled that they are no longer the issue. However, this book is *not* about IT or information systems, or about information management. Both of these topics are specifically and comprehensively addressed elsewhere in the Open University Press titles: *Managing Health Service Information Systems* (edited by Sheaff and Peel, 1995) and *Information Management in Health Services* (edited by Keen, 1994).

The intention of this book is to provide a working definition of DSS as they are used in health services planning and management, and a view of DSS in practice. Our definition – set out in Chapter 2 – emphasizes combinations of information, analytical method and computer power designed and applied to provide help in addressing specific management tasks. This is illustrated in detail with case studies drawn from a wide variety of application areas in the health service.

The future potential for these types of systems is also considered. Because much effort has gone into development and implementation of information systems, it is easy to emphasize the importance of computing power and the applications that it can support. DSS often use only quite basic computing technology and the concept of decision support is founded more on the analytical and decision-orientated *use* of information.

This book brings together case studies covering the development and application of computer-based DSS. Each chapter begins with a significant management task and examines why a DSS approach is applicable. The theories, methods and techniques underlying the DSS are explained and then illustrated with a case study or illustrations of their use in practice. Most are tried and tested; for the others which have only very recently been developed, their full potential is only now being explored.

Who this book is for

The book is intended to appeal to health service managers, professionals and students who should find the mix of theory, method and practice of help in understanding the potential contribution of decision support systems to management. It may also be of interest to computer or information professionals, but it is targeted primarily at those who are interested in understanding how information technologies can be applied to support the conduct of management.

We assume no specialist knowledge from the reader. The style of presentation is essentially non-technical, and the case study illustrations are intended to show how the systems discussed have been created in response to practical agendas.

How to read this book

Readers may prefer to dip into the book rather than to read it from cover to cover, particularly if one or other of the case studies is of especial interest.

To assist in this we have divided it into five Parts. Three of these introduce the case studies. Part 2 includes DSS which support strategic planning tasks – understanding the spatial distribution and effects of health services, planning services and service capacity, undertaking investment appraisal. Part 3 illustrates the use of DSS in operational planning and management – in general practice, in maternity services, in outpatients clinics and other service systems and in resource management at the Clinical Directorate level in an acute service. Part 4 concerns the use of DSS to support policy and organizational learning, using community care and objective setting, respectively, as examples. The chapters in each of these three Parts also follow – at least loosely – a 'patient flow' through the health system from primary care and community care to secondary care settings.

The first and the last of the five Parts are more general. The first comprises two introductory chapters: one sets the context of policy, organization and management in the NHS (as an example of the sorts of changes that are sweeping across health sectors internationally) and also sketches relevant decision making theory; the second discusses in more detail what DSS are and how they work.

The final part looks ahead and features a chapter on potential future developments for DSS and an overall conclusion which tries to be realistic as well as optimistic in its portrayal of their future application in health services management.

Part 1

Context and definition

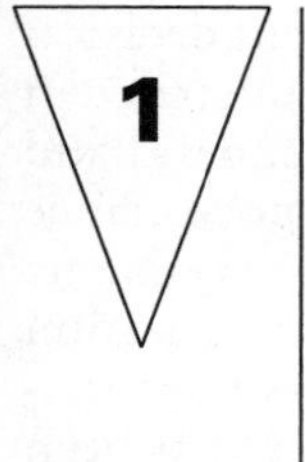

The context of decision making in the NHS

Steve Cropper and Paul Forte

Introduction: NHS management and decision making complexity

If there is one word which describes the decision making process in the NHS it is 'complexity'. It is one of the largest organizations in the UK, with a budget of some £36 billion per year. Taking all its constituent organizations together, it has the largest workforce in the country, highly qualified and skilled with strong professional identities and well-developed, public service value systems. It touches the lives of the whole population in what is often an emotive and sensitive way.

New developments in medical technology, innovations in health care delivery, and changes in consumer needs and awareness place different pressures on the use of NHS resources. Whether a clinician looking after the immediate care of an individual patient, or a health authority allocating resources across provider services and care groups, good management of those resources is crucial. The decision making processes at all levels inevitably involve striking balances: between efficiency and the quality of the service; between services; and between promoting change and maintaining continuity. These balances are often difficult, if not impossible, to resolve to the satisfaction of everyone, particularly given the different interests and values of groups both within and outside the health services. The boundaries separating these groups are not well defined; groups are not necessarily mutually exclusive. However, those boundaries – between clinical and non-clinical staff, between operational managers and policy makers, and between those delivering services and those consuming them – are common sites of controversy.

Clearly, management decisions do not take place in a vacuum. As Harmon and Mayer (1986) argue, the organizational and political contexts of public services have a direct bearing on management decision making. Calls for more informed decision making, greater coherence in policy and organizational structures, and increased openness and accountability have led, most recently, to close attention to governance structures and probity (Ferlie *et al.* 1996). Despite these developments and a faith in rational management, however, investment in the decision making process has, at best, been piecemeal. While there has been sustained investment in information systems and technology, there has been less emphasis on the development of managerial capacity to make good use of these resources.

The term 'decision making' is used throughout this book to include a range of managerial activities such as planning, policy making, and problem solving. These are all fundamental parts of clinical as well as managerial practice. What is particular to *managerial* decision making and the managerial role, however, whether undertaken by general managers or by clinicians, is the focus on exploring the future environment and performance of the organization (see, for example, Royston 1996): this is also the essence of management decision support systems (DSS) to which the remainder of the book turns.

This chapter presents the changing context of NHS decision making. It begins by outlining important influences on it, and theories of decision making which shape it. The discussion of recent investments in NHS decision making processes and an infrastructure to support those processes sets the scene for a more detailed examination, in Chapter 2, of ways in which computer-based DSS can enhance management decision making.

The changing context of NHS decision making

There are a number of strands of context whose changes and interrelations have influenced the nature of decision making in the NHS. Some pre-date the reforms, others were integral to them. While the scale and pace of change since the 1991 reforms (Secretaries of State for Health 1989) has been large and their full effects are still unknown, decision making in the NHS has changed significantly. It will continue to do so as the 'internal market' matures and adjusts in response to changes in health policy and to feedback about what is and is not sustainable. Some broad trends have emerged, however, which are shaping and altering the nature of decision making and these are discussed below.

From public administration to public management

The NHS, in common with other public services, has been subject to radical change in the role, style and location of management over the past 10 to 15 years (Leopold *et al.* 1996). In the case of the NHS, the Griffiths recommendations on general management (DHSS 1983) marked the beginning of this change from an 'administrative' style to one in which private sector management practices had a significant influence – the so-called 'New Public Management' (see Rhodes 1991). Griffiths focused on the issue of responsibility for organizational performance and corresponding structures of authority and accountability. Other persistent themes have included economy and, introduced to the NHS in the 1991 reforms, an emphasis on the disciplines of the market – competition and contestability (Hood 1991). While decentralization goes hand in hand with a countervailing centralization (Metcalfe and Richards 1990), these and subsequent policy changes have all led to an extension and sharpening of responsibility and accountability in *local* decision making. With this has come a new onus on managers to ensure that the information basis on which they operate is adequate to their tasks and responsibilities. As Hood (1991) notes, these changes in public administration were linked to other administrative megatrends – including automation, particularly through information technology – in the production and distribution of public services. In the NHS, a sense of urgency was created by the need to have up-to-date activity and cost data available for the contracting process (Ferlie *et al.* 1996), and there has been significant investment in information technology and systems (Audit Commission 1995).

Organizational boundaries: fragmentation and integration

Metcalfe and Richards (1990: 37) define management as 'taking responsibility for the performance of a system'. All major strands of recent health policy have led the NHS to pay close attention to its system boundaries and its redefined constituent parts, notably purchasers and providers. These roles continue to change with, for example, increasing emphasis on the development of primary care. However, there are conflicting pressures for managers. There is undoubtedly a requirement to ensure that organizational responsibilities are discharged. For example, Trusts are required to ensure return on capital, and to manage activity against resources so as to ensure financial viability and meet national quality standards. The widespread adoption of clinical directorate structures in Trusts has reinforced traditional professional divisions with business identities.

At the same time, there is a growing emphasis on collaborative working to develop and integrate services within Trusts, between Trusts and GPs/purchasers, and between the NHS and other service commissioners and providers. Commercial pressures narrow the focus of managerial concern; collaboration tends to promote a wider view of the system. Such 'whole-systems thinking' – describing the constituent parts of an organization or service, understanding the relationships between them and identifying how management actions will affect them – is perhaps the most difficult task of all. The formalization of organizational boundaries and responsibilities has made it more difficult to maintain an overview of services and to orchestrate analysis of, and responses to, both operational and strategic problems, what Bryson and Crosby (1992) call 'leadership for the common good'.

Political will and executive direction

While management has been strengthened, decision making in the NHS remains politically charged. Central–local relations have given rise to tensions where separation between policy and executive functions is not always clear. Nor, within the executive function, have the rules of subsidiarity been clearly worked out. As rationing decisions in health care have become increasingly explicit (when, before, they were largely implicit), debate about where, within the NHS management structure, decisions should be made continues to surface. On the one hand, there is a desire for local decision making to reflect local needs; on the other, there is a concern to maintain a truly 'national' health service. This is reflected in a continuing sense of uncertainty about the future structure and policy of the NHS, evident at the political level, but translated into central policy and executive strategy. At the local level, the concept of 'policy stress' (Friend 1977) has a strong resonance here, illustrated in a recent critique of NHS central management:

> Whereas the efficiency index requires health authorities to increase workload in the acute sector to satisfy the Treasury's demands, *The Health of the Nation* and the development of community care call for a reallocation of resources away from hospitals . . . Faced with multiple and conflicting demands, NHS managers can be forgiven if they feel confused.
>
> (Ham 1994: 351)

Democracy and accountability

The reforms removed direct local democratic representation from the governing boards of health authorities and did not introduce it onto the newly constituted boards of NHS Trusts. Instead, non-executive directors of all boards are appointed by the Secretary of State. Democratic inputs into health service decision making now take different forms. One route has been broadly 'consumerist' in form and is interested in establishing rights to influence provision and to feedback evaluation of services as experienced by users (NHS Management Executive 1991). Another has sought to promote the idea of an 'active citizenry' capable of debating its aspirations, and contributing to the articulation of values and political purposes (Ranson and Stewart 1994). Each route demands not just appropriate consultation on plans and the widespread publication of decisions (NHS Management Executive 1992a), but that the decision making process itself becomes more public through, for example, open board meetings in Trusts and health authorities, the use of 'citizen juries' and the court system to test decisions made about the management of individual cases. This has been reinforced by calls from the Health Service Commissioner (HMSO 1996) for public decision making where decisions about care affect patients and their families.

Summary

Each of these strands of context, in itself, makes for increased complexity: together, they suggest potentially conflicting responses from NHS managers, who have the responsibility for reconciling their contradictions. However, the means to achieving this reconciliation are ill-defined. Competing and ambiguous objectives, poor information systems and continuously changing organizations combine with the inherent complexity of health care itself to frustrate effective decision making. Changing health policy and management systems will continue to frustrate the search for a stable setting in which management can become institutionalized. The continuing development of community care, the increasing focus on health promotion through 'Health of the Nation', the idea of a primary care-led NHS, the pursuit of evidence-based care through research and development and, changing resource allocation and financial control methods will not allow for stability. The implications of this complexity for the decision making process, and what managers might do to enhance it, are considered below.

Theories of decision making

The literature on decision making theory is extensive (see for example McGrew and Wilson 1982; Kleindorfer *et al.* 1993; Jennings and Wattam 1994 for useful reviews and summaries). It is not intended to explore the field in depth here, but rather to present a selective review of principles.

A common starting point is to distinguish three levels of analysis: individual, group, and organizational decision making. At each level, the scope and complexity of theory required to explain decision making principles and practice is extended, but a basic framework indicating stages of the decision making process forms its core (for example: diagnose the problem; identify options; set out aims, benefits and costs; evaluate options; select preferred option). It is also usual to draw a distinction between *normative* theories (describing how decision making *should* be conducted) and *descriptive* theories (which describe how and in what context decision making *actually* happens). Theories of both types have developed in tandem, informing one another, since an early synthesis of ideas (March and Simon 1958) which has made good sense to theorists and practitioners alike. These foundations of decision making theory

> portray decision-making as intentional, consequential and optimising. That is, they assume that decisions are based on preferences (e.g.

> wants, needs, values, goals, interests, subjective utilities) and expectations about outcomes associated with different alternative actions. And they assume that the best possible alternative (in terms of its consequences for a decision-maker's preferences) is chosen.
>
> (March 1988: 1)

Explaining decisions

Accounts of decisions taken by managers commonly interweave two types of explanation. The first asserts that the decision is demonstrably well founded or intelligible because the option selected 'makes sense' in relation to the goals set and other constraints on choice. In short, a decision is rational when it can be shown that the right solution has been identified and chosen. The second points to the decision making process itself and asserts that decisions arising *from that process* have resulted from an appropriate and testing procedure of analysis and deliberation: no claim is made, however, for the correctness of the decision itself. Simon (1976) distinguishes these explanations as appeals to 'substantive' and 'procedural' rationality respectively; each provides a basis for confidence in the decision taken.

Substantive rationality

Appeals to substantive rationality rest on firm prior evidence that the means offered are effective in meeting the ends sought. It requires agreement that desired outcomes are fully and appropriately specified, and a firm conviction that the means selected will lead to those ends. The current pursuit of evidence-based health care in the NHS also rests on such a notion of rationality; it has more recently been extended as a norm to health policy (Dawson and Maynard 1996; Hayward 1996). As Ham *et al.* (1995: 71–2) argue, 'there needs to be an effective mechanism for transferring the results of research into policy'. This call for more systematic attention to, and use of, existing knowledge aims to make sure that the policy intervention most effective in achieving desired health outcomes is chosen. Where there is no definitive knowledge, mechanisms for exploration of the consequences of interventions are required. Pilot projects, especially when change is likely to be large scale and far-reaching (e.g. total fundholding), offer one way of increasing learning before the wholesale diffusion of new practices. In general, however, there has been little debate about the evidence base of strategic and operational service planning and management in the NHS. Rather, the focus has been on clinical practices at the micro level and on proposals for evidence-based policy at the macro level. While there remains much scope for improving the rationality of both clinical and resource management decisions, there are also limits to its pursuit (Freemantle 1996). As McKee and Clarke (1995: 103) argued: 'perhaps the most difficult issue for all of us concerned in purchasing or providing care is the need for an increased acceptance that a degree of uncertainty is integral to health services'.

Such uncertainty means that substantive rationality will be elusive (Barrett and McMahon 1990). Lack of clarity about the outcomes to be achieved (or avoided), and about the balance across outcomes that should be sought, may be pervasive: recent debates on rationing health care (Mechanic 1995; Crisp *et al.* 1996) are testimony to this. Uncertainty will also extend to judgements about the relative effectiveness of alternatives in bringing about those ends. Also, decisions which at one time seem 'right' can rapidly be undermined by changing circumstances, although belief in them may persist as 'urban myths' (Crail 1996). Where decisions have been taken, the process of implementation will inevitably lead to learning and new understanding, including finding out about any unintended or unforeseen consequences. For example, recent evaluation suggests that increased rates of day surgery are less important than improvements in the efficiency of use of inpatient beds because much daycase activity represents new work rather than substitution for existing inpatient work (Edwards 1996). In another instance, Riley and Kirby (1996) question whether consultant outreach clinics are the anticipated panacea for improving integration between primary and secondary care services. Appeals to substantive rationality – the ability to demonstrate that an option is right, or best – are not likely to be plausible in such circumstances.

Procedural rationality

The alternative, procedural rationality, has a weaker, but still important, claim as a basis for decision making. Rationality is vested in the *conduct of the decision making process* rather than any demonstrable 'rightness' of its outcome (see Dean and Sharfman 1993). Ironically, evidence-based care is judged essentially in these terms. In assessing the findings of a research study, for example, clinicians are advised to check the quality of the research method against the 'gold standard' of the randomized clinical trial and against best-practice conduct of such trials. Procedural rationality demands self-consciousness about the decision making process and the manner in which it is concluded (for example, whether by consensus, with compromise, or where interests are excluded from the weighing of evidence).

The model of management decision making proposed by Simon (1960) – intelligence, evaluation and choice – is a commonly adopted normative theory, translating into a sequence of steps through which decision making should pass:

- formulate the decision problem clearly and explicitly;
- identify systematically aims, objectives, constraints and implicated values;
- identify all options;

- identify and judge the relative value of known costs and benefits from both positive and negative outcomes;
- search for new and relevant information;
- evaluate the extent to which options meet aims and objectives while respecting constraints;
- choose the option which best meets aims, objectives and constraints.

This provides a common way of describing the managerial decision making process. The theory has been adapted to reflect the limitations of decision makers and decision contexts. While the classical theories tend to establish procedures for decision making which emphasize calculation, a body of theory has also developed which recognizes the contexts and complexities of decision making processes and suggests how 'obstacles' to rationality arise and operate in practice (e.g. Sager 1993). Time, attention and analytical capacity are scarce resources, so the search for options tends to be triggered only when a problem is noticed, and stops when a 'good enough' solution is found.

Descriptive theories: from calculation to negotiation and learning

According to this perspective, not only are there limits and checks at each of Simon's (1960) steps, but the integrity of the sequence of steps is also questioned. First, managers pay uneven attention to the different steps in the process. The distribution of managers' attention is shaped by the way they construct problems, by organizational and professional politics and by the social context of decision making. The technical task of finding a solution that works is complicated by the professional and organizational context. Thus Eden (1986) argues that idealized notions of decision making are unhelpful, decision making is a task governed primarily by practical considerations:

> Problem finishing as a descriptive concept is useful to the extent to which we recognize that the practicalities of getting things done are a part of how the problem is defined . . . The nature of the problem will be more significantly influenced by what each person sees as possible courses of action rather than any description of the situation as it is believed to be.
>
> (Eden 1986: 103)

Second, to suggest that decision making can be a steady, progressive process is unhelpful. Friend and Hickling (1987) suggest that a cyclical process, involving fragmentary switching and looping between different modes of decision making, better reflects decision making practice than the prescribed orderly, linear progression. This is consistent with a model of decision making as a developmental or *learning* process. Indeed, there is good reason to suppose that the privileged status given to 'points of decision' is mistaken. Rather, decisions emerge through action and the reasons for them are discovered in a process of learning or sensemaking (Mintzberg *et al.* 1990; Weick 1995). Whether historical or future-orientated, the process can be characterized as follows. When a first attempt at defining objectives, alternatives, criteria, etc. is made, the nature of information required to explore and contain uncertainties becomes better defined. As the supply and quality of information increases, so options will be redefined, goals re-articulated and modified, and so forth. The decision making and sensemaking process proceeds incrementally rather than in a heroic leap; decisions 'develop' as people take action or agree policy where they feel confident in their analysis, and avoid taking decisions where levels of uncertainty do not justify such choice. In this way, decision making need not become paralysed by either the endless search (and often fruitless wait) for 'better' data, or the sheer weight of potential data sources to be considered. However, the process of decision making itself requires significant investment. It is to investment in the decision making process in the NHS that we now turn.

Investments in decision making

Confidence that decision making in the NHS is well founded and well organized remains elusive. Decision making processes at the national level are accused of producing an incoherent health policy, one which tries to respond to too many – often incompatible – demands. The local management agenda has been characterized as one of 'crisis management' driven by instant responses to operational issues. Even where planning frameworks and information systems are well developed, experience suggests that they do not, in themselves, produce thoughtful plans. For example, despite the scale of investment in information systems, and indeed because of it, there are questions about how much benefit has been achieved (Lock 1996).

In terms of management support systems, this requires management of change on a variety of related fronts. In particular, the design, implementation and use of information technology and systems cannot be separated from the conduct of business processes and methods and organizational and management development. Three domains of 'investment' can be identified, combining in various ways to develop and enhance management decision making (see Figure 1.1):

- investment in *intellectual capital* in order to assist development and use of appropriate planning frameworks, management thinking and analysis;
- investment in *enabling technologies* to improve the quality and availability of information required to support management tasks;
- investment to *strengthen organizations* (including cultures, structures and processes) to develop an appropriate environment in which issues can be raised and addressed.

Investment in any and each of these would contribute to the development of decision making capacity in health service organizations – but in limited fashion. At each intersection, the coordination of investment is likely to be more productive, and where all three combine, at the heart of the diagram, then the conditions for effective decision support are most likely to be found.

The technological domain

The importance of the technological domain lies in its technical underpinning of the delivery of information systems which managers require to carry out their tasks. It is an area which has received much attention (and been the subject of much controversy) in recent years, with some £300m

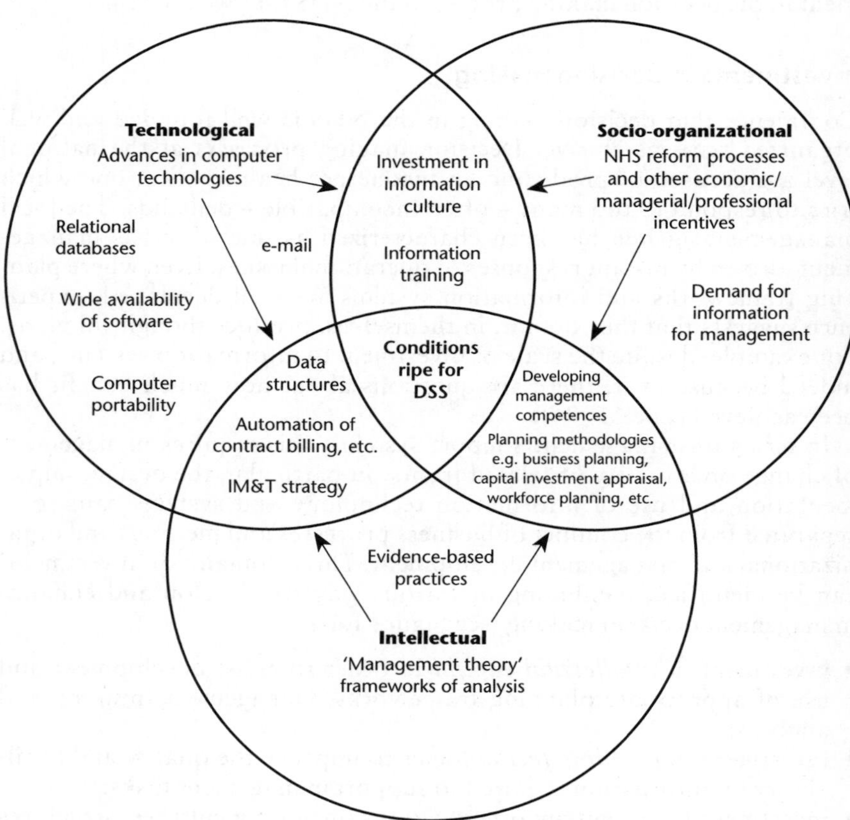

Figure 1.1 Domains influencing health services decision making

per annum being spent during that period on computer-related technologies and large-scale 'demonstrator projects' such as HISS (Audit Commission 1995). The introduction and development of computer-based technologies have been the principal driving force here and, although the emphasis has moved away from hardware in recent years, there are still significant IT infrastructure developments in train (such as the NHS information network and the electronic medical record). Effort has also gone into establishing new areas of data collection and improving its accuracy, timeliness and accessibility (Sheaff and Peel 1995).

Alongside the large-scale IT developments, the proliferation of personal computing technologies (including, more recently, electronic mail and the Internet) has been no less important, particularly in helping to initiate a cultural change in management awareness of the potential use of information and the importance of access to it.

On the other hand, relatively less attention has been paid as to how the information made available by these systems is actually used – or, indeed, whether it *can* be used – by managers. Information technology is not sufficient in itself to ensure this. It can provide the means of accessing and processing data rapidly, but it requires the ability of the manager to'make sense' of it and act upon it. This distinction has not always been explicitly recognized in the NHS (Forte 1994) and is probably one of the reasons why, despite the level of investment in information systems, it is unclear whether the benefits expected have been realized. Technology will continue to develop and be exploited, but technological fixes alone will not produce the forms of management support required.

Socio-organizational domain

The requirements and incentives of the internal market and its management and regulation have largely forced the pace here. Examples include requirements placed on health authorities in setting up and monitoring contracts, the emergence of clinical management structures, and the focus on evidence-based medicine as an agent for change. The highly professionalized nature of health care acts both as driver and restraint. Pressures for change meet an extensive legacy from past organizational structures and working practices to identify and test what Pettigrew *et al.* (1992) called 'receptive and non-receptive contexts for change'. With radical change comes the opportunity to negotiate new forms of organization and relationships, new purposes and directions (Barrett and McMahon 1990). Developments in the socio-organizational domain – changing relationships between professions and between professionals and managers, new organizational structures, resourcing mechanisms and roles – mean that management influence and activity are rapidly changing, stimulated not only by new concepts and methods – risk analysis, business process re-engineering, etc. – from the intellectual domain, but also by control of information technologies.

Intellectual domain

This domain focuses on how individuals, or groups of managers, develop and establish the intellectual capital of management with which problems come to be defined, arguments constructed and agendas set for operational and strategic management in the NHS. The establishment of appropriate frameworks of enquiry and methodologies for supporting management tasks are also important activities in this area. However, this domain, if taken in isolation, runs the risk of becoming an 'ivory tower' where sophisticated concepts and models might be developed but not applied; it might lack the technical capacity to be made operational or fail to carry the necessary wider support and understanding of managers.

Domain boundaries and intersections

Each of the domains influence one another. At their boundaries there is potential for fusion and cross-fertilization of ideas, development of skills and new management activities.

At the interface of *technological* and *intellectual* development, there is a continuing struggle to define appropriate, potentially enduring information structures and technology capable of handling their complexity. The dominant model, indicated in the IM&T strategy (NHS Management Executive 1992b) is one of a comprehensive, integrated information system. This requires developments in both intellectual and technological domains. Debates about clinical and disease coding systems and contracting currencies (such as finished consultant episodes, care packages, health gain and health outcomes) represent intellectual developments which are increasingly capable of being tested and refined in powerful information systems. Yet information systems soon become obsolete: changes in medical technology and practice, in policy imperatives and in organizing processes mean that coding systems and the units of currency will not stand still. While new data capture technologies enable information to be collected rapidly and reliably, and stored, the critical issue is not one of data quantity and quality but, rather, of its organization, commensurability and salience to management and clinicians alike. There is some way to go, even if technology is becoming more flexible and accommodating, before the (changing) needs of the many types of decision maker in the NHS can be met. In the meantime, as Keen and Muris (1995: 57) describe, 'At present, NHS computers can be viewed as thousands of islands, which in many cases can only be linked with great difficulty.' They are sanguine about the potential for harmonization of systems. Indeed, while leading-edge developments in technology may continue to be applied to management problems, a lack of input from the socio-organizational domain means that these are unlikely to break out from experimental or small-scale projects. The continuing stream of informatics 'pilot' and development sites are testimony to this.

At the intersection of the *technological* and *socio-organizational* boundaries lie such activities as information and IT skills development and the more widely understood and popularly understood applications of IT (such as personal computing and the use of e-mail). However, absent here are the intellectual frameworks that might raise the primarily 'office-based' functions to the levels of more complex strategic and advanced operational management applications. A danger here lies in merely automating existing management procedures rather than undertaking a more thorough and considered evaluation of how technology might fundamentally transform them (Zuboff 1988). The NHS IM&T strategy continues the NHS pursuit of IT as a means of developing planning and management capabilities. As Keen and Muris (1995:57) note, 'The introduction of information technology triggers a demand for intellectual skills to be developed.' Significant lessons have been learned from development activities at this interface. In concluding their evaluation of the earlier Resource Management (RM) Initiative, Packwood *et al.* (1991: 151) argued that 'RM is primarily about cultural change . . . It involves accepting responsibility for coping with difficult circumstances . . . Computer technology is subsidiary to this. If cultural change cannot be achieved, RM will not succeed.' Indeed, there is some evidence (e.g. Information Management Group of the NHS Executive 1996) that such findings are being used to inform current efforts to develop comprehensive information systems linked with change management which are seen as a better means of generating effective and resource-sensitive organizations.

Where the *socio-organizational* and *intellectual* domains overlap is where development of frameworks for a deeper understanding and more systematic handling of issues takes place. Much effort is currently focused on ways of determining the activities of the health service most worthy of investment. Development and dissemination of planning methodologies have been built into special workshop programmes and targeted recently as part of both purchaser and provider development. The 'future scenarios' workshops (Office for Public Management 1995) provide an example of this. Other resources provide frameworks for addressing particular management tasks and are intended to prompt further development of a management culture; these have been released as advice on good practice. The early guidance on business planning (NHS Management Executive 1992b) and on risk management (NHS Management Executive 1993) provides examples here. Some of these paper-based systems have been subsequently implemented as a computer-based system. The 'Rubber Windmill' exercise, simulating the workings of the NHS reforms, is one well-known example which subsequently became the computer-based 'Numberside' exercise.

Finally, where the influence of all three of the domains comes together in an appropriate balance, then the role for DSS and their technical and intellectual reason for development becomes clearest and is best served.

Concluding remarks

In this chapter, the context to decision making in the NHS has been characterized as one of complexity, partly because of the intrinsic complexity of health care services and partly because the NHS is a rapidly changing institution. A brief review of ideas, which portray decision making as a process of deliberation and learning as much as calculation, reflects that context: in health services planning and management, there are no firm benchmarks which enable us to judge whether a decision is right or wrong. However, it is possible to assess the quality of management using the decision making process as a proxy – that is, against the principle of procedural rationality. This asks simply, 'Was the decision making process sufficiently thorough and testing for the issue in hand?'

The NHS is investing heavily in infrastructure to support decision making. Arguably, there is a change in culture underway as managers seek appropriate frameworks to guide their analysis of problems and decisions, as continuing investment in information technology and systems lead to more relevant, more accessible, better quality information and as the organization of the NHS responds to pressure for more open, more clearly explicable decisions. The issue is to ensure that these investments are coherent rather than fragmentary, and DSS provide a potentially powerful way of contributing to that process of coordination and development.

References

Audit Commission (1995) *For Your Information: a Study of Information Management and Systems in the Acute Hospital*. London, HMSO.

Barrett, S. and McMahon, L. (1990) Public management in uncertainty: a micro-political perspective of the health service in the United Kingdom, *Policy and Politics*, 18: 257–68.

Bryson, J. M. and Crosby, B. C. (1992) *Leadership for the Common Good: Tackling Public Problems in a Shared-Power World*. San Francisco, Jossey-Bass.

Crail, M. (1996) Lost in the myths of time, *Health Service Journal*, 4 April, 16.

Crisp, R., Hope, T. and Ebbs, D. (1996) The Asbury draft policy on ethical use of resources, *British Medical Journal*, 312: 1528–31.

Dawson, D. and Maynard, A. (1996) Private finance for the public good? *British Medical Journal*, 313: 312.

Dean, J. W. and Sharfman, M. P. (1993) Procedural rationality in the strategic decision making process, *Journal of Management Studies*, 30: 587–610.

Department of Health and Social Security (1983) *The NHS Management Inquiry* (The Griffiths Report). London, HMSO.

Eden, C. (1986) Problem solving or problem finishing, in M. Jackson and P. Keys (eds) *New Directions in Management Science*. Aldershot, Gower.

Edwards, N. (1996) Day for night, *Health Service Journal*, 2 May, 24–6.

Ferlie, E., Ashburner, L., Fitzgerald, L. and Pettigrew, A. (1996) *The New Public Management in Action*. Oxford, Oxford University Press.

Forte, P. (1994) Data rich, information poor: data, information and decision support in the NHS, *European Journal of Information Systems*, 3: 148–54.

Freemantle, N. (1996) Are decisions taken by health care professionals rational? A new systematic review of experimental and quasi experimental literature, *Health Policy*, 38: 78–81.

Friend, J. K. (1977) The dynamics of policy change, *Long Range Planning*, 10: 40–7.

Friend, J. K. and Hickling, A. (1987) *Planning under Pressure*. Oxford, Pergamon.

Ham, C. (1994) Where now for the NHS reforms? *British Medical Journal*, 309: 351–2.

Ham, C., Hunter, D. and Robinson, R. (1995) Evidence based policymaking, *British Medical Journal*, 310: 71–2.

Harmon, M. M. and Mayer, R. T. (1986) *Organization Theory for Public Administration*. Burke, VA, Chatelaine Press.

Hayward, J. (1996) Promoting clinical effectiveness, *British Medical Journal*, 312: 1491–2.

HMSO (1996) *Health Service Commissioner: Selected Investigations Completed October 1995 to March 1996*. London, HMSO.

Hood, C. (1991) A public management for all seasons? *Public Administration*, 69: 3–19.

Information Management Group of the NHS Executive (1996) *HISS: Management of Change*. Winchester, NHS Executive

Jennings, D. and Wattam, S. (1994) *Decision Making: an Integrated Approach*. London, Pitman.

Keen, J. and Muris, N. (1995) Information strategy in the NHS: issues and challenges, *Journal of Management in Medicine*, 9: 57–62.

Kleindorfer, P. R., Kunreuther, H. C. and Schoemaker, P. J. H. (1993) *Decision Sciences: an Integrative Perspective*. Cambridge, Cambridge University Press.

Leopold, J., Glover, I. and Hughes, M. (eds) (1996) *Beyond Reason?* Aldershot, Avebury.

Lock, C. (1996) What value do computers provide to NHS hospitals? *British Medical Journal*, 312: 1407–10.

March, J. G. (1988) *Decisions and Organizations*. Oxford, Basil Blackwell.

March, J. G. and Simon, H. A. (1958) *Organizations*. New York, Wiley.

McGrew, A. G. and Wilson, M. J. (eds) (1982) *Decision Making Approaches and Analysis*. Manchester, Manchester University Press.

McKee, M. and Clarke, A. (1995) Guidelines, enthusiasms, uncertainty, and the limits to purchasing, *British Medical Journal*, 310: 101–4.

Mechanic, D. (1995) Dilemmas in rationing health care services: the case for implicit rationing, *British Medical Journal*, 310: 1655–9.

Metcalfe, L. and Richards, S. (1990) *Improving Public Management*. London, Sage.

Mintzberg, H., Waters, H., Pettigrew, A. M. and Butler, R. (1990) Studying deciding: an exchange of views between Mintzberg and Waters, Pettigrew, and Butler, *Organization Studies*, 11: 1–16.

NHS Management Executive (1991) *Consultation and Involving the Consumer*. London, NHSME.

NHS Management Executive (1992a) *Local Voices – the Views of Local People in Purchasing for Health*. London, HMSO.

NHS Management Executive (1992b) *Business Planning Guidance. Letter to NHS Trust Chairmen, Chief Executives and Directors of Finance*. London, NHS Management Executive.

NHS Management Executive (1993) *Risk Management in the NHS*. London, Department of Health.

Office for Public Management (1995) *Future Patterns: an Approach to Policy and Strategy Development in the New NHS*. London, Office for Public Management.

Packwood, T., Keen, J. and Buxton, M. (1991) *Hospitals in Transition*. Buckingham, Open University Press.

Pettigrew, A. M., Ferlie, E. B. and McKee, L. (1992) *Shaping Strategic Change*. London, Sage.

Ranson, S. and Stewart, J. (1994) *Management for the Public Domain: Enabling the Learning Society*. Basingstoke, Macmillan.

Rhodes, R. A. W. (ed.) (1991) The new public management, *Public Administration*, 69: 1–136.

Riley, K. and Kirby, R. (1996) Practice does not make perfect, *Health Service Journal*, 9 May, 29.

Royston, G. (1996) Modelling for the National Health Service, in P. H. Millard and S. McClean (eds) *Go with the Flow: a Systems Approach to Health Care Planning*. London, Royal Society of Medicine.

Sager, T. (1993) Paradigms for planning: a rationality-based classification, *Planning Theory*, 9: 79–118.

Secretaries of State for Health, Wales, Northern Ireland and Scotland (1989) *Working for Patients: Command Paper 555*. London, HMSO.

Sheaff, R. and Peel, V. (1995) *Managing Health Service Information Systems: an Introduction*. Buckingham, Open University Press.

Simon, H. A. (1960) *The New Science of Management Decision*. New York, Harper and Row.

Simon, H. A. (1976) From substantive to procedural rationality, in A. McGrew and M. J. Wilson (eds) *Decision Making: Approaches and Analysis*. Manchester, Manchester University Press.

Weick, K. E. (1995) *Sensemaking in Organizations*. Thousand Oaks, CA, Sage.

Zuboff, S. (1988) *In the Age of the Machine: the Future of Work and Power*. London, Heinemann.

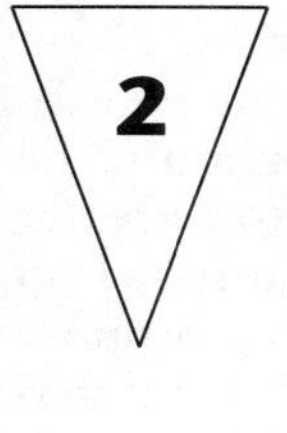

The nature of decision support systems

Steve Cropper and Paul Forte

Introduction

Decision support systems (DSS) have been both heralded as a resource likely to revolutionize management decision making (Turban 1990) and questioned as a technology with serious problems of implementation (Carlson 1982; Wyatt 1995). The truth, we believe, lies somewhere between these assessments.

The purpose of this chapter is to examine the concept of DSS and the distinctive contribution they can make to health services management. It sets the scene for the case study chapters by introducing and explaining DSS terminology, how these systems are constructed, 'work' and may be used to enhance decision making in health services management. This is not to say that there are standard procedures or a standard 'product': DSS differ among themselves, as the case studies in this volume will suggest. The argument here is that while there is a unifying approach which makes DSS what they are, there are nevertheless some significant choices in the way they can be developed, applied and used. These choices affect the likelihood that DSS will be used, valued, disseminated, and whether they might fuel the development of other management support systems. First, however, a definition of DSS is developed to set out their distinctive characteristics.

Defining 'decision support systems'

There is no universally held definition of DSS. At its most general, the term could be used to describe any technology employed to help managers reach decisions related to the conduct of their tasks. Thus written policies and protocols provide guidance to decision makers; a committee or working group is an organizational means of supporting decision making; questions or opinion from a colleague, the results of an economic evaluation, a standard monthly budget statement might also be regarded as contributing to, or supporting decisions. All are, to a greater or lesser extent, definitive or influential – yet not all would qualify as DSS in the terms adopted for this book, however. The definition we propose draws the scope of DSS more tightly, emphasizing appropriate combinations of information, analytical method and the power of computer systems; what counts is the effectiveness of the use of these technologies in decision making processes. Appropriateness is judged in relation to the management task leading to decision making and the way in which such decision making is conducted.

We take decision support systems to be:

> Systems which call for, order and promote deliberation and analysis directly relevant to management tasks where complexity and uncertainty make it difficult to arrive at a reasoned response. A distinctive feature of such systems is their use of computer-assisted modelling methods to help in making sense of current issues, in exploring options for future policy and action, and in assessing their consequences. In general, they can also be reused and translated into decision making processes in different localities.

A simple example of a DSS will serve to illustrate what this definition means in practice. It is a computer-based simulation model used by a number of health authorities to map out and quantify the relationships between 'key variables' in pathways of coronary care in order to inform their purchasing strategies (Bensley *et al.* 1995).

An example of a DSS: pathways of coronary care

The 'Health of the Nation' strategy has made work to meet the coronary heart disease target a universal local priority for health services in Britain. Local needs assessment, relationships and alliances between local health agencies, and evidence on clinical effectiveness have helped in understanding what might constitute an appropriate response. However, the implications for local health services, and particularly acute services, have been difficult to specify. Although epidemiological analyses involve forecasting and target setting, and the contracting process clearly involves analysis of costs attaching to alternative packages of care, the various elements are seldom brought together in an integrated, strategic analysis of future scenarios and options.

Bensley *et al.* (1995) report a decision support system in the form of a computer simulation model linking incidence in angina and acute coronary events to cardiac interventions. Its origins are in a 'pathways-of-care flow chart' developed to help non-clinicians understand how and why doctors work as they do. Quantitative data were added later, and the flow chart was used to estimate the resource effects of changing key variables. In effect, the authors note, the computer software has been used essentially 'to undertake arithmetic bookkeeping calculations' (Bensley *et al.* 1995: 316).

The model draws together various types of information from a number of sources to specify 'default' relationships between variables in the flow chart. The annual incidence of angina, for example, is drawn from a morbidity study by the Royal College of General Practitioners. Other reported studies were used to specify rates of 'acute coronary events', including the proportion of patients who would follow different forms of treatment – angiography, angioplasty, prevention and coronary artery by-pass graft (CABG). Thus the model specifies relationships between variables, using national, regional or sub-regional data, such that 25 per cent of acute coronary events result in sudden death, 75 per cent reach hospital and, of those, 90 per cent are discharged home. As a default, it is assumed that 20 per cent of those discharged become new cases for angiography. The model thus aims to describe the aggregate flow of the population at risk into and through the health care system; it tries to assess the effect and costs of different policies and practices both on health care required and on the number of deaths.

To assess whether, or to what extent, the model was a valid representation of coronary care in the former Yorkshire region, the default relationships were used to generate forecasts of deaths and treatment volumes based on the region's population (aged 35–74) of 1.6 million. The forecasts were then compared with actual figures in Office for Population Census and Surveys records and figures on treatment volumes derived from local surveys. The validity of the model was tested at the smaller population scale of the individual health authority by repeating the same exercise.

The model has subsequently been used by a number of health authorities to assess purchasing options. The data can easily be changed to reflect local patterns or possible impacts, for example, of a major 'heart disease prevention initiative'; they can also take account of changes in GP referral rates, or changes in sudden death rate on the number of deaths and on the cost of treatment of the disease. While the authors (Bensley *et al.* 1995) report several important limitations on use of the model, it has nevertheless been found useful as a means of exploring the effects of different combinations of treatment and prevention. As they argue:

> The first objective of building the flow chart into a simulation model was to answer what-if questions such as 'What is the effect of a ten per cent reduction in the incidence of angina on the number of deaths, angiograms, angioplasties, and CABGs?' Later on, in subsequent versions of the model, the objectives were extended so that the model could . . . explore balances between prevention and

> treatment and those implied between short-term and long-term decision making.
>
> (Bensley *et al.* 1995: 320)

The model is used, therefore, to simulate what would happen if changes in one or more variables in the pathways of coronary care occur.

The definition of DSS expanded

The coronary care pathways simulation is only one type of decision support system: indeed, it is only one form of simulation (see *OR Insight* 1994 for other types and applications). It illustrates the five characteristics of DSS highlighted in our own definition above. Taken together, these distinguish DSS from other forms of information or management support system. To relax any of these requirements starts to move a practice away from DSS towards other forms of organizational, professional or management support. It is not the intention to be purist: developments in technology and in management practice mean that it is unhelpful to draw too strict a boundary around management DSS. However, it is useful to have a starting point which reflects the value to managers of decision-centred systems and to contrast management DSS from other forms of management and decision support.

DSS inform decision makers

DSS themselves do not 'take' decisions. But, in 'promoting deliberation and analysis of information directly relevant to management tasks' they do literally inform decisions. Nagel (1991: 31), for example, defines a DSS as 'an information processing system that is embedded within a decision making system'. It may act either as a channel for existing information or as a means of collating and organizing new information of direct relevance to decisions, or both. To clarify what 'informing' decisions means, it is useful to compare management DSS with two related types of information system: clinical DSS, and management information systems (MIS).

Management vs. clinical DSS

Management DSS differ, in degree, if not in kind, from clinical DSS. In contrast, clinical DSS tend to be 'advisory and optimizing' systems, aiming to ensure the most appropriate clinical procedure and practice is followed. Advice is sought from the system which holds a knowledge base of 'expertise' in clinical theory and practice. It may then be applied, contingently, to the specific case in question. Thus, as Gordon (1996) has argued, while there are many barriers to effective implementation, the essence of clinical DSS is that they are used to hold, disseminate and make immediately accessible valid medical knowledge. One significant variant is that of decision analysis-based DSS. While little applied in the management field in the NHS, this decision support approach nevertheless may be used to gather and organize local knowledge and ignorance (or uncertainty). (For a recent argument about the value of decision analysis in medical decision making, see Dowie 1996; also Lilford and Royston, forthcoming 1997; for an application to management decision making in local government, see Belton 1993 and Morgan 1993.)

Management DSS work in a different way: they are essentially means for the *exploration of decision possibilities*. To start with, they may not necessarily contain a base of expert knowledge. For most significant decisions in health services management, the number of variables to be considered is so great and the evidence so weak that there is seldom a firm knowledge base from which unequivocal advice on the best decision can be derived. Where knowledge is incorporated, it is likely to be sparse. It may be used either as the basic starting parameters in the model (in the coronary care pathways example above, the population at risk) or as 'best estimates' which are open to influence by change in policy, resourcing and practice (for example, rates of sudden death from coronary events). Where they do not contain such knowledge, they serve as means of organizing and analysing information. In doing so, the DSS itself acts as a framework to promote deliberation about the relevance and significance of information available within routine systems and about the information ideally needed for an 'informed decision'. As Lagergren (1987: 3) notes: 'by constructing a formal model we are forced to ask a lot of questions about the system under study that may have been overlooked before. The result is often a deepened knowledge of the system, that might prove as valuable as the insight gained by running the model.' This emphasizes the role of DSS in promoting learning relevant to decisions.

Users have different interests, competencies and ways of using a DSS and may act upon the same output in equally different ways: each may be entirely justifiable. If management DSS provide 'standardization and control' at all, it is at a methodological or procedural level rather than in the form of authoritative, substantive expertise. Clinical DSS, by contrast, tend to emphasize the achievement of consistency and reliability in decisions resulting from their use.

Management DSS vs. MIS

It is also useful to draw contrasts between DSS and the types of management information retrieval and reporting systems that are now commonplace in the NHS (Keen 1994; Sheaff and Peel 1995). Drawing on standard activity recording systems and other primary 'feeder' systems, MIS are intended to deliver relevant data to managers through standard reports (which might highlight where activity or performance deviates from norms, or from planned levels). Increasingly, information systems offer more advanced analytical features which enable 'on-line' exploration of patterns and trends in activity and use of resources and identification of historical interrelationships. Some now include modules which enable projection of trends into the future, and basic 'what if' modelling which allows the effects of different assumptions or options to be assessed: these analytical features blur the boundaries between MIS and DSS.

However, most MIS lack the focus of a specific management task: they serve, rather, as means of collecting, storing and carrying routine information for many users and many different management tasks. The information they carry may be very specific, such as an equipment maintenance register, or the system might integrate many types of information, as community information systems (CIS) and hospital information support systems (HISS) seek to do (Bhuptani *et al.* 1993; Cross 1993). Information required for a decision to be made has to be identified, selected and retrieved with little or no guidance within the information system itself on how to do this. Exploration and analysis of data is left to the user. Where the relationship between decision and data is clear – usually where it is a routine management task – then it is often possible to create routine analytical functions which, for example, generate management reports. As soon as the relationship between data and decision changes, however, and additional data are required, or data are required in a different form, such routines are insufficient. For these reasons, MIS are usually considered helpful in identifying and triggering inquiry into problems, but not in deciding what to do about them (Finlay 1994).

DSS, by contrast, focus on a specific management task. They may even be data-free, initially, but the focus on a particular task means that the type of information required will be clearly identified. In other words, DSS provide 'prompts' towards a disciplined search for data, and for their compilation, often from a variety of sources; DSS enable the construction and analysis of a management problem and decision. More significantly, DSS incorporate means of analysing that information which enable a progressive exploration of the issue in hand.

DSS: complexity and uncertainty

DSS are an appropriate form of investment where 'complexity and uncertainty make it difficult to arrive at a reasoned response'. The purpose of DSS is to improve the effectiveness rather than the efficiency of decision making processes. They should provide, as Eden (1993: 140) suggests, 'ways of helping decision makers make more intelligent decisions'. DSS have most to offer where 'normal' management processes of deliberation, analysis and decision making can come unstuck or produce outcomes in which managers lack confidence. In such circumstances, it is natural to try to simplify the decision task by excluding complexity, making unexamined assumptions, or ignoring uncertainties. The role of DSS, then, is to enable more of the complexity to be recognized and managed within the decision process. In general, they do this by offering

- frameworks and methods of description of analysis which lead progressively to an understanding of the decision to be made;
- control over the process of analysis and deliberation, allowing objectives, constraints and options to be considered in appropriate scope and depth;
- a means of checking possible decisions against data, information and evidence, differing interests, values and perspectives (e.g. purchasers, provider and user/carer) so that they are well-tested and robust; and
- a means of being explicit about factors in a decision, of recording the analysis and, therefore, of offering potentially greater accountability.

Such qualities allow for a greater confidence that decisions made are at least explicable and justifiable, and that they are also less likely to require changing in response to new information, adjustments in policy or independent review.

DSS help in exploring options for future policy and action

Frameworks and methods of analysis lie at the heart of DSS: these are often referred to as 'models'. Models are representations of real processes, events and structures expressed as systems of logical or mathematical relationships between variables. They are not necessarily computerized, but they are abstractions from reality which provide a discipline in understanding the nature of a problem and in exploring options for future policy and action without having to test the options in practice through pilot projects or prototype developments.

Modelling methodologies and techniques are not addressed in detail here, nor is an extensive review of their applications in health care planning and management, but there has been a long-standing interest in such modelling approaches from operational researchers. (Authoritative reviews are provided by Boldy 1987; Gass 1994; Pierskalla and Brailer 1994; Lagergren 1996. For a seminal review of earlier health-related case studies involving modelling methods, see also Boldy 1981 and, more recently, Royston 1996.)

To be of help in decision making, models must capture those characteristics of a decision situation believed to give rise to critical outcomes, or potential points for management intervention: they cannot represent all aspects of the situation, but must capture enough of the complexity to be plausible. When the boundaries of the model are appropriate, the relationships within it appropriately specified and the model results validated against existing knowledge, then it can be used to assess the consequences of particular assumptions. The logical and consistent appraisal of different options can then be undertaken.

Early DSS tended towards sophisticated modelling methods while more recent developments emphasize 'simpler models, more intuitive to managers and an interactive style of usage' (Bunn 1992: 251). There has been an associated shift from a search for methods which generate unique 'best' solutions, to development of approaches which emphasize *exploratory* analysis of decisions. Two methods are integral to this:

- '*what if*' modelling can be used to examine the consequences of deliberate changes to the design of an intervention – 'What happens to costs and throughput if we bought in another consultant surgeon rather than making more beds available?'
- *sensitivity analysis* is a technique for testing whether the robustness of choices is affected by any changes in the assumptions on which they are based – 'How sensitive is this outcome to the loss of one more full-time equivalent to sickness each week? Would we still be able to cover the shifts?'

What DSS lack in comprehensive problem representation and analysis is more than compensated for by the ease with which they can be used in exploring possible options for future action and the assumptions on which their consequences are understood. The greater transparency in models which provide basic templates and frameworks rather than complex, mathematical representations of health care systems, has been seen as a way of ensuring that the expertise of the manager is more effectively used (Lagergren 1987; Eden 1993).

The value of computerization

The original 1971 definition of DSS by Scott-Morton (quoted in Ackermann *et al.* 1993: 46) as 'interactive computer-based systems which help decision makers utilize data and models to solve unstructured problems' has been and remains influential. It is reflected, for example, in Finlay's (1994: 29) recent definition of a DSS as 'a computer-based system that aids the process of decision-making'.

Our definition of DSS as 'computer-based modelling methods' follows this convention. The effective use of models for 'what if' modelling and sensitivity analysis is often only made possible, or tolerable, by the use of computers. The coronary care pathways model, described above, made use of a spreadsheet to automate the calculation and recalculation of the effects of changes in the value of different variables as 'what if' modelling was pursued. The automation of calculations is not a trivial reason for using computers to support modelling efforts: as a minimum, it improves the efficiency of analysis. However, there are more significant reasons to develop computer-based models; these concern the effectiveness of modelling for decision support.

Computer-based models allow an immediacy of analysis which is uncommon in many managerial processes. Changes in the cost, availability, power and portability of hardware, and the mass availability, approachability and sophistication of standard software (perhaps most notably, spreadsheets) have brought modelling within the imagination and capacity of many managers. It is possible to construct or amend and run a model almost on demand in a way that has not been possible until recently. Analysis can be tailored directly to the individual manager's needs – new information and intelligence can be incorporated into the model and the implications for decisions tested. This promotes what Schuck (1985) calls an 'environment of inquiry' in which

> people talk to one another and play with ideas. They pose problems, generate hypotheses, test, experiment, and reflect on the outcomes. Questioning information and consciously reflecting on the problem-solving process result in expanded reasoning capabilities . . . Computer simulations offer opportunities to play without risk to the business. Well-designed software lets people make conjectures and explore consequences.
>
> (Schuck 1985: 72)

This builds on a distinction between 'automating' and 'informating' applications of computers. DSS can do both, but some fundamental differences in types of DSS are noted by Eden (1993: 139):

> the models constructed by management scientists often have been restricted to providing decision makers with analysis, conducted in the 'backroom' and resulting in a written report. Reports and backroom work give the decision maker little room to play with the analysis of the conclusions . . . unless the problem was well structured the decision maker had to force fit the ambiguity of his problem to the formal analysis . . . this is similar to fencing a child in a playpen and providing toys that are pre-designed to constrain imagination and that the toy can be manipulated only as the designer imagined. Now and in the next decade, management scientists will develop increasingly better ways of supporting decision 'on-the-hoof'. This will allow management scientists to help decision makers to play with, and more importantly create their own, flexible toys. They will be able to do so with the freedom and unboundedness of the 'bombsite' as a playground.

These changes, Eden argues, result from recent developments in computing technology and in both specialist and popular software packages. The spreadsheet is perhaps the 'toy' which is best known to managers, widely used for both routine management tasks and *ad hoc* applications (Murphy *et al.* 1995). Useful for 'backroom' data preparation and analysis, it also meets Eden's vision of the building materials for playful experimentation within the 'here and now' of decision making. At its most general, the spreadsheet is simply a blank sheet. Its columns and rows can be given meaning and individual or groups of cells can be filled with content. Where the content is numerical rather than textual, cells can be linked through specification of the relationships between their contents. The process of structuring and entering data into a spreadsheet model offers a discipline, a focus for deliberation and communication and a means of experimentation and analysis.

While DSS help to guide the compilation of information of different types and from different sources, this can lead to concerns that DSS demand too much. Thus,

> The population of users for such a system (senior managers) is one in which time (and patience) are often at a premium and for such users the system often seems like a vast, passive 'data sink' into which precious energy and ideas are sunk but from which nothing ever emerges . . . The net result is frustration and boredom.
>
> (Smithin and Eden 1986: 145)

To shift from a 'more demanding' DSS to a 'more giving' DSS would require systems to offer – as much as to ask for – answers, opinions, suggestions and orientation. Very often, however, there is a minimum threshold of data entry and preparation of the DSS which the user must reach before receiving answers, suggestions or opinions. In looking for ways of adding value to decision making early in the process of use of DSS, it is not appropriate to look for a more prescriptive system, nor to search for systems which can offer definitive responses to inquiries – we have already noted that management DSS cannot expect to replicate the style of clinical DSS. Rather, the design principle must be to find ways of responding to managers' needs as they work through decisions. For example:

- DSS should be capable of responding to a request for analysis and provide feedback or reward at any stage in the process of use rather than after completing input of a full required dataset;
- DSS might prompt and help the user in design and conduct of the decision making process itself;
- DSS might be designed and used to provide a focal point in the decision making process used to test thinking, and to capture, analyse and display representations of the decision in real time.

While many DSS are clearly orientated to important management tasks, they have not always attended to the process and experience of use they demand of managers: many have been too uncompromising in their requirements for disciplined analysis.

Embedding and diffusing DSS

Many DSS address management issues which recur or are found in many localities. That DSS can be 'reused and translated into decision making in different localities' is therefore an advantage. Developments in software platforms mean that DSS are increasingly capable of being rewritten to demand (Eden 1993). Thus basic descriptions of tasks, problems and decisions can be 'roughed out' in a computer-based model with managers during a meeting or workshop and used to inform any research and data collection required to refine and test the description. The development cycle for DSS can now be very short and highly responsive to the learning process as managers draw together their thinking and test it in a formal way. As decision makers use a DSS, they learn more about the complexity of a decision area and how to express its basic character. DSS can become an integral and routine component of the decision making process. Where the decision recurs or is shared by many decision makers, the kind of ability to alter the values of variables (or their interrelationship) that constitutes what-if modelling also makes for reuse and transferability. Where the basic structure of the decision changes, however, more radical adaptation is increasingly possible.

Evaluating the contribution of DSS

Management DSS have not been evaluated to any great extent. Where they have (e.g. Sharda *et al.* 1988), evaluation has focused on their use in well-structured tasks for which it is possible to identify both high quality and poor solutions. In planning and management in the NHS, such benchmarks are rare. While it is desirable to understand the impact of DSS on decisions, such understanding is confounded by the 'sea of complex technological variables, personal transactions, organizational interactions, and environmental contexts' (Norris and Thompson 1991: 14).

Clinical DSS (CDS) have been the subject of more systematic evaluation and, despite their different aims and characteristics, it is possible to learn from that programme of work. Here, evaluation has focused on the diffusion of DSS, on the conditions which will promote their effective and routine use, and on the outcomes of use in terms of quality of clinical decisions. Wyatt (1995) argues that while many clinical DSS have been built and some have shown an impact on processes or outcomes of care, few have passed into routine clinical use. Furthermore 'although DSS are promising tools for disseminating knowledge . . . no amount of sophisticated computing can redeem a system if the knowledge on which it is based is of dubious quality, or if the system's goal is irrelevant to clinical practice' (p. 1). Weaver (1991), writing on the dissemination of clinical DSS, argues:

> Until these technologies are assessed in terms of whether and to what extent they improve the performance of the practitioners who use them, their appearance and the ease with which they can be integrated with established patterns of practice will mostly influence their eventual diffusion and use. More innocuous and conservative CDS systems will likely proliferate quickly, while the introduction of innovative systems that require or produce social change will encounter considerable resistance and will be, at best, gradual.
>
> (Weaver 1991: 48)

While the quality of the solution is an inappropriate benchmark for formal evaluation of management DSS, criteria including the coherence of intent, take-up and, especially, the process and experience of use are of direct relevance. Management DSS may be more or less liberating, more or less convenient or useful, more or less important as a means of initiating and developing planning and management processes, and more or less capable of transfer from one site of use to another. If management DSS are to be judged, however, a starting point is in their manner of use and functioning. While DSS themselves cannot ensure that they are used wisely they might, nevertheless, be expected to enable:

1 greater explicitness about the bases of decision making:
   - greater explicitness and improved communication about goals to be achieved, alternatives available and relations between goals and alternatives;
   - clarification of working assumptions, data and information requirements and linkages;
   - identification and clarification of decisions and events which affect objectives.

2 greater willingness to recognize and an ability to manage complexity:
   - stimulation to think of and consider seriously a wider range of goals and options;
   - an ability to handle multiple goals, alternatives and relations without feeling a need to resort to a single composite goal or simple 'yes/no' alternatives.

3 an improved ability to manage uncertainty
   - encouragement to consider, rather than ignore, worries, sudden thoughts and changes in thinking and to model the effects these might have on the outcome.

DSS design

DSS are useful where the complexity of a decision, or the requirement to display evaluations of a number of options, mean that standard written, verbal or non-automated systems of analysis will be inadequate or cumbersome. Other characteristics of the management task are also important.

Stand-alone vs. integrated systems

The frequency with which decisions are taken, information required and analysis is to be carried out is an important consideration. If decisions recur and the DSS is intended to be used frequently (for example, to assist in manpower rostering in accordance with workload requirements every week or month), then it will be helpful for the DSS either to be contained within or to be physically 'plugged in' to existing data sources. If the DSS is addressing a more 'periodic' process – for example, an annual planning cycle or an occasional 'one-off' exercise – then it is not so imperative that they are directly linked to data sources in the same way; a stand-alone DSS may be perfectly adequate. They may also require data which are not routinely gathered.

Many DSS at least start off in a stand-alone mode for a variety of reasons. One is that they are easier to construct and validate in this form; another is that they are usually more portable like this. Developing physical links to other data sources from the outset, unless this involves a standard process across large parts of the health service, is really a form of local adaptation and is likely to vary, at least slightly, from site to site. It is often easier to leave the DSS in a more generic and portable form.

The process of DSS development

Each of the case study chapters that follow set out and explain the process by which the DSS were developed. A brief overview of the steps involved in DSS development is provided here. In general, the process is not so neat and crisp as use of the term 'steps' implies: DSS development most often follows what might be called an 'unsteady line' towards its destination.

The first step in system development is typically an attempt to represent, qualitatively, the elements of the task. These might appear as stages, or modules, or components of the task. Variables – some within the influence of management action and others outside management influence – affecting the decision are identified and the relationships between them are mapped out, at first roughly and subsequently with as much precision as required or possible. This constitutes a 'logic model' which is then populated with data. The data specify values for the variables and for the strength and form of the relationships between variables. The aim at this stage is to specify a model which can be verified and validated (Pidd 1991; Gass 1994). Verification examines whether the model works as intended: it is the 'logic check'. Validation examines the correspondence between the model and its outputs to available measures of reality: it forms the 'reality check'. It is important at this stage to be explicit about

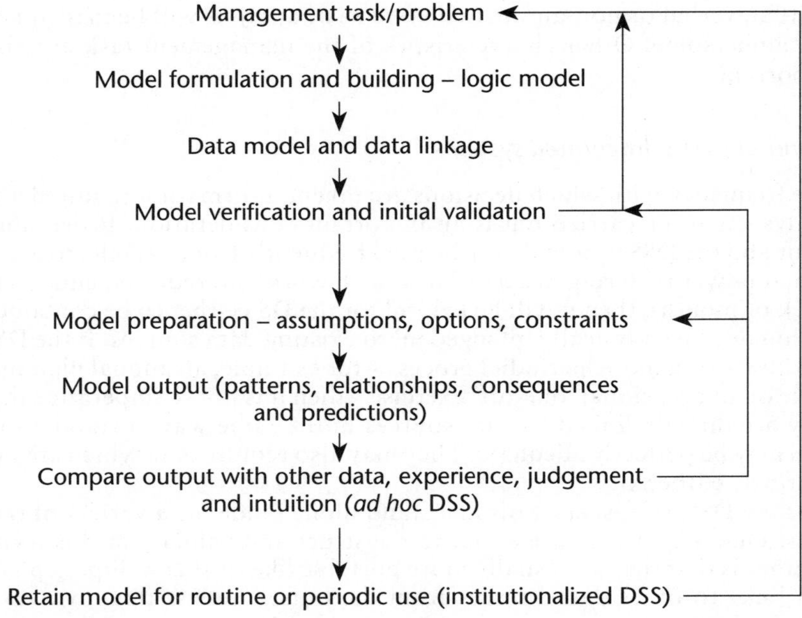

Figure 2.1 Steps in the DSS development process

and critical of assumptions built into the model. When there is sufficient evidence that the model adequately captures the management task, then it may be used for real, either *ad hoc* for a single decision or *institutionalized* within a decision making process.

Management use of DSS – facilitated vs. self-driven

Many accounts of DSS have treated the systems as automating technologies which can be developed and introduced into organizations unproblematically. Increasingly there is recognition that the design and implementation of DSS raises questions about how the analytical process (and DSS) can be related effectively to processes of decision and action. There are a variety of ways in which this may happen, but two types of link set the extremes on a continuum of possibilities.

The first sees the analytical and organizational as parallel activities, linked only when terms of reference are given to analysts and their results fed back into the decision making process (for example, as a report or a presentation). The decision process may be punctuated by a number of such 'backroom' analytical contributions, but these are only one among many influences on the process of deliberation. Over 20 years ago, Mintzberg (1989: 23–4) argued that

> In dealing with complex issues, the senior manager has much to gain from a close relationship with the management scientists of his or her own organization . . . A successful working relationship between the two will be effected when the manager learns to share his or her information and the analyst learns to adapt to the manager's needs. For the analyst, adaptation means worrying less about the elegance of the method and more about its speed and flexibility.

At the other end of the spectrum is the use of DSS as a standard practice by managers. As with other forms of technology, the use of DSS is affected and influenced by the general 'approachability' of the system, including the way in which it is presented and supported (such as the type of self-help guidance for users, or whether there is a technical support line available) and the speed with which it can be used appropriate to its intended function (Suchman 1987).

Concluding remarks

There is always going to be a learning curve with any new tool; the question is whether new users can get sufficient immediate value from a particular DSS or are willing to defer gratification and spend time and resources in becoming familiar with it. This is likely only if the problem being addressed is sufficiently important, and if the gains in confidence, quality of outcome and openness of decision making process anticipated are great. While past experience with DSS helps in assessing the potential of new systems, the process of development or implementation of a DSS requires an act of judgement. Carter *et al.* (1984) suggest several criteria which managers might consider in making such judgement: whether it makes sense of their experience of the decision situation and its context; whether they can commit to it as a framework; and whether they find it useful, realistic and unsurprising in its outcomes. However, the relationship between the user and the system itself is bound up not only with the individual understanding of the DSS but also with the ability of the organization itself to make use of one. Such an ability is signified by a willingness to devote resources to introducing it, training people to use it, finding appropriate first uses and, more widely, embracing a culture which sees DSS as a worthwhile adjunct to the management process. DSS are intended as means of structuring experience, exploring possibilities and testing the coherence of thinking. As Jung argued in *Memories, Dreams, Reflections*, 'The pendulum of the mind oscillates between sense and nonsense, not right and wrong.'

References

Ackermann, F., Cropper, S. A. and Eden, C. (1993) The role of decision support in individual performance review, in P. W. G. Bots, H. G. Sol and R.

Traunmuller (eds) *Decision Support in Public Administration (A-26)*. North-Holland, Elsevier.

Belton, V. (1993) Project planning and prioritization in the social services – an OR contribution, *Journal of the Operational Research* Society, 44: 115–24.

Bensley, D. C., Watson, P. S. and Morrison, G. W. (1995) Pathways of coronary care: a computer-simulation model of the potential for health gain, *IMA Journal of Mathematics Applied in Medicine and Biology*, 12: 315–28.

Bhuptani, B., Collier, B., Hull, M. and Teagle, N. (1993) *Community Information Systems for Providers – Overview Version 2.0*. Leeds, NHS Management Executive, Information Management Group.

Boldy, D. (ed.) (1981) *Operational Research Applied to Health Services*. London, Croom Helm.

Boldy, D. (1987) The relationship between decision support systems and operational research: health care examples, *European Journal of Operational Research*, 29: 128–34.

Bunn, D. (1992) Synthesis of expert judgement and statistical forecasting: models for decision support, in G. Wright and F. Bolger (eds) *Expertise and Decision Support*, pp. 251–68. New York, Plenum Press.

Carlson, E. D. (1982) An approach to building decision support systems, in J. L. Bennett (ed.) *Building Decision Support Systems*, pp. 20–32. Reading, MA, Addison Wesley.

Carter, R., Martin, J., Mayblin, B. and Munday, M. (1984) *Systems, Management and Change: a Graphic Guide*. London, Paul Chapman.

Cross, M. (1993) Hospital information systems: special report, *Health Service Journal*, 17 June, 39.

Dowie, J. (1996) 'Evidence-based', 'cost-effective' and 'preference-driven' medicine: decision analysis based medical decision making is the pre-requisite, *Journal of Health Services Research and Policy*, 1: 104–13.

Eden, C. (1993) From the playpen to the bombsite: the changing nature of management science, *Omega*, 21: 139–54.

Finlay, P. (1994) *Introducing Decision Support Systems*. Oxford, NCC Blackwell.

Gass, S. I. (1994) Public sector analysis and operations research/management science, in S. M. Pollock, M. H. Rothkopf and A. Barnett (eds) *Operations Research and the Public Sector*, pp. 23–46. Amsterdam, Elsevier North Holland.

Gillies, A. C. and Baugh, P. (1995) *Excel in Health Care*. London, Chapman and Hall.

Keen, J. (ed.) (1994) *Information Management in Health Services*. Buckingham, Open University Press.

Lagergren, M. (1987) The art of modelling, *Proceedings of Managing Change in Health Care*. Leeds, European Working Group on Operational Research Applied to Health Services.

Lagergren, M. (1996) What is the role and contribution of models to solving health care management problems? in A. Kastelein, J. Vissers, G. G. van Merode and L. Delesie (eds) *Managing Health Care under Resource Constraints*, pp. 27–44. Eindhoven, European Working Group on Operational Research Applied to Health Services.

Lilford, R. J. and Royston, G. (forthcoming 1997) Mapping the decision maze: decision analysis in the selection, design and application of clinical studies, in *Systems Science in Health Care*.

Mintzberg, H. (1989) The manager's job: folklore or fact, in H. Mintzberg, *Mintzberg on Management*. New York, Free Press.

Morgan, T. (1993) Phased decision conferencing: how a sequence of decision workshops helped a local authority to evaluate decision options, *OR Insight*, 6: 3–12.

Murphy, C., Currie, J., Fahy, M. and Golden, W. (1995) *Deciding the Future: Management Accountants as Decision Support Personnel*. London, CIMA.

Nagel, S. (1991) Introduction, in S. Nagel (ed.) *Public Administration and Decision-Aiding Software: Improving Procedure and Substance*. New York, Greenwood Press.

Norris, D. F. and Thompson, L. (1991) High-tech effects: a model for research on microcomputers in public organizations, in S. Nagel (ed.) *Public Administration and Decision-Aiding Software: Improving Procedure and Substance*. New York, Greenwood Press.

OR Insight (1994) Special issue on simulation in health, *OR Insight*, 8: 1–27.

Pidd, M. (1991) The process of O.R., in S. Littlechild and M. Shutler (eds) *Operations Research in Management*. London, Prentice Hall.

Pierskalla, W. P. and Brailer, D. J. (1994) Applications of operations research in health care delivery, in S. M. Pollock *et al.*, *Handbooks in Operations Research and Management Science*. Amsterdam, Elsevier Science.

Royston, G (1996) Modelling for the National Health Service, in P. H. Millard and S. McClean (eds) *Go with the Flow: A Systems Approach to Health Care Planning*. London, Royal Society of Medicine.

Schuck, G. (1985) Intelligent technology, intelligent workers: a new pedagogy for the high-tech work place, *Organizational Dynamics*, 14: 66–79.

Sharda, R., Barr, S. H. and McDonnell, J. C. (1988) Decision support system effectiveness: a review and an empirical test, *Management Science*, 34: 139–59.

Sheaff, R. and Peel, V. (eds) (1995) *Managing Health Information Systems*. Buckingam, Open University Press.

Smithin, T. and Eden, C. (1986) Computer decision support for senior managers: encouraging exploration, *International Journal of Man–Machine Studies*, 25: 139–52.

Suchman, L. A. (1987) *Plans and Situated Actions: the Problem of Human–Machine Communication*. Cambridge, Cambridge University Press.

Turban, E. (1990) *Decision Support and Expert Systems: Management Support Systems*, 2nd edition. New York, Macmillan.

Weaver, R. R. (1991) Assessment and diffusion of computerized decision support systems, *International Journal of Technology Assessment in Health Care*, 7: 42–50.

Wyatt, J. (1995) Decision support systems – why aren't they used? Paper to Symposium on Medical Informatics: Past, Present and Future. University of Manchester, 22–23 June.

Part 2
Strategic service planning

Introduction

Strategic decisions about health care services take place, substantially and increasingly, at a local level. Health authorities in the NHS are responsible for deciding which services to commission to meet the needs of their population, where they should be located, how they should form a part of the overall pattern of service, who should provide them, at what cost and to what standards. Overall purchasing intentions, published annually, should reflect such decisions. On the provider side, NHS Trusts are required to prepare and publish statements of strategic direction, business plans and business cases for major capital and service developments. These reflect strategic decisions and commitments to offer and provide health care facilities and services – although there are risks attached to the investments needed to make such commitments. Risks include changes in health care technology and practice, in understanding of their effectiveness, or in local service overcapacity.

All of this takes place within a national framework of resource allocation, policy guidance, priorities and service norms. However, there is considerable discretion for local analysis to influence decisions about the number, types and mix of services in individual authorities and Trusts. This is perhaps most powerfully justified by variations in local need and, if only in the short run, in the capacity of local providers to deliver appropriate services.

Strategic service planning tasks include: needs and demand forecasting, service capacity planning in the light of such forecasts and the commissioning of appropriate levels of capacity, assessment of new technologies and service configurations and the likely performance of new services, aggregate human resource planning, location selection, assessment of the distribution of services against need, and assessment of patterns of take-up and utilization of services.

Strategic service planning efforts are influenced by the objectives of health services. Equity, accessibility and an appropriate spatial distribution of services are objectives to which the service is returning, in part following unequivocal evidence that these are significant causes of health inequality. Chapter 3, by Graham Clarke and Martin Clarke, focuses on the spatial dimension to health care planning and provides an authoritative review of geographical information systems (GIS) and spatial modelling methods applied to health services. As questions to do with the structure and spatial disposition of population health needs become more searching, Clarke and Clarke open with a consideration of the geography of morbidity and mortality and examine issues arising when serving patients from fixed point locations – hospitals, etc. (such as the implications for accessibility, and for establishing contracts between purchasers and providers). GIS and spatial models, they argue, can make an important contribution to the planning process, improving health planners' ability to assess the geography of health need, existing service coverage and the likely consequences of options for new service provision. The authors introduce techniques of representation and analysis used in GIS and, in explaining how spatial interaction models increase the potential value of analysis, they expose the form of the model in some basic mathematics. This is the only point in the book that modelling technique is shown in this way, but it serves to indicate that there is a range of sophistication in the mathematics of DSS and to show the analytical functions not normally seen by the user menu-driven information systems. The chapter concludes with a view on areas for further research.

Planning of services across organizational boundaries is a particularly knotty problem for health authorities and social service departments. It has been notoriously difficult to make joint planning arrangements work effectively despite numerous policy exhortations to establish collaborative working practices in planning, implementing and delivering services. As observers including Andrew Nocon at the Social Policy Research Unit in York, and Gerald Wistow at the Nuffield Institute in Leeds have argued, unclear boundaries between agencies, conflicting pressures, a tendency to shift costs and differing approaches to the measurement of need, varying planning capacities, and differing accountabilities all mean that such an approach is difficult to develop and sustain. However, community care planning has been seen as an opportunity to develop a bridgehead. Community care plans are a basis on which health and social services can fashion joint information systems, joint needs assessments and a shared commissioning framework. Chapter 4 by Paul Forte and Tom Bowen on the Balance of Care (BoC) system provides an example of a DSS which provides a framework for and enables the creation of a forum for effective multi-agency strategic analysis, focusing on the long-term care of elderly people. Given the high levels of dependency in this client group there may be very many different ways of providing care.

This, in turn, can have major implications for the type and quantity of the service to be provided and the agency responsible for paying for and/or providing it. The Balance of Care system enables local planning groups to model the widest possible range of scenarios. The model is an integral component of a multi-agency workshop which brings participants together and enables them jointly to model their data and planning assumptions. An application of the model with a group comprising health authorities and a social services department is described. This chapter also considers the role and importance of facilitated workshops centred on using computer-based DSS. BoC has been around for many years, but its relevance has not been diminished by changes in health policy and organization.

The national framework of quality standards – including the Patient's Charter and waiting list initiatives – has been a major concern of managers in acute hospitals. The resource and service implications of meeting such targets are not easy to assess. Investment to address apparent shortages in consultant medical staff has allowed waiting times and lists to be addressed, but it has often brought unexpected consequences, such as increased numbers of referrals and a backlog of patients to be seen in outpatients. Chapter 5 by Tom Bowen and Paul Forte introduces a Business Planning Model developed as a means of helping in the preparation of service development plans with objectives such as meeting Patient's Charter standards and correcting current service deficiencies. The model enables the consequences of corrective action to meet such objectives to be assessed: for example, the consequences for support services such as theatres. Use of this model has involved managers and clinicians working together in a structured way and – incorporated as a component of a managerial skills training programme – has also been a means of management development. There are also implications for identifying gaps in existing data collection and information systems and helping to prioritize where improvements need to be made.

Finally, in this part of the book, we address service development and improvement in the NHS where it involves capital investment. Because it is so significant and because the costs are large, there is pressure on decision makers to ensure value for money and to render a clear account of the decision. There are, however, many uncertainties and risks attached to capital schemes – risk of obsolescence as health care technology changes; risk that the service capacity created is too small or too great against changing patterns of demand, and so on. The Private Finance Initiative has added further complexity and a need for caution to the process of investment decision making. The specification of objectives, the preparation of options which would meet those objectives, identification of the level of benefits (and of the costs and risks attached) are all suggested best practice in capital investment appraisal. Yet 'white elephants' still result. Chapter 6 by Tim Keenan focuses on capital investment appraisal. A decision support system has been developed which takes best practice as a framework for investment appraisal. It offers a tool for exploring options against objectives and against the different assumptions about the future which have been made in the identification and analysis of risk. Use of the system is illustrated by preparation of a business case for reprovision of services for elderly mentally ill people from a long-stay institution into a community setting.

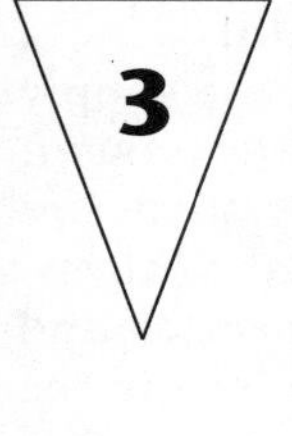

3 Spatial decision support systems for health care planning

Graham Clarke and Martin Clarke

Introduction

For a long time there has been a considerable interest in the geographical or spatial aspects of health care because equity is a fundamental principle of the NHS. Much of the work undertaken by geographers has fallen within five broad areas: spatial epidemiology, the spatial transmission of disease, the link between deprivation and disease, the relationship between access and utilization, and health service resource allocation (see Haynes 1987; Royston *et al.* 1992; Thomas 1992; Mohan 1995). These are clearly important and valuable tasks and have added much to our knowledge of the structures and mechanisms that give rise to spatial patterns of inequality in health status, utilization and resource provision. However, it is argued here that an additional dimension to the geographic analysis of health care systems can be provided through the application and use of computer modelling methods to add to the underlying theory and to generate a forecasting and prescriptive approach. The availability of such methods are of crucial importance to health service managers and planners, especially in the current climate of major changes in the management and delivery of health care.

The chapter is structured as follows. First, the *geographical* concerns raised by the splitting of the NHS into 'purchasers' and 'providers' of health care are highlighted. This is followed by a review of the contribution of geographical information systems (GIS) to health care planning and management. Although there has been considerable interest in their development, it is argued that the level of spatial analysis is low and that more traditional modelling methods offer more powerful insights into health care planning through the combined analysis of geographical variations in health care demand and provision of health care services in specific locations. The resultant patterns of utilization of health care are important to understand, especially when changes to either the supply or demand side are being made. A number of different applications of geographical modelling methods to a variety of health care systems are used to illustrate the main principles and methods of spatial analysis. In the final section the main points of the chapter are summarized and the future research agenda for model-based planning and analysis in the health service is considered.

The geography of health care reforms

The relationship between demand and supply in the NHS has been fundamentally reformed by *Working for Patients* (Secretary of State for Health 1989). The reforms raise some fundamental questions relating to (spatial) equity. The most direct geographical or spatial consequences are the changes to resource allocation procedure: it is clear that certain areas will see increases in their budgets at the expense of other regions. Mohan (1990) investigated these changes in some detail, concluding that rural Britain in general and the 'shire counties' of the South-East in particular will make substantial gains. Other spatial implications are more subtle. One concern arises from the possibility of long distance contracts. Purchasing authorities are now more likely to 'shop around' to try and obtain better standards of care at cheaper prices, and long distance contracts are becoming more common. This raises fundamental concerns over geographical accessibility, since patients (and relatives and friends) may be tied into long journeys to receive care or make visits. Issues of accessibility also surround the creation of a seemingly two-tier system of GPs: fundholders and non-fundholders.

Another major concern arises from the likelihood of increased specialization initiated by the providers of health care. On one hand, smaller hospitals may concentrate on winning contracts that they believe will take full advantage of their expertise and hence maximize their revenues. On the other, there is an increasing trend towards the development of large specialized facilities that are located in a smaller number of hospital locations. This typically requires a reduction in the number of existing units and the assessment of the impacts of this process of rationalization and concentration. While concentration of facilities should lead to the development of 'centres of excellence' and increasingly more effective patient care, it also reduces the overall level of access to these facilities and therefore potentially raises important issues of spatial equity. In addition, it may mean that more routine treatments will be pushed towards primary health care establishments or the private sector.

In the light of these concerns it is critical to monitor the impacts of the purchaser–provider split and offer support for more equitable planning. For purchasers the shift from the management of health facilities to the determination and satisfaction of health care needs of their resident populations requires a better understanding of the geographical dimension of health care needs, utilization and outcomes. In particular there is a need to address the following questions:

1 How do health status variables relate to socio-economic and other variables by small area?
2 How does the actual utilization of health care services relate to the expected utilization by small geographical area?
3 Where do our residents currently receive care?
4 How do the performance of current providers compare with planned objectives and at what costs?
5 How will the pattern of referrals have to change if proposed contracts are to be implemented?

A number of these questions are driven by the realization that, in practice, there are substantial spatial variations in the rate at which health care facilities are utilized. There is now a substantial literature which has demonstrated wide variations in the use of hospital resources as measured by variations in admission rates and length of stay (see the useful summary by Bevan *et al.* 1994). In one sense this would be expected, as variations in morbidity are reflected in utilization of services. However, there is a consistency to the spatial variation in utilization rates that suggests that a more important cause is the availability and access to supply of health care. In other words, everything else being equal, a person is more likely to become a hospital inpatient if they live nearer to (or have better accessibility to) a hospital than one who lives further away. It is, of course, possible to pitch the argument the other way: that health care provision is located in areas of greatest need. Whether this is the case or not is difficult to determine scientifically; the reality is complex and no satisfactory set of explanations has emerged to suggest why these patterns exist. One immediate confounding factor is that many large general hospitals are located in central city locations where both the incidence of disease and levels of higher deprivation exist; a point which is returned to later.

Since hospitalization rates are clearly also influenced by the actions of GPs it is important to analyse their referral patterns. A number of factors have been put forward to explain variations in referral rates by GPs in different locations, such as practice size and characteristics of patients (Armstrong *et al.* 1988). Although there is not yet a firm explanation of referral behaviour, it is often suggested that if GP access to hospital facilities is poor then the GP will attempt to treat the medical episode within the community rather than refer. Conversely a GP with good access to hospital care may more readily pass on the responsibility to a consultant. Inner-city GPs may also have longer list sizes, poorer diagnostic facilities and, perhaps, be less aware of new forms of treatment (see Berkhout *et al.* 1985 for a detailed analysis of referral patterns from GPs in Dewsbury). Taken together these suggested causes may go some way towards explaining part of the spatial variation in utilization rates, but they are clearly not convincing as a total explanation.

For providers of health care the central issue must be the better understanding of where their and their competitors' business is being generated in relation to such geographical variations in demand. Again a possible checklist might be:

1 Where do our existing patients come from? (by age, sex, specialty)
2 Who are our main competitors?
3 What is the potential for increasing the workload by attracting patients currently referred elsewhere?
4 What are the implications of proposed contracts on the future viability of units and specialties within the organization?

The central argument of the remaining sections of this chapter is the need for an information system to provide a framework for examining these and additional 'what if' questions. Much attention has focused recently on the role and potential of geographical information systems to answer these sorts of questions. A brief review follows of what GIS can offer (and perhaps more importantly, what they cannot!)

Geographical information systems in the NHS

Today the GIS industry is a multi-million pound business serving a vast range of diverse organizations associated with spatial data handling; it is threatening to become a major branch of academic geography in its own right. Examples include all aspects of human and physical geography, as the text of Maguire *et al.* (1991) attests. The potential of GIS in the NHS is best illustrated through an examination of what they can offer in terms of spatial analytical functions. These are reviewed under five major headings.

Data storage, retrieval and display

The ability to analyse variations in mortality and morbidity (where such data exist) has been considerably aided by the arrival of widely available GIS packages. Many health authorities have been quick to realize the potential of GIS to store and retrieve spatial information at will. The mapping of incidences of illnesses (identified through utilization data) helps health authorities to monitor trends in disease levels, and identify 'clusters' which may in turn help target campaigns of both preventive and treatment programmes. There has been a great deal of collaboration between academia and health authorities around the country (see Openshaw *et al.* (1987) for an example in searching for leukaemia clusters, and the mapping of spatial variations in health care provision in Merseyside (Brown *et al.* 1991)). Such GIS, based primarily on health

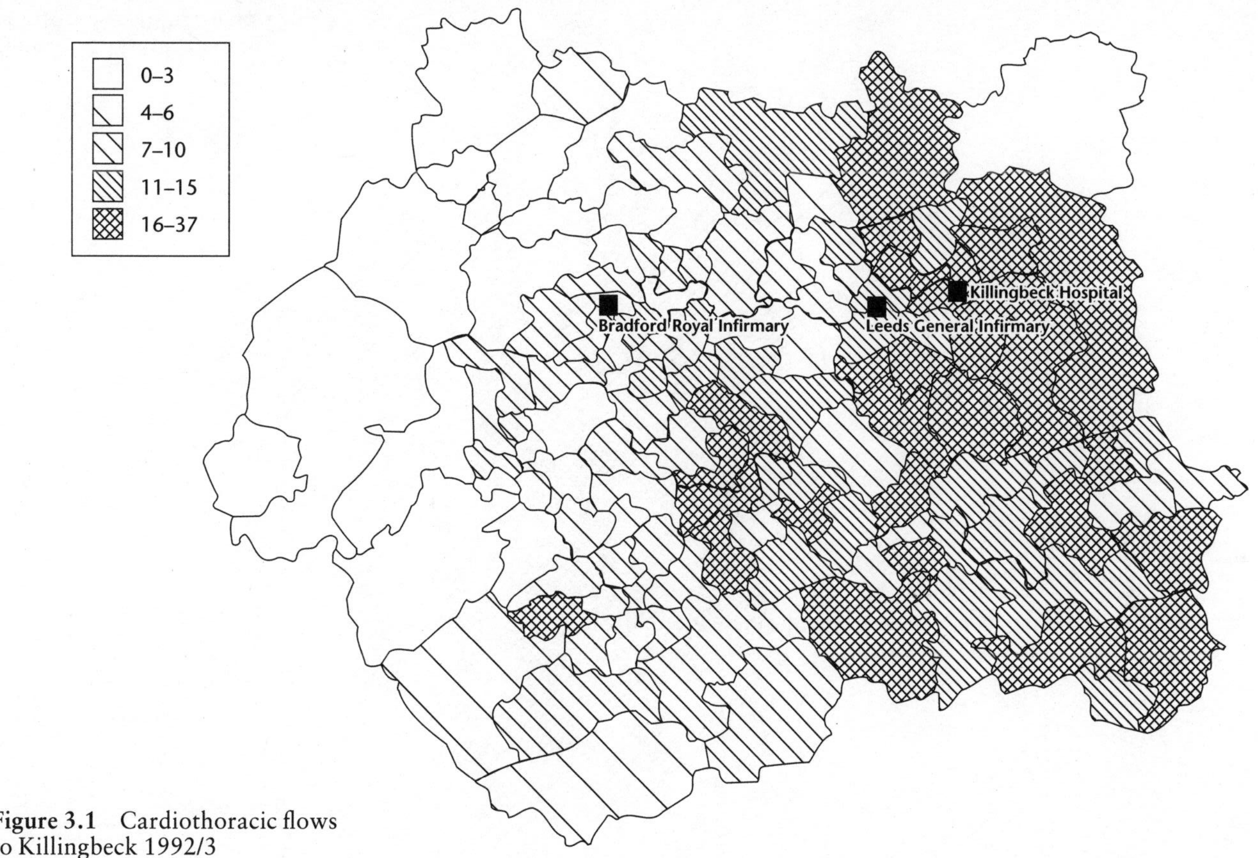

Figure 3.1 Cardiothoracic flows to Killingbeck 1992/3

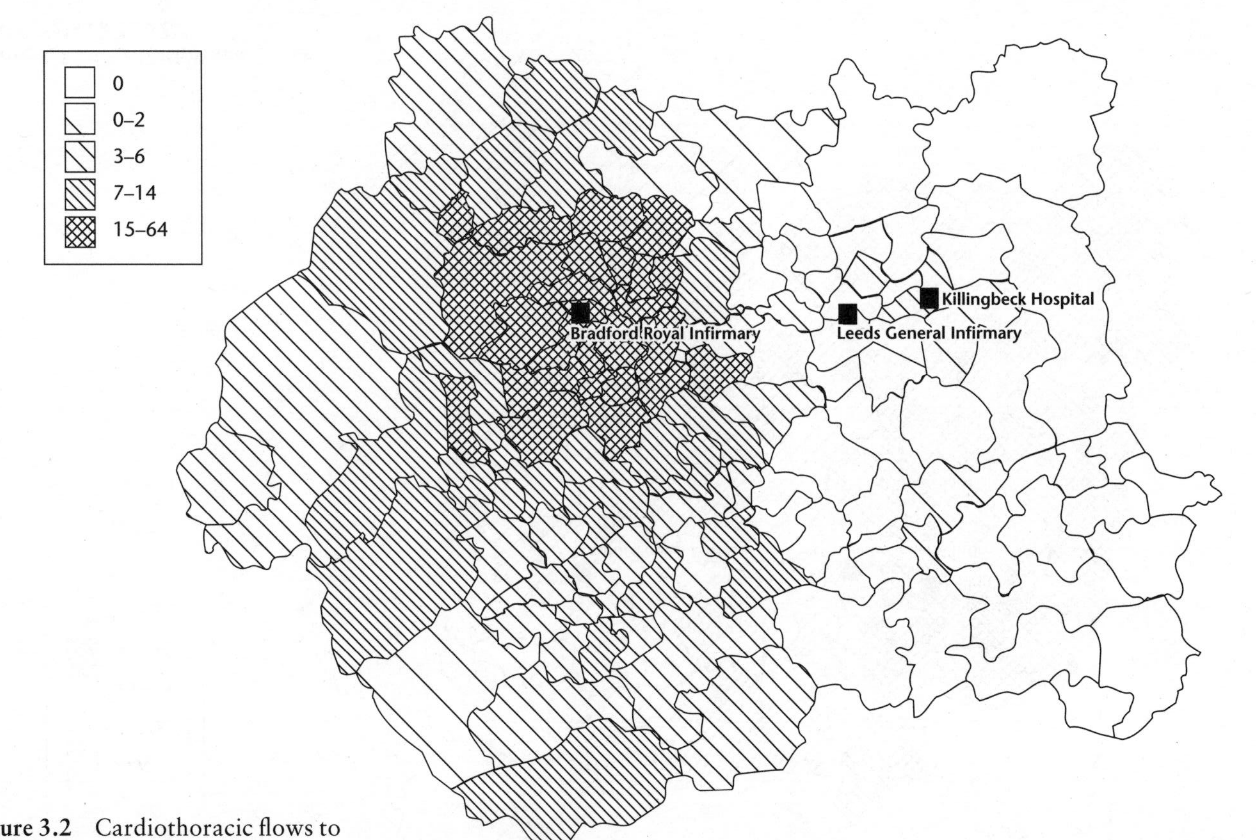

Figure 3.2 Cardiothoracic flows to Bradford Royal Infirmary 1992/3

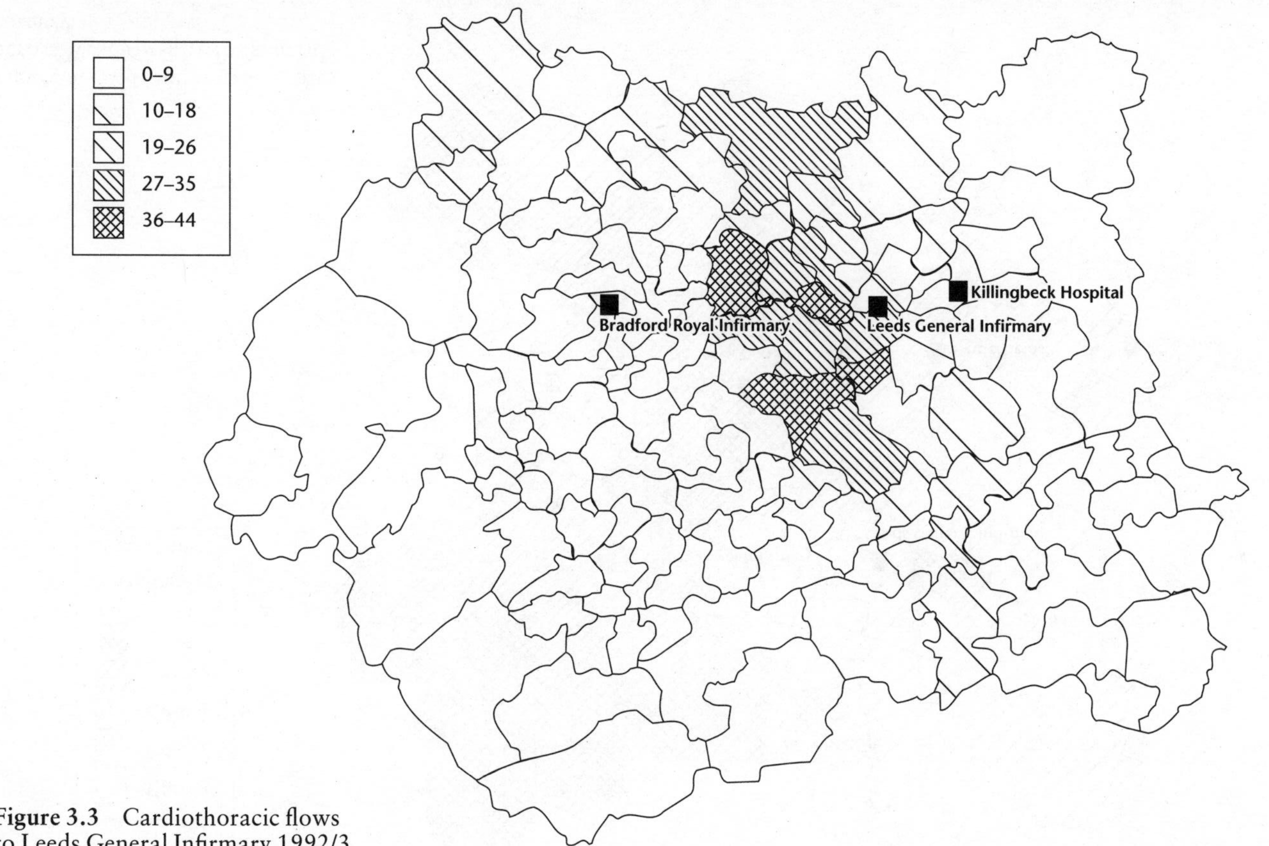

Figure 3.3 Cardiothoracic flows to Leeds General Infirmary 1992/3

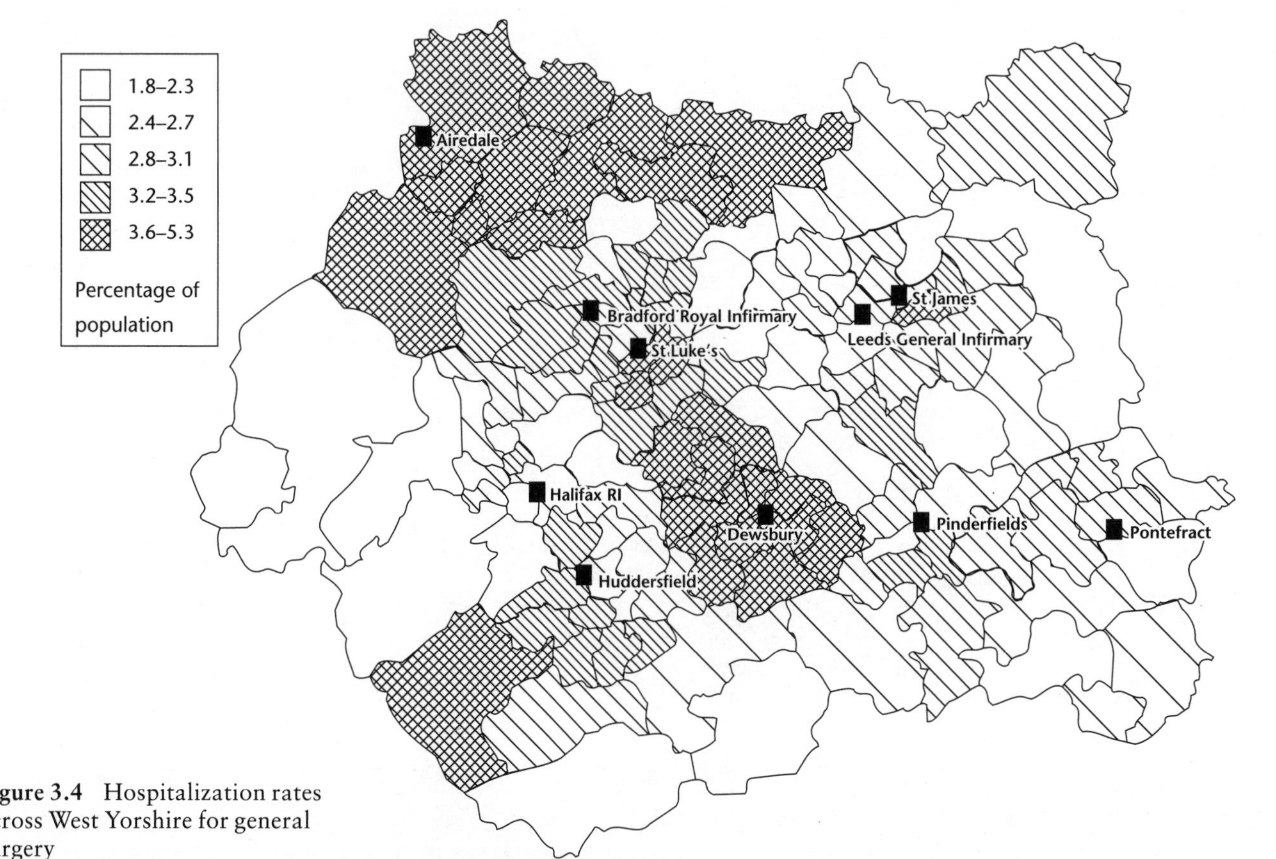

Figure 3.4 Hospitalization rates across West Yorshire for general surgery

care data and geodemographics, also have an important role to play in marketing, especially for private sector hospitals keen to locate new developments in 'optimal' locations (Hale 1991). Thus simply employing the mapping facilities of a GIS can help answer the basic purchaser geographical question of 'Where do our residents currently receive care?' and, for the providers, 'Where do our existing patients come from?' Figures 3.1 to 3.3 show examples of the latter. Here the maps show the catchment areas of three hospitals in West Yorkshire for cardiothoracic surgery: note the very distinctive catchment areas of the three hospitals. These will be analysed in more detail later.

Data linkage

This is one of the most fundamental methods of adding value to data and in most GIS the concept of *polygon overlay* is central to this process. The simplest form of overlay concerns only two variables. For example, a Director of Public Health might be interested in mapping small-area variations in the incidence of childhood leukaemia and overlaying the location of waste incinerators or other noxious industrial activities. Similarly, it is interesting to map small-area variations in hospitalization rates and then simply overlay the location of hospitals. This latter example helps to address another key geographical question: how hospitalization rates vary by small geographical area. Figure 3.4 shows standardized hospitalization rates for all acute specialties in West Yorkshire by postal sector, overlaid with the location of the major acute hospitals. The visual correlation between high hospitalization rates and the location of the hospitals is very striking and tends to support the arguments made earlier. Hirschfield *et al.* (1993) provide another useful example, mapping the location of GP patients in the Wirral with an index which summarizes small geographic areas (into household types: affluent, elderly, poor, etc.). From this they could immediately gauge the social make-up of any individual GP catchment area. If morbidity or mortality rates were also mapped in relation to geodemographic factors then a third purchaser question could be addressed: the relationship between health status and socio-economic variables (see also Bullen *et al.* 1994).

The overlay procedure is often undertaken in conjunction with *spatial buffering,* which enables the user to determine an area at a chosen distance from either a point location (such as a hospital) or a line feature (such as a road). Then, characteristics of the population that live within such a buffer zone can be calculated. This produces very crude catchment area summaries but may be useful in answering basic questions such as number of people within certain drive time buffers of a major hospital (see Figure 3.5).

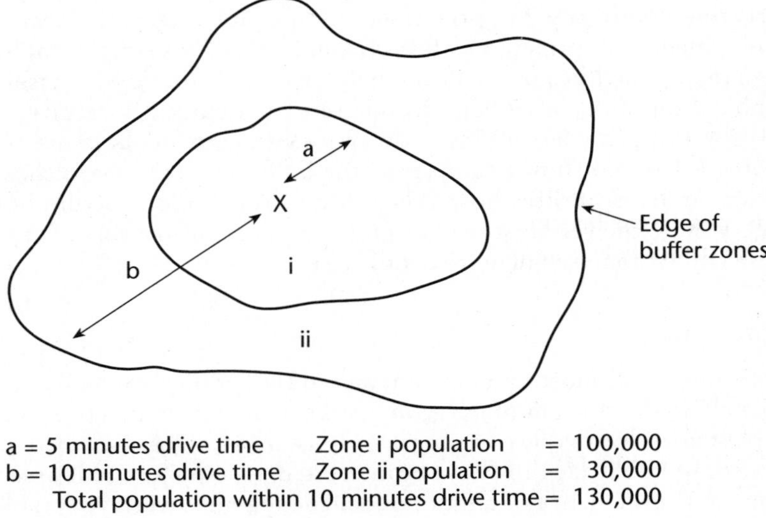

Figure 3.5 Buffer zones around a hospital location (X)

Geocoding

Geocoding refers to the ability of the GIS to store information relating an attribute to any geographical feature and to retrieve this information whenever the user highlights such a feature. This is also referred to as a *spatial query*. On highlighting a specific map location (such as a hospital) the GIS will search through all its information banks to retrieve all recorded information associated with that geographical feature. Although this is unlikely to produce important *analysis* it does speed up the process of data search and manipulation.

Network analysis

This is one of the most frequently used components of GIS and underpins much of GIS use in the utilities and transportation. Once a road system, for example, has been digitized then a GIS can quickly answer questions about routeing: such as what is the quickest way from A to B. The response can be made more complicated by adding *impedance* factors such as speed restrictions, or temporary blockages caused by accidents or road repairs. The most obvious use of network analysis in health care planning is for the optimal routeing of ambulances. These types of system are now in routine operation in many counties (see Jones 1993 and Ward 1994 for excellent illustrations). When combined with other GIS features such as buffering and overlay it is possible to produce sophisticated 'models', for example, to direct evacuation procedures in emergency conditions (see the work of Gatrell and Vincent 1990).

GIS and spatial analysis

As the brief discussion above demonstrates, the level of spatial analysis in GIS packages is currently minimal and much of the use of GIS is descriptive. While this is useful for helping to answer a number of our key questions posed earlier it helps little with impact assessments. From the wealth of published material it seems there are three main ways of trying to improve the level of analysis in the modern GIS community. The first simply involves a greater number of functions being available through proprietary packages – but ultimately many of these are of peripheral interest (such as many of the statistical routines), and such a strategy continues the technology-led approach rather than the solution-led approach to spatial analysis.

A second route, favoured by Openshaw (1992), argues for a new era of spatial analysis based around a more flexible approach to finding spatial patterns and clusters. The idea here is to abandon any *a priori* theory or model to account for spatial patterns (indeed Openshaw advocates that all previous spatial analysis textbooks be incinerated!) and allow new computer software, containing libraries of 'pattern exemplars' (generic algorithms for pattern analysis) to search for such patterns or clusters without any theoretical preconceptions. The motivation for this sort of approach lies in the huge volumes of data currently available and the urgent need for new software to explore all possible patterns and correlations. There have been some impressive successes using this sort of approach, particularly in the well-documented cases of Openshaw's work on finding cancer clusters (Openshaw *et al.* 1987; Openshaw and Craft 1991).

A third route is to move towards integrating GIS with other software through direct or indirect coupling. This involves providing specialist software outside the main package but linking the data storage and graphics of the GIS through new command structures. This approach, when applied to geographical data and problems, forms the heart of *spatial decision support systems*. The definitions and history of their development from management schools is supplied by Densham (1991). He reiterates the fact that spatial problems are generically complex and are usually ill-defined or semi-structured. For these reasons systems are needed which can handle a large variety of different business problems in a user-friendly environment (i.e. no visible computer commands other than a start procedure). Typically GIS are not powerful enough here because of the lack of such suitable analytical functions. What is required is the ability to link spatial models with the strengths of GIS in storage, retrieval and graphics. Birkin *et al.* (1996) label this linkage 'intelligent GIS' and provide a suite of examples from the public and private sector.

Linking models with geographical information systems

There are a number of modelling methodologies which may be applicable for answering the remaining questions set out earlier. Two key approaches are those of *spatial interaction modelling* and *microsimulation*. The former deals with questions concerning flows of patients (or changes to flow patterns), given certain rates of morbidity and hospital location and attraction. Microsimulation is most useful for estimating 'missing' or incomplete data. The bulk of the discussion which follows relates to the spatial interaction modelling (microsimulation is discussed later).

Essentially there are a series of stages in the spatial interaction model process. The first stage is to model the registrations of patients living in census enumeration districts (EDs: usually made up of around 150 households) to GP practices and, hence, to simulate the practices' catchment population. Most research concerning general practice concentrates on referral rates, though studies have been made regarding spatial patterns of registration to practices and the effects of geography upon the utilization of primary health facilities (Knox 1979; Phillips 1979; Hays *et al.* 1990). Also a recent study by Martin and Williams (1992) used a spatial interaction model to study the general practice registration of residents in the Bristol area.

The model itself may be written as:

$$S_{ij} = A_i \; O_i \; W_j \; e^{-\beta_j c_{ij}} \tag{1}$$

where

i is the ED of residence of the patient (the 'origin');

j is the destination general practice;

S_{ij} is the flow of residents registered at practice j who come from ED i;

O_i is the demand (defined as the population of ED i);

W_j is the attractiveness of practice j (defined as its list size);

c_{ij} is a travel cost variable (e.g. the straight-line distance from the centre of the origin ED to the practice);

β_j is a destination-specific distance decay parameter (i.e. describing how the 'attractiveness' of the practice declines as the distance from it increases);

A_i is a balancing factor defined as

$$A_i = 1 / \sum_j W_j e^{-\beta_j c_{ij}} \tag{2}$$

to ensure that patient flows sum to the known patient totals in the origin ED.

The flow of patients from ED to practice is also used as the input to the next stage of the model. This model uses a number of probabilities, generated from the observed data, to predict the number of inpatients by specialty arising in each practice (i.e. it predicts secondary care morbidity by specialty). This section of the model is known as the *morbidity model* and can be written as:

$$S_{ij}^{as} = S_{ij} A_j^{as} \quad (3)$$

$$T_{ij}^{las} = S_{ij}^{as} M_j^{as} B_l^{as} \quad (4)$$

where

a is the age split;

s is the sex split;

l is the specialty;

A_j^{as} is the probability of a patient attending practice j, being aged a and sex s;

S_{ij}^{as} is the breakdown by age and sex of the practice list;

M_j^{as} is the probability of a patient registered at practice j of age a, sex s, requiring an inpatient episode;

B_l^{as} is the probability of inpatient referral by age a, sex s to specialty l;

T_{ij}^{las} is the number of referred patients from ED i, through practice j, to specialty l, by age a, and sex s.

At this point we have simulated the action of the general practitioner and generated demand for health care.

The second half of the model determines to which hospitals each practice refers the inpatients for treatment in a given specialty. The model is written as:

$$T_{jk}^{l} = A_j^{l} T_j^{l} W_k^{l} \beta_k^{l} c_{jk} \quad (5)$$

where

j is the practice;

k is the provider unit (hospital);

l is the specialty of treatment;

T_{jk}^{l} is the flow of inpatients from practice *j*, to hospital *k*, calibrated for specialty *l*;

T_{j}^{l} is the demand (inpatients from practice *j* for specialty *l*) generated above;

W_{k}^{l} is the attractiveness (number of observed episodes) of hospital *k*, for specialty *l*;

c_{jk} is the travel cost variable (straight-line distance);

β_{k}^{l} is the destination-specific distance decay parameter, for hospital *k*, calibrated for specialty *l*

A_{j}^{l} is the balancing factor (as above).

What these models can offer beyond the capabilities of existing GIS is discussed below.

Transformation of data

A basic role of both GIS and models is to provide a framework within which data can be manipulated and transformed. In a GIS environment this may involve simply arithmetic operations to turn, for example, known patient home address records into some measure of market share for a certain hospital (i.e. by calculating the number of patients attending a particular hospital as a percentage of all hospital patients in that locality). Figure 3.6, for example, shows the market share of Leeds General Infirmary of patients requiring hospital treatment in West Yorkshire.

A more detailed approach to data transformation arises through the comprehensive use of model outputs which have been articulated as a system of spatial performance indicators. These help us to address the questions regarding performance outlined earlier. For any service provided, both publicly or privately, two fundamentally different types of performance indicator can be developed. The first can be termed facility-based and relates to the efficiency and effectiveness of the outlet such as a hospital Trust in relation to its catchment population. Catchment populations can be considered as the notional number of individuals that a facility is serving irrespective of where these people live. The crucial argument is that the calculation of catchment populations is dependent on the level of provision in adjacent localities in addition to those available within a particular locality. It can be calculated in a number of different ways from spatial interaction data, i.e.

$$CP_j = P_i \frac{S_{ij}}{\sum_j S_{ij}} \tag{6}$$

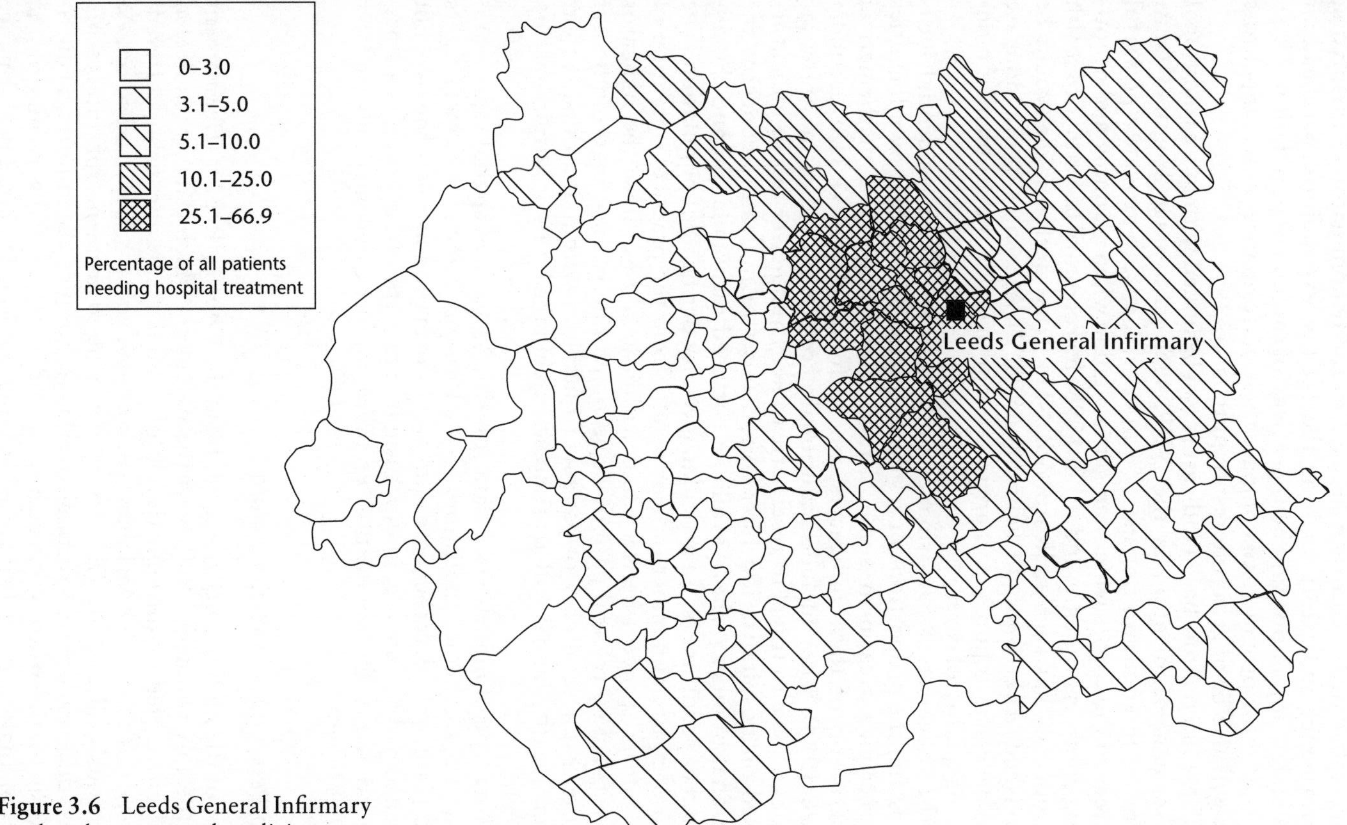

Figure 3.6 Leeds General Infirmary market share: general medicine

Once calculated it can then be used as the denominator in calculating performance indicators such as the facility expenditure per head of catchment population and beds per head of catchment population. These are useful for providers to compare their performance with competitors but will also be of great interest to purchasers.

These interaction-based indicators can be linked with more traditional performance indicators in the NHS, such as average length of stay, turnover interval, waiting lists, cost per case, etc., to provide a powerful battery of indicators which can act as a guide when planning and negotiating contracts for care. Indeed in 1993 the Secretary of State for Health announced that such indicators of NHS Trust performance would be published (*The Times*, 24 February 1993, 2). Measures of outcome are also necessary if purchasers are to attempt to tackle the problem of monitoring quality of care.

The other set of performance indicators relates to residential locations and the proportions of residents treated within their own localities or receiving treatment some distance from home. The mathematical description of these indicators can be found elsewhere (see Bertuglia *et al.* 1994). They include traditional accessibility indicators (how far patients have to travel to receive treatment) and newer sets of indicators based on hospitalization rates. Another set of indicators concerns the notional number of beds available per head of population and the notional expenditure on a particular specialty per head of population. The idea of notional number of beds results from the practical operation of the referral process between and within localities. Since the indicator reflects actual referral patterns it becomes a more meaningful indicator of the real accessibility of patients to facilities within and outside their home locality (and it will also in part explain the levels of hospitalization rates).

This type of model-based data transformation and spatial representation of performance indicators is of enormous value to many managers and planners: it lets them see data and information in a way they are not accustomed to and to gain new insights. Importantly, it provides a starting point for the application of more sophisticated methods in later stages of work.

Synthesis and integration of data

One of the main points emerging from the Chorley Report (Department of the Environment 1987) was the extent to which data are collected and assembled at different levels of spatial resolution using different categories to classify variables, such as age, social status, and so on. As previously discussed, GIS are a powerful instrument for integrating these different datasets through overlay techniques. An important contribution to the overlay procedure would be to add the results of the sort of analysis described in the previous section. That is, a performance indicator framework would provide new ways of transforming data but would itself create a large pool of information that the analyst might find difficult to comprehend fully. A solution to this problem might be to overlay model-based performance indicators in much the same way as conventional GIS data overlay procedures.

However, for many variables, such as morbidity, information is not collected at anything like the required level of spatial detail to make it useful. In these cases models can be employed to useful effect – linking and merging data files and making best estimates of missing information. A new way of measuring morbidity is to use *microsimulation*. Here, households and constituent individuals are re-created from different types of datasets and specified at the highest available level of spatial resolution, i.e. the household itself or small groups of households in the form of enumeration districts. These households and individuals can then be readily aggregated to provide cross-tabulations of any relevant variables at any upwardly compatible spatial scale. The methodology is underpinned by a procedure known as iterative proportional fitting (Fienberg 1970). This population or household reconstruction process has been carried out for a number of very varied application areas (see Birkin and Clarke 1988; Clarke 1996).

Once the household dataset has been reconstructed, the modelling task to calculate likely morbidity patterns can be articulated. From periodic surveys undertaken by GPs it is normally possible to estimate the probabilities of becoming ill for a wide range of specialties given basic demographic factors such as age, sex, social group, ethnicity, etc. Thus each household can be tested for the probability of illness given its own internal demographic profile. This can be achieved through Monte Carlo sampling procedures where a set of random numbers assign illnesses or not, according to such probability matrices. If an individual is assigned an illness then conditional probabilities can in turn be applied to test whether such an illness is likely to require a visit to the GP and then, in turn, hospital treatment. Such morbidity estimates can usefully sit alongside indicators such as hospitalization rates to see whether low or high hospitalization rates are simply associated with high likely levels of morbidity. A good example of the use of microsimulation in health care comes from Williamson (1996). He combines census data with data from various disability studies to estimate the degree of disability among the elderly in West Yorkshire, he then inputs information into various policy scenarios for the provision of care treatment for disabled pensioners.

Updating and forecasting

One of the clear deficiencies of any dataset, and particularly the census, is that it rapidly becomes out of date. No GIS has so far been able to offer users an effective on-line method for updating spatial data. How much of a problem this may pose depends upon the particular application.

Modelling methods which allow for an updating of census and related information are clearly important. In addition, while updating takes us from the past to the present, a further and important requirement is to examine how change may take place in the future. This is important in a number of contexts. For example, health authorities need to know not only what the future structure of the population is likely to be but also to have a reasonably clear indication of the way this structure varies across space. At the very least this information is required at the district level (20 or 30 census wards of approximately 10,000 households each), but it would be much more useful at the individual ward level or even postal district level. While the Office for National Statistics (formerly the OPCS) provides forecasts at health authority levels, more disaggregate forecasts can be modelled using a variety of techniques, from traditional cohort survival methods (see Rees and Wilson 1977) to techniques based on microsimulation (Clarke 1986). These involve updating and ageing small-area populations through the simulation of births and deaths and new household formation. Intra-urban migration can be linked to the changing availability of housing stock through local authority house-building and demolition statistics, as well as through the use of data sources such as the National Health Service Central Register (see Boden *et al.* 1992). Figure 3.7 shows the results of such small-area forecasts for central England. Once constructed these forecasts can be entered into the flow models described above.

Impact analysis

One of the most popular application areas for spatial modelling has been in assessing the impacts of new plans or proposals on the existing situation. This 'what if' simulation has proved valuable in a number of areas in both public and private sectors. (This is, of course, a kind of forecasting – but usually only short-run – concerned with the immediate impact of a new facility.) Traditional GIS are not very good at handling these sorts of questions, but spatial interaction models are ideally suited. In the following examples these models are used to show a number of potential 'what if' applications. The *baseline* model replicates the referral patterns to either GP or hospital based on the current situation. This calibrates the model and enables us to see how well the model can reproduce existing patient flows in the system. The *scenario* model operates by changing the starting conditions in some way. Some examples of such change are illustrated below.

Impacts of a new facility

The first example is drawn from running the models for the specialty of long-term geriatric care in a district of West Yorkshire (District A). In the baseline model there are a total of five existing providers in District A. Their facilities for geriatric care are summarized in Table 3.1. Given the

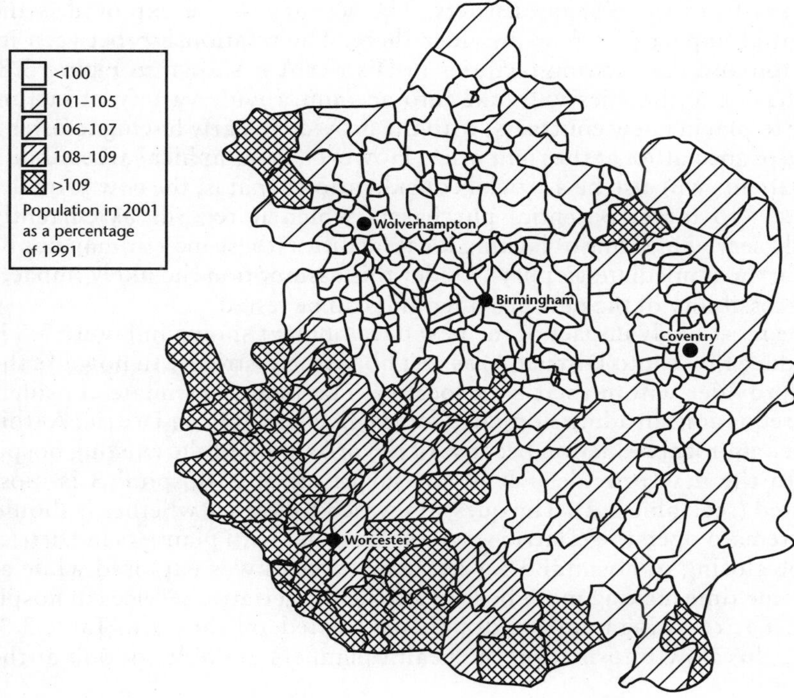

Figure 3.7 Population change by postal district 1991–2001: central England

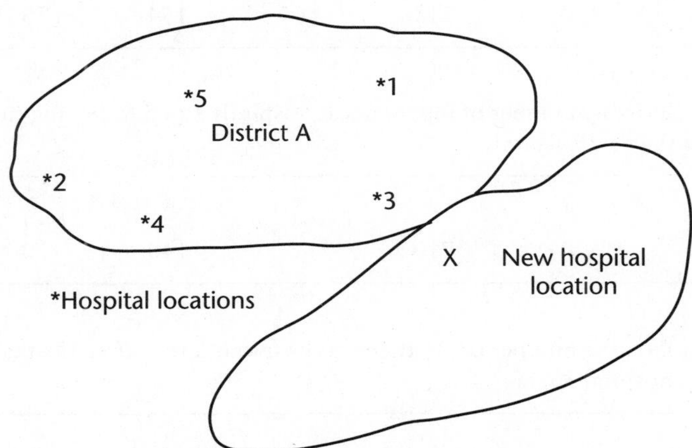

Figure 3.8 Location of a new hospital in relation to hospitals in District A

lack of providers in neighbouring districts there are significant flows of patients from these same districts. The scenario to be explored is the potential impact of a new provider there. The relationship between its location and the existing facilities in District A is shown in Figure 3.8. Purchasing authorities will take into account a wide variety of factors prior to placing new contracts, with the provider clearly having to offer a range of specialties at the right price. However, geographical accessibility for patients will also be a crucial consideration. That is, the new provider is likely to target potential purchasers which it regards as currently poorly served in terms of lacking local facilities (these may or may not be within the immediate vicinity). Under this assumption the likely impacts on accessibility of the new provider unit can be tested.

The most likely impact of the new development shown in Figure 3.8 is to reduce flows into District A, as neighbouring districts can now use the new provider within their own locality. The models estimate considerable reductions in admission rates for the five hospitals in District A (this is not a uniform reduction because of the proximity of the existing hospitals to the new provider). It is not surprising that hospital 3 is most affected (see Table 3.2). The question which follows is whether it should now remain open to geriatric services. Working with planners in District A, the closing of hospital 3 for geriatric services was explored while at the same time making more beds available for geriatric services in hospital 4. The resulting numbers of patients treated are shown in Table 3.3. Using this flow information the health planners are able to look at the

Table 3.1 Existing number of inpatients at hospitals 1 to 5

Hospitals	1	2	3	4	5
Inpatients	0	715	165	154	76

Table 3.2 Existing number of inpatients at hospitals 1 to 5 following the opening of the new hospital

Hospitals	1	2	3	4	5
Inpatients	0	710	48	140	70

Table 3.3 Existing number of inpatients at hospitals 1 to 5 after closing facilities at hospital 3

Hospitals	1	2	3	4	5
Inpatients	0	712	0	169	87

financial implications of changes in likely patient flows in order to decide whether such changes make sense.

Impacts of changing facility size

This looks at a possible scenario regarding the size of provider units. In this case, the attractiveness of the Airedale General Trust (in north Bradford) surgical specialty is increased to reflect greater bed availability, while St Luke's and Bradford Royal Infirmary, and other acute general surgical providers, remain constant. Increasing the attractiveness of Airedale General increases the episodes treated there at the expense of other providers. Those affected are as one would expect given the spatial arrangement of patients and hospital locations.

Figures 3.9a and 3.9b show the pattern of practices referring to Airedale General in the baseline model. The results of the scenario model, shown in Figure 3.9b, are that the increased attractiveness of Airedale General has resulted in the capture of flows of patients previously going to the Bradford hospitals.

Impacts of removing facilities at existing sites

The final example relates to an increasingly important problem faced by the NHS. Earlier, the issue of the provision of cardiothoracic surgery in West Yorkshire was examined. Substantial variations in hospitalization rates for this specialty across the census wards of West Yorkshire and a very strong relationship between high hospitalization rates and facility location were noted. At the time of writing there is a proposal to reduce the number of hospitals performing cardiothoracic surgery from three to two. This involves the closure of Killingbeck Hospital in east Leeds and its incorporation with the existing surgical unit at the Leeds General Infirmary in the centre of the city. The other remaining facility would be the Bradford Royal Infirmary.

The results of using the modelling framework described above to attempt to measure the impact of this change and of alternative proposals on hospitalization rates within West Yorkshire can be seen in Figure 3.10. This demonstrates that the model predicts that a move to the Leeds General Infirmary would result in a substantial reduction in hospitalization rates in the east of the city of Leeds coupled with an increase in the west of the city (the traditional catchment area of the Leeds General Infirmary). However, this would do little to redress the significant imbalances in hospitalization rates that exist in the south-west of the region, particularly in the areas around Halifax and Huddersfield (see again Figure 3.4). The impacts of relocating the Killingbeck facility to the Huddersfield Royal Infirmary were then examined. Figure 3.11 illustrates the impacts on hospitalization rates as predicted by the model. There is a significant reduction in hospitalization rates in the Leeds region (where the rates were already high) but a marked increase in the

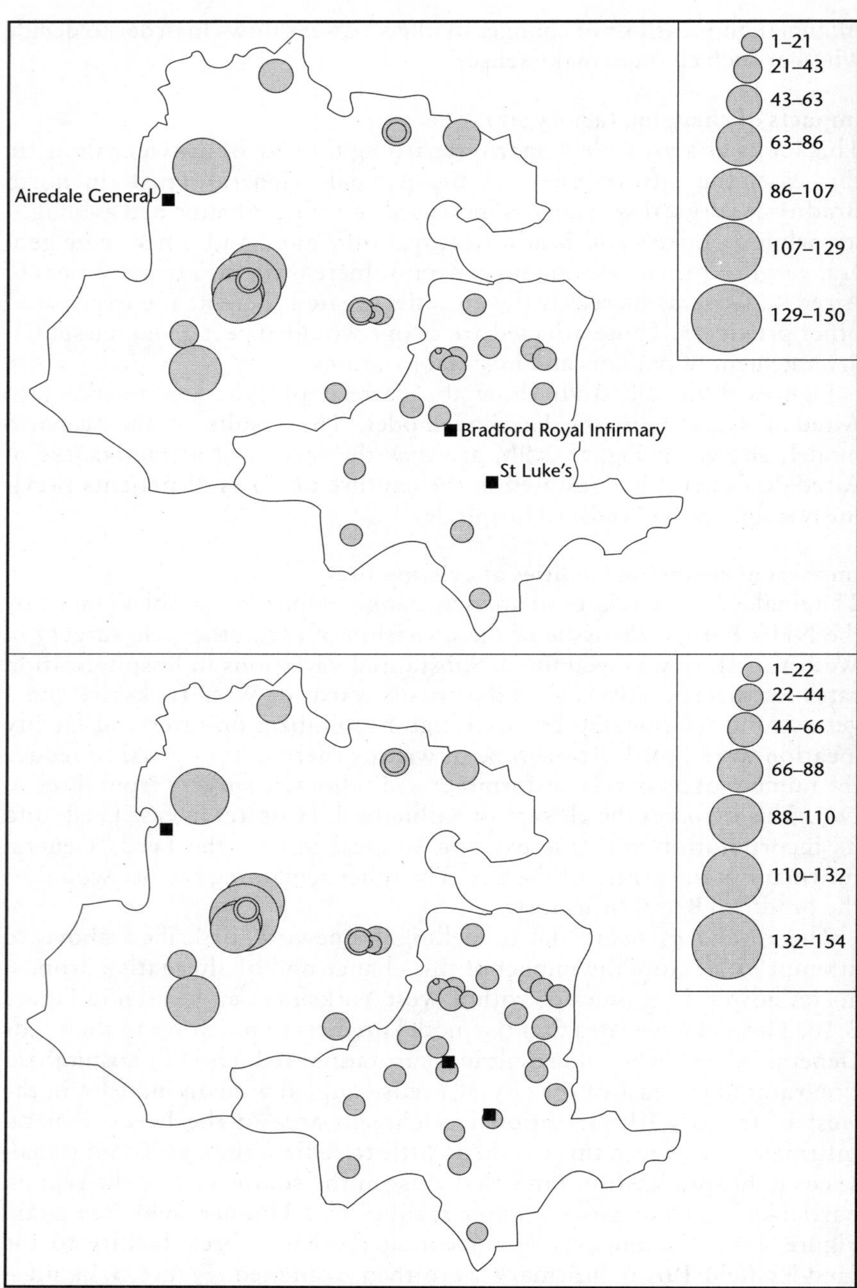

Figure 3.9a GP practice referrals to Airedale General for general surgery
Figure 3.9b GP practice referrals to Airedale General for general surgery following increased attractiveness

Huddersfield and Halifax areas which currently have very low hospitalization rates. From an equity perspective this solution would probably be deemed preferable to the merger of Killingbeck and the Leeds General Infirmary. However, we suspect that arguments about efficiency are deemed more important than equity in the current environment of planning within the NHS. It is through using this type of geographical analysis that the impacts surrounding various options can be explored in some detail; this should lead to better-informed decisions being made in such cases.

These relatively simple examples show how the model can be used to illustrate the implications of changes to primary or secondary facility provision. Multiple changes can be included in each scenario, and entire facilities can be opened or closed. Other parameters, such as residential population and the morbidity variables, could be changed in the scenario to simulate changes in the structure of the population and referral behaviour. Bed availability and mean length of stay can be altered according to the changes in provision by the acute units. From all these changes, performance indicators are (re)generated to enable sophisticated analysis of the health authorities' decisions, and to enable alternatives to be assessed more objectively and efficiently.

Conclusions: towards a research agenda in applied medical geography

The examples illustrated demonstrate the potentially crucial contribution of *geographical analysis* to health care planning and management. While medical geography has a strong and respectable tradition it has perhaps failed to contribute to the decision making process within the NHS to the extent it should have. One obvious reason for this is the lack of recognition within the NHS of the role geography plays in a variety of different aspects of health care.

First, there is the important issue of continuing the tradition in medical geography of spatial epidemiology (see the excellent review in Thomas 1992). For example, in some authorities there is an urgent need to monitor and forecast the spatial distribution of individuals who are HIV positive or who have full-blown AIDS. Williams (1992) has proposed an approach based on microsimulation methodology that would explicitly focus on the process of viral transmission between different sexual orientation groups and drug abusers with a high level of spatial representation. Medical geographers argue forcefully that AIDS is an important subject for analysis and there is therefore a need to demonstrate the contribution that can be made.

A second area relates to the promotion of the marriage between GIS and spatial modelling. It has been argued here that although GIS seem useful for health care applications there is a limit to the power of the spatial analysis routines within such systems. There exists considerable

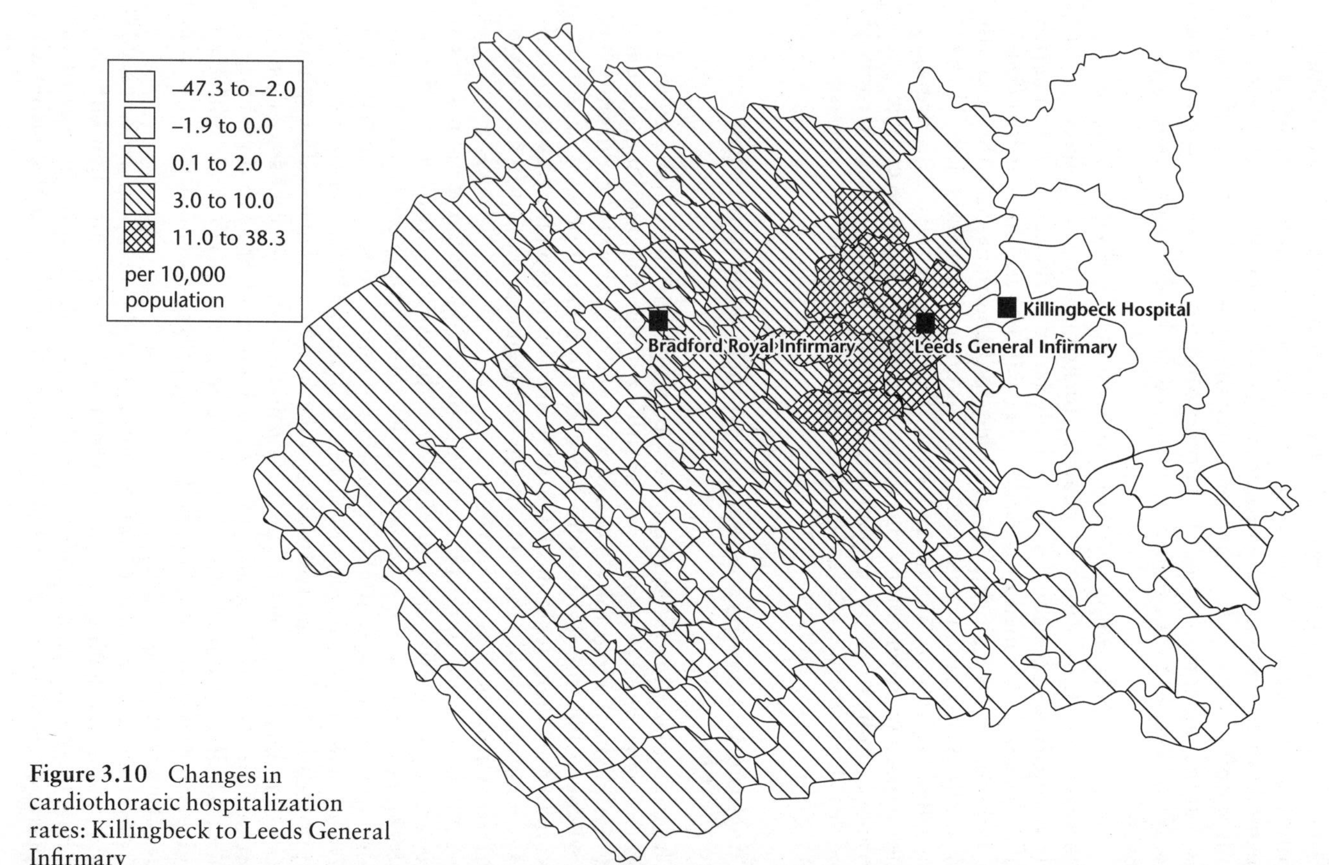

Figure 3.10 Changes in cardiothoracic hospitalization rates: Killingbeck to Leeds General Infirmary

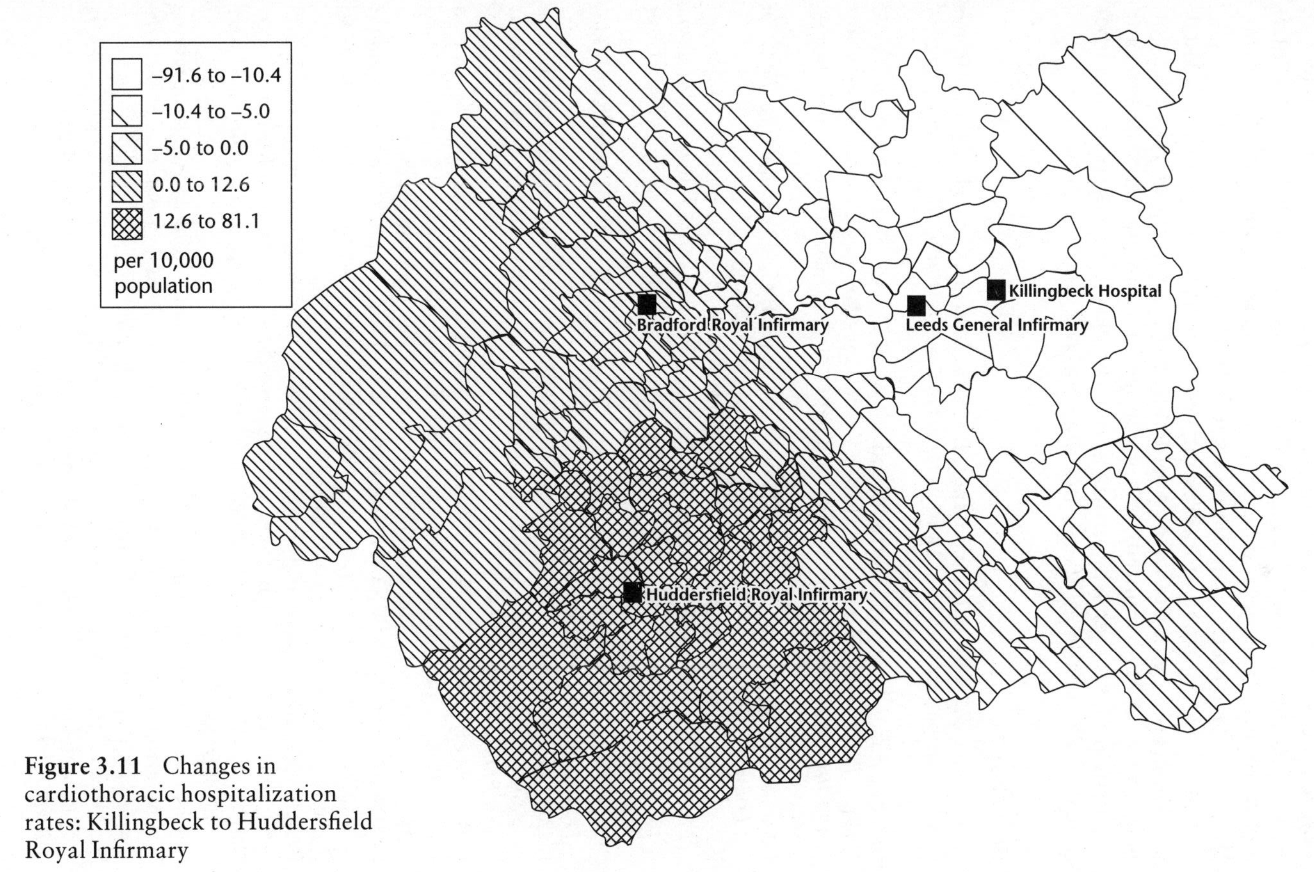

Figure 3.11 Changes in cardiothoracic hospitalization rates: Killingbeck to Huddersfield Royal Infirmary

scope for the development of model-based GIS with their greater analytical power for tackling complex 'what if' questions regarding the provision of health care facilities. In particular, research is needed to implement the framework described in this chapter, perhaps for an entire city or region. If this could be achieved in collaboration with either purchasers or providers, then so much the better.

There is no shortage of interesting research issues in quantitative medical geography; what remains problematic is the setting of priorities and being seen to both contribute to important contemporary debate and perform analysis that will inform and assist decision makers at a number of levels. The challenge exists and time will tell if it is responded to.

References

Armstrong, D., Britten, N. and Grace, J. (1988) Measures of general practitioner referrals: patient workload and list size effects, *Journal of the Royal College of General Practitioners*, 38: 494.

Berkhout, F., Clarke, M., Forte, P. and Clayden, D. (1985) *The Implications of the GP Referral System for Health Authority Planning: Some Observations and the Results of a Survey*, Working paper 407. Leeds, School of Geography, University of Leeds.

Bertuglia, C. S., Clarke, G. P. and Wilson, A. G. (eds) (1994) *Modelling the City: Planning, Performance and Policy*. London, Routledge.

Bevan, G., Brooks, J. and Toth, B. (1994) *Small Area Variations in Use of Hospital Resources in the NHS: Analysis of Variations in Admission Rates and Length of Stay by Case-mix Groups*, Working paper. Bristol, University of Bristol, Department of Social Medicine.

Birkin, M., Clarke, G. P., Clarke, M. and Wilson, A. G. (1996) *Intelligent GIS*. Cambridge, Geoinformation.

Birkin, M. and Clarke, M. (1988) SYNTHESIS – a synthetic spatial information system for urban and regional analysis: methods and examples, *Environment and Planning A*, 20: 1645–71.

Boden, P., Stillwell, J. C. H. and Rees, P. H. (1992) Internal migration projection in England: the OPCS/DOE model, in J. C. H. Stillwell and P. Congdon (eds) *Migration Models: Macro and Micro Approaches*. London, Belhaven.

Brown, P. J., Hirschfield, A. H. and Batey, P. J. (1991) Applications of geodemographic methods in the analysis of health condition incidence data, *Papers of the Regional Science Association*, 70: 329–44.

Bullen, N., Moon, G. and Jones, K. (1994) Defining communities: a GIS approach to delivering better health care, *Mapping Awareness*, March, 22–5.

Clarke, G. P. (ed.) (1996) *Microsimulation for Urban and Regional Policy Analysis*. London, Wiley.

Clarke, M. (1986) Demographic forecasting and household dynamics: a microsimulation approach, in R. Woods and P. H. Rees (eds) *Population Structures and Models*. Hemel Hempstead, Allen and Unwin.

Densham, P. J. (1991) Spatial decision support systems, in D. J. Maguire, M. F. Goodchild and D. W. Rhind (eds) *Geographical Information Systems: Principles and Applications, Volume 1*. London, Longman.

Department of the Environment (1987) *Handling Geographic Information*. Report to the Secretary of State for the Environment of the Committee of Inquiry into the Handling of Geographic Information [The Chorley Report]. London, HMSO.

Fienberg, S. E. (1970) An iterative procedure for estimation in contingency tables, *Annals of Mathematical Statistics*, 41: 907–17.

Gatrell, A. C. and Vincent, P. (1990) Managing natural and technical hazards: the role of GIS, *Regional Research Laboratory Initiative Discussion Paper 7*. Sheffield, ESRC RRL, Department of Town and Regional Planning, Sheffield University.

Hale, D. (1991) The healthcare industry and geographic information systems, *Mapping Awareness*, 5: 36–9.

Haynes, R. (1987) *The Geography of Health Services in Britain*. London, Croom Helm.

Hays, S. M., Kearns, R. A. and Moran, W. (1990) Spatial patterns of attendance at general practitioner services, *Social Science and Medicine*, 31: 773–81.

Hirschfield, A., Brown, P. and Bundred, P. (1993) Doctors, patients and GIS, *Mapping Awareness*, 7: 9–12.

Jones, A. (1993) Using GIS to link road accident outcomes with health service accessibility, *Mapping Awareness*, 7: 33–7.

Knox, P. L. (1979) The accessibility of primary care to urban patients: a geographical analysis, *Journal of the Royal College of General Practitioners*, 29: 160–8.

Maguire, D. J., Goodchild, M. F. and Rhind, D. W. (eds) (1991) *Geographical Information Systems: Principles and Applications*. London, Longman.

Martin, D. and Williams, H. C. W. L. (1992) Market area analysis and accessibility to primary health care centres, *Environment and Planning A*, 24: 1009–19.

Mohan, J. (1990) Spatial implications of the National Health Service White Paper, *Regional Studies*, 24: 553–8.

Mohan, J. (1995) *A National Health Service? The Restructuring of Health Care in Britain since 1979*. Basingstoke, Macmillan.

Openshaw, S. (1992) Some suggestions concerning the development of AI tools for spatial analysis and modelling in GIS, *Annals of Regional Science*, 26: 35–51.

Openshaw S. and Craft, A. (1991) Using geographical analysis machines to search for evidence of clusters and clustering in childhood leukaemias and non-Hodgkin Lymphomas in Britain, in G. Draper (ed.) *The Geographical Epidemiology of Childhood Leukaemias and Non-Hodgkin Lymphomas in Britain, 1966–1983*. OPCS Studies in Medical and Population Subjects, 53. London, HMSO.

Openshaw, S., Charlton, M., Wymer, C. and Craft, A. W. (1987) A mark I geographical analysis machine for the automated analysis of point data sets, *International Journal of Geographic Information Systems*, 1: 335–58.

Phillips, D. R. (1979) Spatial variations in attendance at general practitioners services, *Social Science and Medicine*, 130: 169–76.

Rees, P. H. and Wilson, A. G. (1977) *Spatial Population Analysis*. London, Edward Arnold.

Royston, G. H. D., Hurst, J. W., Lister, E. G. and Stewart, P. A. (1992) Modelling the use of health services by populations of small areas to inform the allocation of central resources to larger regions, *Socio-economic Planning Science*, 26: 169–80.

Secretary of State for Health (1989) *Working for Patients*. London, HMSO.

Thomas, R. W. (1992) *Geomedical Systems: Intervention and Control*. London, Routledge.

Ward, A. (1994) Saving lives in the West Country – using GIS to improve ambulance response times, *Mapping Awareness*, April, 36–7.

Williams, J. (1992) *A Simulation Model of the Spread of HIV and AIDS in the United Kingdom*, Working paper 92/2. Leeds, School of Geography, University of Leeds.

Williamson, P. (1996) Community care policies for the elderly, 1981 and 1991: a microsimulation approach, in G. P. Clarke (ed.) *Microsimulation for Urban and Regional Policy Analysis*. London, Wiley.

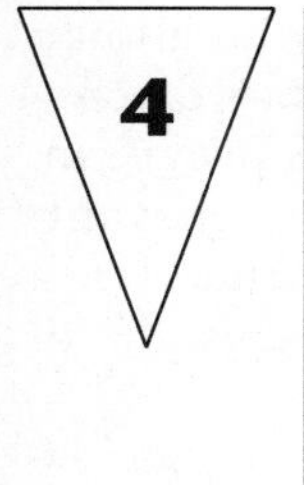

Improving the balance of elderly care services

Paul Forte and Tom Bowen

Introduction

This chapter presents a decision support system designed to address strategic planning issues involving a range of different agencies including health and social services, and the private and voluntary sectors. Responsibilities for setting the appropriate strategic direction, effective service provision and meeting client group needs (in this case, for elderly people) are not always clear-cut and may rest with different agencies. The setting of services for elderly people is predominantly community-based and is characterized by the large number of commissioning and provider organizations, the potential range of services provided, and the often poor quality, compatibility and availability of information on needs and service levels.

First, the main features of the strategic planning process are outlined; this is followed by a discussion of the Balance of Care (BoC) approach, which embodies a computer-based DSS in a facilitated workshop. The DSS helps managers and planners to explore issues arising from the workshop discussions by modelling available data to test assumptions and indicate the resource consequences of different plans and strategies. It enables the undertaking of a wider, deeper and altogether more detailed analysis of planning options and their consequences than might otherwise be possible. Two case studies illustrating the relevance and application of the approach are presented.

Planning long-term care for elderly people

The provision and management of long-term care services for elderly people is taking place against a background of an increasingly elderly population in the UK, an expectation that the costs of providing long-term services for them will inevitably rise, and a complex 'mixed economy' of publicly and privately funded service purchasing and provision. This often makes the establishment and coordination of local policy difficult to achieve. 'Long-term care' refers to services that are required on a continuing basis for an individual and not limited to specific episodes of care (as acute care would be).

The UK, in common with other developed economies, has an increasing proportion of its population over 65 – currently about 16 per cent, and projected to rise to 22 per cent by 2031. Of more concern, however, is the more rapid increase in the number of people over 75 (currently 7 per cent of the population, rising to about 11 per cent in 2031). This age is often regarded as a key turning point for an individual in terms of their functional capabilities and their support requirements, which tend to increase thereafter. Continued increases in life expectancy also appear to be accompanied by an increase in the number of years with chronic diseases (Impallomeni and Starr 1995). The level of dependency on support services can be measured in various ways and is, in effect, an expression of need in the client population. The definition of it used in the BoC system and approach is discussed in more detail later.

The structure of the elderly population itself is only part of the story, however. As much as 80 per cent of total care hours for elderly people are provided by 'informal support' from family and friends (Morris and Wilsdon 1996), but demographic and social changes appear to be reducing the pool of this source of support. Over the period 1981–91 the numbers of people aged 80 and over living alone increased by 10 per cent, with a similar reduction in the proportion living in their children's homes (Murphy and Berrington 1993).

It is likely, therefore, that demand for long-term care services from health and social services, as well as private and voluntary sector provider agencies, will continue to grow. There are many different types of long-term care which may be provided – even to people with the same dependency characteristics. Included under that heading is routine medical care (which might be provided by a community nurse, for example) as well as 'social care' elements (which, ideally, enable people to remain in their community rather than an institutional setting) such as home helps and care assistants. 'Respite' services which provide temporary care for elderly people – often as means of giving their informal carers a break – are also increasingly important. The traditional service providers have always been the NHS and local social services departments but, in recent years, the private sector has also become a significant player, particularly in the provision of residential and nursing home accommodation.

All of this is taking place against a backcloth of restraint in public expenditure. There is a fear that long-term care costs are a 'timebomb' becoming more dangerous as the numbers of very elderly people increase.

Some commentators disagree with this view: Abel-Smith (1996) reported that the care costs of people dying aged 80 and over are only 80 per cent of those who die in the age range 65–79 and that only 8 per cent of increases in health service costs over the next 20 years will be attributable to an ageing population. Hunter (1996) considers that it is the management and planning of these services, rather than the actual numbers of elderly people, which is of more importance in controlling costs.

The large array of commissioning and providing organizations involved inevitably makes it difficult to plan and coordinate requirements. The fragmentation of responsibility has had unintended consequences at local and national levels, in terms of both finance and quality of care provided. A good example of this – and one which largely triggered the Community Care Act in 1990 – was the steep rise in the number of claimants for residential care benefits, from 12,000 claiming £10m in 1979, to 268,000 claiming £2,347m by 1993 (Department of Social Services 1994). As far as health authorities and social service departments were concerned this was not from their budgets – they were getting 'free' new services in the form of privately financed residential and nursing home provision, which boomed as a consequence.

The planning issues

Against this background, the combined effects of the NHS reforms and the Community Care Act have been, on the one hand, to disperse responsibility for service provision through the contracting process and, on the other, to focus responsibility for assessing individual long-term care requirements with social services departments. At the operational level there is usually a good degree of coordination in service provision with other agencies (Henwood 1995), but the same cannot be said of the strategic level, where any 'cost-shifting' between agencies (which might pass at the operational level) cannot be sustained.

The two levels are closely related – there is little point in operating a good needs assessment framework which appropriately matches services to the needs of an individual if, halfway through the year, it becomes clear that the overall resources available simply cannot support that level of provision across the whole elderly population. Failure to embrace a wider, more long-term perspective also means that consequences for other services are overlooked or not properly addressed. If, for example, elderly patients in hospital for acute care cannot be discharged home because of insufficient community-based support services, then 'bed-blocking' usually results. As well as being an expensive and inappropriate setting for the care of elderly people, there is a knock-on effect for other client groups, who may not be admitted because there are no available beds.

Other important issues also have to be resolved at the strategic level. A major concern is that of defining funding responsibility 'boundaries' between agencies. There are no national guidelines, so any arrangements have to be established locally and can vary from place to place. These boundaries are also significant for clients; long-term care provided by the NHS is free whereas that funded by social services is usually means-tested and requires a contribution from the client. Some two-thirds of localities had still not resolved this issue five years on from the Community Care Act (Saper and Laing 1995).

Complexity also stems from the range of 'care packages' which may be provided to an individual; each potentially requires different combinations not only of services but of providing (and sometimes funding) agencies. At the operational level it is important to ensure some degree of choice, but at the strategic level of service commissioning the issue is to establish the broad direction for service provision to ensure there are no gaps in coverage of the elderly population, and that the highest quality service is being provided for the lowest possible cost.

The simple reason, therefore, why the strategic planning perspective is not well established is that it is a difficult, time-consuming and 'messy' task; it is impossible for one person – or even organization – to maintain a coherent overview. The usual difficulties created by a lack of information are compounded by the number of interested parties involved (statutory, private and voluntary sectors; client and carer groups). This, in turn, makes people unwilling to take the lead in strategic planning and helps to promulgate the idea of strategy as remote from reality and not of immediate importance. Difficulty in finding a common language between agencies makes it hard to translate general care statements of intent (such as 'more care in the community') into strategic and subsequent operational plans. It rapidly becomes difficult to try to keep an overall picture of how plans will impact on the quantity and quality of the services different agencies will have to provide, also the quality of care that will result, and who will have to pay for it (see Nocon 1994).

Joint planning and other multi-agency issues such as these have been recognized for at least the past 30 years (Challis *et al.* 1988). What has changed, however, is their relative importance on the local management agenda. This can be attributed to a variety of circumstances including increasingly devolved management structures, more focused responsibilities for providing care, budget concerns, changes in clinical management practice, and rising expectations among the public. Clearly, there will be differences in the exact nature and causes of problems encountered over time between agencies and from place to place, but the essential issue of tackling the balance of care between different services, agencies, resources and dependencies, is neither unique to any one locality, nor does it fundamentally change over time.

The BoC system was developed as a way of trying to help managers handle this complexity. It offers an analytical framework which addresses the common elements of the issues encountered in each locality. At the same time it is wholly adaptable to addressing local data and agendas within this framework.

Dependency data

A major problem that commissioning agencies (in particular) face is poor availability and accessibility of information on existing service levels and their costs, and how these relate to the needs of the elderly population. The number of community nurses per 10,000 people over 65, for example, indicates nothing about whether this resource is appropriately targeted to those who require it – and a large proportion of the population may not have any need at all. What is important is to relate information on services to levels of *dependency* in the population.

A working definition of dependency can be taken on two principal dimensions: the incapacity of the individual, and the level of informal support (from family and friends) which is available to them. For an individual, there are three important characteristics: physical ability (mobility and the ability to carry out daily living tasks); mental ability (dementia or behavioural disorder); and incontinence. Different combinations of these will generate different service requirements.

The role of informal support is much more difficult to assess, but it does have an important mediating effect on whether, or to what degree, statutory services provision becomes involved. Informal carers often absorb much, if not all, of an individual's social care requirements, and their presence or absence will have a significant impact on the response demanded of other – formal – services. The two dimensions of dependency taken together will have important implications for the type and quantity of services required, the location of the provision and which agency is responsible.

The Balance of Care approach and system

The BoC approach focuses attention on the resource implications of the long-term care requirements of elderly people according to their level of dependency. The overall approach has a long pedigree, with original concepts going back to the 1970s (Canvin *et al.* 1978; Taket 1991). It takes a broad view of planning which ranges from the definition of local planning issues and the gathering together of appropriate people and data, to using a computer-based system and the interpretation and application of the results through subsequent discussion. Within that approach, the BoC system refers specifically to the computer-based modelling component which has been through several transformations in its structure and technological base from mainframe in its early years to a microcomputer-based format, first by the then Department of Health and Social Security (Bowen and Forte 1987), and more recently by Secta Consulting (1996).

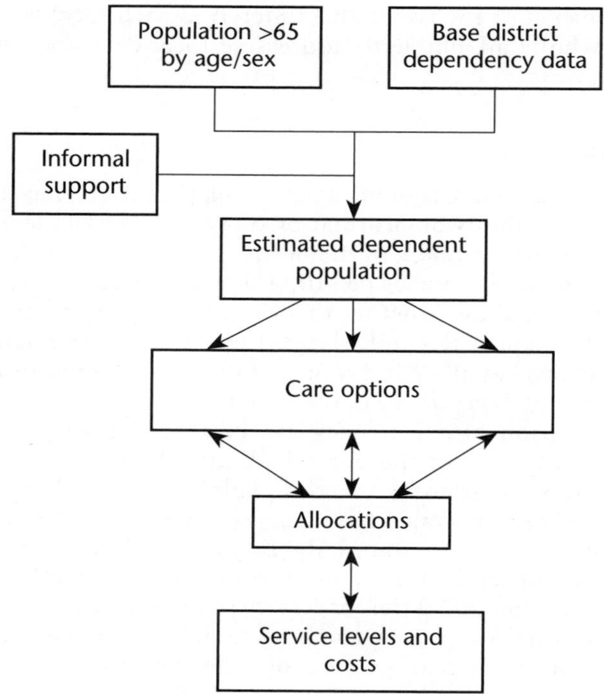

Figure 4.1 Structure of the Balance of Care system

The mainframe version had a more complex model structure but, owing to the lack of suitable data, required a detailed local dependency survey to be undertaken beforehand in order to be able to operate. This process was usually found to be a valuable exercise in itself but it was expensive and time-consuming to conduct, and it was difficult to make extensive use of the data collected.

The poor routine availability of these data still remains a sticking point in local planning. The microcomputer version has a simpler structure (see Figure 4.1) and was designed from the outset to enable people to progress their plans without having to conduct a survey first.

The system comprises two principal components: a population model, and a care options model. The population model allows dependency levels in the over 65 population to be estimated in the absence of any such local data (which can, of course, be used instead if available). It uses a combination of census data and dependency data collected in a previous Balance of Care project survey (the 'base district') to generate estimates in 16 different dependency categories for any given locality. Epidemiological studies such as those by Bond and Carstairs (1981) and the World

Health Organization (1983) show that, within the planning horizon (at most ten years), the probability of a given level of functional dependency is related to age. Informal support, however, cannot be related to age and sex in the same way. Rather than ignore the issue, the system enables the user to consider what the local levels might be like and explore alternative assumptions about this factor based on local knowledge.

This is not the only way of estimating dependency, of course. Others have developed statistical models (see Whynes and Baines 1996, for a recent example) and there have been continuing – if rather slow and patchy – improvements to information systems to enable this data to be collected routinely. The BoC system encourages users to use local information whenever possible, and other estimates or actual data can easily be input directly into the model if available.

Given this expression of demand, a variety of 'care options' can then be specified for each dependency group using the care options model. The user can then allocate the population of that group to relevant care options in a variety of ways; he or she can calculate the implications in terms of cost or facilities needed to meet that allocation. The list of care options is not exhaustive (in particular, innovative practices will lead to the specification of new options), and the views about the appropriateness of care options will vary according to local conditions and care policies. Importantly, the system can take on board not only the views of health professionals and managers but also the service clients and career groups if they are involved in the workshop; it does not require extensive knowledge of how the community care system works in order to have a view about how it operates in practice – the BoC can incorporate these views as required. This is an increasingly important consideration in service planning for all agencies (Barnes and Wistow 1994).

An example of potential care options for a dependency group is illustrated in Table 4.1. In this case a person in this dependency group is assumed to have severe physical disability, occasional incontinence and no dementia. Social support circumstances are assumed to be good. The data requirements of the system are geared to the management issue under consideration; in theory at least, most of the data will be collected routinely (apart from dependency data as noted above). However, the ability to access it can vary quite significantly from place to place. In principle, information on the quantity, location and cost of services is more straightforward to obtain. In practice, however, data are often held by different agencies in different systems (not all of which are computer-based), and there may be different data definitions to contend with as well. While it can be inconvenient to assemble the data, nonetheless it is usually possible to do so. The BoC system, importantly, aids this process first by focusing attention on data relevant to the planning issues; second, it enables people to progress in their planning without having to wait for every item of data to be gathered and verified. It is very easy to

Table 4.1 Potential care options for a dependency group

Service	*Care options*			
	Option 1	*Option 2*	*Option 3*	*Option 4*
Geriatric ward (weeks per year)	52			
Residential home (weeks per year)		52		
Day hospital (attendances per week)			2	
Home visits (hours per week)			5	5
Home help (hours per week)			12	16
Preference order	2	4	1	3
Annual cost (£)	7,190	1,230	3,669	1,760

Source: Report of a study on community care 1984.

enter data into the system, so initial estimates or 'best guesses' for data items can always be used to start with and updated as time goes on.

A number of simple, built-in routines allocate the population of a particular dependency group to care options automatically on the basis of specified preferences or lowest cost, but the user can also specify individual allocations either in conjunction with the automated routines or completely independently of them.

The system provides analyses of the care options across all dependency groups showing, for example, how the cost consequences of a particular scenario impact on dependency levels or on funding or provider agencies. Implications for the quantities of particular services is also provided, both in total and by individual dependency group. Users can start, therefore, by obtaining an overall impression of the potential impact of a particular scenario, and then gradually zoom in on this view to see how it affects individual dependency groups or services. This enables assessments to be made of the appropriate mixes of services in terms of service levels, costs, and how they relate to dependency and locality within the study area. At this point authorities have to reconcile conflicting objectives of cost efficiency and service effectiveness, and take into account other constraints which may be imposed by existing patterns of service delivery and manpower. It is possible to return to the care options or allocations, make adjustments as desired and recalculate the results in a matter of seconds. Users can thus enter an iterative cycle of testing assumptions until they are satisfied that any strategic objectives and constraints have been recognized.

Applications of the Balance of Care approach

Reported projects using the Balance of Care approach have been carried out in a number of UK health authorities (see, for example, Boldy *et al.*

1982). Many pre-dated the original microcomputer system and involved undertaking detailed surveys of dependency and the existing use of services. In this section the focus is on applications undertaken with the microcomputer version (see also Forte and Bowen 1994).

Respite care in Sandwell

A specific example of the BoC system in recent use comes from Sandwell in the West Midlands where it was used to underpin a major strategic assessment of 'short break' services for older people and their carers. The study was jointly undertaken by Sandwell Health Authority and Sandwell Social Services Department (1996). The definition of 'short break services' includes temporary relief for carers as well as recuperative breaks for older people; it comprises 24-hour care services outside the home as well as a range of domiciliary-based services such as day and night sitting. These types of service are becoming an increasingly important – and rapidly expanding – area of service provision and, as the strategy document noted, the gap between what is available and what is required continues to get wider.

The BoC approach was used to try and better understand the nature of that gap and what might be required to start bridging it. Starting from a needs-led approach the system was used to provide initial estimates of dependent elderly people (which were subsequently altered using local data). This was used as the basis for potential respite care requirements and the establishment of a strategy for up to the year 2000, including spending requirements. The importance of the Balance of Care approach in this exercise was not just to handle the numbers but also to provide a structure (through the definition of dependency groups) around which different groups and interests could focus and express ideas, concerns and explore different options using a 'common language'.

Table 4.2 shows the estimates produced using the system of the overall level of services across all dependency groups that would, ideally, be needed. This is based on the estimated numbers of dependent elderly people and the level of short-break care service (including type and quantity of service) which was regarded as appropriate to the levels of dependency identified in Sandwell. (Note that in Table 4.2 the required level of service is in relation to short-break services only and does not include, for example, hospital beds that might be additionally required for long-term care.)

Given known local funding sources over the next two years (amounting to £250,000), it was envisaged that resources would be targeted on increasing the existing capacity of the night sitting service by 70 per cent (which would cover 12 per cent of estimated need, up from the existing coverage of 7 per cent), and a fourfold increase in the number of day sitting hours to enable 11 per cent of estimated demand to be met (up from the existing 3 per cent). This is in addition to other short break service

Table 4.2 Short break service requirements in Sandwell

Service type	*Level of service required*	*% currently available*
Elderly care hospital beds	37	41
Psychiatric hospital beds	15	33
Social services elderly persons residential home places	113	20
Private nursing home places	57	3
Private residential home places	34	3
Day sitting (hours)	178,000	3
Night sitting (nights)	75,000	7

priorities which were also identified for ethnic minorities and older people with mental health problems.

This is a good example of organizations in a locality taking on board the Balance of Care system and adapting it to their management requirements. However, past experience has demonstrated that the take-up of the system 'from cold' – that is, without any additional support – is relatively poor. In the Sandwell case there had been a prior 'facilitated workshop' using the system and it was this which gave them the confidence subsequently to use it themselves in the respite care application. The workshop programme, which was developed with this in mind, has been developed not as a simple 'system tutorial' but as a means of demonstrating the potential of the BoC approach in a real application using local data and issues as its focus and directly engaging local planners, managers and professionals.

The Balance of Care workshop programme

The workshop helps to reinforce the development of links between local agencies by bringing together key players, and by recognizing and accommodating the importance of each of their contributions: this applies not just across organizations, but across disciplines as well. Having someone familiar with the computer system to facilitate the workshop means that attention can be focused during the workshop on addressing the planning issues themselves.

In one workshop held in the north Midlands, representatives from social services, from the three health authorities and the family health services authority within its boundary and from the local community Trusts formed a 'core group' of 16 who attended all workshop sessions. These were spread over four days. The first session comprised an initial demonstration of the model to a group of about 40 people so there could be a wider understanding of the overall aims of the workshop and what their core group colleagues would be addressing in future sessions. Planning issues, data sources and responsibilities were also identified for subsequent stages.

The second session took place a few weeks later when the core group reassembled for an intensive two-day session. Sub-groups were formed to consider the demographic and dependency characteristics of the elderly population as estimated by the model as well as information on current service levels and costs drawn from a variety of local sources. The task of translating care policies – published and otherwise – into service implications with respect to dependency levels was led by a consultant geriatrician. This is the central feature of the approach: getting people to focus on appropriate quantities and types of service with respect to different dependency characteristics, and trying to move away from the strong bias which tends to exist towards service-based planning (i.e. basing future plans on existing patterns of service and facilities).

While this work was underway, data, planning assumptions and ideas were continually entered into the system by the group facilitator. Gradually, the resource implications began to unfold over the two days as data and planning ideas were entered, their effects calculated and opinions revised and refined. The computer screen was projected onto a screen so all participants could see the results immediately, make 'real time' suggestions to try out different assumptions and watch them analysed instantly. This method of working was very fruitful; many more ideas could be tested out than would have otherwise been the case with an equivalent paper-only exercise. A lot of debate was stimulated which, apart from focusing on the results, also brought to light all sorts of questions about data sources, namely their accuracy, how they could be improved, and where there were obvious gaps. At the end of the second day an action plan for taking forward the main points emerging was drawn up and a copy of the model, data and print-out left with the Social Services Department. Table 4.3 summarizes some of the principal potential areas of change that emerged, with some services needing to increase while others might be reduced in scale or adapted to other functions (such as respite care).

Table 4.3 North Midlands: potential consequences for services

Service	*Present*	*Future*
Long stay hospital beds	340	100
Long stay psychiatric places	220	50
Residential home places	1,800	700
Day centre places	670	1,500
Home care assistants	2,200	3,400
Private psychiatric nursing home places	0	200
Respite care beds	48	500

Source: Unpublished study.

The third session of the workshop took place about two months later with a presentation of the model and local results to a group of operational-level health service staff including community nurses and residential home managers. In the interim, people had already started to refine their ideas and to think about translating the exercise from the county to a locality basis; most importantly, they had gone on to use the model for themselves without further external support. This was an important outcome, as a key aim of this workshop programme is not just to provide a 'one-off' event, but to get the principles of the approach more firmly embedded into the routine local planning and contracting process. Several months later the outcomes of the workshop were informally reviewed with some of the participants. A number of positive effects were cited, ranging from input to the development of a respite care policy to staff training. The participative nature of the workshop was found to provide a good way of involving operational care provider staff directly in the planning process, particularly through the focus on needs assessment and the discussions around the specification of care options where their operational-level knowledge was particularly valuable. Moreover, the approach was felt to complement the work of established planning structures while, at the same time, adding more rigour to the use of existing information (and highlighting inadequacies where they occurred).

In more general terms the workshop was also acknowledged to have helped strengthen relationships between planning authorities. The BoC system provided a strong focus for this. Even where it did not provide an 'answer', it contributed significantly to a clearer understanding of the underlying components of planning problems by exposing hitherto implicit assumptions about data and aspects of policy. The ability to incorporate user and carer ideas and preferences was also appreciated.

Inevitably there were difficulties in assembling data and agreeing assumptions to be made. Apart from the all-important local commitment, the approach requires an intensive time input during the workshops to be effective. Some thought also needs to go into tailoring the model for particular local circumstances – for example, considering what different care options might be required for different ethnic groups. Ultimately, though, the fact that it took this effort and time is not a fault of the approach itself but rather a recognition of the complexity of the issues involved.

The Social Services Department have gone on to use the BoC approach in a variety of local exercises, particularly for the development of care options. It can be said that the BoC approach has permeated their thinking on a range of strategic issues ranging from needs assessment to care delivery.

Concluding remarks

An important feature of DSS, like the Balance of Care system and approach, is their ability to enable users to gain insights into the overall resource consequences of policy directions, and to pave the way for further, more detailed work which will often fall outside its immediate scope.

The structure of the computer system is such that it can maximize the use of any additional information which is locally available from surveys or other data sources and that it can be used at different levels of sophistication appropriate to the particular problems faced locally. Some authorities, for example, have found it useful simply as a starting point for looking at ways of improving existing local information on dependency levels and service utilization, and have found that a demonstration and group discussion of the model is sufficient in itself to stimulate ideas. Others have gone on to a more detailed examination of care policies, quantifying care options and substituting local data where available as outlined in the examples above. There are no hard-and-fast rules as to what constitutes an 'application'; this will vary across districts and with local priorities.

The idea of an applications workshop within which the most recent BoC system version is used has been the most significant development in trying to ensure that users of the system can exploit its full potential. In the introductory chapters to this book the conditions best suited to DSS applications were discussed, which reflects the experience of applying the BoC system over the years. With the first release of the microcomputer system it was expected that managers would be able to use it directly themselves without much in the way of applications support. Subsequent experience has suggested that the model is better understood with initial support and so the idea of integrating it with a facilitated workshop – which is much more than a system tutorial – came about.

'Would the same approach work in my area?' The short answer is yes; in common with other DSS described in this book, both the approach and system are designed to be easily tailored to different local circumstances. However, no DSS or workshops can substitute for a lack of local commitment to the planning process by any of the key players. Nor can BoC – or any other DSS – succeed easily if there are constant problems in continuity caused by the constant ebb and flow of reorganization and people changing jobs and responsibilities. All organizations blame each other at one time or another for the lack of progress; unfortunately although this has long been recognized to be unhelpful it continues to happen today (Ransford 1996).

The Balance of Care approach and system cannot give perfect answers to complex strategic planning issues at the push of a button and was not designed to do so. However, it does make a good starting point for the development of strategic thinking and action. Where a robust joint planning framework is already active, it can highlight areas of potential development for effective solutions and help to present them in more imaginative ways. As the quality and quantity of the information base for community services increases so does the potential to tackle short-term planning and organizational issues. The Balance of Care system can be used to support such activity and stimulate the move towards better local information systems.

Finally, a question: if you don't use something like the Balance of Care approach to enable you to develop and quantify your strategic plans, what will you use instead?

References

Abel-Smith, B. (1996) The evaluation of health care costs: how did we get there? in *Health Care Reform: the Will to Change, Health Policy Studies no. 8*. Paris, OECD.

Barnes, M. and Wistow, G. (1994) Achieving a strategy for user involvement in community care, *Health and Social Care*, 2: 347–56.

Boldy, D., Russell, J. and Royston, G. (1982) Planning the balance of health and social services in the United Kingdom, *Management Science*, 28: 1258–69.

Bond, J. and Carstairs, V. (1981) Services for the elderly, *Scottish Health Service Studies no. 42*. Edinburgh, Scottish Home and Health Department.

Bowen, T. and Forte, P. (1987) *The Balance of Care Microcomputer System: Guidance for Users*. London, DHSS Operational Research Service.

Canvin, R., Hamson, J., Lyons, J. and Russell, J. (1978) Balance of care in Devon: joint strategic planning of health and social services at AHA and county level, *Health and Social Services Journal*, 18 August, C17–C20.

Challis, L., Fuller, S., Henwood, M., Klein, R., Plowden, W., Webb, A., Whittingham, P. and Wistow, G. (1988) *Joint Approaches to Social Policy*. Cambridge, Cambridge University Press.

Department of Health and Social Services (1981) *Report of a Study on Community Care*. London, DHSS.

Department of Social Services (1994) *Income Support Statistics. Quarterly Enquiry, May 1993*. London, Department of Social Services.

Forte, P. and Bowen, T. (1994) Improving the balance of elderly care services: recent applications, in J.-C. Rey and C. Tilquin (eds) *SYSTED94: Dependency, the Challenge for the Year 2000*. Lausanne, Swiss Institute of Public Health.

Henwood, M. (1995) Strained relations, *Health Service Journal*, 6 July, 22–3.

Hunter, D. (1996) New line on age-old problems, *Health Service Journal*, 20 June, 21.

Impallomeni, M. and Starr, J. (1995) The changing face of community and institutional care for the elderly, *Journal of Public Health Medicine*, 17: 171–8.

Morris, N. and Wilsdon, T. (1996) Who pays for long-term care? *London Economics Newsletter*, 1: 1–3.

Murphy, M. and Berrington, A. (1993) Household change in the 1980s: a review, *Population Trends*, 73: 18–26.

Nocon, A. (1994) *Collaboration in Community Care in the 1990s*. Sunderland, Business Education Publishers.

Ransford, J. (1996) People aren't goods! *Institute of Health Service Management Network*, 3: 2.

Sandwell Health Authority and Sandwell Social Services Department (1996) *Joint Strategy for Short Breaks for Older People and their Carers*. Sandwell, Sandwell Health Authority and Sandwell Social Services Department.

Saper, R. and Laing, W. (1995) Age of uncertainty, *Health Service Journal*, 26 October, 22–5.

Secta Consulting (1996) *Balance of Care Familiarisation Pack*. Sutton Coldfield, Secta Consulting.

Taket, A. (1991) Resource allocation models and health service systems: an exploration, in W. Morgenstern, E. Chigan, R. Prokhorskas, M. Rusnak and G. Schettler (eds) *Models of Noncommunicable Diseases*. Berlin, Springer-Verlag.

Whynes, D. and Baines, D. (1996) Predicting activity and workload in general practice from the demographic structure of the practice population, *Journal of Health Services Research Policy*, 1: 128–34.

World Health Organization (1983) *The Uses of Epidemiology in the Study of the Elderly. Report of a WHO Scientific Group on the Epidemiology of Ageing*, Technical Report 706. Geneva, WHO.

Software availability

The Balance of Care system is written in Microsoft Excel. For further information about the Balance of Care system and workshop programme please contact Secta Consulting Ltd, Charter House, 56 High Street, Sutton Coldfield, B71 2UJ. Tel: 0121 321 1717, fax: 0121 321 1535.

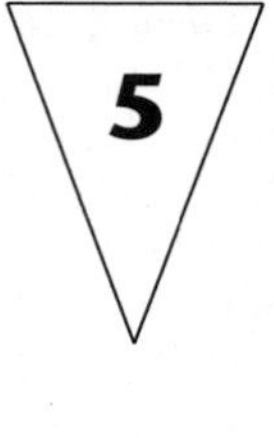

Activity and capacity planning in an acute hospital

Tom Bowen and Paul Forte

Introduction

In the NHS it has become commonplace to hear of long waits for admission to hospital for routine surgery or to see a specialist on an outpatient basis, and hospitals often report associated bed shortages and staffing difficulties. Clearly overall issues of resourcing loom large here, but problems can arise because of imbalances in the range of services available: there may be enough beds but not enough operating theatre time, or staff to undertake the operation, or the opposite may be the case. Hospital managers have the challenging job of ensuring that an appropriate balance of services is provided, and that they are making a good case – when justified – to health authorities and other funding bodies for increased resources.

This is a very complex task. If changes are made to either the quantity or quality of a service, managers need to consider what the implications may be for demand in related services, and the implications for both income and expenditure. Hospital services are like a leaky pressure system – if escaping steam is shut off in one place it will probably start escaping in another. For instance, if extra outpatient clinics are run, some reduction in the waiting time for patient appointments should result. But if more patients are seen, then it is also probable that there will be more decisions to admit, which will increase the pressure on beds and theatres, and of course on many other clinical services. Without complementary measures in these services, the inpatient waiting list is likely to rise. And if all these balancing acts are successful, the perception of a much improved service invariably encourages more referrals from GPs and the cycle starts all over again. It may be obvious where the consequences will reappear, but equally, the levels of complexity of hospital systems may mean that predictions are, at best, partial. (The discussion by Wolstenholme and Crook in Chapter 12 provides a clear review of such types of system complexity.)

In Brighton managers had recognized these complexities for a long time. They were exacerbated by a shortage of modern hospital buildings, which required even individual departments to operate across a number of hospital sites. The imminent establishment of a new management structure to run the hospitals as an NHS Trust provided a focus for exploring innovative ways of supporting managers in these tasks. Guidance from the NHS Management Executive (NHSME 1992) to Trusts emphasized the importance of preparing annual business plans in negotiations with purchasers. In Brighton such a formal process had already been initiated and some responsibility for business planning had been devolved to clinical directorates. However, the ability of the directorates to make clear and compelling cases for service developments both at directorate and senior management levels was not at all well developed. To continue to develop this process, and to prepare for the move to Trust status, the (then) Unit General Manager of the Brighton hospitals wanted to:

- improve the analytic capability of the organization;
- improve the information systems; and, most importantly,
- help managers increase their business skills, and in particular their skills in putting together and presenting a business case.

At that time there were particular pressures from health authorities to reduce waiting times both for outpatient appointments and for inpatient admissions, in line with the Government's Patient's Charter targets, and this led to additional emphasis on the integrated planning of activity and capacity levels.

This chapter is concerned with ways of helping managers follow through, and quantify, all the major elements required for a successful new development. It describes a DSS – the Business Planning Model – that was first developed and used in Brighton Health Care NHS Trust, and the various related training initiatives that were established to help managers put together successful business cases. It particularly focuses on medium-term developments, of the sort which are now negotiated within the annual service contract round between health authorities and NHS Trusts. The following sections set out:

- the business planning tasks (and some complicating factors);
- the structure of the activity and capacity model that was built;
- some simple approaches that were used to calculate future activity levels;
- the more complete, but necessarily more complex, model of patient flows that was implemented;

- a description of some of the analyses, and resulting actions, that were taken in one treatment specialty;
- an outline of a one-day training exercise – the business planning game, which incorporates use of the model – for all staff who may be involved in putting together a business case.

The chapter concludes with some views about how to ensure that the level of detail in any analytical exercise is kept in step with the information and business skills of managers and clinical staff alike, and with the quality and quantity of data available through management information systems.

Developing a business planning capacity

The Brighton managers felt that, to reach a stage where highly focused negotiations with purchasers could occur, a lot of preliminary work was desirable. Ideally the Trust should have identified:

- internally agreed target levels of provision;
- the activity levels to deliver those targets;
- possible ways of making more efficient use of existing resources;
- where increased (or decreased) provision would be required;
- the knock-on implications for the support services (laboratories, imaging, etc.);
- estimates of the expenditure implications, hence the additional income requirements.

To identify if there are better ways of using resources, and to establish the feasibility of increasing or decreasing provision, it is essential that clinical staff are fully involved in the process of putting together the business case. Only they can agree to specific changes in clinical practice that could contribute to enhanced delivery, and their familiarity with the organizational processes on the ground may illuminate options for logistical change that will have escaped the attention of managers.

All of this requires a way of looking at the mechanics of the service that may be unfamiliar to both managers and clinicians. Sometimes it is called an examination of the 'dynamics of the business'. To achieve this managers and clinicians need to agree what the key elements of the service are, how they interact and how they may be influenced. In practice this is almost certain to lead to greatly increased demands for information which, in the post-reform NHS, is increasingly capable of being delivered as new and more comprehensive information systems come on stream. Any Trust that has established full contract management facilities, and is working to an agreed activity plan consistent with its contracts, should now be able to describe the flows of patients through its services.

Of course life is not always so simple, and it is equally commonplace that an examination of current activity patterns highlights areas where data are insufficient. This can be a very constructive route into the specification and development of new or enhanced information systems, since the business need for the data should then be understood by all parties, and there is then much greater prospect of full support for the implementation effort and changes to working processes that may be required. Traditionally the NHS has established its information systems without sufficient 'ownership' of the business requirements from those involved in delivering and managing the services.

A major programme of management training was also established, in the form of a series of specially designed seminars linked to the business planning round. These set out fundamental principles of business planning in the context of directorate level requirements. The seminars became part of an integrated information skills training programme, which ensured that an individual could address related IT training needs (basic PC skills, use of spreadsheets, etc.) as particular business and analytical skills were built up. As with many exercises focused around decision support systems, it is important to ensure that a common understanding between all parties is reached regarding the key elements of concern, rather than just calculating the 'right answer'. Statistical accuracy is not always the most important consideration, provided that participants are comfortable that the 'business' is being portrayed in a believable fashion.

The Business Planning Model

If patient services are provided through the 'traditional' pattern of inpatient and outpatient facilities, the flow of patients can be represented diagrammatically, as in Figure 5.1, which also identifies some of the resource consequences. Originally this description of patient flows was described as a *model of activity and resource use,* and was generally accepted by clinicians and managers alike as a good representation of how services are accessed. As work progressed the title was changed, perhaps a little grandly, to the Business Planning Model, to emphasize the connection with the annual business planning round and associated contract negotiations, and the need for managers to look in some detail at potential changes to activity and capacity before building income and expenditure forecasts for future years.

The Business Planning Model works in a similar manner to other business planning methods (see, for example, Bennett 1994) as a way of understanding the framework of services and as a means of exploring, quantitatively, the consequences of different levels of service now and in the future. It also attempts to make possible an extended analysis of the business beyond immediate departmental boundaries.

The model should be familiar to anyone working in the hospital sector. A patient with a perceived medical problem will first consult their GP. If the GP feels that a specialist consultation is appropriate, referral to an appropriate consultant will follow. The hospital will then arrange an

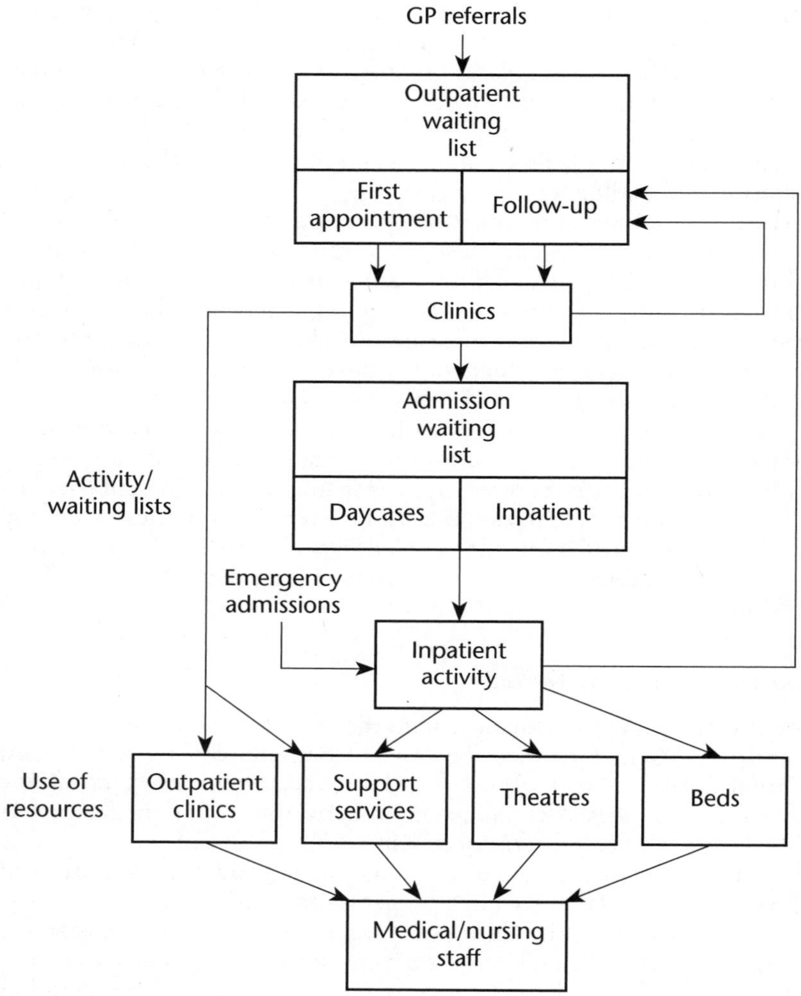

GP referrals
Outpatient waiting list
First appointment
Follow-up
Clinics
Admission waiting list
Daycases
Inpatient
Activity/ waiting lists
Emergency admissions
Inpatient activity
Use of resources
Outpatient clinics
Support services
Theatres
Beds
Medical/nursing staff

Figure 5.1 Structure of the Business Planning Model

outpatient appointment, either very rapidly (if the presenting symptoms suggest urgent treatment may be required), or whenever a clinic slot is next available (if the condition is viewed as 'routine'). Although few hospitals run formal waiting lists for outpatients it can be helpful to establish the total numbers waiting for a first (or subsequent) appointment, since this provides one indicator of unsatisfied demand.

Once a patient attends clinic for the initial consultation, one of three actions can follow:

- there may be a *decision to admit*, and the patient will be placed on a waiting list for treatment, either as a daycase or as an inpatient requiring at least one overnight stay in hospital. Increasingly patients are given a confirmed admission date while attending outpatients, but as for outpatients there will still be a period of waiting (hopefully only hours or days for patients with urgent medical conditions);
- a *follow-up appointment* may be made, either to monitor the condition or to review the diagnosis in the light of any diagnostic tests or other therapies that may be prescribed;
- no further specialist treatment may be needed, in which case the patient is then *discharged* (a patient may be discharged at any point in the treatment process but, to avoid overcomplicating Figure 5.1, not all of the possible discharge points are shown).

Follow-up appointments are then subject to the same possibilities as first appointments. In some specialties (such as ophthalmology, endocrinology and cardiology) patients may have a large number of follow-ups in order to monitor chronic conditions.

Patients admitted from the inpatient waiting list are described as 'elective', and will join in hospital all those patients admitted as emergencies. In a typical acute hospital something like 50 per cent of admissions will be as emergencies, including most medical patients. Following elective treatment patients may be given a follow-up outpatient appointment, although increasingly nowadays post-operative care will be overseen by the patient's GP, or occasionally none may be required. Review in outpatients may indicate a requirement for further outpatient or inpatient treatment.

The lower half of Figure 5.1 identifies the resource implications of activity occurring in either inpatient or outpatient facilities:

- outpatient attendances make a call on the clinic's facilities, and are also likely to require various clinical support services (laboratory tests, imaging tests, physiotherapy, dietetic advice, etc.);
- inpatients, by definition, require beds either on the ward or the daycase unit; they invariably make demands on clinical support service, and surgical patients will also require operating theatre time.

All these services require numbers of staff to deliver them, and the additional running cost of an expanded resource is often largely a function of the changed staffing requirement.

Initial development work

To introduce the modelling approach, and to make initial estimates of the values of the different variables for each treatment specialty, a workshop was run for directorate support managers in early autumn 1992. The workshop addressed the question of what needed to be done if the

Patient's Charter target standards for inpatient and outpatient waiting times were to be achieved by the end of the following financial year. It involved the managers in undertaking some 'back of the envelope' calculations. At that time the targets were that no patient waited over 13 weeks for a first outpatient consultation, or waited more than 18 months for admission following the decision to admit being taken.

A list of planning variables such as bed occupancy rates, length of stay, and the percentage of patients seen as daycases were provided for each specialty. Each manager reviewed the one or more specialties for which they had responsibility and, with the aid of a set of simple example calculations, calculated or estimated values for these basic variables. This was, essentially, a paper-based version of the model, although concentrating on key variables and their interrelationships only. As a learning process, demonstrating some of the key characteristics and interconnections involved, it worked well. It was the first time many of the Trust's newly appointed business support managers had come into contact with this type of analytical approach to understanding patterns of activity and use of resources in their specialties. It was felt, therefore, that a gradual build-up to more complex modelling was an appropriate way to go about developing their skills.

On another front, a purpose of the exercise was to help identify at an early stage which were the specialties that required more detailed attention (in terms of management action), and to make possible an early assessment of whether it might be practicable to put together a more formal and detailed business case to the local health authorities and GPs for additional specific funding to achieve the Patient's Charter targets.

Prior to the workshop a more complex prototype implementation of the model had been undertaken built in Microsoft Excel (version 5.0) spreadsheets and developed in-house by the information and systems development unit. This included a range of variables (part of which is shown in Figure 5.2). These variables represent the main components (or parameters) of the flow diagram model and the 'change rates' of the activities linking them. The rates were derived from a combination of historic activity data over the previous two years and, where the data were required but did not exist, initial estimates supplied by the managers and clinicians were used instead. As data were refined or obtained (sometimes through specific analysis of a sample of raw data records) the quantities could be simply updated as appropriate. Any changes made to them automatically updated the model and adjusted the table and graph displays accordingly.

It was agreed to pilot the model in Ophthalmology, and Trauma and Orthopaedics, both of which had major – but different – problems in meeting existing, let alone planned, levels of demand. The Ophthalmology study follows below; the Trauma and Orthopaedics study was used as the basis of the business planning game described later.

Activity/ resource	*Variable*	*Current level in Ophthalmology*
Outpatient clinic usage	Clinic sessions held	216
	People seen per clinic held	11.1
	% clinics for new appointments	15%
Outpatient waiting list	Opening list at April 1991	1606
	New GP referrals	300
	% of first appointments not attending (DNA)	11%
	% DNA staying on list	85%
	Number removed from list	n.a.
Follow-up appointments	Opening follow-up list at April 1991	n.a.
	First appointments needing follow-up	80%
	Follow-ups needing further follow-up	77%
	% of admissions needing follow-up	99%
	% of follow-up appointments DNA	12%
	Follow-up DNA staying on list	85%
	Number removed from list	n.a.
Inpatient waiting list	% of first appointments admitted	15%
	% of follow-ups appointments admitted	15%
	Average follow-up visits after admission	6.00
	% decisions to admit that are daycases	45%
	Number of inpatient elective admissions	105
	% inpatient admissions DNA	0%
	% inpatient DNA staying on list	90%
	% of inpatient appointments cancelled by hospital	10%
	% of inpatient hospital cancelled staying on list	100%
	Number removed from list per month	40
Daycase waiting list	% of first appointments admitted (daycases)	15%
	% of follow-up appointments admitted (daycases)	15%
	Number of daycase elective admissions	110
	% daycase admissions DNA	10%
	% daycase DNA staying on list	90%
	% of daycase appointments cancelled by hospital	10%
	% of daycase hospital cancelled staying on list	100%
Emergency admissions	Monthly emergency admissions	30

Figure 5.2 Variables used in the Business Planning Model

Application of the Business Planning Model

The Ophthalmology service of Brighton Health Care is run from the Sussex Eye Hospital, a separate building adjacent to the main acute hospital site. While this allows some flexibility in terms of bed and theatre capacity, a situation had been reached in which both inpatient and outpatient waiting lists were inexorably rising. There was a general perception among both clinicians and managers that an increase in the consultant complement was needed. However, there remained a nagging concern that the continual increase in numbers of 'regular' patients being seen year after year would soak up the additional staffing, without any significant fall in the waiting lists. Indeed it was conceivable that the lists could rise further if the new consultant attracted more GP referrals.

It was decided to run the Business Planning Model to explore various elements of this outpatients problem. The Ophthalmology business support manager, together with support from the systems development unit, put together the initial data from the NHS Trust activity database supplemented by estimates of specialty-specific activity rates not recorded. At various meetings over the succeeding three weeks the model was run several times and various scenarios developed for sharing with the consultants and other medical staff.

Four scenarios are shown in Figures 5.3 to 5.6. Each figure replicates the principal summary area of the spreadsheet presentation as it was viewed on the screen. It shows the values of certain key variables, together with related graphs showing the trends in inpatient and outpatient waiting lists. The convention adopted throughout the model was to display historical data for the preceding 18–24 months and project these forward for a further 24 months according to the assumptions that the user of the model chooses to make. Thus the 'current position' is always read at the mid-point of the time axis. This is also the point where the (usually) 'uneven' line reflecting actual past activity changes to a straight-line projection.

The variables and their values displayed above the graphs are directly related to the graphs below and any changes in their values will impact upon the trend in the future projections shown by the graph. Historical data and estimates form a starting point and can be simply changed by the user as required to model the potential effects. In other parts of the spreadsheet tables can be viewed instead, and there are six other screens which summarize in graph and table form other activity areas of the model, such as bed and operating theatre usage and the balance between elective inpatient and daycase activity and emergency admissions.

Scenario 1 (Figure 5.3) represents a 'do-nothing' option. Activity is assumed to remain at current levels, as is the balance of workload between inpatients, daycases and emergencies. The number of first appointments therefore continues to fall short of the number of GP referrals, and hence the outpatient waiting list continues to grow. By March 1994 it was anticipated that the numbers waiting would have grown to over 2,500, and that this would lead to non-urgent patients waiting 39 weeks for their first appointment. At the same time the inpatient waiting list would continue to grow.

Clearly some increases in activity were essential if the ophthalmology service was to move towards the Patient's Charter standard of 13 weeks,

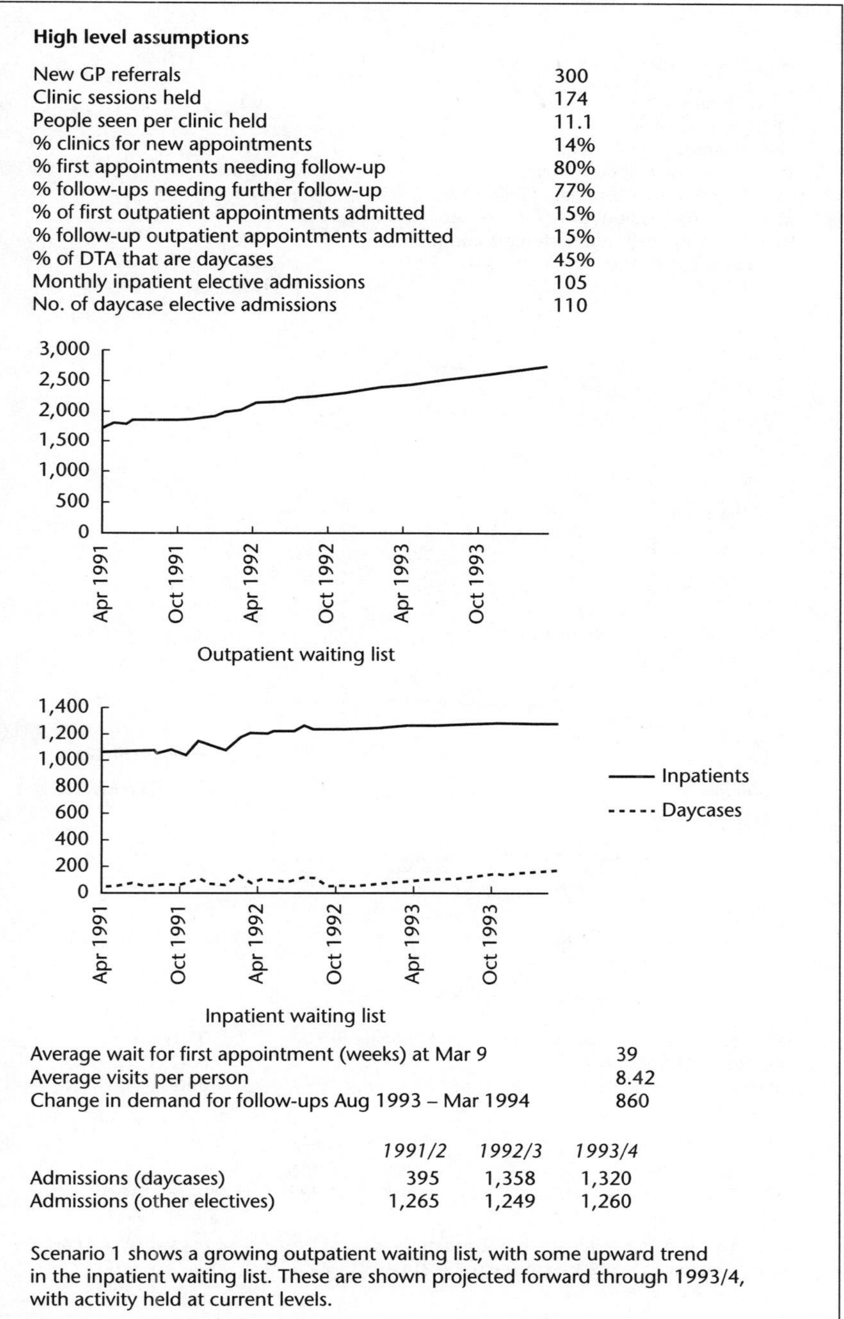

High level assumptions

New GP referrals	300
Clinic sessions held	174
People seen per clinic held	11.1
% clinics for new appointments	14%
% first appointments needing follow-up	80%
% follow-ups needing further follow-up	77%
% of first outpatient appointments admitted	15%
% follow-up outpatient appointments admitted	15%
% of DTA that are daycases	45%
Monthly inpatient elective admissions	105
No. of daycase elective admissions	110

Average wait for first appointment (weeks) at Mar 9	39
Average visits per person	8.42
Change in demand for follow-ups Aug 1993 – Mar 1994	860

	1991/2	*1992/3*	*1993/4*
Admissions (daycases)	395	1,358	1,320
Admissions (other electives)	1,265	1,249	1,260

Scenario 1 shows a growing outpatient waiting list, with some upward trend in the inpatient waiting list. These are shown projected forward through 1993/4, with activity held at current levels.

Figure 5.3 Ophthalmology scenario 1

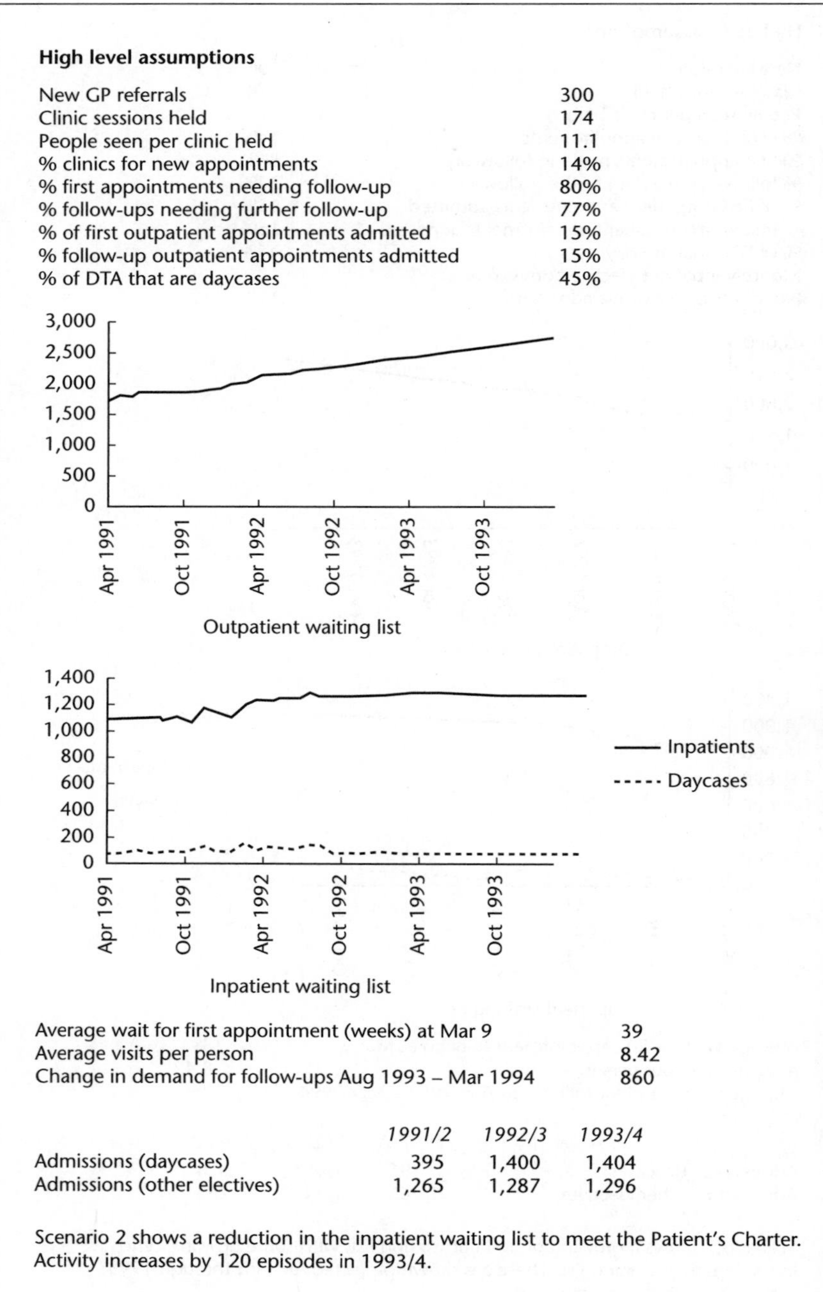
High level assumptions
New GP referrals 300
Clinic sessions held 174
People seen per clinic held 11.1
% clinics for new appointments 14%
% first appointments needing follow-up 80%
% follow-ups needing further follow-up 77%
% of first outpatient appointments admitted 15%
% follow-up outpatient appointments admitted 15%
% of DTA that are daycases 45%
3,000
2,500
2,000
1,500
1,000
500
0
Apr 1991
Oct 1991
Apr 1992
Oct 1992
Apr 1993
Oct 1993
Outpatient waiting list
1,400
1,200
1,000
800
600
400
200
0
Apr 1991
Oct 1991
Apr 1992
Oct 1992
Apr 1993
Oct 1993
Inpatients
Daycases
Inpatient waiting list
Average wait for first appointment (weeks) at Mar 9 39
Average visits per person 8.42
Change in demand for follow-ups Aug 1993 – Mar 1994 860
1991/2 1992/3 1993/4
Admissions (daycases) 395 1,400 1,404
Admissions (other electives) 1,265 1,287 1,296
Scenario 2 shows a reduction in the inpatient waiting list to meet the Patient's Charter.
Activity increases by 120 episodes in 1993/4.

Figure 5.4 Ophthalmology scenario 2

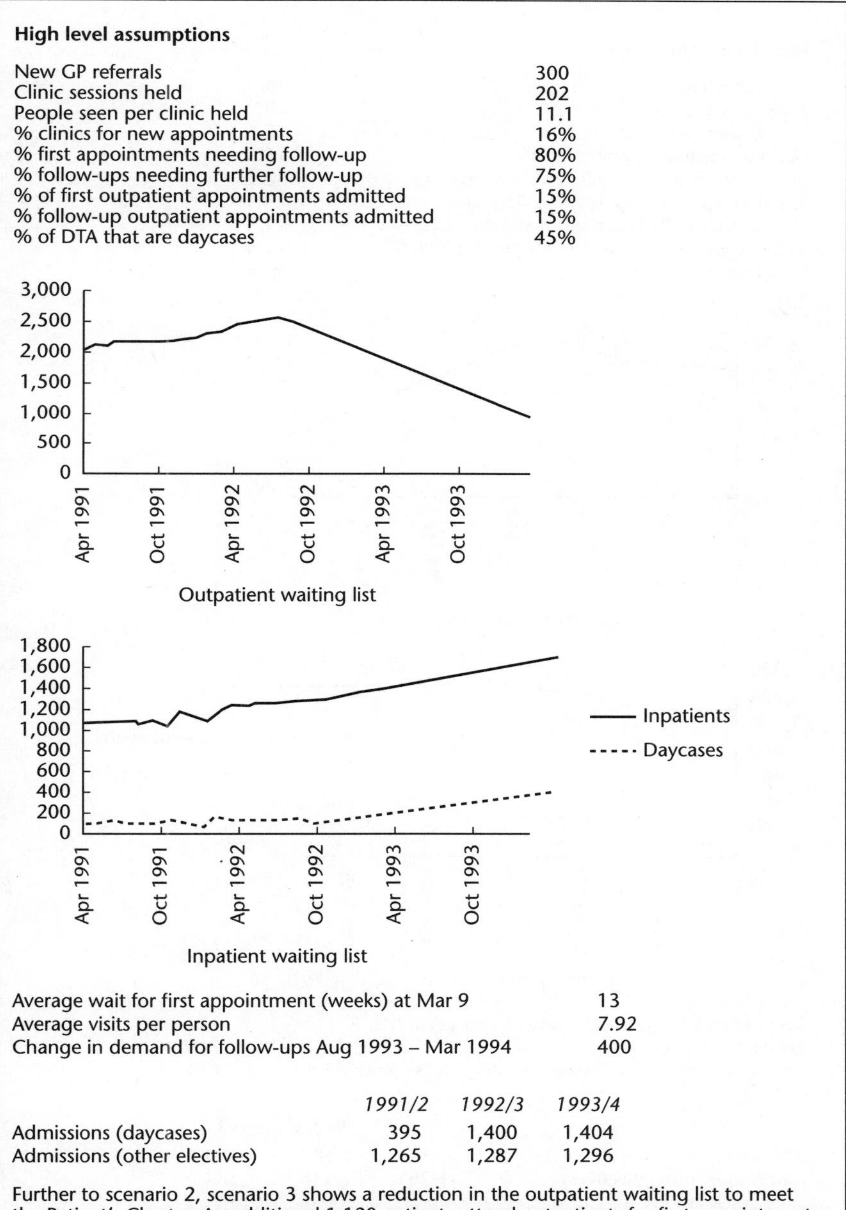
High level assumptions
New GP referrals 300
Clinic sessions held 202
People seen per clinic held 11.1
% clinics for new appointments 16%
% first appointments needing follow-up 80%
% follow-ups needing further follow-up 75%
% of first outpatient appointments admitted 15%
% follow-up outpatient appointments admitted 15%
% of DTA that are daycases 45%
3,000
2,500
2,000
1,500
1,000
500
0
Apr 1991
Oct 1991
Apr 1992
Oct 1992
Apr 1993
Oct 1993
Outpatient waiting list
1,800
1,600
1,400
1,200
1,000
800
600
400
200
0
Apr 1991
Oct 1991
Apr 1992
Oct 1992
Apr 1993
Oct 1993
Inpatient waiting list
Inpatients
Daycases
Average wait for first appointment (weeks) at Mar 9 13
Average visits per person 7.92
Change in demand for follow-ups Aug 1993 – Mar 1994 400
1991/2 1992/3 1993/4
Admissions (daycases) 395 1,400 1,404
Admissions (other electives) 1,265 1,287 1,296
Further to scenario 2, scenario 3 shows a reduction in the outpatient waiting list to meet the Patient's Charter. An additional 1,120 patients attend outpatients for first appointments. Capacity is provided by a combination of 28 extra clinic sessions per month; increasing new appointments from 14% to 16% of the total; reducing the follow-up rate for other appointments from 77% to 75%. The inpatient waiting list rises substantially.

Figure 5.5 Ophthalmology scenario 3

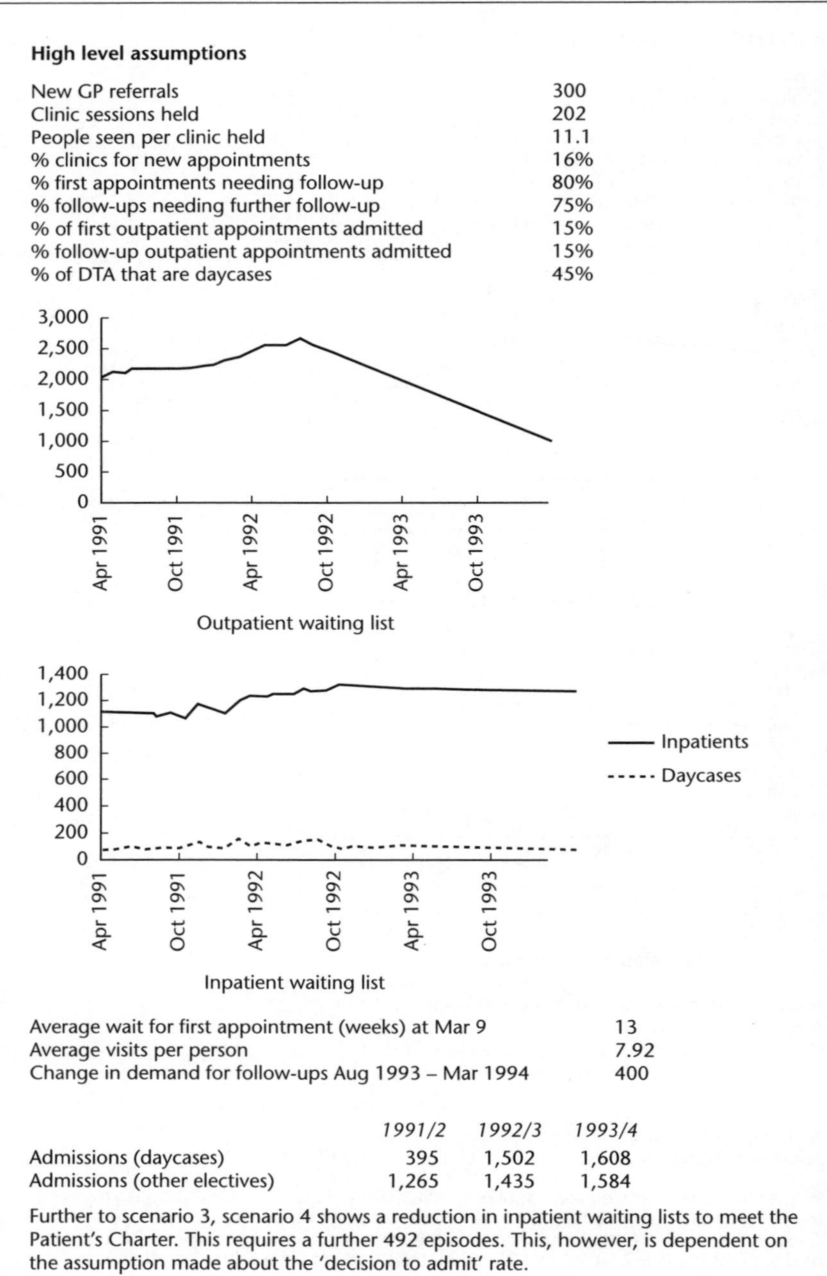

Figure 5.6 Ophthalmology scenario 4

let alone reach it. Scenario 2 (Figure 5.4) shows that the increased inpatient and daycase activity required to halt the upward trend in the inpatient waiting list would be an extra 120 admissions per annum. Note, however, that the outpatient waiting experience would continue to deteriorate.

At this point attention returned to the outpatient side. In principle it would be possible to achieve the Patient's Charter target by a substantial increase in consultant and support staff. However, it was known that the health authority would be unenthusiastic about funding such a change if there was no clear demonstration that better organization of services and any possible changes to clinical practice had been explored. A range of responses were discussed and explored using the model:

- the average interval between follow-ups could be increased, thereby allowing more slots to be used for first appointments;
- outpatients could be discharged after fewer visits: often follow-ups were seen by junior staff who might be reluctant to discharge, but it might be possible to tighten up protocols, or additional consultant staff would enable more active management of follow-ups;
- other clinical staff could see the patient on first appointment in order to make an initial assessment of need and urgency. This was seen as the most promising way to make a rapid improvement to outpatient waiting times, and it was proposed to introduce nurse practitioners to see some of the non-urgent referrals to outpatients;
- the possibility of increasing clinic size was examined but rejected: clinics already operated with very short time slots and many overran. (The review did, however, highlight the possibility of more flexible appointment systems which in the future could provide a more responsive service to patients.)

Scenario 3 shows the combined effect of a number of these changes (Figure 5.5). Capacity is increased by 28 sessions a month, to be met by an extra part-time consultant post and additional nurse practitioners. The proportion of appointments filled by new referrals is increased from 14 to 16 per cent with a compensating reduction in the number of follow-ups. This change is shown to be sufficient to make a large reduction in the outpatient waiting lists (in fact Patient's Charter targets would be reached). However, there would be a significant knock-on effect on the inpatient side, with a major rise in the numbers waiting for surgery. This is of course hardly surprising: more referrals are being seen and it follows that there will be more decisions to admit (in this scenario it was assumed that the admission rate remains at 15 per cent of all outpatient attendances).

Finally, scenario 4 (Figure 5.6) summarizes the approach taken to stabilize the inpatient waiting list. This required an additional 492 admissions, and it was proposed that the bulk of the additional work should be carried out on a daycase basis. This additional work would clearly require some additional consultant ophthalmologist input. The move to daycase surgery was seen as both desirable from the patients' point of view and clinically acceptable given the increased use of laser technology. The health authorities and the GP fundholders would approve since it could provide much needed additional activity at an affordable cost. And it also helped move towards another of the Patient's Charter targets: that over 50 per cent of cataract operations should be carried out on a daycase basis.

These proposals were broadly supported by health authorities, and led to new service contracts being agreed at higher levels of activity and higher levels of funding. An additional part-time consultant was appointed and nurse practitioner clinics were set up. Happily the impact on outpatient waits was as predicted and it was possible to cope with the extra admissions without increasing inpatient waiting times.

Of course this is not the end of the story. The NHS is highly responsive to improvements in service provision. Having started a virtuous circle, increased demand from GPs began to materialize leading to further pressures for expansion of the service. Demand has continued to rise, most notably from beyond the previously existing catchment area.

The business planning game

Coupled with practical exercises as described above, a one-day training exercise using the model was established to provide an introduction to clinicians and managers in how to develop and present a coherent business case, using orthopaedics as the case study. The detailed objectives were to:

- demonstrate how *data* which are already available can be used as a basis for planning, and also to highlight further areas where data need to be reorganized or collected;
- show how the Business Planning Model can make use of these data and use them to form the basis of a *decision support tool*;
- highlight the links and *interdependencies* between different parts of the organization, and the way that change in one part of the organization may impact elsewhere;
- provoke creative thinking on specialty-level management *actions* that could be taken to improve the performance of a Trust.

As is commonplace with such exercises, it is not expected that large amounts of time should be spent using the model. It has the role of providing structure and helping participants chase through the implications of different proposals.

A case study relating to the orthopaedic specialty is presented to participants with elements similar to those described earlier. PCs are available with the Business Planning Model, fully populated with the relevant orthopaedic activity data for the previous two years, and supporting documentation. The baseline scenario is that, within the hospital, the possibility of additional theatre sessions for trauma (emergency) patients is being discussed. No ward closures or other changes to the hospital's overall bed allocation is expected, and there are no proposals to change existing 'bed borrowing' arrangements between specialties to cope with peaks in emergency demand. Information on a variety of potential external factors is also introduced. For example, proposals are outlined for a 'hospital at home' scheme which could allow earlier discharge of inpatients and hence reduce bed requirements.

From this starting point, participants are formed into teams and asked to:

- review the current situation in orthopaedics;
- consider the implications for activity to meet Patient's Charter objectives;
- consider the resources available to carry out these plans, and how they can be managed to achieve the plans;
- identify the cost implications and where any additional funding might come from.

At the outset it is stressed to participants that the available data are neither perfect nor complete, but are currently the best available. Teams need to think creatively about ways of improving services, and should bring their own professional perspective to bear on plans. Where the model does not handle particular service implications (e.g. for laboratory and imaging services), some attempt at quantification is still required.

Teams are asked to prepare formal 15-minute presentations for the 'Board', to be delivered at the end of the day. The presentation is an integral part of the day and teams have to present their plans and explain its underlying reasoning to a panel of judges representing top management. Teams are expected to be aware of the wider resource implications of their plans and to be able to present their case effectively to a health authority or other funding organization. As with all good games the winning team receives a prize.

Having run the game a number of times, both in Brighton Health Care and for managers from other Trusts, it is interesting to note the way in which different teams organize themselves. Some teams concentrate on identifying the very creative ideas that might 'break the logjam'. Others spend a lot of time trying to 'get the numbers right'. Often teams do not reach the point where income and expenditure implications can be appraised prior to presentation. The trick of course is to try to cover all these elements to an adequate level within the constrained time available. This simulates the practical constraints of real life!

Concluding remarks

The use of the Business Planning Model and its associated business planning game illustrates some of the ways in which decision support systems can exploit the power of modern PC software and facilitate the development of more sophisticated approaches to activity and capacity planning in the hospital sector. The DSS starts as an aid to calculating key components of future business plans, but it can influence the management development agenda across a broad range of issues.

The impact on training programmes is especially marked. In Brighton the work helped to focus on a range of training needs that managers may have. At one level there is a need to understand fully the 'business dynamics', especially the interdependence of the various factors that a manager may or may not directly control. Then there is a need to enhance the analytical skills of managers, particularly when it comes to the interpretation and further analysis of routine management information. This triggers an examination of IT skills, especially competence in basic PC, spreadsheet and word processor functions, and associated facilities such as electronic mail. As part of a coordinated training programme, the business planning game can bring together all these elements.

Similarly there can be significant impacts on information systems development. High level examination of management data will always draw attention to any deficiencies in data quality and collection methods. This allows much easier resolution of operational difficulties with existing systems, since the importance of getting it right will have become clear to clinicians and managers alike through the planning process. Equally, the detailed planning is likely to spotlight gaps in existing information availability and thus provide clear statements of user requirements for future developments and procurements.

Finally, and most importantly, all of these developments are concerned with enhancing the capability of managers to make significant improvements to the range of services they can provide within the available resources. By using the Business Planning Model, managers can work closely with clinicians to understand and resolve internal issues regarding the organization of services, and then identify what changes can effectively be made in the overall provision of services. As with all DSS, the use of the model cannot make the managers' decisions for them, but can help to ensure that good internal decisions are made and strong external bids for resources can be advanced.

References

Bennett, A. R. (1994) Business planning: can the health service move from strategy into action? *Journal of Management in Medicine*, 8: 24–33.

NHSME (1992) *Business Planning Guidance, Letter to NHS Trust Chairmen, Chief Executives and Directors of Finance*. London, NHS Management Executive.

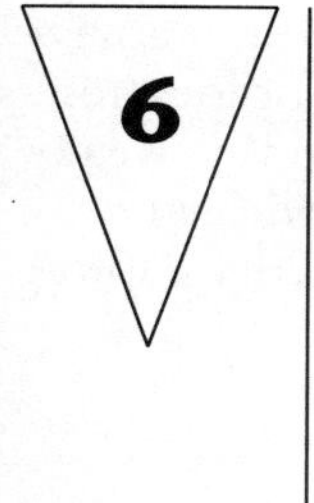

Capital investment appraisal in the NHS

Tim Keenan

Introduction

Because the demands for investment in public service infrastructure increasingly seem to exceed the funds available, the need to get the best value for money from scarce capital resources becomes paramount. There is also a growing recognition that mistakes with public investment decisions can no longer be afforded. The NHS must seek to 'back winners', though the criteria for success will be broader than the strictly commercial benchmarks of the financial world.

This chapter looks at how a decision support system – Business Case – was developed. It outlines Business Case's role in supporting a major capital investment appraisal and decision process in one Trust.

Investment decision making in the NHS – a historical perspective

In the past, two features have characterized major capital investment decision making in health care: opaqueness and procrastination. The process for arriving at the biggest decisions of all – where to build a new hospital and what size it should be – was usually impenetrable and gave rise to suspicions of politically influenced 'back-door deals' rather than robust investment appraisals.

However, procrastination was perhaps more damaging, with investment projects typically joining a queueing system to await their turn for public capital funds; sometimes projects would have to wait for a decade or longer for a decision. The full cost to the public sector of such processes was immense as they would be likely to have several reappraisals during the waiting period. Schemes which started out as large scale, new build district general hospital (DGH) developments often ended up as smaller, 'site rationalization' projects and, occasionally, vice versa.

Arguably, every region of the country has its 'white elephant' – a new hospital facility which is wholly inappropriate in size, design or location. The recent reduction in size of acute hospitals is testimony to this weakness in the process. The waste implicit in such obviously poor decisions is the motivating force behind the relatively recent drive to improve capital decision making.

Recent developments in health care investment appraisal

Before the 1991 reforms capital was a 'free good' in the NHS: that is, the cost of capital assets was not incorporated into the revenue budgets of health authorities. Following the reforms, capital charges were introduced which required the newly created NHS Trusts to charge depreciation and make an annual 6 per cent return on their capital assets. This produced a radical change in the appraisal of investment opportunities. Biggest was no longer best, as owning assets which were not fully utilized started to cost money; white elephants were now becoming exposed.

Capital charges have posed difficult questions for the NHS. Questions such as 'what additional benefits actually accrue from more capital-intensive hospitals?', 'which investments really do improve patient quality and value for money?' and 'which investments are future-proof' now have to be closely addressed. The ability of an asset to earn a return is largely related to its use and the intensity of that use. As a result, proportionately more capital is now invested in assets with a direct patient benefit; it is rarer now for scarce capital resources to be invested in building offices or administrative facilities because the additional expense tends not to generate a financial return (Department of Health 1991).

In an attempt to bring together the skills and techniques of public and private investment appraisal, the NHS Executive issued the seminal *Capital Investment Manual* (NHS Executive 1994). The philosophy behind this document, and subsequent guidance, has been to reverse the two central weaknesses of previous decision making by ensuring that it is more open and accountable and by speeding up the approval/rejection process.

Drawing upon classical option appraisal processes from the private sector, health care organizations are now asked by the NHS Executive and the Treasury to follow a two-stage process. First, they must show that there is a case for change and that the proposed change is sustainable (an 'outline business case', or feasibility study). If the outline is approved by health authorities and the NHS Executive, then the second stage is to work up the proposals into detailed costed designs and implementation plans (a 'full business case').

The extension of the Private Finance Initiative (PFI) to health care in 1995 provided both a further impetus and increased complexity to the investment appraisal process because a successful PFI project needs to address the provision of services as well as assets. This is necessary because greater innovation in service provision is required in order to overcome the higher cost of private sector capital. In turn, this means that the appraisal process has to be flexible enough to allow radically different options to be evaluated, yet sufficiently sophisticated to assess the value to the public sector of transferring future risk exposure to PFI partners. In the context of PFI a DSS needs to be able not only to appraise proposals but, critically, to provide modelling assistance during often protracted and complex negotiations. The need, therefore, is for a vehicle for learning about and modelling possible ramifications, risks, benefits and costs of alternative health care investment opportunities, and to provide a structured and auditable process through which proposed investments can be challenged and accountability ensured.

Decision support for capital investment appraisal

Anyone embarking upon an appraisal of significant investment opportunities in the UK health sector in these rapidly changing times should expect variables such as demand, clinical performance, facility requirements, costs and operational solutions to change many times before and after the final decision is taken. In such circumstances 'living and breathing' modelling software which links these and other variables is clearly essential. The alternatives to an integrated decision support tool are either manual calculations or, more usually, for different professionals to develop 'one-off' spreadsheets: the health planner would develop a demand and activity model; the estates advisers would develop a facilities planning model; the accountants would generate a financial and costing model; and financial advisers and quantity surveyors would probably use separate risk evaluation systems. In such circumstances each professional tends to operate in isolation, with poor integration of results. Modelling the impact of changes in one area on another is virtually impossible, and as a result the whole process of option appraisal is time consuming and expensive.

The theoretical basis for NHS investment appraisal

A DSS needs to reflect a theoretical basis for decision taking. In the field of public sector investment decisions – health care infrastructure investment appraisal in particular – the choice of theoretical bases is severely limited by one practical constraint: namely, the degree of difficulty and controversy associated with valuing, in financial terms, the health gain associated with any service development proposal.

Significant health care investments tend to be justified on the grounds that they improve operational efficiency and/or service quality and effectiveness. However, placing robust financial values against quality and effectiveness has been slow to progress from the realms of academic research to day-to-day health care decision making, largely because the techniques are regarded as insufficiently reliable to ensure consistent appraisals across the country. Therefore, the most appealing theoretical model for investment decision taking, *cost-benefit analysis* (CBA), is rejected in favour of a more practical, less contestable model which avoids some of the intellectual challenges CBA currently faces. This alternative, in effect, separates the cost/financial appraisal from the benefit/quality appraisal of options for change. On one hand it at least sidesteps some of the problems of CBA; however, on the other, it does not produce a clear-cut answer because it does not result in a comparable set of figures for each option.

This means the final decision as to whether the benefits of change justify the costs ultimately depends on human judgement. The role of method and software in this context is to support (but not fundamentally to change) an established decision making process. The system cannot produce a definitive answer to an option appraisal; it can, rather, be seen as an aid to thinking through the process, producing information structured to aid rational deliberation and decision making.

Development methodology

The DSS (Business Case) discussed here originally started out as a collection of tools used by a specialist health care management consultancy firm to assist NHS Trusts and health authorities in their option appraisals. To the consultancy firm, repeatedly undertaking investment appraisal work, the desired benefits were clearly to improve productivity on assignments, to enhance quality of work, to ensure consistency in client support and to create added value to aid the sales effort. There would be little incentive for individual NHS organizations to develop such a tool as they would only be appraising large scale investments occasionally.

The process of DSS development and testing was fairly traditional. A high level specification of need was produced by a small user group which led, in turn, to a detailed specification and prototype system. This was then used by the management consultants on a large number of assignments, during which many modifications were made to the system and additional functionality incorporated. At the end of the prototyping phase (which lasted a year) the firm was left with an application which delivered all the needs of its consultants, but which was somewhat unwieldy given the number of functions added during this phase.

A major requirement which evolved during the prototyping and was not envisaged in the original specification, was the need to accommodate the wide diversity in the availability of information across NHS organizations. Somehow the software needed to be sufficiently sophisticated to cope with a teaching hospital setting with a fully comprehensive information system while, at the same time also being usable by a small DGH with little more than aggregate information to hand.

The next stage was to rewrite the user specification in the light of the prototyping experience and to reprogram the application from first principles, building in maximum 'user-friendliness'. The design objective was to enable Trust managers to operate the software comfortably after a one-day training course. A telephone helpdesk facility was also considered necessary, and refresher courses were also offered for those who required them.

In releasing the system to the NHS it was important to recognize that the user would not be a management consultant experienced in the field of investment appraisals, but a potentially inexperienced Trust business manager undertaking a first option evaluation on behalf of a multidisciplinary team. Two NHS Trusts agreed to trial Business Case for six months, at the end of which a series of modifications were proposed, programmed and tested before the application was put on general release. The resultant software was then validated through a formal programme of testing before being released for general use, some 18 months after the project began. To date it has been used in support of investment projects totalling over £900 million.

Defining the decision making process

The structure of the system reflects the staged decision making processes recommended by the NHS Executive in the *Capital Investment Manual* (NHS Executive 1994). This incorporates best practice option appraisal processes as recommended by the Treasury, combined with techniques used in private sector projects (HM Treasury 1991). Essentially, this involves a three-stage decision process: proving the case for change; identifying and evaluating the options for change, and recommending a preferred one; and identifying the optimal method of financing the project (i.e. whether through public or private finance). These processes, and the way in which the DSS was developed to support them, are described below.

Stage 1: the case for change

As physical assets can have a useful life of 60 years or more, it is important to ensure that changing requirements are accounted for as best as possible. Historically, this analysis has always been the weakest feature of all NHS investment decisions, not least because of the difficulty in looking up to 20 years ahead and trying to assess how factors such as demand, clinical performance, service delivery and new technology will impact upon the need for health facilities of a particular size. The evidence of this can be seen in the experience of newly commissioned acute hospitals, many of which have sought more resources to build extra

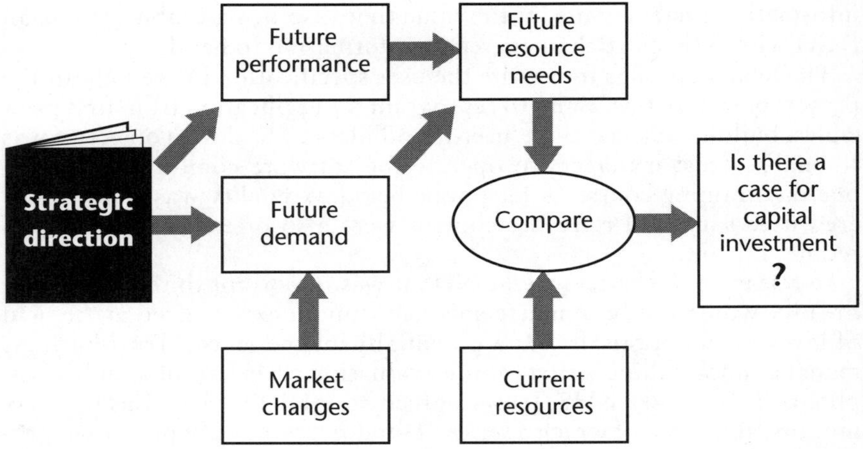

Figure 6.1 Making the case for change

daycase theatres within the first two years of opening. The rapidly changing dynamics of the internal market in recent years have even caused newly completed facilities to be under threat of closure the moment they are opened (*Guardian*, 3 September 1996: 2). So making a coherent case for change is important and is the first stage in the process (Figure 6.1).

In assessing the future need for resources such as beds, theatre sessions, daycase facilities, etc., it is necessary to define some key variables within the DSS:

- *Planning currency*. Hospital activity is disaggregated in the system to enable planning to take place at different levels (for example, the focus of interest might be on inpatients, daycases, outpatients; theatre or clinic sessions; specialty and sub-specialty analyses; healthcare resource groups (HRGs); operative procedures and clinical diagnoses). The ability for the user to select the planning currency is very important as it allows high level planning to take place initially with minimal data, and for the accuracy of these plans to be tested by gradually increasing the detail of the planning level. The aim is also to avoid a failing of many other service planning tools, which is to have to load the model with large amounts of data before any meaningful results can be obtained.
- *Demand*. The facility to make assumptions about changes in future demand patterns of any of the planning currencies is essential. Such future demand assumptions should reflect projected demographic change, anticipated technological advances, and the impact of competition and changes in clinical practice.
- *Performance*. In this context, performance means efficiency improvements in the delivery of health care and management of facilities.

Facilities required in the future will partially depend on the productivity of assets, so it is therefore necessary to make assumptions, at any of the planning currency levels, about variables such as average length of stay, operations per theatre session, turnover intervals and ward occupancy. The expectation in health care investments is that hospitals first compare (or 'benchmark') their performance against others, and set future performance challenges accordingly. A common target is for health care providers to set future performance targets at or around the 90th percentile of similar providers. The source of these data has traditionally been the health service indicators although, in recent years, 'benchmarking clubs' have proliferated in the NHS, offering the possibility of higher quality and more up-to-date comparable data. However, models of delivery of health care services and productivity rarely change overnight, and therefore it is necessary to model the impact of gradual and differential improvements over time.

- *Departmental relationships*. A key feature of the system is to model the relationship between overall patient activity and the impact upon the need for diagnostic and support departments. The approach is to define assumptions about the impact of individual cases at the level of clinical coding (such as the International Classification of Diseases scheme (ICD10), or that developed by the Office of Population Census and Surveys (OPCS4)) upon throughput in support departments such as Radiology or Haematology. The model then permits future scenarios to change such assumptions to reflect the expected impact of change, such as increased daycases, the introduction of new technology and, most importantly, changed clinical practice/new methods of service delivery.

In building a decision support system to relate these variables accurately, the starting point is to construct a model and populate it with current and historic data to assess whether it 'predicts' the existing facilities used to treat current throughput. Often such a check highlights data quality issues (such as inaccuracies in clinical coding) which need to be adjusted before future modelling can begin. Once the system is proven accurately to predict current resource usage with actual data, it can then be used to predict future resource usage based on assumptions as to how demand and performance are likely to change (see Figure 6.2).

The modelling methodology uses nine potential scenarios for combinations of assumptions for future demand and performance (Figure 6.3). Normally the assumptions for input into the model are produced on an individual specialty/case mix basis by clinical directorates, taking into account benchmarking information and known purchaser plans. In practice the whole process tends to be iterative, taking up to six months to complete – giving further emphasis to the advantages of using a computerized model. It is often the case that the early iterations of the model produce a wide range of possible outcomes such as 'the Trust

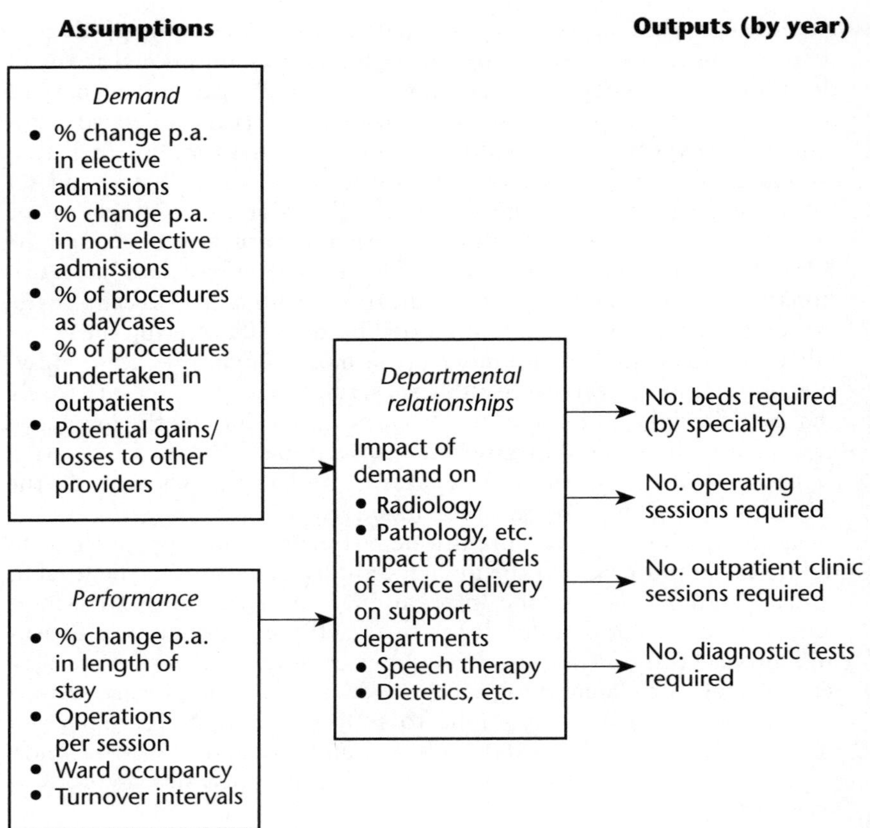

Figure 6.2 Structure of the model

requires between 600 and 750 inpatient beds by the year 2000'. As assumptions are clarified and consultations progress, the range of outcomes tends to reduce to more manageable proportions.

Outputs from the model therefore can be used to support the case for change by:

- demonstrating the *improved efficiency* which can be achieved from a capital investment (e.g. how reconfigured services and facilities might reduce length of stay or increase the proportion of procedures treated as daycases);
- defining the *range* of future facility requirements, and highlighting how this may change over time;
- informing planners and architects of the scope of the *flexibility* they might need to incorporate into estate plans for the facilities, in order to accommodate the feasible range of future requirements;

- providing a means by which future facilities requirements can be *updated* throughout the business case process to reflect changes in demand, performance or clinical practice.

In developing this aspect of the system, consideration has been given to the context in which the application would be used. User trials showed that it was important for the application to work effectively in a 'live' context at meetings, particularly to show the impact upon facility requirements (such as beds, theatres, etc.) of changed assumptions. For this reason emphasis was placed during the design phase on speed of processing and quality of visual displays. Pilot studies showed that the tool was equally likely to be used in meetings/workshops as in a back-room capacity.

The ability to run several scenarios concurrently is useful as it provides a mechanism for Trusts to accommodate differing views of the future. Typically a facilitator supported by the software tool will attempt, on an individual specialty basis, to elicit from clinicians and business managers how they expect demand and performance to change over time.

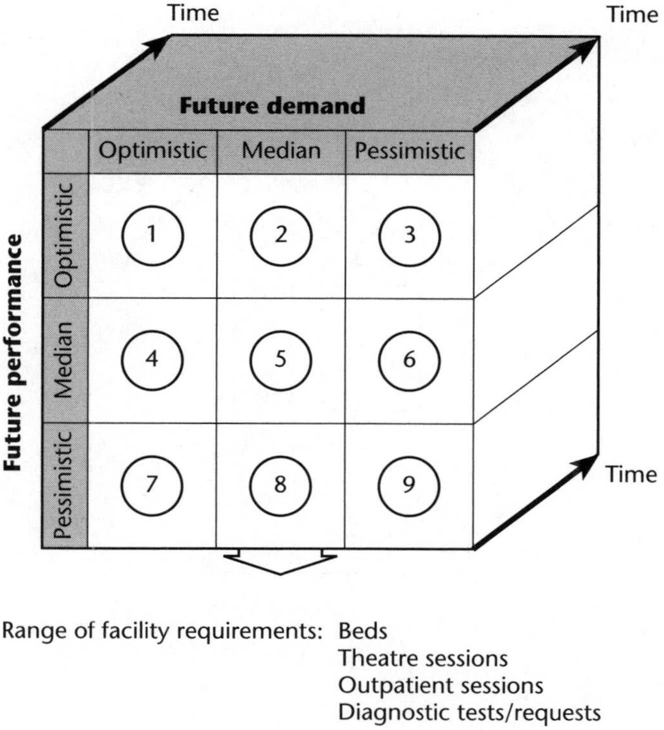

Figure 6.3 Developing scenarios to be tested

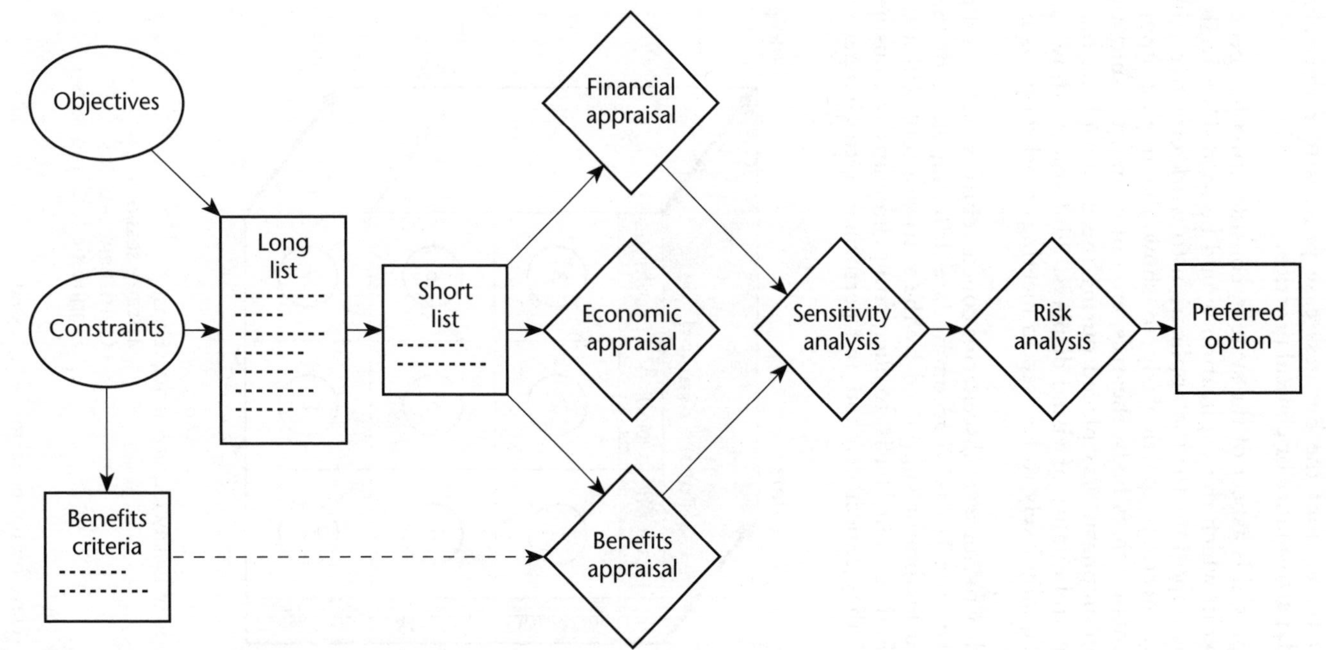

Figure 6.4 The option appraisal process

The impact on facility requirements can then be fed back to assess instantly how reasonable the assumptions predicted by the model seem. In helping clinicians plan for the future in this way, the facilitator would normally start with an assessment of the present situation. This is where benchmarking of relative performance is most important as it helps set the context for the determination of future performance targets.

Stage 2: option appraisal

Where there is a *prima facie* case for capital investment in a health care facility, the decision support software then provides a structured analytical tool to support detailed appraisal of alternative options (Figure 6.4).

Again, this element of the DSS draws heavily upon recommended best practice in evaluating options for change. Through a step-by-step approach towards selection of a preferred option, it aims to avoid the historical weaknesses of health care business cases, including pressures from 'shroud waving' clinicians offering warnings of dire consequences which might result from a failure to invest in a particular option. (This often occurs when only one option for change is being considered.)

These stages in which this is done are illustrated below with reference to a case study based on a real investment project undertaken between July 1994 and September 1996 in an NHS Community Trust. (Because commercially sensitive information relating to PFI bids is illustrated later, the Trust has been made anonymous.) Malchester Priority Services NHS Trust was responsible for a large Victorian mental health institution and former poor house, which had once treated over 1,000 patients. By 1994 its heavily underutilized buildings accommodated about 200 elderly mentally ill inpatients, provided 150 day places and housed Trust offices. The need to provide the new services in a more appropriate community-based setting was considered pressing. This drive was led by the health authority and supported by the GPs and the NHS Executive. As the district is semi-rural with poor communications, a more dispersed provision of services to improve accessibility with a mix of residential and day care provision for elderly mentally ill people was envisaged. The Trust needed to appraise options for change and, in an outline business case, submit proposals which would not only seek the closure of the institution, but also radically change the shape of service provision for the resident elderly mentally ill patients.

Define investment objectives

Options cannot properly be appraised unless it is clear what they are trying to achieve. Investment objectives need to be service-led rather than 'estates' driven and, as a result, there may be several possible estate solutions. In Malchester the objectives were to provide mental health and related services in a non-institutional setting.

Table 6.1 Defining investment constraints

Time	The new model of mental health services should be implemented by the end of 1999
Capital cost	The capital cost should not exceed £8 million
Affordability	The revenue costs implications should be broadly neutral
Quality	New facilities and service models should not be institutional in nature

Note: The time constraint was set by the NHS Executive in order to ensure that a capital receipt for the sale of the former institution land was received in time to fund other capital developments in the region. The capital cost constraint was set by the regional office of the NHS Executive, reflecting the perceived maximum capital monies which might be made available for the scheme. The affordability constraint was set by the local health authority, and effectively meant that any reshaped services should cost no more than at present (and, ideally, less, as the health authority expected significant reductions in building overheads resulting from the closure of the institution). The quality constraint was agreed by all, though voluntary agencies (such as MIND) were particularly insistent on the deinstitutionalization issue.

Define constraints

A clear definition of any absolute constraints affecting the decision process is essential to ensure that the appraisal is efficient (i.e. unrealistic options are ruled out early on) and accountable (i.e. constraints are fair and defensible). The system helps by prompting for areas where constraints are typically defined (such as time and cost). Examples identified in the case study are shown in Table 6.1.

Define benefit criteria

Non-financial factors against which options for meeting the objectives can be assessed are required. The DSS adds structure and order to discussion and measurement of these elements (see Table 6.2). In Malchester this was done through a workshop to which all interested parties were invited (including service purchasers and providers; voluntary agencies; patient/carer representatives; the local authority; GPs; and the NHS Executive). The system assists this process in two ways: by prompting typical health care investment benefits for consideration; and by asking users to link each relevant benefit to a key word in the investment objective statement (to demonstrate that desired benefits are in fact derived from project objectives). If there is a mismatch the system prompts the user to examine the consistency of the logic.

Table 6.2 Defining benefit criteria

Accessibility	• to patients and carers • to Trust staff • to primary care teams
Acceptability	• to the public • to patients • to primary care teams • to partners in service delivery
Equity	• to patients • to staff
Effectiveness	• improved health gain • use of staff and estate • facilitating inappropriate admissions and earlier discharge
Responsive	• to patients' needs • accountable to stakeholders • user-friendly in style of service delivery • flexible and expandable
Integration	• with regard to national mental health policy

Produce a 'long list' of options

The DSS supports a 'brainstorming' stage to identify all potential options capable of meeting the defined service objectives. The aim is to ensure that a full range of options – from the radical to the immediately obvious – are considered. This introduces greater accountability and transparency into the decision process because it ensures that reasons for not considering certain options in detail are made explicit and can therefore be challenged. It also encourages lateral thinking about options and may result in a wider range of them being selected than might otherwise have been the case. The long list is reduced to a short list by rejecting options for explicit reasons, such as a poor match with investment objectives; unfeasible options; and a failure to satisfy time or cost constraints.

Again, there is support for the user through screen prompts suggesting options for consideration (such as market testing the service, sharing provision with others, joint ventures with the private sector, discontinuing the service, greenfield site solutions, mobile service provision). It also ensures that an audit trail of reasoning, referenced to desired benefits and objectives, is retained to justify the rejection of long-listed options. Indeed options cannot be rejected without consistent reasons being defined, and all options satisfying the defined constraints and objectives are automatically short-listed.

Table 6.3 Evaluating non-financial benefits

Criteria		*Option 1 3 community units*		*Option 2 4 community units*		*Option 3 Do minimum (refurbishment)*	
	Weight (W)%	*Score (s)*	*Wxs*	*Score*	*Wxs*	*Score*	*Wxs*
Accessibility	21	4	84	8	168	0	0
Acceptability	11	4	44	7	77	1	11
Equity	9	5	45	7	63	2	18
Effectiveness	25	6	150	7	175	1	25
Responsiveness	18	5	90	7	126	0	0
Integration	16	8	96	8	128	2	32
Total score	**100**		**509**		**737**		**86**
Ranking			②		①		③
Benefits ratio			69%		100%		12%

Note: The short list comprised three options to replace the Victorian institution. Option 1 involved building three community-based units across the district (two in principal towns; the third in a rural area). Option 2 involved building a fourth unit also in an outlying rural area. The 'do minimum' option involved extensive refurbishment to the existing institution in an attempt to 'deinstitutionalize' it. The above table represents the evaluation team's initial assessment of the non-financial merits of options, with option 2 most preferred.

Evaluate the non-financial merits of options

The DSS follows a weighted scoring system which will permit project teams, first, to weight the relative importance of benefit criteria and, second, to scope short-listed options against how well they meet the criteria (see Belton 1991). The process of weighting criteria can be undertaken either as a group activity exercise, or individually, and arriving at an average group view. The option with the highest overall weighted score from either approach is the one, all other things being equal, likely to deliver the highest overall level of benefits. The actual benefits appraisal matrix in the case study example is shown in Table 6.3.

Sensitivity testing of the benefits appraisal

The DSS is very useful as a means of testing the sensitivity of the benefits appraisal to changes in assumptions. Dissenting views can be tested to see if, for example, the result would change if the weightings attached to a particular criteria were significantly altered. Similarly, disagreements over scores attached to options can also be tested to see if changes would materially affect their ranking. In Malchester the ranking did not change and so the team drew confidence in the conclusion that option 2 would offer the most benefits (see also Phillips and Phillips 1994).

Evaluation of the financial and economic merits of options

Business Case includes both capital and revenue costing modules. An appraisal of options puts them in the form of two perspectives:

- the 'accountant's view': the impact on service prices (i.e. affordability to purchasers);
- the 'economist's view': Net Present Cost (i.e. value for money in the use of public capital, where the lowest Net Present Cost is the most economically advantageous).

The results of this analysis for Malchester are displayed in Table 6.4.

Testing the sensitivity of the financial appraisal

The ability to ask 'what if' questions is essential in determining the degree of financial risk inherent within each option, and also in helping to ascertain what contingency sums need to be set aside in order to accommodate risks. The system instantly recalculates the consequences of such questions as:

- What if capital costs overshoot by 10 per cent?
- What if the construction programme is delayed by six months?
- What if the capital receipt for existing land is delayed or is lower than expected?

Table 6.4 Financial and economic appraisal

	Option 1 *3 community units*	*Option 2* *4 community units*	*Option 3* *Do minimum (refurbishment)*
Accountant's view Impact on prices (per annum)	–£200,000 ①	–£150,000 ②	+£50,000 ③
Economist's view Net Present Cost	£193m ①	£195m ②	£204m ③

Note: Not surprisingly this shows that building and running three units is cheaper than four; but it also shows that the 'do minimum' option is more expensive than either a new build option (due to the high running costs of the refurbished and oversized Victorian buildings). The accountant's view showed that options 1 and 2 would lead to a reduction in prices for mental health services for the elderly, with option 1 showing an additional £50,000 saving per year over option 2. The economist's analysis showed a similar ranking of options. So, from a financial perspective, option 1 appeared to offer the best value for money.

- What if the staffing costs of the new service have been underestimated?
- What if future demand projections are under- or overstated?

In Malchester this analysis showed that the overall result was particularly sensitive to two variables – the purchase price of land (on which new units were to be built), and the staffing consequences for the new service pattern.

Assess the risks of options

The system enables generic risks to be defined and disaggregated. Following a simple qualitative risk assessment methodology, overall risk exposure is defined as the product of *risk impact* (the consequences arising if a risk occurs) and *risk likelihood* (the probability of a risk occurring). For each option it is then possible to score its inherent risk. Usually, such analysis will be used as part of a two-stage process: first, to identify major risks and put in place risk management strategies; and second, to identify any residual risk after such strategies have been defined. It is on the basis of the residual risk that options are assessed.

A further refinement of the software is that more precise probabilities and financial values can be added (using a variety of alternative methodologies). These could be added to the scheme costs and set aside as a planning contingency. It is then possible to return to the financial and economic appraisals to see if, by adding in the cost of risk management strategies and any contingency sum, the ranking of the options changes.

Select the preferred option

Business Case supports decision making; it does not take decisions. Therefore the end product of the analysis will always require judgement in the selection of a preferred option. However, these judgements can be referenced to an auditable analytical base, and may be framed in a variety of terms (such as whether the additional costs of one option are justified in terms of the extra benefits it delivers, or whether the degree of risk exposure attached to an option is justifiable – see Table 6.5).

Stage 3: identify the optimal method of financing the project

Having arrived at a preferred option, the system can then provide support for the final stage of the investment appraisal process: to evaluate private sector (PFI) proposals to finance the project against the publicly funded alternative. The PFI proposals can be tested by repeating stage 2 with one important addition – a strengthened assessment of risk transfer. This is because, when comparing publicly and privately financed alternatives, one of the most significant differences is the level of risk each party is prepared to take. The decision making process requires risk transfer (i.e. risks passed on to the private sector) within PFI proposals

Table 6.5 Selecting the preferred option

Risk	*Option 1* *3 community units*	*Option 2* *4 community units*	*Option 3* *Do minimum (refurbishment)*
Benefits rank	②	①	③
Benefits ratio	69%	100%	12%
Pricing rank	①	②	③
Net Present Cost rank (i.e. value for money)	①	②	③
Risk rank	①=	①=	③

Note: The Malchester case study resulted in the above analysis which, at first sight, seems to produce an indeterminate result. The option with the highest benefits is not the cheapest, so arriving at a preferred option is still a question of judgement. The balance to be made is between the additional benefits of option 2 over option 1 compared to the additional costs. By going back through the analysis, it is possible to highlight where these benefits may accrue. Ultimately, however, this approach provided decision makers with a more informed basis upon which to decide whether the extra £50,000 per annum cost of option 2 justifies the 31 per cent expected increase in patient benefits. Although the Trust would have preferred option 2 to be selected, the final decision rested with the health authority which, after considerable discussion, decided to support option 1. Clearly, to gain a complete assessment from the health authority perspective, one should take into account the benefits which would accrue from the reinvestment of these savings in other health care services.

to be evaluated at two levels: a high level, qualitative assessment; and a more detailed, quantitative assessment.

The DSS enables the sophistication of risk analysis to increase as the negotiations with PFI partners progresses by including a methodology to address both of these requirements. The *qualitative risk assessment methodology* also follows a weighted scoring system which evaluates each risk in terms of:

- protection against the likelihood that the 'downside risk' will exceed 'upside risk';
- the degree to which the variability of outcome can be reduced;
- the degree to which future flexibility is provided, helping risks to be more easily managed.

The scoring mechanism adopted allows for the proposals to be compared not only with each other, but also against a 'theoretical' publicly financed option. This is needed for benchmarking purposes because PFI bids must compete not only against each other in the option appraisal but also against a publicly funded option if they are to be sanctioned as 'value for money' by the Treasury. The scores range from +10 (where the PFI option completely transfers risk out of the public sector), through a score of zero (where there is no change to the risk allocation at all), to –10; here the risk is transferred wholly to the public sector.

Table 6.6 Qualitative evaluation of risk transfer aspects within Malchester Priority Services NHS Trust PFI proposals

Risk area	*Risk type*	*Weight (W) %*	*PFI bid 1* *Score (s)*	*PFI bid 1* *Wxs*	*PFI bid 2* *Score*	*PFI bid 2* *Wxs*
1 Development and construction	Downside > upside	8	2	16	2	16
	Less variability	8	2	16	2	16
	More flexibility	9	1	9	4	36
Subtotal		25	5	41	8	68
2 Operating	Downside > upside	6	4	24	4	24
	Less variability	6	5	30	5	30
	More flexibility	8	3	24	3	24
Subtotal		20	12	78	12	78
3 Market and volume	Downside > upside	5	7	35	2	10
	Less variability	5	3	15	2	10
	More flexibility	5	1	5	1	5
Subtotal		15	11	55	5	25
4 Obsolescence	Downside > upside	5	0	0	0	0
	Less variability	5	6	30	8	40
	More flexibility	5	2	10	3	15
Subtotal		15	8	40	11	55
5 Regulatory and policy	Downside > upside	3	2	6	2	6
	Less variability	5	3	15	3	15
	More flexibility	2	2	4	2	4
Subtotal		10	7	25	7	25
6 Economic	Downside > upside	5	(3)	(15)	(3)	(15)
	Less variability	5	(2)	(10)	(2)	(10)
	More flexibility	5	0	0	0	0
Subtotal		15	(5)	(25)	(5)	(25)
Total		**100**		**214**		**226**

Note: Malchester Priority Services put its preferred option (option 1) out to tender to PFI bids. Two bids were shortlisted; the above analysis represents the qualitative assessment of the risk transfer proposal within each bid. The analysis shows that PFI bid 2 involves greater risk transfer than bid 1. Both proposals show a significant positive score, reflecting real risk transfer to the private sector.

In the Malchester case, the publicly funded scheme scored zero against each category, and therefore the overall positive score for either of the PFI options reflects a net transfer of risk to the private sector (see Table 6.6).

The quantitative risk assessment methodology can be used when details of the preferred bid are worked up in negotiation. The starting point is to establish a detailed risk register noting pertinent details about each potential risk, such as:

- description of a risk event;
- identification of how a risk may occur;
- probability of a risk occurring;
- probability of financial impact, should a risk occur;
- likely timing of a risk event;
- risk management measures.

The DSS can run risk simulations for the project as a whole, allowing for the random occurrence of individual risks and plotting an overall distribution of risks. The software also enables dependencies between risk events to be taken account of in simulations, and allows users to determine which risks are mutually exclusive and which are conditional upon other risks.

The introduction of this risk assessment approach serves to underline how previous decision making processes ignored risks inherent in public investments. The Malchester case study showed that an investment, until recently, could have been approved without anyone knowing that it contained a risk exposure of some £27.3m.

Concluding remarks

The application of modelling tools to some of the most significant investment decisions made by health care providers and purchasers shows how they can be used to support decision making, without replacing it. The tool discussed here also highlights how a sophisticated DSS can actually change decision making processes for the better by introducing both structure and accountability when presented in a straightforward and participative manner.

Furthermore, the use of a DSS in this way demonstrates how software designed to work in a 'live' as well as 'backroom' context can materially improve the quality of decision making by providing information and analysis at the time and place it is most needed. In the context of major negotiations between the NHS and large private sector consortia such software will be essential in protecting the interests of the public sector and in speeding up the negotiation process.

Finally, and perhaps most significantly, the DSS illustrated here demonstrates the advantages of pooling the analytical skills of the wide range of professionals involved in the NHS investment appraisals. In the long term, therefore, such systems can be expected to help streamline the process of investment appraisal by reducing the structural inefficiency of accountants, planners, quantity surveyors, economists, clinicians, business managers and administrators all working as 'islands of expertise'.

Such a multidisciplinary DSS therefore proves the adage that 'the whole is greater than the sum of the parts'.

References

Belton, V. (1991) Multiple criteria decision analysis: practically the only way to choose, in A. G. Mumford and T. C. Bailey (eds) *Operational Research Tutorial Papers*. Birmingham, The Operational Research Society.

HM Treasury (1991) *Economic Appraisal in Central Government: a Technical Guide for Government Departments* [The Green Book]. London, HMSO.

Department of Health (1991) *The Economic Appraisal of Property Options: a Manual of Procedures and Techniques*. Leeds, Department of Health.

NHS Executive (1994) *The Capital Investment Manual*. Leeds, HMSO.

Phillips, L. D. and Phillips, M. C. (1994) Facilitated work groups: theory and practice, *Journal of the Operational Research Society*, 44: 533–49.

Software availability

The system is written in Microsoft Excel. Further details can be obtained from Secta Consulting Ltd, Triton House, Hare Park Lane, Liversedge, West Yorkshire WF15 8HN. Tel: 01274 852160, fax: 01274 852159.

Part 3
Operational service planning and management

Introduction

Part 3 examines how DSS can be developed and used to assist in the operational planning and management tasks facing business managers, service managers and clinical managers in NHS Trusts, general practice and other health care provider settings. Running health services at this level comprises a set of logistical tasks to ensure the availability of such things as beds, staff, equipment, records, tests and patients. Appropriate planning, monitoring and control are required, and the manner in which these are pursued is linked both to the framework of strategic objectives and to financial and other resource constraints. In more detail, these logistical tasks include workforce management (including overall staffing patterns, short-run shift rostering, corrective allocations for skillmix, etc.); stock control and use of equipment and materials; and activity scheduling (including outpatient appointments and inpatient elective surgery lists).

The behaviour of such service systems is often poorly understood and, even where there has been considerable analytical work to establish broad principles and the factors which are involved, there are few instances where absolute truths can dictate operational management practice. This suggests a role, again, for exploratory DSS which allow local versions of complexity to be made explicit, monitored and managed on the basis of thoughtful option appraisal. The complexity of operational management is due to a variety of factors including fluctuations in demand patterns; short-term uncertainty in availability of resources (e.g. absent staff); multiple constraints and objectives (including budgetary, policy, statutory and contractual limitations); effects of quality standards; preferences for particular clinical practices, and so on.

As in strategic service planning and management, the case for DSS rests on their ability not just to highlight, but also to help manage such complexities. The five applications of DSS to operational management tasks that follow are varied. They comprise use of the integrated information resource available in general practice in assessing the likely demand for new services; two different aspects of workforce management in maternity services; management of outpatients and other hospital service systems activity; and resource measurement and modelling in neurosciences.

Primary care represents a significant area of activity, with 90 per cent of health care episodes taking place solely in this sector of the NHS. In addition, nearly 10 per cent of the total costs of the NHS can be attributed to drug costs, and much of this is initiated in primary care. Chapter 7 by Paul Bradley looks at the role of decision support systems in this sector, where 80 per cent of GP practices have computers. Features of existing systems include person-based records, the adoption of standardized coding procedures, and the development of electronic guidelines and protocols. Major considerations, however, are not just how these facilities are currently used by GPs, but how they could be further developed; not just for audit and review purposes but also for operational management and strategic planning of resources at the primary care level. The chapter illustrates how the information resource can be analysed and used to assess likely levels of demand for a new practice-based service.

Chapter 8 by Patricia Meldrum and colleagues illustrates the potential of DSS in an area of planning which is crucial to the efficiency, quality and effectiveness of health services – workforce planning. The application shows how a computer-based planning system, developed as a spreadsheet application, can provide support in an area where policy change has altered the conventional 'rules of thumb' for staffing in a number of ways. The research to develop the DSS provides the basic framework of variables, relationships between them and parameters for the set of options that decision makers might seriously consider. This powerfully illustrates how a DSS can be used to support dissemination of information about policy or best practice as well as providing specific modelling capacity (in this case to explore workforce requirements). The chapter focuses on midwifery services and presents a system which supports analysis of workforce requirements given differing assumptions about level of demand and skillmix.

Chapter 9 by Roger Beech, Alicia Mejia and Rabia Shirazi presents a second DSS developed to address workforce planning and management in midwifery services. Where the previous chapter was concerned with overall staffing levels required to deliver midwifery services (and the costs attached), this one illustrates how analysis of the differing staff requirements generated by *Changing Childbirth* (Department of Health 1993) and its proposal for a system of named midwife (or, at least, a system of team midwifery) to ensure continuity of care can be structured and made accessible to operational managers responsible. The chapter describes the management problem, the process of system design, the system as it has been developed and its use in practice.

The running of outpatient clinics is a recurrent problem in many health care services. The classic consequence is that a patient may wait for an hour in a crowded waiting room for a two- or three-minute consultation. The problem is well recognized and has led to the publication of Patient's Charter standards that patients should be seen within 30 minutes of their appointment time. A number of ways of organizing outpatient services to meet this specification have been proposed. The DSS approach discussed by Dave Worthington in Chapter 10 is a 'what if?' method which enables clinic managers to see the likely consequences of alternative ways of running clinics without having to implement them 'for real' first. Mathematical models, simulation and 'common-sense' calculation are all introduced, demonstrated and assessed using material from three case studies. From these, lessons are drawn concerning: creating opportunities for change; simple versus complicated models; qualitative and quantitative data; and who can be expected to use the models.

With the NHS reforms and the distinction between purchasers and providers has come greater responsibility for financial management and issues of broader resource management at lower levels in the management structure. This chapter discusses these issues and describes a DSS at the clinical directorate level of a teaching hospital. It is not sufficient to focus on overall numbers of episodes treated in a directorate, but to understand the link between resource usage and the mix of complexity of the cases being handled. Health resource groups form a basis for measuring casemix, but a prior issue was how to record the information. Chapter 11 by Peter Lees and Lisa Macfarlane describes the development of a DSS, based on a database made possible by use of novel data capture technology – barcoding – from which it was then possible to construct resource profiles and derive costs for the individuals or groups of patients. Developing a means of recording and analysing this not only facilitates audit and accountability but also makes possible the forward planning to try and match resources with expected demand. A first use of the DSS to explore skillmix patterns in nursing practice and to inform deliberation about options for change is described; plans for future development and use are also set out.

Reference

Department of Health (1993) *Changing Childbirth, Part I: Report of the Expert Maternity Group*. London, Department of Health.

7 Decision support in primary care

Paul Bradley

Introduction

Decision support is a relatively new concept in general practice. This is somewhat surprising given that, in essence if not name, it is already an everyday component of the practice of medicine in primary health care. The delivery of health care, at the most fundamental level of doctor–patient consultation, involves the provision of medical history (or data) to the doctor by the patient. The elicitation of physical signs by appropriate examination, coupled with other clinical data, is combined by the practitioner who applies personal knowledge to generate information (the diagnosis) upon which decisions (management and treatment) can be based. However, the widespread use of computers in general practice and the NHS reforms have given a new impetus to decision support that extends that simple concept. In particular it needs the power of information management and technology to inform and support decision making based upon hard evidence about, and real information derived from, primary care.

The image of a general practitioner (GP) as a single medical practitioner involved in a collection of individual doctor–patient episodes is increasingly out of date, particularly since the introduction of the NHS reforms and the New Contract for GPs which was introduced around the same time. Previously, general practitioners had been concerned with the delivery of health care to the individual and had little reason to be concerned with the health care issues of the population as a whole. The New Contract which followed *Promoting Better Health* (Secretaries of State 1987) introduced new responsibilities for primary care concerning the health of the population more generally, including the setting of practice-based targets for childhood immunizations and cervical cytology, and placing a greater weight on the provision of preventive care with new responsibilities: screening newly registered patients and elderly people; reviewing patients who had not attended the surgery in the previous three years; and supporting a range of health promotion activities. This placed new demands for information to be able to administer and organize these processes as well as to monitor and ensure conformance with the requirements of the New Contract. The complexity and volume of information now required by the management team is such that only integrated computerized clinical and administrative systems can provide an adequate management information system and develop the building blocks of information to provide decision support.

Practices are now seen as representing one component of a primary health care system with a much wider remit than before. GPs are now tending to operate as a member of a primary health care team (PHCT) whose composition and range of skills varies from place to place, but might typically include doctors, practice and community nurses, receptionists and managers, physiotherapists and community psychiatric nurses. The GP fundholding scheme, introduced by the 1991 reforms – and now accounting for about 56 per cent of all GPs (*British Medical Journal* 1996), has placed more economic power in the hands of general practice to shape the quality and scope of health care delivery through the direct purchasing of services from secondary and community care health care providers, and the management of prescribing and staffing budgets.

These factors, along with increasingly aware consumers, have increased the requirement to have information to inform decision making; for controlling and coordinating the PHCT; liaising with the community and the secondary care sectors to ensure high quality, cost effective health care for patients; and for understanding health care needs and aspirations of the wider community.

This chapter examines information and its role in decision support in a primary care setting. After discussing the growth of computer-based information systems in general practice, subsequent sections look at their uses in relation to management tasks in a primary care context. These are grouped into those focusing on the individual client (where much of the information required is clinically based); those concerning the practice as a business (where information on whether it is likely to meet its targets, for example, is important); and on the role of the practice in the wider community (population-based health care). The examples given are based on the experiences of a group practice, the Lache Health Centre in Cheshire.

The growth of GP computing

Although the increase in the number of practices using computers has been marked since the late 1980s in response to the NHS reforms and the introduction of the New Contract, the growth in computing had already begun some years before with the 'Micros for GPs' project, which examined the potential of computers to provide administrative and managerial support in general practice. The scheme, sponsored by the Department of Trade and Industry, provided 50 per cent funding for a number of practices to purchase computers and stimulated an increased interest in general practice computing (Howarth 1986).

However, it was two of the major GP suppliers, AAH Meditel and VAMP, who recognized the commercial potential of computerized data collection by GPs. The majority of the population – some 98 per cent – is registered with named general practitioners at any one time, and it is estimated that 90 per cent of the population are seen at least once every three years by their GP. In addition, since 90 per cent of all health care interventions take place in the primary care setting, the health care data held in general practice represent a rich repository and a potentially valuable information source (Pringle and Hobbs 1991). When data for individual practices are aggregated across several practice populations then this forms an ideal and highly representative source of data for population-based studies and analysis.

The computer companies saw an opportunity to create health care databases which would be continuously updated through routine primary health care data collection. They offered to provide free computer systems to practices in return for anonymized patient morbidity and prescribing data with a view to selling this information on to government and pharmaceutical agencies with an interest in this information.

These projects proved to be a significant spur to the introduction of computer terminals to the consultation room desktop but did not, however, deliver the original commercial objectives in the long term. This was almost certainly because the NHS reforms required GP computerization to take place on a much more extensive scale. The companies continued as computer system suppliers, rather than data processors and information suppliers (see Figure 7.1).

The move towards desk-top consultation use has been accompanied by a shift in the nature of computer use from essentially 'back-office' functions to becoming a key element in the development of the electronic medical record (EMR). The EMR has increasingly been used in doctor–patient consultation to record details of health care delivery and to support that process. This change in culture has been reflected in the findings of a number of surveys conducted by or on behalf of the Department of Health between 1987 and 1993 (see Table 7.1).

These changes in the use of the facilities offered by GP systems point towards a new emphasis on the collection of comprehensive data. Routine collection of clinical data at the point of consultation (in over 33 per cent of practices) enriches the EMR of an individual, and the data held in it can subsequently be aggregated with others to describe the health care activity of the practice as a whole. Routine use of systems to

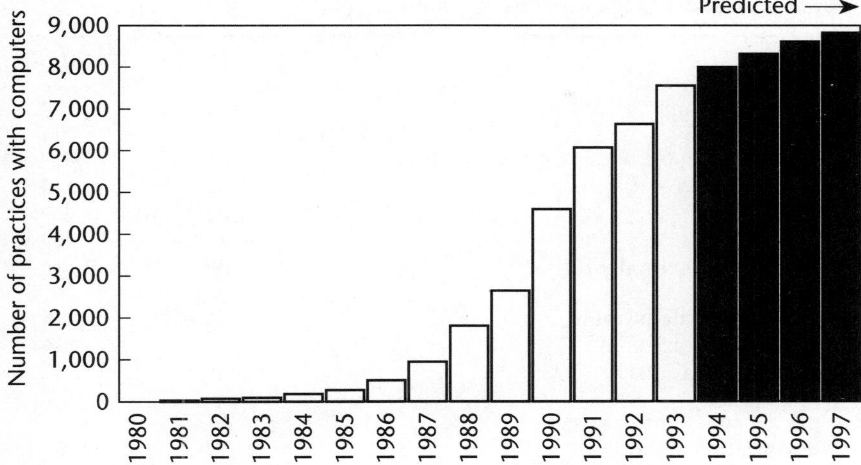

Figure 7.1 The growth in GP computing
Source: Bradley (1993a).

view clinical data (in 66 per cent of practices) enables practitioners to react to computerized prompts and reminders. This adds value to the consultation by facilitating opportunistic preventive care and health promotion with individuals. The potential of such systems to supply information to the practices and health authorities has also begun to be realized. Approximately 80 per cent of practices using them to produce annual reports and undertake clinical audit.

Practices are now having to monitor and report quarterly on their immunization rates for children and cytology status for women. The high level of performance required to attract maximum payment for the practice requires a strongly proactive approach to identifying and calling those for whom an immunization or a smear is due. In addition, the necessary PHCT members need to be informed and coordinated to ensure maximum uptake. The introduction of fundholding places even greater demands upon practices to collect and utilize data in support of contracting; monitoring that activity is taking place with secondary providers and is of sufficient quality is vitally important. For the management within the practice the handling of the budgets for staff, secondary and community care services and prescribing is a major commitment. These budgets need to be matched against the activity of the practice and the management needs to be informed of this both to monitor the level of financial commitment and to prepare business plans and bids for funding for the following year and beyond. It is essential that the management within the practice is aware of the current and predicted health needs of the practice population so that services can be enhanced,

Table 7.1 Change in the uses of GP computing (%)

	1987	*1991*	*1993*
Repeat prescribing	90	91	98
Registration	73	97	94
Clinical records (total)		85	90
full		26	29
partial		22	19
partial, but eventually full		37	42
Entry of clinical data (total)	38	56	66
all consultations		30	34
some consultations		26	32
Use during consultations	11		
viewing clinical data		52	63
Acute prescribing	17	48	58
Call and recall		87	84
immunization recall	61		
cervical cytology	72		
searches			
contraceptive recall	47		
Data collection for annual report		68	80
Audit		59	77
Word processing	64		
Referral letters		34	51
Research		27	34
Protocols of care		14	29
Other searches	60		
Morbidity recording	52		
Practice accounts	19	17	24
Payroll			28
Dispensing labels	14	13	13
Dispensing	11		
Dispensing – stock control		3	4
Other uses	5	9	8
Appointments	5		
Home visit schedules	5		

Sources: DHSS Information Technology Branch (1987) and Information Management Group (1993).

diminished, contracts shifted, negotiations planned and contracts specified as appropriate.

The potential of decision support systems in general practice

The reforms of the NHS have three underlying principles: that health services should be primary care-led; patient-responsive; and that the delivery of care is based on need. The potential for decision support in relation to achieving these goals in general practice exists at a number of levels. The first, and perhaps most obvious, focus is to facilitate *decision making in the consultation*. Within the consultation, the clinical professional performs a number of tasks in which decision making could benefit from access to high quality, up-to-date information. These tasks are wide-ranging: prescribing (including evidence-based effectiveness, interactions, contra-indications); referral issues (including waiting times, current position on contracts, protocols and guidelines); diagnosis (expert advice); and investigation (including appropriateness, interpretation, guidelines, methodology, access).

Second, at *the management level within the practice*, the abstraction of information from data routinely collected in the context of clinical care provides decision support for the tasks of contracting, negotiating contracts and budgets, monitoring financial commitment and quality-of-care issues.

Third, outside the individual practice, there exists the potential to extract and aggregate data from a number of practices to provide key information for *wider planning* of services based on the needs of the local population.

Decision support in the consultation

Generating clinical data

Generally speaking, all clinical data derive from a contact between the patient and the PHCT. The contact may be initiated by either party – for example, the patient requesting a prescription, or the PHCT sending for a patient for a routine intervention – and it might take place in the surgery, home or by letter or telephone. As a result of this contact, data are generated; perhaps concerning a prescription, the recording an intervention, or of other medical details. It is these data which describe the nature and the extent of primary health care.

Storing clinical data

The traditional record in general practice has been the 'Lloyd George' folder, a card envelope containing entries relating mainly to clinical episodes (usually handwritten). This makes the past history of the patient available at the time of consultation or when specifically selected, but fails to provide easy access to the information it holds at other times. As a result, clinical audit exercises of any significance require laborious retrieval and examination of individual or sample records. Attempts to get better access to individual information over the years have included age-sex registers, morbidity-specific card file indices, colour coding of record envelopes, pathology books, referral registers, and so on. Each system has provided more rapid access to the data, but the disadvantage is that each represents only one facet of health care data. Therefore, a single patient attending for a cervical smear, tetanus booster and an asthma check-up would have data entered or updated in three separate registers and the medical record.

The integrated medical record system

A computerized information system reduces the labour-intensive nature of data collection and maintenance. This is because the EMR, in general practice, has developed as a *person-centred* record (as opposed to a *function-centred* facility such as the patient administration systems commonly found in secondary care settings). This means that data are entered only once into a single record and this record can hold different types of data relating to the patient; their clinical history; administrative data such as their address; preventive and health promotion data, and so on. The different data can be entered into the system by relevant members of the PHCT with the appropriate access and, with the increasing use of the computer in the consultation room in 'real time', more clinical data are recorded directly onto it. As a result the EMR is evolving into a sophisticated database of clinical, demographic and epidemiological data; and, increasingly, the information held on it can be used to 'add value' to decision making such as real-time access to expert advice, or assistance in developing a strategy for screening information that will assist them in providing high quality medical care to their patients.

Types of decision support in the consultation

Decision support based on the EMR offers patient-focused care that can be broadly classified as passive or active.

Passive decision support

During the consultation, on-screen reminders can be used to draw attention to occasions where particular interventions for the patient are overdue, or where background information is missing from records. A significant number of omissions can be pursued opportunistically in this way: the collection of periodic health data; reminders for patients who have defaulted from screening and prevention programmes; and prompting for interventions which might be overlooked by the clinician, such as

System 5	No. 10803	Fictitious, Mrs I A M		25/ 2/96	14:34
House Name, 17 The Road, IA3 3NS			sex F	dob 4/10/64	age 31y

	Review/Follow-up		
13/12/94	*PROMPT* Cervical smear needed	13/12/94	P
17/ 1/96	*PROMPT* Tobacco consumption	17/ 1/96	B
	PROMPT O/E – Blood pressure	17/ 1/96	T
18/ 1/96	*PROMPT* O/E – weight	18/ 1/96	T
	PROMPT O/E – height (do a weight after)	18/ 1/96	T
	PROMPT Alcohol consumption	18/ 1/96	B
25/ 2/96	PROMPT * Abnormal biochem/haem	26/ 2/96	A
23/ 4/95	FP1001 claim due next visit	23/ 4/96	A

Figure 7.2 Electronic reminders providing passive decision support

long-term monitoring of medication. Figure 7.2 illustrates an example of a screen from a passive decision support system. The upper part identifies the patient, while the central portion of the screen shows the clinical details as presented when that patient's record is first displayed on the screen. Reminders shown here are drawing attention to overdue screening procedures (smear needed), missing health data (smoking status), aspects of clinical care (a recent abnormal blood test) and administrative procedures (a contraceptive claim is due shortly).

Although a rather minimalist approach, it can at least help to ensure that policies can be applied in the course of normal work activities; which is welcome for PHCT members. Figure 7.3 shows the effect of this method on recording the collection of background health data at the Lache practice over time. An incentive for recording was the fact that it was necessary for the practice to collect and report it in order to qualify for highest level health promotion payment. Relying entirely on passive reminders proved very effective in achieving this target.

Active decision support

More 'active' decision support can be exploited using built-in electronic guidelines. These present PHCT members with predefined plans or templates to help ensure that appropriate clinical practice is undertaken in given circumstances. An example is in the management of diabetes, where conditional branching (that is, where the programme responds to

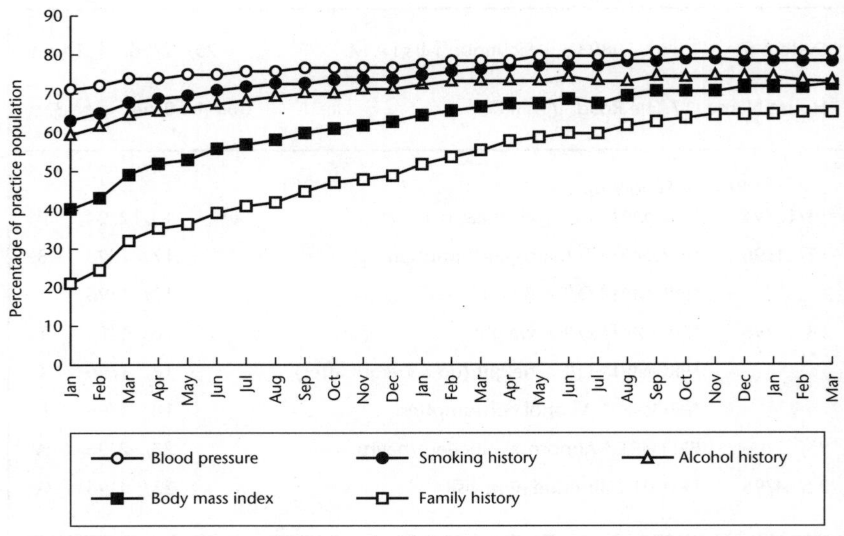

Figure 7.3 Recording of basic health promotion data 1994–6

a particular user input in different ways) can be used to make sure that appropriate care is offered to patients who are treated by diet alone; diet and tablets; or diet and insulin. Guidelines themselves can come from a variety of sources. They may be written by the practice, developed in cooperation with local primary and secondary care providers, or be derived from national guidance. They are usually activated by the individual user or, more usefully, can be triggered automatically on predefined inputs by the team member (for example, a code for follow-up diabetes assessment). Figure 7.4 shows a simple measure of the effect of introducing such a protocol in a single practice. Prior to 1991 – and despite the recognition that knowledge of the type of treatment prescribed for individual patients with diabetes was important information – no patient had this specific fact recorded (although it could be obtained indirectly by analysing the patient's prescribing regime).

In June 1991 an electronic protocol was introduced that required the user to record the type of diabetes treatment; this resulted in 90 per cent of all patients having the fact recorded within that year. However, the protocol did not prompt for the data to be recorded again, with the result that in succeeding years recording of treatment declined. As diabetes is a condition for which the type of treatment may change over time, it is good practice to check at each consultation on the current status. It was eventually realized that the protocol did not do this and it was changed to prompt the user to check treatment at each review. The change was

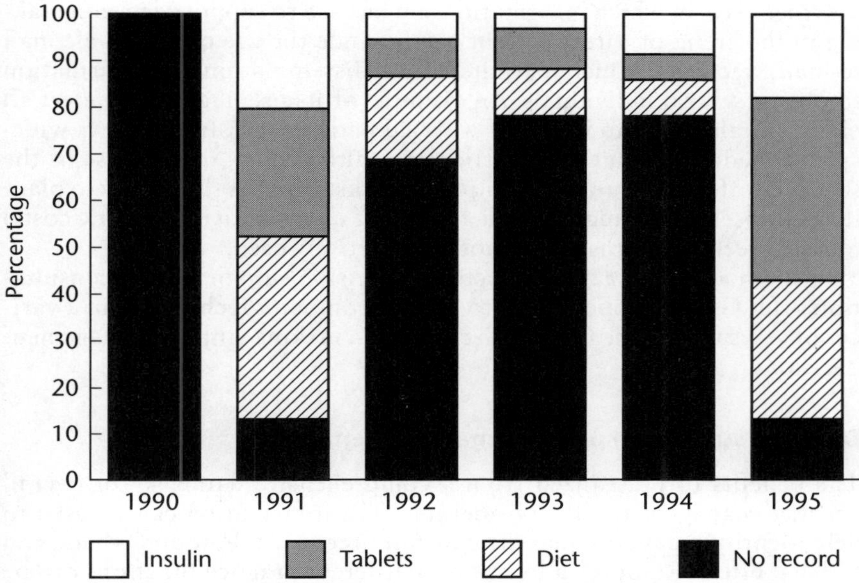

Figure 7.4 Assuring the quality of care: diabetic patients with a record of the type of treatment within each year

implemented in 1995 and promptly produced a 90 per cent recording level once more (with an expectation that this will be maintained in the future).

The potential for such a facility to influence prescribing habits in local practices is another potential application area, with guidelines being used to suggest appropriate therapies for a range of common conditions (such as the best choice of antibiotic in the management of urinary tract infection). A system, known as Prodigy, which will work across a number of GP systems is being piloted at the time of writing (Purves 1996).

'Real time' on-line information refers to facilities where a user has instant access to an information resource on the local system without recourse to connecting to remote databases via modems. There are a growing number of reference sources for GPs available on CD-ROMs, including Personalized Medical Reference (McMoran and Prince 1993) and MENTOR, that enable users to look up particular medical conditions of interest. With graphical user interfaces (such as Windows) and multimedia workstations, the range of medical electronic publications and data sources is set to increase, such as Medline; journals (*The Lancet* and *British Medical Journal*); the electronic British National Formulary (for prescribing); and evidence-based medicine reports such as the Cochrane Database of Systematic Reviews (Chalmers 1993).

Other ways in which information can be used to support decision making in the arena of direct patient care include the use of electronic mail (e-mail) facilities which permits rapid dissemination of information to one or several individuals. An example of its use might be to alert all clinicians ahead of an influx of worried patients (as often follows widespread media coverage of a particular health topic). Another use of the facilities offered by modern computer workstations is the ability to place items of useful information (e.g. a graph of comparative antibiotic costs) on the screen when it is on but not being actively used.

In summary, both active and passive decision support in the consultation offer GPs the opportunity to exploit computer technology in a variety of ways to provide them with support in making clinical management decisions.

Decision support in practice management

The benefits to be realized from a comprehensive database for overall practice management are considerable. The information can be used to help identify types and quantities of resources used, how and where, and to what effect. Resource allocation to different practice functions can be determined in the light of that knowledge, and there is a better capability to control and coordinate planning and make assumptions about future needs. Additional responsibilities for wider population health care, noted earlier, have increased the value of aggregated information to practices. Practices are no longer a fragmented 'cottage industry' provided by non-accountable practitioners. The new culture within the NHS views practices as small independent business units, each having a need to develop business plans, to manage budgets, to develop information systems and to monitor quality of care (Greenhalgh and Company Ltd 1994).

Practices now commonly prepare business plans with both tactical and strategic implications for future development and growth, bringing together financial, resource, manpower and health care planning. As an employer the practice has statutory responsibilities which it must fulfil; it is also in contract with the NHS to provide a range of services for which payments are made in a variety of different ways. Particular targets need to be met, defined aspects of activity need to be reported on, and quality of care monitored through clinical audit. A framework for examining areas of practice activity (Figure 7.5) illustrates the complexity of potential information demands to be met by any practice seeking to have objective evidence available. This framework is an expansion of the areas of structure, process and outcome identified by Donabedian (1980) as areas of potential clinical audit.

The type of information used in decision making varies depending upon the nature of the management task. For example, at the operational level, a doctor starting a surgery needs the names of patients attending, not an analysis of the workload pattern for the last year, whereas long-

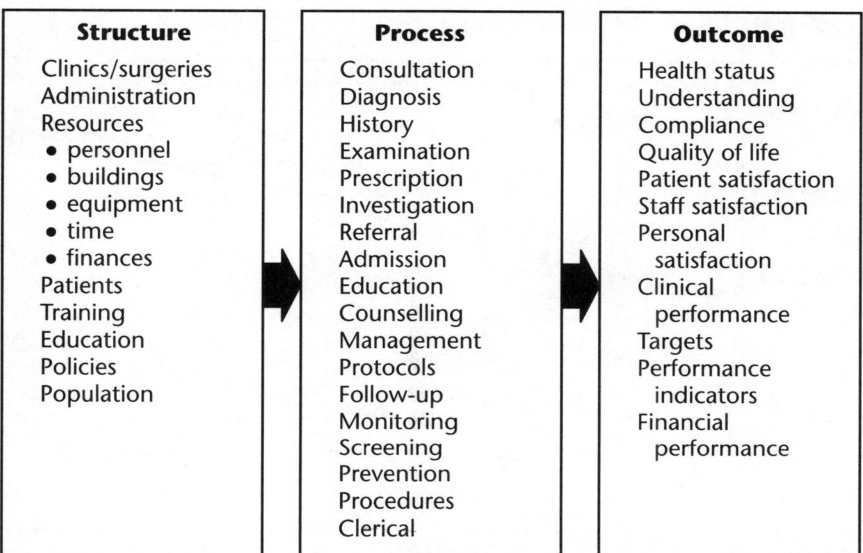

Structure
Clinics/surgeries
Administration
Resources
• personnel
• buildings
• equipment
• time
• finances
Patients
Training
Education
Policies
Population
Process
Consultation
Diagnosis
History
Examination
Prescription
Investigation
Referral
Admission
Education
Counselling
Management
Protocols
Follow-up
Monitoring
Screening
Prevention
Procedures
Clerical
Outcome
Health status
Understanding
Compliance
Quality of life
Patient satisfaction
Staff satisfaction
Personal satisfaction
Clinical performance
Targets
Performance indicators
Financial performance

Figure 7.5 The extended audit chain
Source: Bradley (1993b).

term planning of the appointments system (a strategic level task) would require the workload patterns. Data collected as part of the core activity of the practice support the production of relevant information through analysis and appropriate summary. Computer-based systems make this much easier through the use of graphs, charts, lists or tables.

A good example of this occurs in the preparation of practices for fundholding, where internal and external data sources are used to produce the information required to set the funds for referral and prescribing activities. At an early stage the practice needs to start collecting and collating data on referral activity, demographic and morbidity data relating to the practice population, practice staff and services, historical prescribing patterns, current prescribing policies and formularies, and their likely impact on prescribing budgets. A synthesis of these data alongside the plans for the practice will form the basis of setting the budgets and setting the goals the practice wishes to achieve. The information will also be used to influence negotiations and contract setting with provider units and to set the baseline for monitoring provider unit performance as well as providing the yardstick against which the practice will judge its own achievement.

In a similar manner, prescribing within the practice can be continuously monitored to predict and influence prescribing patterns. While data from the Prescription Pricing Authority can be used to influence prescribing activity through discussion, peer review and clinical audit, these data are usually three months out of date by the time they are

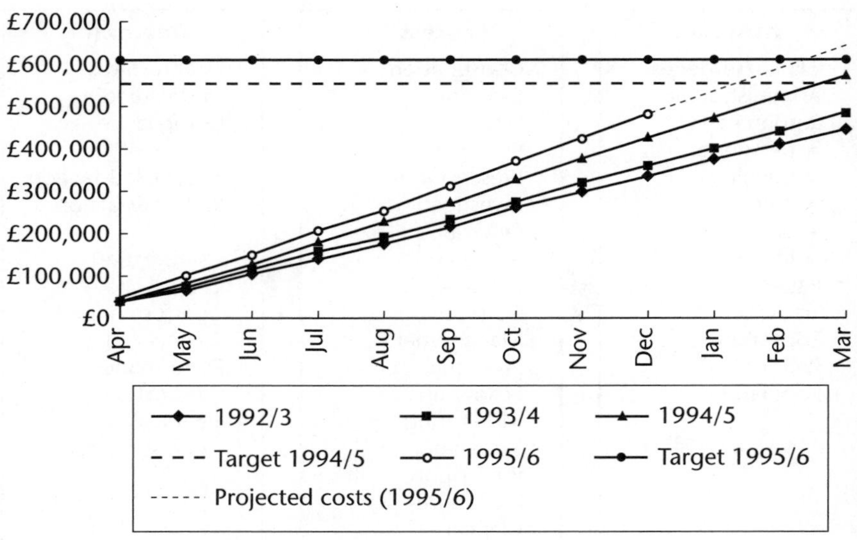

Figure 7.6 Monitoring prescribing costs, Lache Health Centre, 1992–6

received. Using a practice information system, however, it is possible to identify costly or inappropriate prescribing and departures from agreed formularies, prompting action to influence the prescribing process. Indeed, this is an ideal means of developing prescribing policies through the creation of a practice-based formulary. In addition discussion within the PHCT and negotiation with other health care professionals outside the practice – such as hospital consultants who have a major influence on prescribing decisions – can result in a more cost effective and appropriate prescribing, although to maintain this requires ongoing commitment to examination of prescribing issues (see Wyatt *et al.* 1992; Dowell *et al.* 1995). Figure 7.6 illustrates how continuous analysis of prescribing costs was used at Lache to monitor costs against the target budget and show the overall change over time. Trends or deviations from the expected course of events are highlighted by the system and remedial action can be taken.

Not only is it possible to look at past performance, but the richness of practice data can facilitate 'what if' projections, identifying potential areas of expansion and growth in terms of activity or costs. For example, an analysis of the female population of the practice showed a relatively low consultation rate for menopausal problems, given the size of the female population and an even lower rate for the use of hormone replacement therapy (Figure 7.7).

It was considered that rising expectations on the part of the female population lead to an increase in this rate in the future and so it was decided to establish the past trends for consultations relating to the

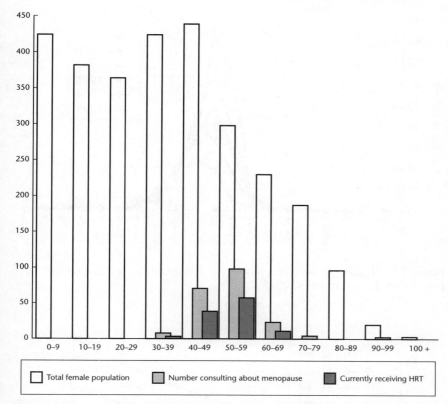

Figure 7.7 Analysis of menopausal women receiving HRT (by age group)

menopause and to predict the workload and drug cost effects over the next five years. The analysis demonstrated the past growth in consultations (approximately 25 per cent per year) for the years 1990–5, particularly among younger women (Figure 7.8).

This seemed to predict that there would be a corresponding increase in workload and cost of prescribing hormone replacement therapy (new versions of which are more costly to provide). Using this information the practice can begin to address these issues well in advance of pressure on drug budgets or practice resources (Figure 7.9).

Decision support beyond the practice

The principles of the NHS reforms require access to high quality information to permit effective planning and delivery of health care across a population greater than those of individual practices. Given the widespread computerization in primary care and the continuous nature of contacts between the PHCT and patients in primary health care (as

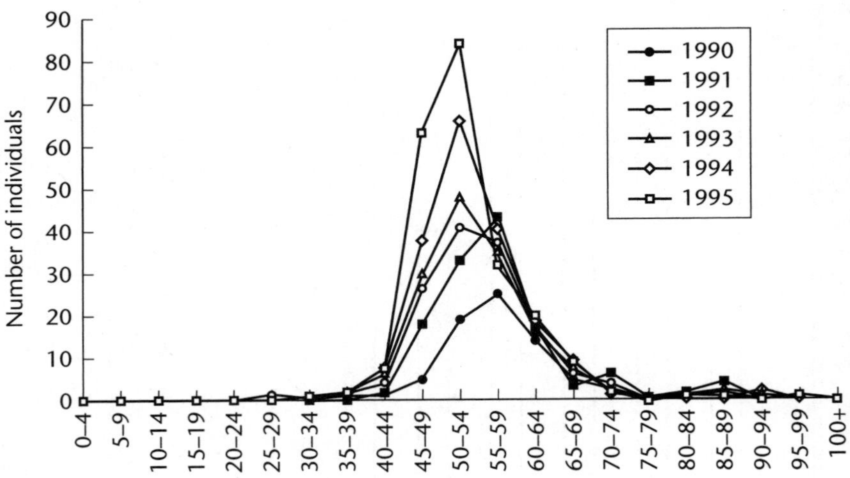

Figure 7.8 Analysis of consultations for the menopause of female practice population (by age group) 1990–5

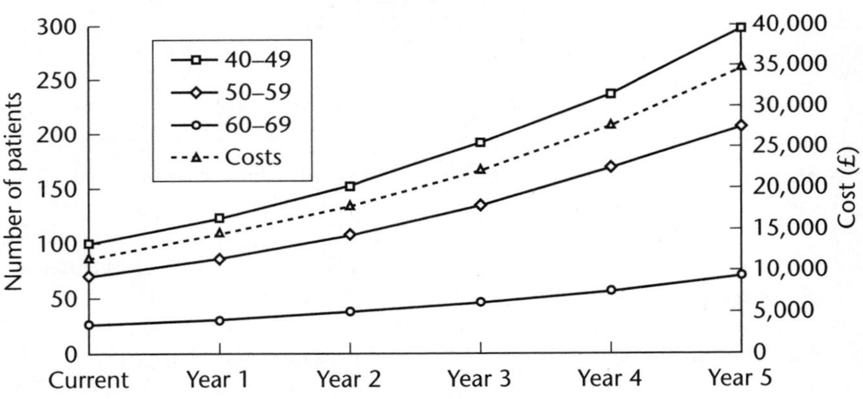

Figure 7.9 Predicted workload and drug costs for women on HRT treatment

opposed to the episodic nature of secondary care contacts), primary care databases have the potential to provide most of the information required for needs-assessment purposes across the NHS. The Department of Health is currently running a project to look at the feasibility of extracting and using general practice data to support the rest of the health service, and the Miquest project is developing a software tool which will enable data to be extracted from a variety of GP systems by means of a single structured query language approach (Allan 1993). This would mean, for example, that the results of the searches on databases could be exchanged electronically and enable aggregation and analysis to produce locality-based needs information. In Somerset, the possibility of such data collection has been used to build a database of primary health care morbidity derived from 11 practices (Pearson *et al.* 1996). The data were found to be reliable and accurate and were subsequently used to assist purchasing decisions and to alter contract placements in one specialty.

However, there are a number of hurdles to be overcome before the availability of such locality-based information will become more widespread. More practice computer systems need to meet the Requirements for Accreditation (Information Management Group 1995) in order to be compliant with the initiatives being undertaken as part of the overall Information Management and Technology strategy of the Department of Health (Information Management Group 1992). Current practice systems need to be technically updated, and both systems and training in their use needs to be properly funded. This will inevitably mean increased training and provision of expert resources or mentors to practices, and the changes will require additional infrastructure to facilitate and manage the process. Investment in such schemes will provide access to information that has previously remained elusive and will enable the creation of strategic alliances between primary care and secondary care providers, and health authorities and other health care purchasers. This basis means that the delivery of health care will be based on a 'true' assessment of population need and resource allocation decisions can follow more closely as a result: monitoring activity and quality of health care will be much more straightforward. The only requirements to facilitate such a scheme are the will, imagination, finance and commitment to develop and share information systems that can support decision making at this level of health care management.

Concluding remarks

Decision support for primary care is still in its infancy. Many practices view information technology with some suspicion and management have not fully perceived the breadth or depth of information that can be made available, concentrating instead on those functions that support daily activities (Goves *et al.* 1991). Furthermore, many doctors have probably never been trained in the complexities of data and information handling; given the demands of everyday practice, they are unlikely to have the time to acquire these skills. However, changes in primary care are such that doctors and other members of the PHCT will need to develop these skills in order to make best use of the high quality information that is beginning to emerge from their information systems. Organizations outside practices – initially slow to recognize the potential of primary health care data – are now showing increasing interest, because the value of these data is proven and their potential to influence the planning and delivery of care is recognized. There are still difficulties both inside and outside practices to be overcome – some attitudinal, others educational – but with appropriate investment in technology, training and the infrastructure required, the potential of a primary-care-led NHS supported by information derived from primary care is a realizable goal.

References

Allan, K. (1993) MIQUEST – enabling health data, in *Proceeding of the Annual Conference of the Primary Health Care Specialist Group of the British Computer Society*. Worcester, Primary Health Care Specialist Group.

Bradley, P. (1993a) The primary health care specialist group perspective, in *Proceeding of the Annual Conference of the Primary Health Care Specialist Group of the British Computer Society*. Worcester, Primary Health Care Specialist Group.

Bradley, P. (1993b) Towards holistic audit, *Journal of Informatics in Primary Care*, January: 3–6.

British Medical Journal (1996) More GPs become fundholders, *British Medical Journal*, 313: 442.

Chalmers, I. (1993) The Cochrane collaboration: preparing, maintaining and disseminating systematic reviews of the effects of health care, *Annals of the New York Academy of Sciences*, 703: 156–63.

Donabedian, A. (1980) *Exploration in Quality Assessment and Monitoring*. Ann Arbor, MI, Health Administration Press.

Dowell, J. S., Snadden, D. and Dunbar, J. A. (1995) Changing to generic formulary: how one fundholding practice reduced prescribing costs, *British Medical Journal*, 310: 505–8.

Goves, J. R., Davies, T. and Reilly, T. (1991) Computerisation of primary care in Wales, *British Medical Journal*, 303: 93–4.

Greenhalgh and Company Ltd (1994) *Using Information in Practice Management: Business Planning*. Macclesfield, Greenhalgh and Company Ltd.

Howarth, F. P. (1986) Micros for GPs, *British Medical Journal*, 292: 307–8.

Information Management Group (1992) *IM&T Infrastructure Overview*. London, NHS Management Executive.

Information Management Group (1995) *General Medical Practice Computer Systems – Requirements for Accreditation – Version 3 (1995/96)*. Leeds, NHS Management Executive.

McMoran, S. and Prince, C. (1993) Personalised medical reference, *Journal of Informatics in Primary Care*, January: 13–15.

Pearson, N., O'Brien, J., Thomas, H., Ewings, P., Gallier, L. and Bussey, A. (1996) Collecting morbidity data in general practice: the Somerset morbidity project, *British Medical Journal*, 312: 1517–20.

Pringle, M. and Hobbs, R. (1991) Large computer databases in general practice, *British Medical Journal*, 302: 741–2.

Purves, I. (1996) Personal communication.

Secretaries of State for Health, Wales, Northern Ireland and Scotland (1987) *Promoting Better Health*. London, HMSO.

Wyatt, T. D., Reilly, P. M., Morrow, N. C. and Passmore, C. M. (1992) Short-lived effects of a formulary on anti-infective prescribing – the need for continuing peer review? *Family Practice*, 9: 461–5.

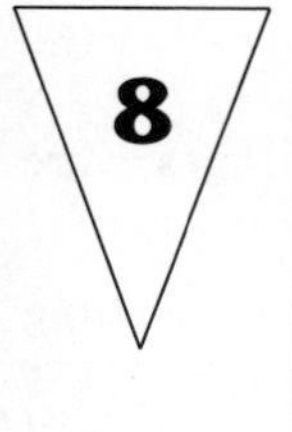

The MatS maternity staffing model

Patricia Meldrum, Sara Twaddle, Patricia Purton and Barbara MacLennan

Introduction

MatS is a spreadsheet-based model developed over two years and distributed in 1995 to purchasers and providers of maternity services in Scotland as an aid to decision making when reviewing services. This DSS enables managers to estimate the impact on staffing and costs of introducing changes in the delivery of care. It may also be used to estimate how current staffing levels compare against the levels associated with accepted best practice.

This chapter briefly reviews recent changes in the organization of maternity services and the resulting concerns that led to the development of the DSS. It outlines the benefits of a modelling approach to the problem and details the process by which the model was developed. A case scenario illustrates how the DSS is structured and how it may be used. This scenario takes an issue which was of concern to a large maternity hospital and illustrates how the model provided information required by managers charged with developing maternity services.

The management problem: planning maternity care services

A number of official reports published recently in the UK made recommendations concerning the future organization of maternity services and the delivery of maternity care (House of Commons Health Committee on Maternity Services 1992; Department of Health 1993; Scottish Office Home and Health Department 1993). The main recommendations were to move away from the high technology, high intervention method of care that had developed and to 'demedicalize' maternity services, increase community-based care, increase informed choice for women, improve continuity of care and carer, and recognize the professional role of the midwife as a practitioner.

These official reports were published at a time when changes were already taking place in maternity services. These included:

- a reduction in the length of postnatal stay, with many women going home on the second or third postnatal day. This increases both the workload of community-based midwives and the intensity of work of hospital-based midwives;
- changes in the role of the midwife, with some midwives running their own antenatal clinics and delivery units (MacVicar *et al.* 1993; Hundley *et al.* 1994).

While generally welcomed, these recommendations and developments have raised concerns about their impact on staffing and costs. It was felt that there was a role for a model that would enable providers and purchasers of services to estimate the implications of any change in services easily and to open up a dialogue about the sorts of changes and implications that would be acceptable. A grant was awarded by the Health Services Research Committee of the Chief Scientist Office of the Scottish Office Home and Health Department (the national grant awarding body for all aspects of health services research in Scotland) to develop the model and to distribute it to providers and purchasers within Scotland.

The main purpose of the model is to describe and quantify service provision in a particular provider unit, to estimate whether or not desirable changes would be possible given available resources and, if not, to estimate the additional resources required. The model has three main elements – staffing, costs and demand for services – which, in combination, reflect key management problems.

Maternity care services

Maternity care can be divided into three stages: antenatal care, intrapartum care (which includes the birth itself, and the times immediately before and after it) and postnatal care. At each stage, care may be provided in a number of different locations and by a range of different providers:

- *hospital* – this includes units led by consultants, general practitioners and midwives. Most midwife-led units are within or alongside consultant units;
- *community* – this includes hospital outreach clinics held in the community, GP clinics and midwife clinics in general practices or community clinics;
- *home* – some women receive some antenatal care at home, some choose to deliver at home and all women have some of their postnatal care at home.

There are a number of different care options available to women:

- *traditional* – the traditional model of hospital delivery and length of stay of at least 48 hours;
- *planned early discharge* – hospital delivery and discharge in less than 48 hours;
- *DOMINO* or *home birth* – see the definition in the Appendix at the end of the chapter.

In Scotland, antenatal care is currently provided by a system of shared care between general practitioner, obstetrician and midwife. In 1992 nearly all births (99.5 per cent) occurred in hospital, with 70 per cent being delivered by midwives (Scottish Needs Assessment Programme 1994). Postnatal care is predominantly provided by midwives, initially in the hospital and then at home until at least the tenth postnatal day.

There are a number of issues that arise when considering ways of implementing changes. Possible changes to maternity services include:

- changes in the place of care (e.g. from hospital to community);
- changes in the care provider (e.g. from obstetrician or GP to midwife);
- changes in the amount of care – recommendations continue to advocate a reduction in numbers of antenatal visits and a tailoring in the number and frequency of postnatal visits.

Each may involve reorganization of the delivery of services and may require changes in the staffing level and mix.

Benefits of a modelling approach

Managers responsible for making decisions about the provision of care in this complex system face a number of restrictions. The MatS model can assist in dealing with a number of these concerns.

It enables more informed decision making by estimating the impact of different methods of delivering care on staffing and costs. It is expected that one of the main users of the model will be the head of midwifery services (HOMS) charged with managing the delivery of services within a given budget. The HOMS is likely to have access to all of the data required, although these may have to be gathered from a number of sources in the hospital and the community. In pilot testing the only piece of information that sites did not have available was local intervention rates. However, the model will default to using national average figures.

It enables different provider and purchaser groups which are involved in the decision making process to discuss the issues and implications using a standardized instrument and structure. It is expected that hospital managers and health authority purchasers will find the DSS useful as a source of information on potential variations in services and costs. However, these groups will require to consult with the HOMS in order to obtain the required level of detailed information about services needed to run the model. This should provide a means of opening up a dialogue about service provision and potential ways of changing services.

It enables users to see what models of care are possible within budget limitations. Users can adjust the trade-off between quality (including women's choice) and cost to see which is most acceptable.

Where information is shared, providers and purchasers can see how the unit performs in comparison to similar units. If staffing levels are different, examination of the data entered may highlight different policies that go some way towards explaining the differences in staffing in apparently similar units.

Scope and limitations of the model

Realizing that the main users would be managers of midwifery services in hospitals, the MatS model was designed to be a 'user-friendly' decision support system which could be used by people with little time and little computer experience. The model was developed in Microsoft Excel version 5 and comes with detailed guidance notes written so that it can be used by people with little or no experience of the package.

Its main focus is to determine the midwifery staffing required to provide a service as defined by the manager using the system. Midwives are the largest single staff group and the group most likely to be affected by a change in care provision. In order to simplify the DSS in terms of its development and use, it does not address the wider issues of medical or managerial staffing requirements and only includes auxiliary nurses or health care assistants working as assistants to the midwives. Furthermore, the model deals with the obstetric service only and does not address the midwifery staffing for special care baby units (SCBUs), neonatal intensive care units or for surgical procedures other than Caesarean sections.

Developing a maternity staffing model

Work to develop an understanding of the operation of maternity services sufficient to construct and validate the MatS model was carried out in three stages. The main methods used in each stage are summarized in Figure 8.1.

Understanding maternity services

First, a literature review was conducted to determine recommended good practice in maternity services and activity levels recorded in other studies. An initial postal survey of HOMS throughout Scotland had shown that units had different ways of defining the types of care provided. In order to standardize the inputs to the model, a list of standard definitions approved by the Royal College of Midwives for commonly used terms was

Understanding maternity services →	**Building the model →**	**Testing the model**
General review Literature review *Local provision* Information from purchasers and providers	*Staffing norms* Postal Delphi survey *Activity norms* Good practice figures from literature review National average figures from central data source	*Calculate activity levels* Use data entered by user Calculate annual activity using good practice or national average figures *Apply staffing figures* Use results from Delphi survey Calculate annual total hours required *Calculate WTE staff* Convert hours to whole-time equivalent staff

Figure 8.1 MatS: the process of development

drawn up (Meldrum *et al.* 1994) and used in developing the model (see Appendix). Findings from the literature review could then be incorporated into the calculations underlying the model, and are shown as the 'Standard figures' in Table 8.3 later in this chapter.

For inputs where no good practice recommendations were available, such as the average postnatal stay following a Caesarean section, Scottish national average figures were used (Scottish Health Services Common Services Agency 1994). Activity figures were calculated using the good practice recommendations and national average figures shown in Table 8.3. Care options felt to be infeasible by the different professional groups contacted were removed from the model and figures were calculated for those remaining.

Detailed information on local maternity care options was gathered through semi-structured interviews with representatives of all purchaser and provider organizations throughout mainland Scotland. It included some options that were felt to be feasible and others that were felt to be infeasible. Further information about feasible care options was obtained from postal questionnaires returned by 19 of the 22 clinical directors in mainland consultant obstetric units who were contacted. The views of a sample of 218 general practitioners (from a sample of 276) across Scotland were also obtained using postal questionnaires.

Building the DSS

When asked how staffing decisions were made, heads of midwifery and other provider representatives mostly said that they were made through the professional judgement of the HOMS. Therefore it was felt that the most appropriate means of obtaining information on staffing levels would be to use the expertise of that professional group.

A panel of 13 midwives with wide managerial and academic experience was recruited from throughout the UK. Members of this panel took part in a postal Delphi study to elicit and progressively refine their expert judgement. In a series of 'rounds' a questionnaire invited each member to indicate how they would staff particular wards, clinics and other aspects of services for a given range of activity levels. After each round of the questionnaires was returned, respondents were fed back a summary of the results from the whole panel and a copy of their own replies. They were asked to change their own answers if they felt that was appropriate. In this survey, a broad consensus was reached after each panel member had returned four rounds of the questionnaires. The mean of the values indicated in responses to the final round of questionnaires were used in the model.

The model focuses on three grades of staff:

- *midwife coordinator* – the equivalent to sister grade midwives (G grades and occasionally F grades), with a clinical and managerial role;
- *midwife* – a fully qualified midwife (E and F grades);
- *untrained assistant* – an assistant to the midwife, equivalent to the current auxiliary or health care assistant role (A and B grades).

These do not follow the current system of nursing grades exactly but, rather, reflect a view held by many within the profession that the current clinical grading structure is unhelpful since 'a midwife is a midwife'. Indeed it is anticipated that the structure may change in the future (Review Body on Nursing Staff, Midwives, Health Visitors and Professions Allied to Medicine 1995). The model has been designed, therefore, to produce results in terms of the three more 'generic' grades of staff above.

Testing the model

The DSS works by first calculating annual activity levels for each intervention, e.g. antenatal clinics, based on the data entered by the user. Annual activity levels are calculated using these data and the good practice and national average figures. Staffing figures, calculated in terms of the number of staff hours required to carry out that activity on an annual basis, are then applied to these activity levels based on the results of the Delphi survey. This is translated back into a whole-time equivalent number of staff required to provide the service, after adjusting the required hours upwards to take account of holidays, sickness and other time away from the workplace. At present the model does not consider continuity of carer: this is the issue addressed in Chapter 9 by Beech, Mejia and Shirazi.

Lessons from piloting the model

The model was piloted in six different types of hospitals: a large city-based general hospital with some teaching involvement; a large city-based teaching maternity unit; a smaller city-based non-teaching maternity hospital; a smaller non-teaching maternity unit serving a mixed urban–rural population; and two smaller mixed specialist hospitals serving mixed urban–rural populations. It was revised in light of problems highlighted and suggestions made. Table 8.1 shows how staffing figures for the sixth hospital, using the final version of the model, compared against the actual staff numbers in post. Three general conclusions can be drawn from this and from the other pilot sites.

In several sites, the total number of community staff calculated by the model was similar to the number in post. However, the skill mix was different in most cases, with most having a much higher ratio of midwife coordinators to midwives than calculated. This reflects the fact that, historically, almost all community-based midwives have been G grades. However, the view expressed by a number of heads of midwifery and reflected by the Delphi panel is that this is no longer appropriate, and more staff of lower grades will be working in the community as posts arise.

In some cases, the number of untrained assistants calculated by the model was lower than the number actually employed by the unit. This may be explained by the fact that the model only deals with auxiliaries in their role as assistants to the midwives, and this may not include some of their core duties.

In most of the pilot sites, the overall numbers of staff predicted by the model were slightly lower than the staff actually in post. Part of the reason for these lower numbers is the lower numbers of untrained assistants, as discussed. It might also be the case that some users did not have access to local data on intervention rates requested by the model. If some of the local intervention rates were higher than the figures used, this would partly explain lower staffing figures predicted by the model.

Table 8.1 Percentage difference* between predicted staff numbers and actual staff numbers in Hospital 6

	Midwife coordinators	*Midwives*	*Total skilled staff*	*Untrained staff*	*Total staff*
Hospital-based	–13	9	5	–19	–2
Community-based	–76	490	7	0	7
Both locations	–44	27	5	–19	–1

*Positive percentages show how much higher predicted staff numbers are than actual numbers, and negative percentages show how much lower.

The process of piloting the model also provided information about its acceptability to the HOMS, part of the final target audience. The ease with which they were able to use the model differed with their level of experience in using a keyboard and using Windows-based software. Some were not at all comfortable and said that they would ask their secretary to use the model in future, entering the data provided. Others were more comfortable using the keyboard, but did not have experience of using a mouse and a Windows environment. The guidance notes were subsequently rewritten to give more details about how to use the mouse and also to explain how to use the model without using the mouse.

In terms of the information requested, there were some initial difficulties with the model not accurately reflecting the sort of data that would be collected and available to the HOMS. This was addressed by rewriting parts of the model to remove questions asking for data that were not available and using Scottish average figures in the calculations instead. Feedback from the final pilot sites was that most of the data requested were available. However, the HOMS did have some difficulty with providing information on the average number of midwife hours per month spent on direct care other than in wards and clinics (e.g. health education sessions, telephone enquiries, general advice, etc.) and on indirect care (e.g. administration and travelling time). They reported that while this data could be collected from individual midwife records, it would be time consuming and they found it easier to enter an informed estimate. In spite of this difficulty, it was felt important to keep these questions in the model because they covered a whole range of activities that otherwise could not be built into the calculations with any degree of accuracy.

Applying the model

A composite case, developed from work at a number of units, is used to illustrate how the model can be used to address maternity services planning.

More than half of the antenatal clinics at a large city-based teaching hospital serving an urban-based population were midwife-only clinics, and more than half of all antenatal care was provided in the community. Hospital managers were keen to move still more care into the community, in line with recommended best practice. Midwifery and medical staff also accepted that numbers of antenatal visits for low risk women were higher than those recommended by official guidance. While most managers and senior staff believed that introducing these changes in service would result in cost savings, the magnitude of the savings was unknown, as was the relative impact on hospital and community staffing. Staff were keen to have this information so as to discuss possible ways of reallocating the freed resources and, consequently, to consider if these changes in policy could be justified locally.

User inputs to MatS model	**Outputs from MatS model**	
Determinants of local service	*Annual staffing requirement* →	*Staff costs*
Local demand – numbers – care options Local organization of services Local geography	Midwife coordinators Midwives Untrained assistants	All 3 staff grades

Figure 8.2 MatS: data inputs and outputs

The HOMS used the model to estimate the impact on staffing and costs of reducing the number of antenatal clinic visits for this group, and of shifting more of the antenatal clinics out of the hospital and into community clinics. It was accepted that some aspects of care would remain unchanged at that time – for example untrained assistants did not work in the community because of a holistic approach to patient care in the community and because home assessments had to be done by a fully qualified midwife. Another local requirement was that all booking visits took place at hospital.

The HOMS ran the model twice. For the reasons discussed above, the MatS model may not predict exactly the same numbers of staff as are currently in post. Since the HOMS was considering changes in service provision, it was important, first, to run the model based on maintenance of existing services in order to establish the baseline data. Running the model a second time allowed the HOMS to estimate the difference in staffing and costs following changes in the service. Throughout this account, data generated by the model relate to the hospital and community services both before and after any proposed change in practice.

The DSS is organized so that the first stage involves the user entering data about the determinants of the local service. Outputs are then produced in terms of the requirement for the three grades of staff and associated staff costs. This structure is shown in Figure 8.2.

Entering data on type of unit and hospital and community workload

In response to a series of on-screen questions, the HOMS typed in information about the type of unit, how it is organized and about the level of hospital and community workload. The information collected at this time and the data entered by Hospital A are shown in Table 8.2. Only data that varied as a result of the proposed policy change are entered in the 'after' column.

The information collected covers all possible uses of the midwives' and untrained staff's time in the hospital and in the community. The data

Table 8.2 Type of unit and workload

Information requested	*Hospital A – before*	*Hospital A – after*
1 Type of population	Urban-based	—[1]
2 Type of unit	Consultant unit	—
3 Estimated births per year	4,200	—
4 Estimated number primiparous[2]	40%	—
5 Organization of antenatal clinics	Mixed booking/return clinics	—
	(numbers per week)	(numbers per week)
	5 hospital consultant clinics	4 hospital consultant clinics
	5 outreach consultant clinics	5 outreach consultant clinics
	7 hospital midwife-only clinics	4 hospital midwife-only clinics
	6 outreach midwife-only clinics	7 outreach midwife-only clinics
	Staffed by community midwives	—
	No community booking visits	—
6 Community antenatal visits	10 GP clinics	—
	35 midwife-only clinics	—
7 Total midwife hours per month on other direct care	Hospital – 190 hours Community – 210 hours	Hospital – 160 hours Community – 230 hours
8 Midwife hours on indirect care	Hospital – 130 hours Community – 160 hours	Hospital – 110 hours Community – 190 hours
9 Do auxiliaries work in the community?	No	—
10 Days a week daycare available	5 days	—
11 Structure of hospital wards	Mixed wards	—
12 Minimum staffing for theatre	3 midwives + 1 assistant	—
13 Who staffs elective theatre?	Obstetric staff	—
14 Availability of elective theatre	5 days a week; 8 hours a day	—
15 Expected ward occupancy rate	65%	—

(cont.)

(Table 8.2 cont.)

16 Amount added for down time	9%	—
17 Annual number of students	15 midwifery, 20 CF[3]	—
18 Annual obstetric budget	£3,145,000	—

[1] — = no change.
[2] Women having their first baby.
[3] Common Foundation, Project 2000.

collection framework is designed to ensure that the model can be used by units providing care in different ways. Each piece of information is used in the calculations and all questions must be answered by the user, even if the only valid response is 'Not applicable'.

Choice of default 'good practice' figures or local figures

The next stage of the model is illustrated in Table 8.3. The two columns on the left show standard figures taken from the literature or national average figures. These are copied automatically into the two columns on the right, headed 'Local figures', but the user is prompted to overtype any of the figures on the right hand side which are known not to reflect local practice. All of the figures relate to the average activity (number of visits, length of stay, etc.) per woman. In this case, the HOMS made changes in the right hand columns the first time that the model was used ('before' figures). The second time it was used, she changed the figures on the right hand side back to the standard figures, as shown in bold to reflect the proposed change in policy.

The opportunity to check these default figures against local practice means that the model can more accurately deal with local situations, but users equally may choose not to change some of the figures that they know to be incorrect in order to see the impact on staffing and costs of moving towards best practice or national average figures.

User defines the type of maternity service to be modelled

At the next stage the HOMS was presented with a series of questions about the type of service provided at the unit. The data requested are shown in Table 8.4. The first three questions deal with the demand for intrapartum care options other than the standard hospital delivery. At the time of interviewing hospital managers to collect background information on models of care provided, many felt unable to advertise these non-standard options to women because the additional community staffing required would be prohibitive. Most units had a low percentage

Table 8.3 Standard figures and local figures for aspects of care

	Standard figures (after)		*Local figures (before)*	
	Prims[1]	*Multips*[2]	*Prims*	*Multips*
1 *Hospital/outreach clinic visits (number)*				
High risk women	6	6	6	6
Low risk, including DOMINO and home	2	2	4	3
2 *Day care (number of visits)*				
Women with antenatal risk factors	2.75	2.5	2.75	2.5
3 *Inpatient days (number)*				
High risk/antenatal risk factors	3.9	1.9	3.9	1.9
4 *Community clinic visits (number)*				
High risk	5	5	5	5
Low risk	7	5	9	7
DOMINO	7	5	9	7
Home birth	7	5	9	7
5 *Routine home antenatal visits (number)*				
High risk	1.2	1.2	1.2	1.2
Low risk	1.2	1.2	1.2	1.2
DOMINO	1.2	1.2	1.2	1.2
Home birth	5.2	5.2	5.2	5.2
6 *Home assessment visits (number)*				
High risk	0	0	0	0
Low risk	0	0	0	0
DOMINO	0	0	0	0
Home birth	1	1	1	1
7 *Intranatal (length of stay)*				
DOMINO (hours)	12	12	12	12
Vaginal delivery (days)	4.8	3	4.8	3
Caesarean section (days)	8	8	8	8
Other instrumental delivery (days)	5.6	4.1	5.6	4.1
8 *Postnatal home visits (number)*				
DOMINO	7	7	7	7
Home birth	8.1	8.1	8.1	8.1

(cont.)

(Table 8.3 cont.)

Planned early discharge	5.7	5.7	5.7	5.7
Routine discharge	5.7	5.7	5.7	5.7
Caesarean section	2	2	2	2
Assisted delivery	5	5	5	5
9 *Intervention rates (prims and multips)*				
Induction rate	20.42%		20.42%	
Assisted delivery rate	11.86%		11.86%	
Caesarean section rate	13.86%		13.86%	
No intervention	59.17%		59.17%	

[1] Prims – primiparous: women having their first baby.
[2] Multips – multiparous: women having their second or subsequent baby.

Table 8.4 Type of maternity service

Information requested	*Hospital A – before*	*Hospital A – after*
1 Percentage booked for DOMINO	2%	—
2 Percentage booked for home birth	0.5%	—
3 Percentage booked for early discharge (excluding DOMINOs)	3% in 12 hours or less 10% in 13–24 hours	— —
4 Extent of team midwifery	Community-based teams only	—
5 Extent of midwife-only antenatal clinics	Midwife-only hospital and community-based antenatal clinics	—
6 Extent of midwife-only intrapartum care	Midwife-led intrapartum care in consultant unit only	—
7 Cost of midwife coordinator, midwife and untrained assistant (salary plus oncosts)	Standard salary figures	—

of women using these options, and this was mainly women who knew how to ask for this type of care. When using the model, users may choose to enter the figures for their current activity or enter estimated figures if women were offered more choice. The other questions in this section relate to models of care that users may be working towards, in line with official recommendations. Once again users may choose to enter the current situation or the option that they wish to work towards and see the impact that it would have on staffing and on costs. In this case the HOMS entered data relating to her current situation. This was not affected by the change in policy, and so the 'before' and 'after' data were the same.

Model produces tables of results

After the data entry stage was complete, the model was run to produce tables of results. These show the numbers of midwifery and untrained staff required in the hospital (Table 8.5a) and in the community (Table 8.6a), the cost of these staff (Tables 8.5b and 8.6b) and how this compared against the initial budget figure (Table 8.7). Staff numbers are shown in whole-time equivalents (WTE). The figures in bold are the results that changed following the change in policy. For example, pregnant women assessed as 'low risk' are currently asked to attend for more

Table 8.5a Hospital staffing

	Midwife coordinator		*Midwife*		*Untrained staff*	
	Before	*After*	*Before*	*After*	*Before*	*After*
Consultant clinics (hospital)	0.4	0.4	0.6	**0.5**	0.5	**0.4**
Consultant clinics (outreach)	N/A	N/A	N/A	N/A	N/A	N/A
Midwife-only clinics (hospital)	0.7	**0.4**	1.4	**0.8**	0.6	**0.4**
Midwife-only clinics (outreach)	N/A	N/A	N/A	N/A	N/A	N/A
Parentcraft and other 'direct care' activities	0.0	0.0	1.4	**1.2**	0.0	0.0
'Indirect care' activities	0.0	0.0	1.0	**0.8**	0.0	0.0
Time for booked DOMINO/home births	N/A	N/A	N/A	N/A	N/A	N/A
Daycare	1.0	1.0	2.6	2.6	1.0	1.0
Inpatient care	6.8	6.8	42.8	42.8	17.1	17.1
Labour/delivery suite	5.7	5.7	42.8	42.8	11.4	11.4
Theatre	0.0	0.0	4.5	4.5	1.5	1.5
Additional time for students	0.0	0.0	0.9	0.9	0.0	0.0
Total	**14.6**	**14.3**	**98.0**	**96.9**	**32.1**	**31.8**

Table 8.5b Costs of hospital staffing

	Minimum WTE		*Cost*		*Beds*
	Before	*After*	*Before*	*After*	
Midwife coordinators	14.6	**14.3**	£346,575	**£339,453**	
Midwives	98.0	**96.9**	£1,911,000	**£1,889,550**	
Untrained staff	32.1	**31.8**	£373,901	**£370,406**	
Ward beds required					91
Total	**144.7**	**143.0**	**£2,631,476**	**£2,599,409**	**91**

antenatal clinic visits than recommended as best practice in the literature (see the second row of figures, Table 8.3). The HOMS showed this by typing in her own figures in the 'Local figures' column as she ran the model for the first time (4 and 3 for primaparous and multiparous, respectively). The second time she ran the model, she overtyped those figures with the 'Standard figures' to test what differences a reduction in visits to levels consistent with recommended practice would imply.

The cells in the tables that show 'N/A' relate to activities that were not provided by hospital staff. Outreach clinics were staffed by community midwives and are shown in Table 8.6a. 'Time for booked DOMINO/home births' was not applicable in this case because this only applies if antenatal care is organized in a different way for these women than for other women.

The proposed change in policy was estimated to result in a reduction of 0.3 WTE midwife coordinators, 1.1 WTE midwives and 0.3 WTE untrained staff in the hospital. This gave a cost saving of approximately £32,000.

Savings of over £71,000 were predicted in the community, resulting from a reduction of 1.2 WTE midwife coordinators and 2.2 WTE midwives in the community. Larger savings fell in the community because the reduction in the average number of visits per woman had a larger impact there than the shift of small amounts of activity to the community from the hospital.

Table 8.7 shows the total staffing costs and compares this against the budget currently available. If the total cost calculated is over budget a message appears on screen to say that the scenario selected is not feasible within existing resources. In these cases, users may choose to run the model using a different scenario or to continue the analysis as a means of estimating the additional resources required to develop services in line with the options chosen. In the case of the hospital, the change in policy resulted in estimated cost savings of more than £100,000, keeping the service costs within budget.

Table 8.6a Community staffing

	Midwife coordinator		*Midwife*		*Untrained staff*	
	Before	*After*	*Before*	*After*	*Before*	*After*
Antenatal clinics – GP/obstetrician	0.4	0.4	0.8	0.8	N/A	N/A
Antenatal clinics – midwife-only	2.7	**1.4**	6.1	**3.4**	N/A	N/A
Consultant outreach clinics (obstetrician)	0.4	0.4	0.7	0.7	N/A	N/A
Consultant outreach clinics (midwife-only)	0.6	**0.7**	1.4	**1.6**	N/A	N/A
Parentcraft and other 'direct care' activities	0.0	0.0	1.6	**1.7**	0.0	0.0
'Indirect care' activities	0.0	0.0	1.2	**1.4**	0.0	0.0
Home booking visits	N/A	N/A	N/A	N/A	N/A	N/A
Antenatal home visits	0.0	0.0	1.8	1.8	0.0	0.0
Postnatal home visits	0.0	0.0	5.9	5.9	0.0	0.0
Delivery episodes (DOMINO and home birth)	0.0	0.0	0.3	0.3	0.0	0.0
Additional WTE staff for DOMINO and home birth	0.0	0.0	0.0	0.0	0.0	0.0
Additional time for students	0.0	0.0	0.9	0.9	0.0	0.0
Total	**4.1**	**2.9**	**20.7**	**18.5**	**0.0**	**0.0**

Table 8.6b Costs of community staffing

	Minimum WTE		*Cost*	
	Before	*After*	*Before*	*After*
Midwife coordinators	4.1	**2.9**	£97,326	**£68,840**
Midwives	20.7	**18.5**	£403,650	**£360,750**
Untrained staff	0.0	0.0	£0.00	£0.00
On-call and call-out cost for DOMINO and home birth			£9,531	£9,531
Total	**24.8**	**21.4**	**£510,507**	**£439,121**

Finally, the model calculated the additional cost (or cost saving) per DOMINO and per home birth incurred purely because these women chose a DOMINO or home birth rather than the traditional model of care (Table 8.8). The change in policy had no effect on these costs.

Table 8.7 Total staffing and costs

	Minimum WTE		*Cost*	
	Before	*After*	*Before*	*After*
Midwife coordinators	18.7	**17.2**	£443,901	**£408,294**
Midwives	118.7	**115.4**	£2,314,650	**£2,250,300**
Untrained staff	32.1	**31.8**	£373,901	**£370,406**
On-call and call-out cost	—	—	£9,531	£9,531
Total	**169.5**	**164.4**	**£3,141,983**	**£3,038,531**
Total fixed budget			**£3,145,000**	**£3,145,000**
Excess income			**£3,017**	**£106,469**

Table 8.8 Additional costs incurred by booked DOMINOs and home births

Bookings for DOMINO	2.0%		Number of women		84	
Bookings for home birth	0.5%		Number of women		21	
	Additional WTE staff		*Additional cost*		*Additional cost per case*	
	Before	*After*	*Before*	*After*	*Before*	*After*
DOMINO						
Hospital-based staff	0.0	0.0	£0	£0		
Community-based staff	0.2	0.2	£3,900	£3,900		
On-call and call-in costs			£1,915	£1,915		
Total	**0.2**	**0.2**	**£5,815**	**£5,815**	**£69**	**£69**
Home birth						
Hospital-based staff	0.0	0.0	£0	£0		
Community-based staff	0.1	0.1	£1,950	£1,950		
On-call and call-in costs			£705	£705		
Total	**0.1**	**0.1**	**£2,655**	**£2,655**	**£126**	**£126**

Implications of the results

The analysis suggests that relocating antenatal care from the hospital to the community and reducing antenatal visits in line with recommended good practice services would result in estimated cost savings of over £100,000 and a release of staff time both in the hospital and in the community. After discussions with managerial and other senior staff, the HOMS was able to use the model to explore ways of redeploying these resources so as to increase implementation of national policy guidance, such as offering more women the full range of options for care or by introducing changes reflecting particular local concerns. This involved running the model a number of times, changing a range of different inputs to the model to reflect differences in services – for example increasing the number of women choosing to have a DOMINO or introducing more client-specific health education sessions. Options that were calculated by the DSS as falling within the available budget were then considered, and final recommendations discussed with other groups in the hospital and with purchasing organizations.

Conclusions

The MatS model was developed to allow users to estimate the impact of changes in service delivery and organization on staffing levels and costs. It was designed to address the types of issues of concern to purchasers and providers who are faced with the responsibility for implementing official recommendations concerning the development of services, in circumstances where the local make-up of services means that the method of implementation is likely to vary. It enables users to consider a number of different means of achieving a particular goal and to compare the potential impact of these options. If two or more users choose to compare information, the model can help explain differences in staffing in similar units and may highlight the factors that result in these staffing differences.

The model has been shown to predict numbers of staff in post reasonably accurately. The predicted skill mix is often different to that found in practice because attitudes among midwifery managers, reflected in the figures given by the expert Delphi panel, are changing towards a lower skill mix, particularly in the community. It may be that the model predicts the sorts of skill mix that will be seen in the future, as posts are reviewed following the departure of current staff.

In the case scenario described, the model showed that by making changes in antenatal care that were in line with recommended practice, savings could be realized. The model could then be used to consider appropriate ways of reallocating these savings so as to achieve further service goals.

While the DSS has been piloted in several maternity units and widely disseminated, neither the extent of effective take-up nor the effectiveness of the MatS model have been evaluated. Any evaluation should be concerned with a number of issues: the reliability of the model, how easy it is to use, the time taken to use it, the confidence that users place in the results and whether or not it has been used to influence decision making. A postal survey of the purchasers and providers who were supplied with the model and other users who purchased it would be one way forward, although this should be followed by more in-depth interviews with a sample of those who have used it and those who have considered using it but have not been able to do so. Feedback from these two groups should provide information on the strengths and weaknesses of the model and highlight lessons that could be applied to similar projects.

The main lessons learned from the process of developing the DSS are that time should be built into similar projects for dissemination, training and support, and evaluation. Spending time demonstrating the model to users on a one-to-one basis rather than to large groups would have been a particularly useful process, given that a number of potential users may have very limited experience of using computers and the 'what if' method of DSS.

Acknowledgements

The development of MatS was funded by the Health Services Research Committee of the Chief Scientist Office of the Scottish Office Home and Health Department. We are grateful to all the heads of midwifery, purchasers, hospital providers, clinical directors and general practitioners who provided information for this project, the members of the Delphi panel for their input and to Robert Calderwood, John MacFarlane, Gillian McIlwaine and Jane McKinley for their advice and direction. We would also like to thank Bridget Stuart and Ann Lees for advice.

References

Department of Health (1993) *Changing Childbirth: Report of the Expert Maternity Group*. London, HMSO.

House of Commons Health Committee on Maternity Services (1992) *Second Report for the Session 1991–1992* (HCP29). London, HMSO.

Hundley, V. A., Cruickshank, F. M., Lang, G. D., Glazener, C. M. A., Milne, J. M. and Turner, M. (1994) Midwife-managed delivery unit: a randomised controlled trial, *British Medical Journal*, 309: 1400–4.

MacVicar, J., Dobbie, G., Owen-Johnstone, L., Jagger, C., Hopkins, M. and Kennedy, J. (1993) Simulated home delivery in hospital: a randomised controlled trial, *British Journal of Obstetrics and Gynaecology*, 100: 316–23.

Meldrum, P., Purton, P., MacLennan, B. B. and Twaddle, S. (1994) Moving towards a common definition for maternity services: standard definitions for common terms, *Midwifery*, 10: 165–70.

Review Body on Nursing Staff, Midwives, Health Visitors and Professions Allied to Medicine (1995) *Twelfth Report on Nursing Staff, Midwives and Health Visitors*. London, HMSO.

Scottish Health Services Common Services Agency (1994) *Hospital and Health Board Comparisons in Obstetrics 1991–1993*. Edinburgh, Information and Statistics Division, Common Services Agency.

Scottish Needs Assessment Programme (SNAP) (1994) *Increasing Choice in Maternity Care in Scotland: Issues for Purchasers and Providers*. Glasgow, Scottish Forum for Public Health Medicine.

Scottish Office Home and Health Department (1993) *Provision of Maternity Services in Scotland: a Policy Review*. Edinburgh, HMSO.

Software availability

Copies of the MatS model are available from The Royal College of Midwives Scottish Board, 37 Frederick Street, Edinburgh EH2 1EP.

Appendix: Royal College of Midwives definitions

DOMINO scheme
This term is based on the definition 'domiciliary in and out'. It is a plan of care where the community midwife assesses the woman in her own home prior to accompanying her, at the appropriate time, to the maternity unit for delivery. The mother and baby return home at six to eight hours after the delivery and continue with the domiciliary midwifery care.

Early discharge
A planned transfer home, at six to eight hours, of a postnatal mother and her baby, from a maternity unit to care by the domiciliary midwifery services. This discharge is planned during the antenatal period.

Home confinement
The delivery of a baby in the woman's home, as opposed to a GP unit, or a maternity unit (consultant unit).

'Low risk' woman
A classification of pregnant women which predicts probable normal antenatal, intranatal and postnatal outcomes.

Midwife clinic
Antenatal care provided by the midwife in a hospital clinic, GP centre or client's own home setting. The midwife assumes responsibility for normal women and plans, implements and evaluates the care, in partnership with the client. In the event of complications the woman is referred for medical opinion/care.

Midwife-led unit
A unit, e.g. labour ward, in which the pattern of normal midwifery care is planned, implemented and evaluated by teams of midwives usually led by a midwife who may be called a midwife 'consultant'. Women will be referred to obstetric colleagues on the detection of an abnormality.

Source: *Midwifery* (1994) 10: 165–70.

9 A decision support system for planning continuity of midwifery services

Roger Beech, Alicia Mejia and Rabia Shirazi

Introduction

For every woman, pregnancy and birth are a unique experience. Pregnancy is not a disease but a normal event that is important not only to the pregnant woman but also to other members of the family. Two recent Government reports have addressed the issue of how maternity services should be organized in order to improve quality, in terms of the process of care. A key finding of a report by the House of Commons Health Committee (1992) was that there should be a more personalized type of care during pregnancy, labour and the postnatal period. The committee also emphasized that the professional best qualified to provide this care was the midwife.

As a response to this report the Government (Department of Health 1992: 70) set up an expert panel to 'to review policy on NHS maternity care, particularly during childbirth, and to make recommendations'. The report of the panel argued that

> Every woman should have the name of a midwife who works locally, is known to her, and whom she can contact for advice. She should also know the name of the lead professional who is responsible for planning and monitoring her care. Within 5 years, 75% of women should be cared for in labour by a midwife whom they have come to know during pregnancy.
>
> (Department of Health 1993: 76)

This recommendation was adopted as Government policy; hospitals have therefore been required to consider what measures they would introduce to achieve the desired levels of continuity.

The management task: planning for continuity of care

In midwifery-led services, care is provided at three stages (antenatal, labour and postnatal) by a midwife or team of midwives. If care is provided by the same midwife (or *named midwife*) in all three stages it is known as *continuity of carer*. In practice this is not always feasible and so a team of midwives might be used instead; in this case we talk of *continuity of care*. With this approach pregnant women become familiar with each one of the midwives of the team during their pregnancy, and the baby is delivered by one member of the team. Discontinuity of care occurs when a midwife of the team is not available to take on an antenatal or postnatal appointment or to deliver the baby (in which case a midwife of a different team would be involved).

Although the Government set the policy, no guidance on how the desired levels of continuity could be achieved was provided. This is a complex problem that requires careful planning. While aiming to provide a good service to the pregnant women, the manager (or person in charge of implementing maternity services) has to take into consideration limitations, such as:

- *Financial* – any implementation of maternity services has to stay within a budget. For this reason, many hospitals do not allow midwives to do extra hours even if, in the case of long deliveries, it implies the baby being delivered by a different midwife from the named midwife.
- *On-duty time* – even without the financial limitation, midwives cannot be on duty for 24 hours every day.
- *Personal reasons* – midwives also have a private life.

Alternative responses to guidelines on continuity

There are significant differences in the way maternity services have been organized to achieve the goals set by the Government. These include:

- size of the midwife team;
- caseload per midwife;
- whether or not a named midwife is used;
- midwives' duty rotas;
- policy on who delivers the baby (named midwife, midwife on call, or any other member of the team);
- duties of the midwife on call: labour only, or antenatal, postnatal and delivery duties;
- whether there is a second midwife on call who will deliver babies when the first midwife on call is already delivering a baby.

Commenting on these operational responses, Kroll observed:

> I am amazed at the variations on the concept [of team midwifery]. The size of the team is anything from six to 26 midwives . . . The

> responsibilities of the team vary as to . . . whether they are community- or hospital-based or integrated teams. Team care may be offered in labour only, or in the antenatal and postnatal period with no guarantees that a team member will be available during the intrapartum period.
>
> (Kroll 1993: 26)

While there is clearly a lack of consensus as to how to implement the Government recommendations, there is perhaps the greatest need for a means of exploring the implications of alternative arrangements for achieving continuity of care or carer. With that information available, managers can then decide which arrangement best suits their needs. The decision support system (DSS) described in this chapter is based upon research conducted at a hospital in south-east London. First, the DSS is described by considering the inputs, methods of analysis, and outputs of the system. Then, using data from that hospital the results of alternative planning scenarios are then described to illustrate the potential value of a computer model for planning midwifery care.

The development of a DSS for planning continuity of maternity care

Implementing the proposed changes requires a variety of questions to be answered. Some questions concern *the provision of continuity of care/carer* such as:

- For a given number of pregnant women seen in the hospital per year, what should the team size be?
- What is the best way to ensure that the baby will be delivered by a midwife known to the pregnant woman?
- How well can continuity of carer and continuity of care be achieved?
- What happens if the number of women seen by the hospital in a year increases?

Other questions concern *working arrangements*:

- What is the proportion of time that the midwives will be idle?
- What is the weekly number of hours that they will work and what is the number of hours that they will spend delivering babies?
- What are the effects and implications of the different midwives' rotas?

Given these questions, senior staff at two London hospitals wanted to know whether continuity of midwifery care was feasible and, if so, how it could best be achieved. One of these hospitals was chosen as the pilot site, and analysts continued to work closely with staff there during the model development.

Answering the questions posed by the managers of midwifery services requires a model that represents as accurately as possible key characteristics of the process of maternity care. Specifically:

- The requirements of pregnant women and the availability of midwives *change over time*: for example, the frequency of antenatal appointments increases as pregnancy progresses and the availability of individual midwives changes due to factors such as duty rotas, holidays and sickness.
- A degree of uncertainty, or *randomness* is associated with the length of a given pregnancy and with the duration of labour, as well as with the number of referrals of pregnant women to the hospital or maternity unit. These numbers will not be constant and are best described as a probability distribution, or by time-dependent probability distributions (in some hospitals, there is a *seasonality* effect, and more babies are delivered in September and in March).
- There are already several *different implementations* of team midwifery, and a model needs to be flexible enough to cope with these variations.

These three key factors suggested simulation as the most appropriate analytic tool for the development of the DSS. A *simulation model* creates a replica of the real-world system that is to be analysed. It can cater very easily with randomness associated with the real world, and while not providing an *optimal answer* or solution, it is particularly useful when the aim is to answer '*what if*' questions. The user can explore different scenarios, estimate the likely effect of changes in the parameters of the system, and carry out a *sensitivity analysis* to identify those parameters that are critical to the behaviour of the system. One of the advantages of a simulation model is that it allows existing policies and practices to be evaluated; at the same time, it enables alternatives to be tested, without the inconvenience and expense of implementing and evaluating them in real life.

Model inputs

Inputs can be broadly categorized into non-hospital-dependent and hospital-dependent. *Non-hospital-dependent* inputs cover the clinical aspects of pregnancy and labour. The model assumes that the length of pregnancy and the duration of labour are not going to change in a significant way from hospital to hospital; for this reason, once they have been identified (in this case using historical data from a hospital in south London) they do not need to be changed.

Hospital-dependent inputs describe particular characteristics of the hospital or situation that is to be evaluated. Two types of hospital-dependent inputs are considered: numerical (data inputs) and logical (policy inputs).

Data inputs cover the scheduled number of antenatal and postnatal appointments of pregnant women and the midwives' duty rotas. These rotas specify for each week, for each day of the week and for each midwife whether she is off duty, on duty, on call, or second on call (when there is a second midwife on call). If she is on duty, it also specifies whether the midwife will be doing clinics, home visits or delivering babies.

Other inputs to the system, besides the weekly rota are:

- expected number of new referrals per week;
- average home visit time per pregnant woman;
- starting time for each one of the three daily shifts: morning, afternoon, and night;
- if possible, an alternative rota for those weeks when there is a midwife on holiday;
- maximum number of patients seen at a clinic;
- maximum number of patients seen in a visiting time period;
- maximum number of postnatal visits during the weekends;
- weeks of holidays for each midwife in the team.

These data are entered to describe the baseline situation at any new hospital. Users can also change these variables in order to assess how continuity is affected by modifications in the demands for, and the availability of, resources.

Policy inputs provide a means of representing different ways of implementing maternity services. The simulation model caters for them by setting different parameters to be 'true' or 'false'. Note that when the policy includes a midwife on call, her only duties are to deliver babies; and that all policies include at least one midwife on call at night to cover deliveries. In more detail, the DSS program considers the following alternatives:

- There is/is not a midwife on call during the day as well as at night.
- Only the midwife on call will deliver babies or any of the midwives of the team can deliver a baby during the day.
- There is/is not a second midwife on call during the day.
- There is/is not a second midwife on call during the night.
- Antenatal appointments take place preferably at a clinic (or antenatal appointments are arranged with the named midwife if possible, even if this implies a home visit).
- The named midwife will always be called to deliver a baby even if she is off duty (or the policy aim is *continuity of care* rather than *continuity of carer*).

Different combinations of these parameters enable the user to construct and then evaluate alternatives to the already existing implementations of team midwifery. For example, currently there are midwives on call during the day and during the night: babies are delivered by the midwife who happens to be on call. The manager may wish to explore the effect of having only one midwife on call during the night delivering babies, with babies being delivered by any of the midwives of the team during the day. By changing the appropriate parameters it is then possible to compare the system in use at the hospital to the new system.

Model analysis and outputs

The maternity services model automatically keeps track, for each pregnant woman, of the time when the next antenatal appointment (or labour or postnatal appointment) is due. When it is, the model checks if the named midwife is available (i.e. is not off duty, on holiday, or fully occupied because she is seeing other women). If she is not available then it records a *discontinuity* of carer. It also checks whether there is another midwife of the team to take on the appointment or the delivery of the baby. If there is no midwife available it will record a discontinuity in the continuity of care.

For a particular policy, how well continuity of *carer* is achieved can be measured by estimating the percentage of appointments (antenatal and postnatal) and of deliveries with the named midwife. Similarly, how well continuity of *care* is achieved can be measured by estimating the percentage of appointments and of deliveries with any of the members of the team.

Validation of the model

There are two main stages in the validation of a model:

- *Exposure of the logic or model verification* – during its development there should be checks to ensure that the representation of the real system being modelled is accurate and that the model closely reflects the behaviour of the real system. For the midwifery model this was achieved by discussing the structure of the model and its methods of calculation with local midwives.
- *Exposure of the results* – validation of the results ideally requires data to compare actual and predicted outcome. Such data are often not available. At the time of writing, no records exist of the number of deliveries with the named midwife and with any of the members of the team. This information should become available in the near future as research in this area is currently being carried out by another research team at the same hospital. Validation of baseline results has so far been based on informal discussions with the senior midwife. These indicate that the results produced by the model for the current implementation are acceptable.

Validation of the logic, data and results of a model should be regarded as an ongoing process. It is often only by continuous use of the system that a full understanding of the model and the topic that it is addressing is obtained by both users and analysts.

Using the model to plan and test service changes

In the south-east London hospital where the model has been developed there are currently two teams each comprising six midwives: babies are

Table 9.1 Levels of continuity of carer and continuity of care

	Continuity of carer: % of appointments with a named midwife	*Continuity of care: % of appointments with team midwife*
Antenatal	83	100
Labour	20	99
Postnatal	42	95

delivered by the midwife who is on call. Antenatal clinics are held once a week at the hospital (or in a local GP surgery) and women go there for their check-ups irrespective of which midwife is holding the clinic (i.e. there is no attempt at providing continuity of carer during the antenatal stage). Usually women are visited daily for at least three or four days after giving birth. After this, they will be visited every other day excluding weekends. However, if there are no midwives from the woman's team available when a postnatal visit is due, the visit is postponed until such a day as a midwife of the team is available, i.e. there is an attempt to ensure continuity of care. This policy was analysed and the consequences of the simulation concerning the levels of continuity of care and continuity of carer examined. These are set out in Table 9.1. The results are based on a caseload of 230 babies delivered per year by the team of six midwives (on average, a caseload of 38 babies per midwife).

The strength of a simulation is that it enables the user to explore the implications of both changes in the way services are delivered and changes in demands for care. With the current version of the system it typically takes around 30 minutes to assess the implications of a new planning scenario.

To illustrate the potential of the midwifery model, the impacts on continuity of care and carer are now assessed for changes in caseload, team size and the number of women that can be seen by a midwife per shift.

Scenario 1: change in caseload and team size

Assuming there is no change in either the duty rotas of the midwives or the planned appointments that women receive, Figures 9.1, 9.2 and 9.3 show the change in the continuity of carer and continuity of care levels as a function of changes in the caseload for the antenatal, labour and postnatal periods respectively. Two team sizes are considered: team sizes of six and seven.

In all cases, as might be expected, continuity of care is greater than continuity of carer. Figures 9.1 and 9.3 also show that during the antenatal and postnatal periods levels of continuity are greater when there are larger teams, because the ratio of mothers to midwives is lower. Figure 9.3 also shows that continuity of care/carer is lower for postnatal care, which cannot accurately be scheduled in advance.

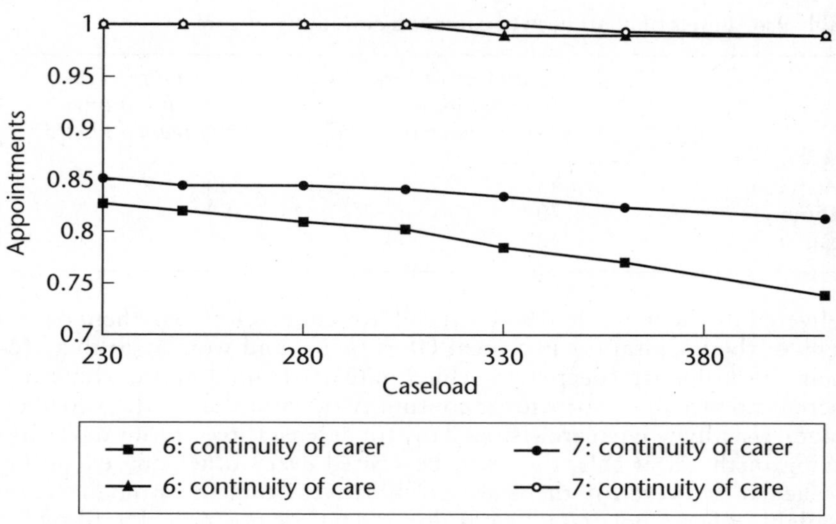

Figure 9.1 Antenatal care: levels of continuity

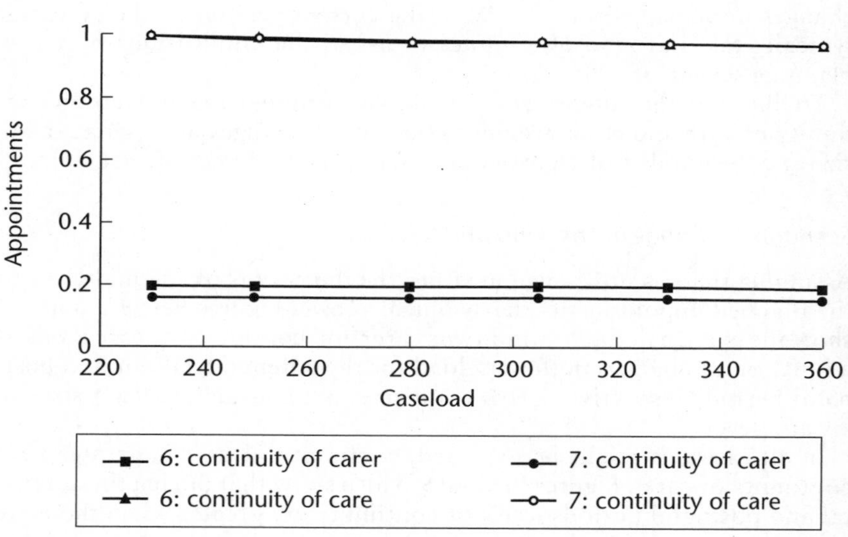

Figure 9.2 Labour care: levels of continuity

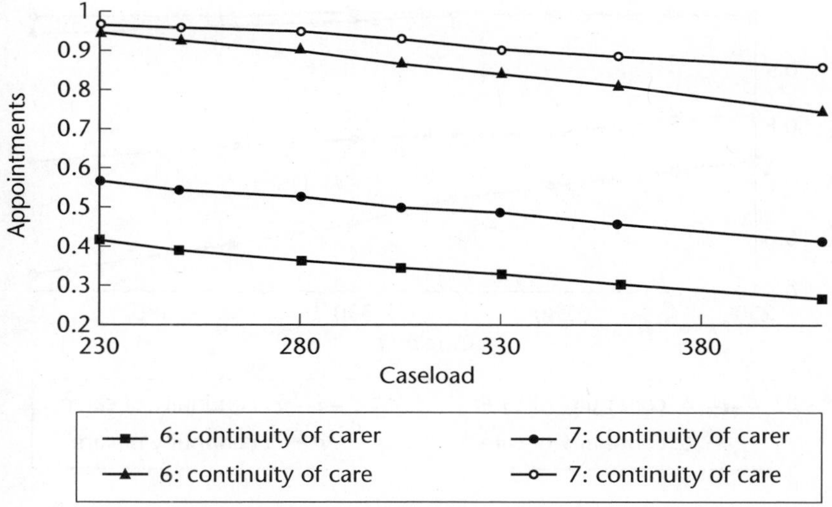

Figure 9.3 Postnatal care: levels of continuity

Figure 9.2 indicates that continuity during labour is unaffected by caseload. This is because it is largely determined by the duty rota, with babies being delivered by the midwife on call. What does influence levels of continuity during labour is midwifery team size. Unlike antenatal and postnatal care, continuity of carer and of care are greater for smaller team sizes. With a smaller team size the probability of having the named midwife on call is greater.

Using this type of output a manager could assess what actions were required to cope with a projected increase in caseload. These results suggest that high levels of continuity of care are still achievable in spite of large increases in caseload.

Scenario 2: effect of a decrease in the number of pregnant women seen in clinics and home visits

The model can also be used to consider the effect of a reduction in the number of pregnant women seen in clinics and home visits. A typical hospital clinic has ten appointment slots (i.e. up to ten pregnant women can be seen during a morning or an afternoon clinic). During a typical morning or afternoon of home visits a midwife can see at most six women (pregnant or recently delivered).

Figures 9.4 and 9.5 show the effect upon the levels of continuity of care and carer of a reduction of 25 per cent in the number of midwives available, this affecting the number of women seen in antenatal hospital clinics and in typical home visit sessions.

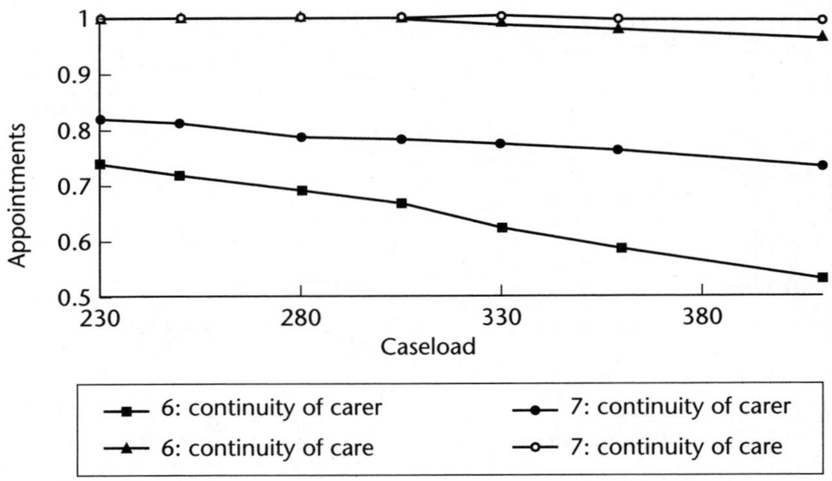

Figure 9.4 Antenatal care: reduced capacity

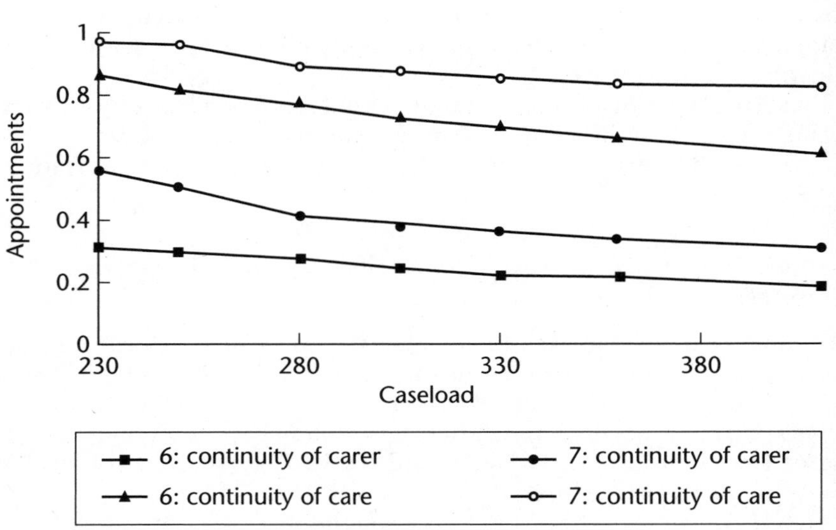

Figure 9.5 Postnatal care: reduced capacity

In comparison to the results shown in Figure 9.1, lower levels of continuity are achieved particularly at higher levels of caseload. This is because with less appointment slots available it is not always possible for a pregnant woman to see the named midwife or, even, a midwife of the team. The results shown in Figure 9.5 are similar to those shown in Figure 9.3 except for the lower levels of continuity of care and carer.

Concluding remarks

Achieving continuity of midwifery care is a complex planning problem. There are differences in the way this problem has been addressed – not only from hospital to hospital but also within the same hospital. The current approach to policy and option appraisal is to implement and then evaluate it. Such an approach may prove to be expensive as well as causing disruption to the provision of maternity services to pregnant women. Use of a model can help to avoid cost and disruption. At the request of users, the model has so far been used to consider: the impacts on continuity of an increased number of referrals for care; the merits of the two alternative midwifery policies currently existing within the pilot site; and the feasibility and implications of increasing the duration of clinic appointments. Managers' interest in the last question stems from a potential rise in the number of antenatal tests that can be offered to women and the need to explain the purpose of these tests and the results that they generate.

The process of use of the model is iterative. As results are produced, they are discussed with managers responsible for the service. New assumptions arising from that discussion are tested, and the results again fed back to the manager; and so on. Only after thorough testing using the model would a new service arrangement be introduced in practice.

This chapter has illustrated how a simulation model can be developed and used as a decision support tool to tackle this problem. It should be noted, however, that throughout the process of research and development, both analysts and users were on a learning curve. Analysts learned about the nature of midwifery services, while users are finding out more about the potential of computer models and how they can be used to identify strategies for improving services.

Models are not common in the NHS. Therefore, even though a model may now exist, the potential areas of application may not be immediately obvious to users. The simulation model described here is not for the daily organization and scheduling of services, but has a more strategic role. It could be argued that use of the model can help NHS managers to stand back and extend their normal planning horizons and this can bring a shift in thinking that is beneficial. Finally, given the existence of the software, the model could be introduced into a new hospital relatively easily: many of the data it requires are readily available, if not appropriately integrated. The system can help to respond to the requirements for continuity of midwifery care and in so doing, to improve midwifery services.

Acknowledgements

The authors would like to thank the people who helped us with their support throughout the development of the model: Helen Fawcett, Charles Wolfe, Paula Lacombe, David Balmer and the senior midwives of Lewisham Hospital, Whipps Cross Hospital, Maidstone Hospital, Heatherwood Hospital (Ascot), among others.

References

Department of Health (1992) *Maternity Services: Government Response to the Second Report from the Health Committee, Session 1991–92* (Cm 2018). London, HMSO.

Department of Health (1993) *Changing Childbirth. Part I: Report of the Expert Maternity Group*. London, Department of Health.

Health Committee (1992) *Maternity Services: Health Committee Second Report, Session 1991–92*. London, HMSO.

Kroll, D. (1993) The name of the game – team midwifery now, *Modern Midwife*, May/June, 26–8.

Queue management: what has a DSS approach to offer to improve the running of outpatient clinics?

Dave Worthington

Introduction

This chapter introduces some examples of DSS that have been used in addressing a particular class of health service problems: queue management. Because queue management problems, even apparently similar ones, take many forms in practice, it is important not to make any strong presumption that any single type of DSS approach should be used – an open mind is needed. The chapter also illustrates and discusses factors that have led to the success or otherwise of these approaches: the aim is to enable managers to evaluate DSS as an idea and a practice, and to provoke initial thoughts on what would be required to make effective use of DSS approaches. Those presented range from straightforward ideas that managers may wish to use for themselves, to methods where familiarity with the 'modelling process' is essential and hence where managers are more likely to be involved in the commissioning of a DSS project.

A brief overview of queue management in health services is used to introduce three important insights drawn from a more general literature on queue management. The following section reminds the reader of the basic DSS project methodology and gives three brief examples of DSS approaches to health service queue management problems. These concern: beds required for intensive care units, hospital waiting list management and hospital outpatient clinics. Two subsequent sections consider the role of DSS in hospital outpatient clinic problems in more detail, via two contrasting DSS case studies, both concerned with improving the running of particular outpatient clinics. The chapter finishes with a brief discussion that will help managers to evaluate, use, develop or commission a DSS, and some general conclusions about the use of DSS in managing health service queues.

Queue management problems

Queue management as a management task

In almost any profession, concern about 'queue management' quite rightly comes a poor second to concerns about the professional quality of the service delivered. A primary concern of a social worker is to deal properly with children at risk even if it means cancelling all other appointments for that day. A primary concern of a doctor holding an outpatient clinic is to provide correct diagnosis and advice to the patient in front of him or her, even if the waiting room is already full.

Against this backdrop of very clear priorities it has been easy in the past to take the view that the public should just be grateful for what they receive, and that their inconvenience as individuals can be ignored for the sake of the general good. However, closer inspection reveals that while professional priorities must be respected there are many instances where the levels of inconvenience to the public are caused by poor organization, and that in many cases it is possible to provide a reasonably convenient service as well as a high quality professional service. This argument has been reinforced in recent years by a number of 'Citizen's Charter' documents, including the Patient's Charter (Department of Health 1991), setting service level standards in many service sector organizations which focus directly on 'convenience' as a measure of quality.

Health service queues

Queueing systems are a well-established problem area for operations management and for decision support systems. The term 'queue' can be misleading because a queueing system does not necessarily have a visible queue (Figure 10.1). Some authors use the more informative name 'service systems', as it gives better weight to their key characteristics, namely:

- a service on offer which requires time and resources to deliver,
- customers who want to receive the service from time to time,
- if the customers are 'lucky' and arrive to find a server free, they receive the service without queueing; if they are 'unlucky' they have to queue or are turned away.

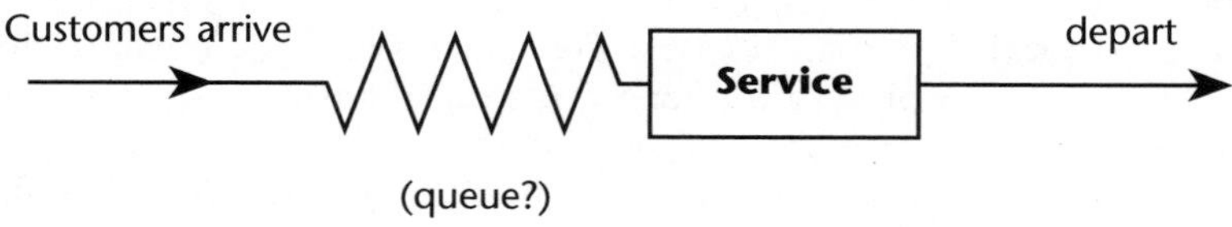

Figure 10.1 The key characteristics of a queueing system

Many queueing systems do have physical queues (e.g. supermarket tills), some have notional rather than physical queues (e.g. hospital waiting lists), and some are designed so that queues, notional or otherwise, are virtually impossible (e.g. ambulance service). Given the definition above, the list of queueing systems in the health service is as long as the list of services that it provides, for example:

- patients waiting to see a GP, practice nurse, health visitor, etc.;
- patients waiting for an X-ray;
- patients attending an accident and emergency department;
- patients requiring a bed in an intensive care unit or coronary care unit;
- patients needing an organ transplant;
- patients on a hospital waiting list;
- patients at an outpatient clinic;
- emergency hospital admissions;
- specimens for analysis in a pathology department.

Furthermore, queues remain one of the most tractable means of measuring and assessing the performance or failure of many health service systems, e.g. waiting lists, Patient's charter standards, emergency/urgent case overload and shortages of (paediatric) intensive care beds.

Queue management insights

The modelling approaches described later in this chapter are derived from the theoretical framework of Queueing Theory, pioneered by a Danish mathematician in the early 1900s, and originally applied to telephone systems. Nowadays the range of applications is wide, including loading and unloading of ships, aircraft landing and taking-off, resourcing and locating emergency services, program scheduling in computer systems, production processes and designing digital communication systems. For further background reading on queue modelling see Anderson *et al.* (1985) or Worthington (1990).

Fundamental results from this area provide insights into queue behaviour, suggest general solutions to queue management problems, and also provide a basis for DSS contributions. From a vast mountain of queueing theory, three insights of particular relevance to health service queue management problems are selected for inclusion here:

1. When faced with a queue management problem, the basic options for decreasing or increasing the amount of congestion and its impacts are:
   - increase/decrease number of servers;
   - increase/decrease service rate per server;
   - decrease/increase arrival rate;
   - reduce/increase variability in length of service times;
   - reduce/increase variability in inter-arrival times;

- introduce queue discipline (e.g. 'First in, first out' (FIFO), urgent customers served first, customers requiring short service times served first);
- keep customers happy (e.g. warn them how long to expect to wait, explain why waits are long, entertain them!).

2 However, whatever measures are taken to control queues, the unpredictable (i.e. random) nature of the actual demand for services from one period of time to the next and from one customer to the next means that there will always be relatively 'good' hours/days/weeks and relatively 'bad' hours/days/weeks.

3 In many queueing situations there is a trade-off between the service level to customers and the utilization of resources. All other things being equal, a service system which has relatively low waiting times for customers will have relatively large server idle time, and vice versa.

The implications of these insights and the methods of queue analysis from which they derive are clearly relevant in the health services, where service level targets are being set for many services and where the consequences of possible changes need to be explored. A task for management is often to balance resource usage and quality improvements appropriately.

DSS approaches

A DSS can be defined as any intelligent use of data and information to help inform decision makers about the likely consequences of decision options. A DSS may involve a computer, but can also involve other forms of structuring and analysis of aspects of a problem, as will be seen later.

General DSS project methodology

When faced with a queue management problem it is important to be open-minded about whether a DSS-based approach is appropriate, and if so, which one. A typical methodology in any DSS project will involve:

- obtaining a proper understanding of the problem;
- extracting the key factors and issues that need to be 'modelled';
- developing an appropriate model (where a model already exists, calibration for local circumstances will still be an important step);
- using the model to investigate the likely implications of alternative decisions;
- using model results to inform decisions;
- implementing decisions.

This is a useful checklist, although that is all it can be. Almost all real projects will require *ad hoc* variations, including iterations among the stages and very unequal amounts of time and effort devoted to the different steps. Indeed, for some problems a decision to abandon a DSS approach after stage 1 may well be correct. That said, almost all health service queue management problems have the potential for a DSS approach. Three very different examples, for which DSS approaches are well documented, are introduced below to illustrate the point.

Applications of DSS approaches to health service queues

Beds required in an intensive care unit

The provision and management of intensive care units (ICUs) is a recurrent issue for health service management. ICUs are a very expensive service because of the equipment involved and the very high staffing levels that they require. However, if there are insufficient intensive care beds, there is a relatively high chance that all beds will be in use when another patient, needing intensive care, arrives. The consequences of such an event can range from a marginally early discharge of a patient from ICU to another ward with no significant detrimental effects, to redirection of a new patient to the nearest available intensive care bed, with potentially dire consequences for the patient.

DSS can be used to investigate various aspects of this problem. A number of accounts of such studies are available (see Bibliography), each with results that depend on the local characteristics of demand for intensive care beds and local admission and discharge practices. Figure 10.2 is based on results presented by Wharton (1994) and shows how the

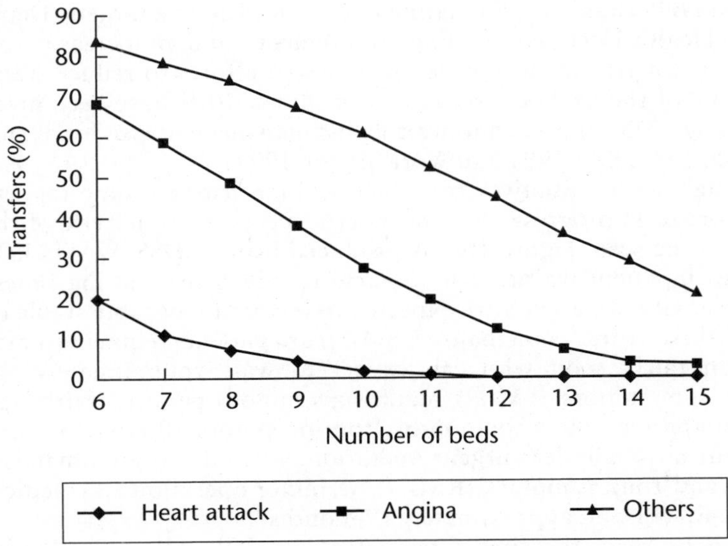

Figure 10.2 Proportions of three groups of patients transferred prematurely from intensive care

percentages of three different groups of patients who would need to be transferred prematurely on arrival of another patient with greater need depend on the number of intensive care beds. For example if there were eight beds, 6 per cent of heart attack, 49 per cent of angina and 74 per cent of other patients would need to be transferred prematurely. If there were 12 beds, the service level achieved would be much better, with only 0.2 per cent of heart attack patients needing to be transferred prematurely and corresponding improvements for angina and other patients. The nature of this result is as predicted by the third of the general queue management insights outlined above. In this example the DSS has been used to put specific form to the general finding.

Hospital waiting list management

Hospital waiting lists have been a major issue for the NHS ever since its inception. Many attempts have been made to reduce them by use of such measures as increasing the number of servers (e.g. beds) or increasing the service rate per server (e.g. reducing lengths of stay). Typically these measures have not worked, often because short-term improvements in waiting times have also attracted an increase in arrival rate (e.g. more referrals for treatment or a lowering of the threshold at which NHS inpatient care is considered) causing the level of congestion to grow again. Frankel and West (1993) offer a general discussion, Worthington (1987) an analysis from a queue management perspective, and Worthington (1991) gives a particular example of the problem.

Recent NHS changes, culminating in Patient's Charter targets (Department of Health 1991), contracting requirements, and an increased range of options for treatment have led to renewed efforts to reduce waiting lists. Some of the likely consequences of these efforts have been investigated using a DSS approach to waiting list management (see for example Ellis *et al.* 1990, Ellis 1991 and Worthington 1991).

Although some initiatives to reduce waiting lists are now reporting good short-term progress, the longer-term success or otherwise of them remains to be seen. Figure 10.3 is produced using a DSS, WAITLIST: it shows an inpatient waiting list scenario in which the waiting times of four categories of patients are expected to remain reasonably stable over the next three years. 'Soon majors' (SMAJ) are patients requiring a major operation fairly soon who can expect to wait approximately three months; 'soon minors' (SMIN), requiring a minor operation fairly soon, will wait approximately six months; 'routine majors' (RMAJ), needing a major but medically less urgent operation, will wait approximately 26 months; and 'routine minors' (RMIN), i.e. minor operation and medically less urgent, will wait approximately 17 months.

As can be seen, the first three categories fall within the Patient's Charter target (currently 18 months), but the waits for routine majors are well in excess. Using WAITLIST again, Figure 10.4 demonstrates the

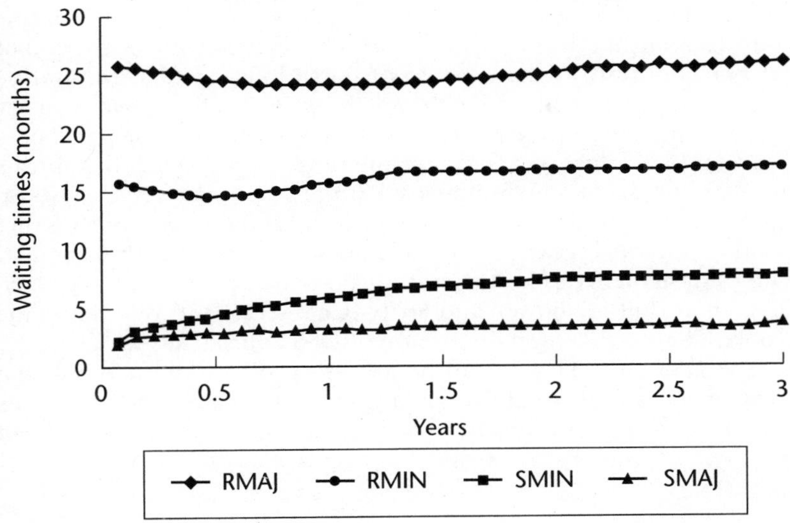

Figure 10.3 Projected inpatient waiting times (stable scenario)

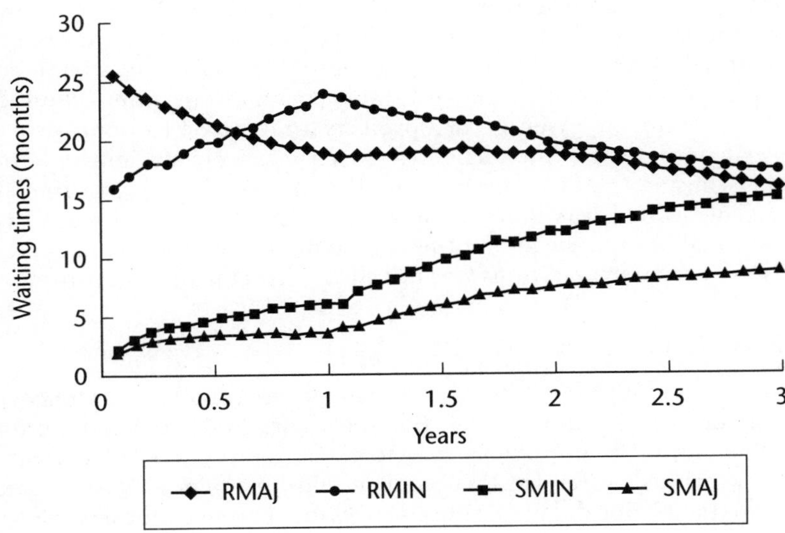

Figure 10.4 Projected inpatient waiting times (achieving targets – just)

effect of changing patient priorities to reduce the waits of 'routine majors' to 18 months within the next year. This is successful at the end of the first year, but only at the expense of much longer waits for 'routine minor' patients. The figure also shows the effects of further priority changes to bring the 'routine minor' waits back down to 18 months during the second and third years. Again the target is achieved, but in this case at the expense of much-increased waits for both types of 'soon' patients, with 'soon minor' patients about to exceed the 18-month target at the end of the third year. These are 'knock-on' effects within the list. The wider consequences for hospital and other health services are not considered here, but see Bowen and Forte (Chapter 5) and Wolstenholme and Crook (Chapter 12) for a discussion of DSS approaches which do.

Thus, the DSS (WAITLIST) can be used to project the likely waiting time consequences of waiting list management options, so that decisions can be made in the light of longer-term implications as well as short-term targets.

Hospital outpatient clinics

Outpatient clinic waiting rooms have also long been the focus of criticism of the NHS. Not only do patients endure long waits in them, they also have plenty of time to dwell on the possible unsatisfactory reasons for their wait, and to discuss them with fellow sufferers. They have also been the subject of much DSS work, starting with early simulation modelling by Bailey (1952) and encompassing many more and less sophisticated approaches since then (for example, NHS Management Executive 1992; see also Bibliography). Much of this work has concentrated on the design of appointment systems, although some approaches have also attempted to study the general organization and management of outpatient clinics.

Below, accounts are given of two projects undertaken to improve the running of outpatient clinics. The first was a relatively straightforward study in which a 'better' appointment system was found and implemented. The second was more complex, the cause of long clinic waits extending well beyond the appointment system. In this latter case, implementation of recommendations was not such a straightforward process.

Case study 1: plaster check clinics

The outpatient clinics involved in this study were referred to as 'plaster check' clinics at the Royal Lancaster Infirmary (Brahimi and Worthington 1993). The clinics' main purpose was to check the progress of patients who had previously attended the Accident and Emergency Department; for some patients, this did in fact entail checking their plaster casts. These clinics were held most days of the week, and usually had one doctor. The study was undertaken at the request of the outpatient department manager who was concerned about the long patient waits and hoped that it would be possible to devise a 'better' appointment system without unnecessary experimental trials.

Visits to the department confirmed that most clinics suffered from a high degree of congestion, with patients often waiting well over half an hour, and sometimes much longer, for a consultation which could last less than two or three minutes. Typically, however, the clinics finished on time, providing some evidence for the outpatient manager's initial impression that it would be possible to improve the scheduling of patients within the clinics. Hence while the researchers remained open-minded, it was possible to follow the project methodology, outlined above, reasonably closely.

For all patients due to attend a total of seven clinics, three during one fortnight and four from a second fortnight two months later, data were collected on:

1 appointment times,
2 arrival times,
3 times that consultations started, and
4 times that consultations finished.

Simple comparisons showed no significant differences in patients attending the different plaster clinics, so it was judged to be appropriate to model all clinics in the same way and to calibrate any DSS using the combined data for all 114 patients. The data were collected by the researchers, with the added benefit that they gained a thorough understanding of the problem in the process. However, with a small amount of organizational effort, data items 1 and 2 can often be collected by the appointments desk staff, and items 3 and 4 can be noted by nursing staff as one patient leaves the doctor and another goes in.

Simple analyses of the data showed that about 10 per cent of patients did not attend, but of those who did the majority arrived early or on time. The probability distribution of observed consultation times is shown in Figure 10.5. These results together with the first model, described below, were presented and discussed in a meeting with the outpatient department manager and some of the nursing staff.

The first model (Figure 10.6) was a simple graphical representation of one of the clinics. The leftmost line on the graph plots the number of patients who have arrived at the clinic against time of day. For example, three patients had arrived by 9.00 a.m. (the clinic start-time), the fourth had arrived at about 9.05 a.m. and the 23rd and final patient arrived at about 10.10 a.m. The rightmost line then plots the times at which each of the 23 patients completed their consultation. For example the first consultation finished at about 9.10 a.m., the second at about 9.25 a.m. and the 23rd at about 11.15 a.m.

This graph proved to be a very effective DSS, providing much insight into the problem for both the researchers and the clinic staff. In particular, it shows very clearly how the numbers and waiting times of patients build up during the clinic. For example, the height of the line *AB* (14)

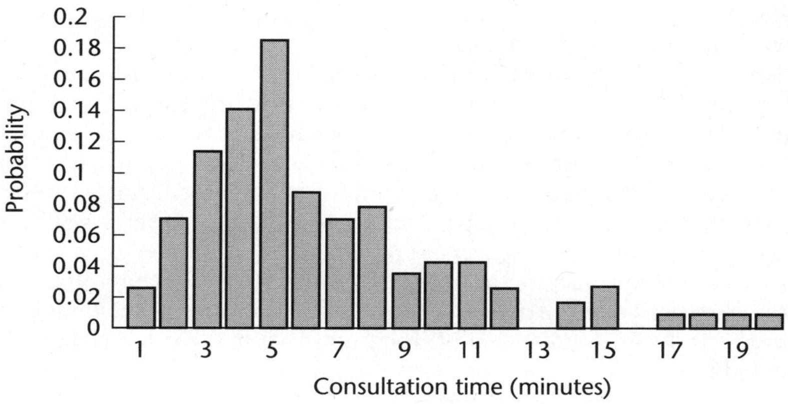

Figure 10.5 Probability distribution of observed consultation times

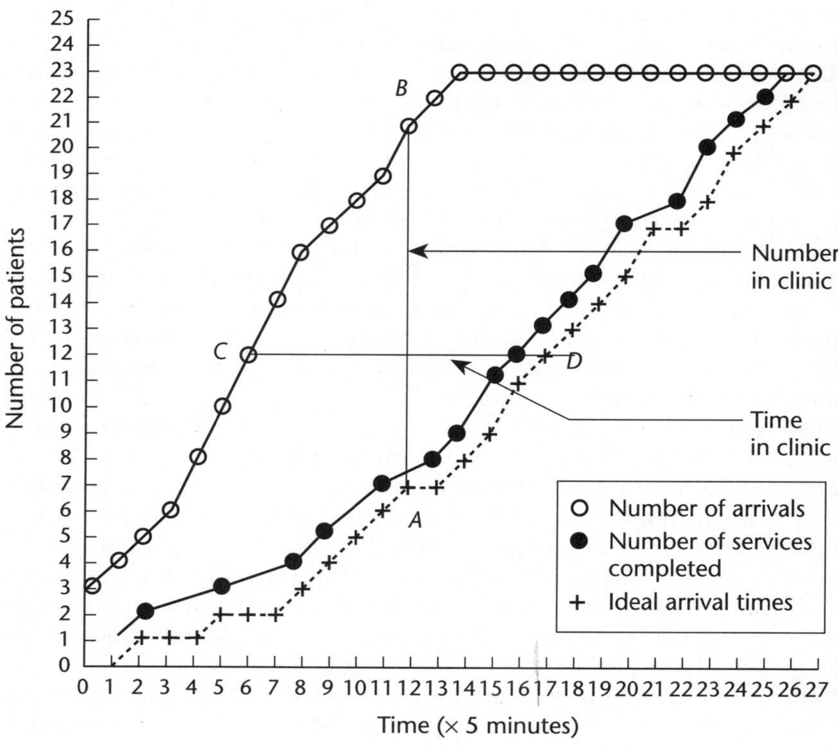

Figure 10.6 Graphical re-creation of an actual clinic

shows how many patients were in the clinic at the time (12 x 5 minutes = 1 hour); and the length of line *CD* (11 x 5 = 55 minutes) shows how long the 12th patient spent in the clinic. If this clinic was typical, the message was clear: patients' appointment times cause them to arrive much earlier than is necessary. The ideal appointment times for this clinic are indicated by the intermediate line, i.e. just above the consultation completion line – but it is only possible to say this with hindsight. In practice, consultation completion times are not normally known in advance, so if appointment times follow this 'ideal' line too closely there is a chance that a shorter than expected consultation will leave the doctor with no one to see. Equally a patient who arrives late or fails to attend would also leave the doctor idle.

The graphical model and preliminary data analyses were very valuable in the project: the work was transparent to the hospital staff (it could in fact be repeated by them if they so wished), and it led to a shared understanding of the problem and the nature of the solution being sought.

The next stage was to investigate the likely effects of alternative appointment systems on numbers of patients waiting, their anticipated waiting times and doctors' idle time, allowing for the known natural variation in clinic workloads. The graphical method would not have been able to take proper account of natural (random) variation, so instead, a computer-based DSS called CLINIQUE was used by the researchers in conjunction with the outpatient manager.

CLINIQUE is a purpose-built DSS for modelling appointment systems, based on recent queue modelling research (Brahimi and Worthington 1991a). It incorporates statistical information on patients' consultation times and non-attendance rates to predict system performance measures for appointment systems specified by the user. To my knowledge this is the only software of its kind, although some simulation packages, e.g. CLINSIM (Paul 1994), can also be used (with some effort) to model outpatient clinics. The strengths of CLINSIM are its ability to model staffing levels and clinic layouts, but its handling of appointment systems is relatively crude.

Example results from CLINIQUE produced for the final meeting with the outpatient department manager are shown in Figure 10.7 (the anticipated queueing times of patients under the existing appointment system) and Figure 10.8 (the anticipated queueing times for an appointment system with larger gaps between patients). In both figures the 'mean' line indicates what would happen at an average clinic, the 'upper 2.5 per cent' line indicates what would happen at a 1 in 40 'bad' clinic, and the 'lower 2.5 per cent' line indicates what would happen at a 1 in 40 'good' clinic. It can be seen that with the existing system (Figure 10.7), queueing times would on average climb to about 11 x 5 = 55 minutes, at 'bad' clinics queueing times could reach 80 minutes, and even at 'good' clinics queueing times would reach 35 minutes. On the other hand, with the more spaced appointment system (Figure 10.8), waiting times would be considerably

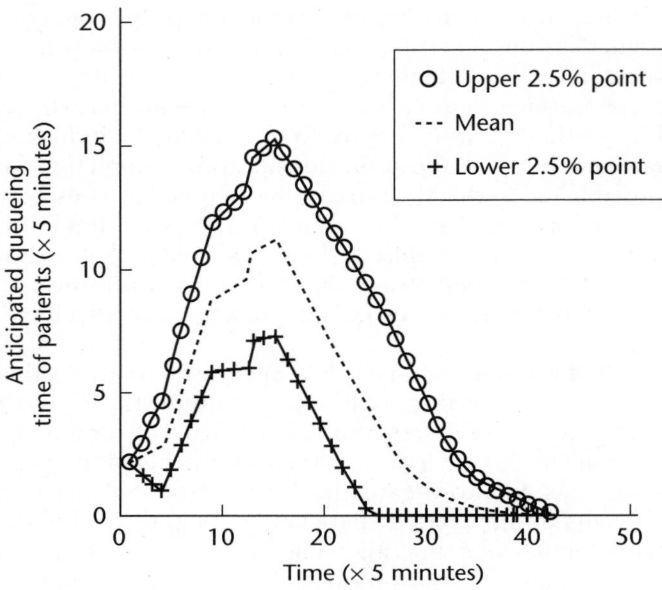

Figure 10.7 Anticipated queueing times – existing appointment system

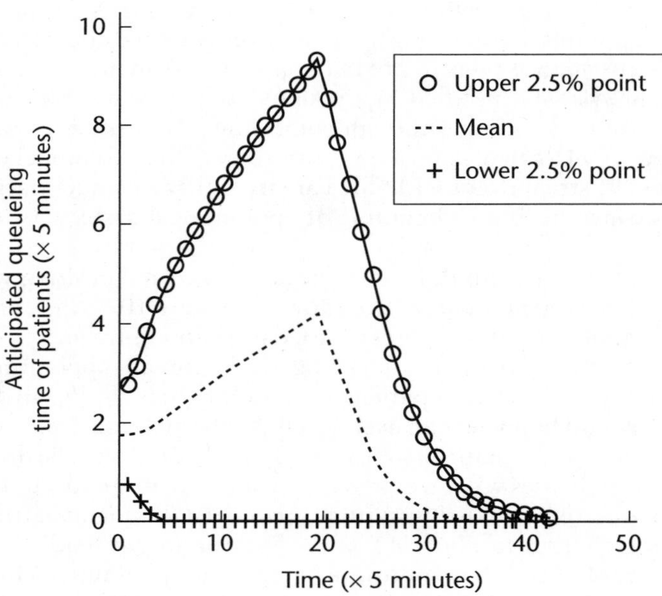

Figure 10.8 Anticipated queueing times – 'better' appointment system

less, with the 'average' clinic climbing to 20 minutes, 'bad' clinics only climbing to less than 40 minutes, and 'good' clinics having zero queueing times. This final point was of some concern to the hospital staff as it meant that occasionally patients would not have to queue, and by implication the doctor might have to wait for a patient. Other graphical output from CLINIQUE, not shown here, was used to reassure staff that this chance would be small and quite acceptable!

Implementation

The combination of this sort of graphical evidence, together with some more general common-sense advice concerning issues such as late arrival of doctors, was well received by hospital management. It was sufficient to convince them and the medical staff that there was scope for substantial improvements in patients' waiting times without significantly increasing doctors' idle times. Implementation of revised appointment systems along the lines suggested was undertaken by the booking clerks under the direction of the hospital management with no significant problems.

In the follow-up to the project a few months later the question was asked about how the doctors had taken to the new system. The very apt reply was that the doctors had not noticed the change – but the patients had! In addition, the researchers were not required to undertake any further similar studies. The main messages of the study had been understood, they were fairly straightforward and were being applied by the hospital management and booking clerks to other similarly structured clinics in the hospital without the need for further modelling work.

Case study 2: ophthalmology clinics

The outpatient clinics that were the subject of this second case study were those of a consultant ophthalmologist at the Royal Preston Hospital (Bennett and Worthington forthcoming). In the face of the introduction of the Patient's Charter the ophthalmology consultant had an increased responsibility to improve the standard of service offered to patients visiting his outpatient clinics. He was aware of problems such as regular, overbooked, late-running sessions and was concerned that a significant number of visitors to the clinic experienced waits before seeing a doctor far in excess of the 30-minute target of the Patient's Charter.

The consultant felt that many of the problems encountered at clinics were because the existing simple appointment system was unsuitable for his somewhat more complex sessions: many patients saw a doctor more than once or received a variety of treatments during a single visit. This study was initiated by him in the expectation that the project would concentrate on developing a more sophisticated appointment system.

In this case study use of the general project methodology, outlined earlier, was particularly important to ensure that the researchers were open-minded about the possible causes of congestion at the clinics and how they might be overcome. In particular, emphasis on gradually improving understanding of the problem with the problem owners proved to be very important. As understanding improved, ideas were discussed with clinic staff and, when appropriate, models (DSS) were developed to highlight key issues or to demonstrate possible solutions. Four of the models that proved useful in this study are briefly described.

A vicious-circle model

Figure 10.9 shows a diagrammatic model which suggests that, in the long term, many problems in the clinics resulted from a 'vicious circle' of events. Starting with the leftmost box, the Appointments department were unable to create sensible daily clinic schedules because of the large volume of patients requiring treatment at any one time. As a result, every clinic session was overbooked and so clinics became congested, with large numbers of patients having to wait for lengthy periods. Doctors and other resources were overburdened; and, when there were last-minute capacity reductions (such as doctors' absence through illness), clinic staff and Appointments staff spent much time and effort in cancelling and rescheduling patients' appointments.

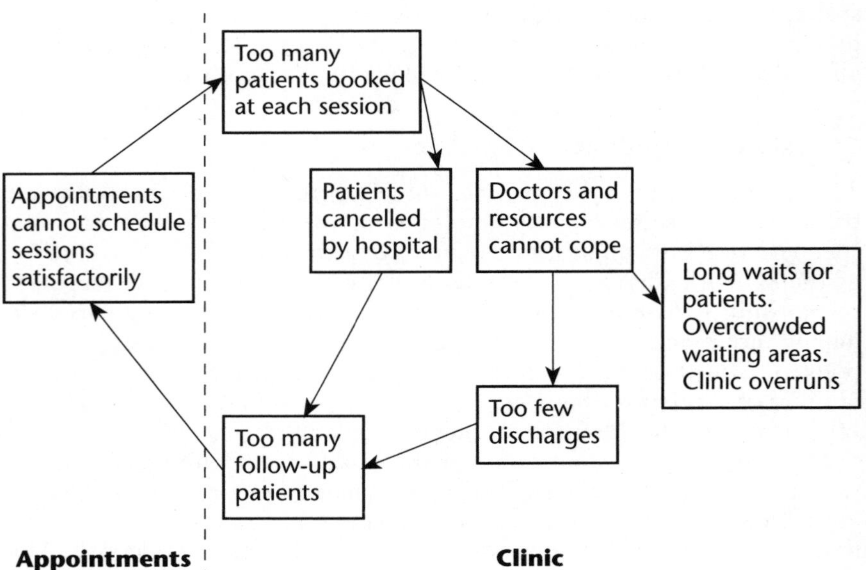

Figure 10.9 A vicious circle of dependencies within the outpatient clinic setting

The effect of overburdened doctors was severe: few discharges could be made. A consultation which results in a discharge is typically more lengthy than a routine appointment, so doctors under pressure would avoid discharging to save themselves time. The low discharge rate resulted in an escalating list of follow-up patients in addition to the list of new patients who had not yet visited the clinic. As the number of patients requiring future appointments grew, so the problem developed and the 'vicious circle' continued. It was clear that in the long term the situation could only be improved by breaking out of the circle, or by converting it to a 'virtuous circle'. Two possible types of action were identified in consultation with clinic staff from examination of the model, one from each domain of the system:

- Appointments – employ new scheduling arrangements which will lead to improvements;
- Clinic – match the demand for appointments to capacity by reducing demand or increasing capacity or a combination of the two.

These possibilities were investigated using a variety of DSS approaches, including the following models.

Clinic build-up model

By collecting and graphically presenting data produced by the Appointments department for a number of clinics, it was possible to build up a clear picture of how bookings for clinics were made. Figure 10.10 shows that appointments for a session were made as early as nine months in advance. A period of gradual increase in the number of appointments made occurred up to around 75 days prior to a clinic, after which time

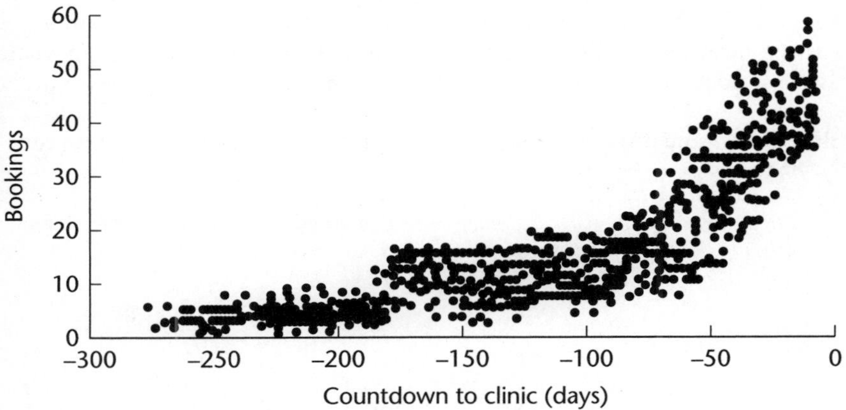

Figure 10.10 Build-up of clinic size prior to a session

there was a sharp rise in bookings made. The clinic's intended capacity (for about 33 patients) was always exceeded by the day of the clinic, but this could occur up to two months earlier. In the worst of cases by the day of the clinic the session could be almost 100 per cent overbooked.

The scatter graph in Figure 10.10 proved to be a very useful tool for highlighting the severity with which demand outstripped clinic capacity. The graph also enabled staff to focus on potential problems, such as mass cancellation and rescheduling of appointments, which could be caused by doctors giving insufficient notice of intended absence. Finally, the graph could be used to determine a definite deadline by which notice of holidays ought to be given, namely ten weeks in advance.

Spreadsheet model

A simple spreadsheet model was employed to investigate the potential impact of adopting a policy for patients classified as routine, where doctors aimed to extend patients' length of time between visits, and hence reduce the pressure on clinics. The aim was to obtain a rough estimate of potential savings using available data and to avoid the collection of additional data. A full analysis would have required accurate values for the time from appointment request to appointment (for routine patients) and of the length of time over which routine patients needed to be monitored. Instead, relatively simple calculations were used to produce fairly robust estimates of the annual savings in numbers of appointments that would be achieved by increasing the gap between appointment request and appointment by three, four, five or six months. These calculations were conveniently carried out on a spreadsheet and the results for different assumed current gaps are presented in Table 10.1. Although the precise value of the predicted annual savings depends on the particular value of the current average gap (which was unknown), the order of savings can be seen to be the same for a whole range of possible values. An increase of three months would save approximately 430 appointments per year, whereas increases of four, five and six months would save approximately

Table 10.1 Annual appointments saved by increasing the time to next visit for routine patients

Assumed current gap (months)	*Increase in time between routine appointments (months)*			
	3	4	5	6
6	480	576	654	720
7	432	523	600	664
8	392	480	553	617
9	360	443	514	576

520, 600 and 660 per year respectively. Given that the current numbers of appointments exceeded the actual annual clinic capacity by approximately 900, the practical message was clear: while increased gaps would help reduce the problem, it would not be enough, and other methods would also be required to bring demand within capacity.

CLINIQUE model

Once it had been established that the fundamental problem was to match the demand for outpatient appointments to clinic capacity, it was again possible to use CLINIQUE to investigate whether the existing appointment system would then be appropriate. Graphical results, similar in nature to those in case study 1, showed that once overbooking was removed, the existing appointment systems would be likely to strike an acceptable balance between patients' waiting times and doctors' idle times.

Implementation

The study as a whole led to a list of 13 recommendations that were presented at the end of the project to staff involved in various aspects of running the clinics. Three of the recommendations suggested ways of tackling the 35 per cent excess of demand for appointments over capacity. For example:

> *Increase the capacity for patients* by extending the time interval until the next appointment for routine patients by three months or more. It is expected that this will reduce the demand for appointments to 20 per cent above capacity.

The remaining ten recommendations related to possible measures for improving the day-to-day operation of the clinics. For example:

> *Doctors to specify a range of dates for each follow-up appointment, particularly for patients returning within two months.* This will assist Appointments staff in making the best possible clinic scheduling arrangements.

Because of the wide-ranging nature of the recommendations and the time constraint on the project it was not possible for the project team to be involved in an 'implementation stage'. Indeed there was no implementation stage as such, for a variety of reasons. Because the project recommendations were developed during the project in collaboration with the ophthalmology department staff, a number of the ideas had already been adopted before the project finished. Other proposals, particularly those involving staff from other parts of the hospital, could only be adopted when suitable opportunities arose.

Two and a half years since the project was completed, most of the recommendations have now been implemented in some form or another: the consultant ophthalmologist also has a much clearer understanding of the causes of the remaining problems. However, his efforts to address these have been partially frustrated by the lack of cooperation from other parties involved. In addition it has not been possible to observe any before-and-after effects on performance measures, such as waiting times, because they have been largely masked by further pressures on the department to take new groups of patients and to deal with short-term staff shortages.

Discussion

The lessons to be drawn from this chapter will depend on the background and interests of the reader. Health service staff concerned to improve the performance of clinics may have found some useful ideas about the practical problems of managing queues; researchers may have learned something about the pros and cons of different models and methodologies.

There are important lessons, though, for someone who might be involved in an evaluation of DSS as an approach to queue management, and who might wish to use, commission or develop a DSS in the light of its potential and its pitfalls. The following analysis has been aided greatly by the reactions to the material in this chapter, paraphrased below, of groups of health service managers taking part in the Keele University MBA (Health Executive) programme.

Case study 1 was chosen especially because it turned out to be a reasonably clear-cut problem of a poor appointment system, for which the application of a DSS approach led to real and measurable improvements. It demonstrates that:

- poor appointment systems do exist;
- improvements are sometimes possible with little confrontation, and can be resource-neutral;
- modelling is a useful tool, but typically needs some modelling expertise to help focus modelling efforts and to interpret results;
- the data required exist and are simple to collect;
- the solution can be almost obvious;
- while the transfer of good practice between clinics is clearly good news for the health service, evidence suggests that often it does not transfer readily between sites. Rather, local studies are necessary to tailor solutions to the local context and to involve managers so that they own the study and its results.

Case study 2 was chosen because while it also describes the successful application of a DSS approach, reinforcing messages from the first, it also serves to add a cautionary note to those messages. The problem was obviously much messier, the methodology required was more varied and the benefits much less easy to identify, never mind to measure. In particular it suggests that:

- different types of clinics (and indeed the same types of clinics at different hospitals) require different DSS approaches;
- different clinics may require a range of solutions, sometimes involving more widespread changes than those anticipated at the start of a project;
- improvements will not always be resource-neutral;
- involvement of stakeholders in a project is important, although not necessarily easy;
- the benefits of a DSS approach are not always dramatic or measurable and should be seen as part of an overall process of improving health service practices.

More generally, ICU beds and waiting list management are two of many further examples of health service queue management applications of DSS. The lessons derived from the outpatient case studies have relevance to these two examples and to the wider issue of applying a DSS approach to inform the management of health service queues. The reader is encouraged to reflect upon the comments arising from the two case studies, replacing references to clinics with other examples of health service queues (i.e. services).

Conclusions

The aims of this chapter have been to consider a particular type of health service problem, queue management; to introduce examples of DSS approaches that have been applied to it; and to discuss factors that have led to the success or otherwise of some of the DSS. There is considerable scope for a DSS contribution to queue management, but there are many (often local) factors that affect the suitability and success or otherwise of particular DSS approaches.

Faced with a queue management problem the manager must keep an open mind about DSS approaches, or indeed other approaches, that might be useful. The key methodological ideas to be borne in mind in this area are a fairly general 'project methodology' together with an awareness of key 'queue management insights'. These indicate types of practical solution to queue management problems: they should be used to help guide the direction of a DSS project, or indeed to discourage a project that would only serve to 'prove the obvious'.

Any DSS must be recognized as a simplification of the real situation. Hence before using a DSS to inform decisions a manager must be able to convince himself or herself, with help from 'modelling experts' if necessary, that the simplifications underpinning the DSS project provide an adequate representation of their real problem. Once achieved, this understanding will enable managers to recognize when to implement or modify 'good practice' (even if invented elsewhere), and also how to make effective use of DSS for their own problems and decision making.

When considering a DSS approach to the particular problem of improving the running of outpatient clinics, is the crucial issue

- simply a poor appointment system,
- a mismatch of service capacity and demand, or
- general poor organization?

In the first instance, methods similar to those described in case study 1 – using a DSS such as CLINIQUE – are recommended. In the second and third circumstances, a more open style of investigation such as that described in case study 2 is recommended. The starting point, however, should always be simple common sense.

Acknowledgements

Thanks are especially due to the clinic staff in the plaster check clinics at the Royal Lancaster Infirmary and the ophthalmology clinics at Royal Preston Hospital for their interested involvement in the case studies described. Thanks are also due to other staff at those hospitals for their help and cooperation, and indeed to hospital staff in other clinics where we have worked, whose problems and solutions have helped shape this chapter. Finally, thanks goes to Joanne Bennett, Stephen Leigh, Jane Manser and Sophocles Voyazas (Masters students in the Department of Management Science at Lancaster University) and to Mammar Brahimi (PhD student) who carried out the outpatient studies upon which this chapter is based.

Bibliography including references

Queue management

Anderson, D. R., Sweeney, D. J. and Williams, T. A. (1985) *An Introduction to Management Science*, 4th edition, Chapter 13. St Paul, MN, West Publishing.

Brahimi, M. and Worthington, D. J. (1991a) The finite capacity multi-server queue with inhomogeneous arrival rate and discrete service time distribution: and its application to continuous service time problems, *European Journal of Operational Research*, 50: 310–24.

Worthington, D. J. (1990) 'Useful' queueing models, in R. W. Eglese and L. Hendry (eds) *Tutorial Papers in Operational Research*. Birmingham, Operational Research Society.

Intensive care beds

Dacre, M. (1995) 'The provision of intensive care for male and female patients', Chapter B3, unpublished M.Sc. dissertation, Lancaster University.

Davies, R. (1994) Simulation for planning services for patients with coronary heart disease, *European Journal of Operational Research*, 71: 323–32.

Hannan, E. (1974) Planning an emergency department holding unit, *Socio-Economic Planning Sciences*, 9: 179–88.

Harris, R. A. (1986) Hospital bed requirements planning, *European Journal of Operational Research*, 25: 121–6.

Lowery, J. C. and Martin, J. B. (1992) Design and validation of a critical care simulation model, *Journal of Society for Health Systems*, 3: 15–36.

Moores, B. and Sissouras, A. A. (1975) The optimum number of beds in an emergency care unit, *Omega*, 4: 59–65.

Wharton, F. (1994) *A Model for Designing Intensive Care Units*. Working paper no. HUMS/FW/22. Hull, School of Management, Hull University.

Waiting lists

Cromwell, D. and Mays, L. (1995) *A Critical Review of the Literature on the Management of Elective Surgery*. Center for Health Service Development, University of Wollongong, Australia.

Department of Health (1991) *The Patient's Charter*. London, HMSO.

Ellis, B. W. (1991) Factors influencing waiting lists and cost of surgical treatment, *Annals of Royal College of Surgeons of England*, 73: 74–7.

Ellis, B. W., Rivett, R. C. and Dudley, H. A. F. (1990) Extending the use of clinical audit data: a resource planning model, *British Medical Journal*, 301: 159–62.

Frankel, S. and West, R. (1993) What is to be done? in S. Frankel and R. West (eds) *Rationing and Rationality in the NHS: the Persistence of Waiting Lists*. Basingstoke, Macmillan.

Worthington, D. J. (1987) Queueing models for hospital waiting lists, *Journal of the Operational Research Society*, 38: 413–22.

Worthington, D. J. (1991) Hospital waiting list management models, *Journal of the Operational Research Society*, 42: 833–43.

Outpatient clinics

Bailey, N. T. J. (1952) A study of queues and appointment systems in hospital outpatient departments, *Journal of the Royal Statistical Society*, 14: 185–99.

Bennett, J. C. and Worthington, D. J. (forthcoming) A flexible approach to improving outpatient clinic organisation, submitted to *Omega*.

Brahimi, M. and Worthington, D. J. (1991b) Queuing models for out-patient appointment systems – a case study, *Journal of the Operational Research Society*, 42: 746–66.

Brahimi, M. and Worthington, D. J. (1993) Improving outpatient appointment systems, *International Journal of Health Care Quality Assurance*, 6: 18–23.

Cox, T. F., Birchall, J. F. and Wong, H. (1985) Optimising the queueing system of an ear, nose and throat outpatient clinic, *Journal of Applied Statistics*, 12: 113–26.

Department of Health (1991) *The Patient's Charter*. London, HMSO.

Ho, C. and Lau, H. S. (1992) Minimising total cost in scheduling outpatient appointments, *Management Science*, 12: 1750–64.

Jackson, R. R. P., Welch, J. D. and Fry, J. (1964) Appointment systems in hospitals and general practice, *Operational Research Quarterly*, 15: 219–37.

Jansson, B. (1966) Choosing a good appointment system – a study of queues of the type (D,M,1), *Operations Research*, 14: 292–312.

Lehaney, B. and Paul, R. J. (1994) Using SSM to develop a simulation of outpatient services, *Journal of the Royal Society of Health*, 114: 248–51.

NHS Management Executive (1992) *Queue Action*. Leeds, NHS Management Executive.

O'Keefe, R. M. (1985) Investigating outpatient departments, *Journal of the Operational Research Society*, 36: 705–12.

Paul, R. (1994) The CLINSIM simulation package, *OR Insight*, 8: 24–7.

Rising, E., Baron, R. and Averill, B. (1973) A system analysis of a university health service outpatient clinic, *Operations Research*, 21: 1030–47.

Robinson, L. W., Gerchak, Y. and Gupta, D. (1996) Appointment times which minimize waiting and facility idleness (personal communication).

Taylor III, B. W. and Keown, A. J. (1980) A network analysis of an inpatient/outpatient department, *Journal of the Operational Research Society*, 31: 169–79.

Vissers, J. and Wijngaard, J. (1979) The outpatient appointment system: design of a simulation study, *European Journal of Operational Research*, 13: 459–63.

Software availability

WAITLIST is a PC-based DSS for investigating hospital waiting list management scenarios. CLINIQUE is a PC-based DSS for investigating the effects of alternative clinic appointment systems in terms of patient waiting times, patient queues and doctor idle time. For further information contact: Dave Worthington, Department of Management Science, The Management School, Lancaster University, Lancaster LA1 4YX, England. Tel: +(44) (0)1524 593872, fax: +(44) (0)1524 844885, e-mail: d.worthington@lancaster.ac.uk

11 Decision support systems in neurosciences: measurement and analysis of clinical activity

Peter D. Lees and Lisa Macfarlane

Introduction

This chapter describes how a busy neuroscience centre set about improving the management of its resources, both to keep costs down and to ensure those costs were appropriately covered through its contracts with purchasers. A unique approach was taken to identifying the costs of caring for the different types of patient admitted, in particular the costs of nursing care.

Four broad sections are set out below. Under 'Management issues' the need for more and better information is described, both in terms of funding the day-to-day efficiency of the service and for setting appropriate contract quantities and prices for the year. 'Methodology' explains how data were captured to build a sufficiently detailed decision support database. The third section describes how the data were analysed and used. It is divided into three sub-sections. The first focuses on refining prices for different categories of patient (or casemix) using healthcare resource groups (HRGs) to ensure that annually negotiated contracts would cover expected demand (and costs) for services. The second part of the analysis concentrates on nursing skillmix and patient profiles on a day-to-day basis to support decisions about the operational management of the unit. The third discusses how the measures and analyses of activity were considered and then translated into action through a series of specially convened nursing workshops. Finally, the 'Discussion' section evaluates the usefulness of the method and how it has been – and continues to be – used within the neuroscience unit.

Resource management issues in a clinical directorate

Two key management issues faced the Wessex Neurological Centre (WNC) in 1992/3: how to ensure that the money received from purchasers was sufficient to provide a quality service to the patients needing treatment, and how to contain increasing costs and make best use of available resources.

Setting contract prices

In the preliminary stages of management reform of the NHS, the Resource Management Initiative placed financial management and accountability at the level of service delivery by establishing clinical directorates as devolved management units within hospitals (see Packwood *et al.* 1991). The later split between purchasers and providers then gave Trusts and – in many cases by implication – clinical directorates the responsibility of securing their income via negotiated contracts. The WNC, in common with other directorates, was faced with a requirement to cover its costs and negotiate contracts using notional prices that did not necessarily reflect actual expenditure. This suggested a need for a measure of health care (or 'price') which reflected its true cost, was attached to an individual patient for the care received, and which was more than an apportioned Trust budget allocated to finished consultant episodes (FCE).

In theory, a Trust should be able to balance its books overall while experiencing variations in over- and-under expenditure across the different directorates. However, in the case of neuroscience, the existing budget (initially used to set baseline prices) had been overspent at an increasing rate. Unless costs could be contained or prices raised, further over-expenditure would be at the increasing expense of other Trust services. To agree a price for specific services, the directorate team needed to know what their service actually cost to run and what components within the service were causing costs to increase. Just as a degree of variation could be managed at Trust level, so, too, it was expected that high-volume low-cost cases would balance out the lower volume complex cases at directorate level: prices were therefore based on the average cost of all cases on the assumption that fluctuations in the costs of care would balance out over a financial year. Initial contracts (known as 'block' contracts) were based on this 'average' price. However, as the over-expenditure problem continued, it was suspected that the number of more complicated (and costly) cases was increasing without a corresponding increase in price (Neil-Dwyer *et al.* 1992). It was impossible to *know*, however, if overspending on contracts was due to a deficient baseline budget or unrealistic contract prices or both. More importantly, it was impossible to negotiate contracts to cover the costs of increasing numbers of more complex cases because the information did not exist at a sufficiently sophisticated level – either about the cost of caring for different types of patient, or about forecast levels of activity for specific conditions.

The neuroscience directorate had to find a means of ensuring it could recoup the costs of any increase in numbers and for case complexity; because prices had to reflect costs reliable casemix measures needed to be identified and tested. This process had already started with the development of healthcare resource groups (HRGs) by the National Casemix Office (National Casemix Office 1994). These were intended to represent groupings of patient treatments which were clinically similar and which consumed broadly similar resources. At this stage, however, length of stay was the only readily available proxy for resource use, so it was agreed to use this project to test the validity and reliability of this proxy measure and to identify any other significant cost triggers or weighting mechanisms. In May 1994 the NHS Executive issued guidance on costing for contracting, confirming the importance of accurate specialty costing (National Steering Group on Costing 1994).

Using available nursing staff effectively

At the same time as juggling financial problems, the WNC was also experiencing an increasing shortage of specialist nurses (and later a shortage of doctors too). Nursing costs made up 46 per cent of the WNC budget, and it was therefore important to manage nursing resources carefully if costs were to be kept down. An effect of the staff shortages was a higher burden on available staff: sickness and absence rates consequently rose. Increased reliance on agency staff also increased costs, quality of care (in terms of continuity of care) was reduced, and nurses of the right calibre or with appropriate skill levels were not necessarily available when needed. Dependence on the goodwill of already overstretched staff, and a diminished sense of teamwork and ownership added to a 'spiral of decline'. While easy to recognize, there were few clues to suggest how it could be avoided – especially with junior doctors' hours also under review.

The management issues could be summarized then as a rising caseload of increasing complexity; unknown but evidently increasing costs; contract prices based on a top–down apportioned budget whose accuracy was questionable; increasing staff costs; and increasing pressure on limited resources. This project was defined as a means of collecting, processing and analysing data to support business planning decisions about costing and pricing the service and effectively deploying internal resources (both staff and facilities).

Methodology

A first step was to revisit the roles and responsibilities of all staff. In the first instance it was decided to look at the way skilled nurses were being deployed within the WNC and identify any scope for change or more effective use of their time.

A project to record and analyse cost and activity data was set up to identify the costs of providing neuroscience care across different neurological conditions and neurosurgical procedures, and to test how well HRGs actually acted as a way of grouping care on the basis of cost (Carpenter 1995). Derived costs could then be compared with actual contract prices. As variable costs were the main issue – it was assumed that overheads and fixed costs would still remain to be apportioned – it was decided to identify and individually cost each activity associated with caring for patients entering the WNC. As the bulk of activity (and expenditure) was carried out by nursing staff, the project concentrated primarily on collecting data on ward nursing costs, plus physiotherapy, theatres, drugs, tests and consumables. These would represent the 'observed' content of the resulting decision support system database. From this it would also be possible to match nursing skillmix in relation to neuroscience casemix to enable better management of elective caseload and to ensure the right skills and facilities would be available when needed. This might also help to make best use of scarce skills through more selective employment of agency nurses and more appropriate use of highly trained specialist nurses.

Traditional work study techniques of measuring human resources input were excluded owing to cost, inaccuracy or inconvenience: the use of observers would have proved very expensive, inconvenient and irritating to staff given the scope of the project and the different locations involved; self-recorded diaries were felt to be too open to inaccuracy, and video techniques were again seen as unworkable in the various environments. Instead barcoding was chosen as a viable option (Schmaus 1991a; Weilert and Tilzer 1991). Similar use of the technology had been made in the United States (Schmaus 1991b), though not in the UK and, after preliminary piloting, the technique was adopted.

Method of data collection

Portable barcoding pens with 32K of RAM memory and an internal clock and calendar were issued to all nursing and physiotherapy staff on each shift on three surgical wards and a medical ward as well as the Intensive Therapy Unit (ITU). Unique barcodes were produced for locations (such as a ward or theatre), for individual personnel (including their grade and professional group), and for individual patients. Barcodes were also produced for each activity, and related to either direct or indirect patient care following discussion with representatives from each staff group. A pilot run verified the activities, tested the technology and acted as a 'dress rehearsal' for the staff. The final set of barcodes were laminated and packaged in pocket-sized booklets for staff to carry as well as being attached to patient beds and mounted at strategic points on the ward (e.g. near telephones).

At the beginning of a shift operators swiped their unique barcode, the location code and the shift code. Then, for each direct care activity they swiped the patient's unique code, the activity they were about to perform and, at the end of that activity, the 'finish' code. For indirect activities (such as clerical, cleaning and housekeeping tasks, ward reports and telephone calls) there was no need to record a patient code as the tasks were not related to individual patients. A liquid crystal display in each pen enabled users to validate entries; immediate errors could be 'undone' by swiping the relevant barcode backwards.

The data contained in the pens were downloaded every two to three days via a 'datawell'; a data transfer device that took the data from the pen and fed them directly into the receiving database. They were then validated by ward staff. Clearly erroneous data were excluded (where, for example, activities had not been 'finished') and the data were 'trimmed' before analysis. This process involved the judgement of an expert panel and statistical analysis of the timings of each activity.

The project included the development of new purpose-specific software written in FoxPro (Foster 1994) to facilitate direct download of the data from the barcode pens, and to automatically provide validation, summary and analysis. Unlike existing spreadsheets or database packages, the system enabled the coding structures for the data to be easily set up. The built-in validation process enabled users to specify criteria and select batches of data for checking, and an *ad hoc* and standard reporting facility meant that initial feedback of results to staff could be immediate. Once data were validated, they could easily be transferred to other standard applications for further statistical analysis and graphical display and presentation.

Using the DSS for resource management

A database containing 96,000 activity timings was created (accounting for 80 per cent of admissions during the four-month study period). Each timing was costed according to staff grade plus consumables, drugs, tests and specific theatre costs. The database was further enhanced by downloading casemix data from the 'Directorate' information system. This attached patient-specific details of primary diagnosis, operative procedure and length of stay to each recorded patient profile. Additional variables such as age, sex, and referring GP, could have been added but were not pertinent to this particular study.

Identifying the costs of care

For every patient, a daily profile was obtained of the activities and the variable costs associated with their inpatient care.

Table 11.1 shows an extract from the costed activity database that was built up from the activity timings. This was achieved by attaching a cost

Table 11.1 Costed activity database

Patient	*LOS (days)*	*HRG*	*ICD9*	*OPCS*	*Nursing* (£)	*Physio* (£)	*Ward consum-ables/ drugs*(£)	*Theatre staff* (£)	*Anaes. consum-ables/ drugs*(£)	*Test* (£)	**Total direct costs* (£)
1	47	A01	191.6	A05.2	511.1	60.8	2123.7	278.6	920.0	42.0	3936.3
2	8	A01	239.6	A12.4	56.6	0.7	5.4	1241.5	709.0	494.0	2507.2
3	15	A01	431.0	V03.5	569.4	0.0	140.6	865.4	359.0	783.0	2737.7
4	20	A01	194.4	B06.9	70.8	0.1	73.1	1009.7	888.4	602.0	2645.9

Source: Unpublished WNC report.

Notes
LOS: length of stay
HRG, ICD9, OPCS: treatment codes
*Total direct costs exclude Senior House Officer costs

to each timed activity (such as apportioned nurse cost by grade, drug, operation or test cost). These patient profiles were then grouped by diagnosis and by operative procedure to illustrate the daily, cumulative and average cost of treating, for example, a patient with a subarachnoid haemorrhage, and the variation in cost according to whether or not they underwent surgery (costs increase significantly if an operation is required). Patient data were then also grouped by HRG. For each condition, it was possible to identify the cost of care and what event during a patient's treatment triggered a new or increased cost. For example, one patient was admitted for three days and required only tests and observation. Another came in with the same diagnosis but more complex symptoms and required more complicated tests and lengthier observation. A third patient with critical symptoms of the same diagnosis required tests, surgery, intensive care and observation. All patients were coded under the same diagnosis but required very different resource inputs.

For the first time, the directorate could see what it cost to treat its patients and how costs varied by casemix. An individual 'price' could be attached to high-cost complex cases, avoiding a rise in the average cost and keeping low-cost treatment at competitive rates.

Analysis by HRG and an independent clustering exercise enabled a view to be taken about the homogeneity or otherwise of the groupings, whether alternative resource groupings existed that better represented real costs, the appropriateness of length of stay as a proxy for resource use and identification of length of stay weightings. For example it was found that while costs rose during a patient stay, they did so at a decreasing rate; overall, and excluding the cost of surgery, the first three days tend to be the most expensive (that is, the most resource-intensive) so shorter lengths of stay would not proportionately reduce costs. When setting an 'average' price on the basis of an 'average' length of stay, this could now be taken into account by assigning cost weights to ensure the majority of costs were attached to early days of inpatient care.

Table 11.2 Total direct costs (£) for top four HRGs (version 2)

HRG	*No. cases*	*Mean cost (£)*	*Std. deviation*	*Q1*	*Median*	*Q3*	*Mode*
a01	48	1480.0	850.1	925	1320	1885	600
a02	182	1062.4	702.4	608	880	1358	610
a03	25	1132.8	616.3	800	950	1290	640
a04	13	1005.4	605.2	580	820	1350	580

Source: Unpublished WNC report.

Notes

Q1, Q3: first and third quartile values

Table 11.2 shows how the dataset was summarized by HRG. The mean value for each HRG taken on its own gives a rather misleading picture; it is important to note the range of costs within and between each group. By analysing this spread of resources, it was clear that certain groups would be better split into two or more separate groupings (because the cost variance was so high) while others would be better amalgamated into a single group. As a result, HRG-based contracts could now much more closely reflect cases of similar cost.

Making better use of scarce nursing skills

The data collected in the system were analysed to understand more about the use of nursing care and, in particular, about patterns of work, skillmix in relation to casemix, and tasks and activities across different professional boundaries. The results were then used as a basis for internal discussion with nursing and physiotherapy staff. (N.b. skillmix here refers strictly to grade mix.) Activity analyses were by:

- ward
- shift
- nursing/physiotherapy grade
- grouped activity (top ten only)
- individual activities
- direct and indirect activities
- unproductive time (e.g. walking between tasks).

Table 11.3 sets out the average time (hours) spent per category of task per shift for all grades on the surgical wards and is shown here to demonstrate the level of detail collected. All tasks could be similarly analysed by grade of staff, location or by patient category (whether by HRG, ICD9 or OPCS classification systems).

This indicates that, on average across all grades, 32 per cent of nursing time was spent on work other than specific direct or indirect patient care activities. This represents unproductive time, such as walking or waiting,

Table 11.3 Average time (person-hours) per task per shift for all grades

Task	*Early shift*	*Late shift*	*Night shift*	*Total*
Neuro observation	11.4	11.4	20.0	42.8
Mobility and nutrition	11.4	10.0	14.4	35.8
Reports	11.4	7.1	6.7	25.2
Phone calls and housekeeping	11.4	7.8	3.6	22.8
Hygiene	16.8	6.0	8.4	31.2
Medicines	6.8	5.6	11.0	23.4
Elimination	3.6	3.6	4.2	11.4
Clerical	4.9	3.6	3.2	11.7
Wound care and emergencies	2.8	1.4	2.5	6.7
Cleaning	1.3	1.2	2.0	4.5
Escorting	1.8	1.2	0.6	3.6
Assisting and psychological support	1.0	1.1	0.7	2.8
Total	**84.6**	**60.0**	**77.3**	**221.9**
Total shift person-hours @ 5% undermanning	**129.2**	**88.9**	**109.7**	**327.8**
'unproductive' time per shift* (%)	34.5	32.5	29.5	32.3

Source: Unpublished WNC report.
*This includes legitimate time between finishing one activity and starting the next.

but also includes time spent between activities (the data pens were not in continual use every minute of every shift).

Table 11.4 shows the percentage of each grade's time spent on each category of activity on the neuromedical ward. Here unproductive time was specifically recorded. For the medical ward this shows a 20 per cent unproductive rate and an anticipated 23 per cent under-recording level.

Nursing workshops

Throughout 1994/5, a series of meetings was held to discuss the implications of the data with staff and to identify possible solutions to a number of recurring problems, such as the lack of nursing staff (particularly neuro-specialist agency nurses), lack of equipment, increasing patient dependency, interruptions and disruption to routines. Following discussion with the senior clinical nurse and subsequent meetings with WNC sisters, a workshop was organized to take forward key issues. Each ward and shift was invited to send representatives. The workshop was organized into five parts, including a recap of the project so far, a description by the senior sister on the medical ward of their experience of the project and the use they had made of the data, a discussion led by the project's

Table 11.4 Percentage of time per grade and category of task

Activity	*Agency*	*Student*	*ENB*	*A*	*D*	*E*	*F*	*G*	*Overall*
Walking	9	8	7	9	9	10	6	12	9
Waiting	0	1	1	1	1	1	0	0	1
Interruption	0	0	0	1	1	1	1	2	1
Personal hygiene	1	1	1	1	1	1	1	1	1
Inactive	10	10	9	10	8	6	4	6	8
Prep and clean-up	0	0	0	0	0	0	0	0	0
Direct care	23	29	20	26	28	19	16	28	24
Indirect care	16	37	40	39	30	31	45	49	34
Unrecorded	40	15	22	12	23	31	26	2	23
Total	**100**	**100**	**100**	**100**	**100**	**100**	**100**	**100**	**100**

Source: Unpublished WCN report.

research nurse about potential uses of the data (with some practical examples taken from the database), group work and agreed actions. At the outset nurses expressed the fear that they did not have the skills to analyse the data or to use them; they questioned the use of finding solutions if there was no money to implement change. Importantly, however, by the end of the workshop, the nurses had used the data to highlight queries and had come up with very practical solutions that not only would cost nothing but would use their time more efficiently.

The data confirmed (or denied) and quantified often-voiced opinions. For example, the amount of unproductive nursing time due to lack of basic equipment held on the wards was quantified and, following discussions, ward stores were reorganized. Recognition of the amount of time nurses spent walking led to a reorganization of the ward layout. Interruptions to patient care – including the disruption caused by other professionals' irregular work patterns, such as consultant ward rounds – were identified as a nursing care issue. These could be quantified and steps taken to reduce them. Patterns of work were re-examined and more administrative duties were shifted to night duty shifts when there was spare capacity. Night staff also took on pharmacy ordering, stocking the intravenous cupboard, checking resuscitation equipment, entering admissions onto the computer and updating documentation. Analysed by grade, the data raised queries about 'inappropriate' activities; for example, it was found that D grade nurses in ITU spent significant amounts of time inducting new staff and that neurological observations took up a high proportion of time across all grades. The proportion of hands-on care could also be examined by grade. Data were analysed by day of the week and showed, for example, that activity on the medical ward always peaked on a Thursday but that no plan had ever been devised to cope with this. Lack of early information about admissions had left senior nurses 'firefighting' more than they felt they had to. Now earlier access to admission lists has given an opportunity to enable skills to be better deployed on the day.

Overall, nursing staff reported that they liked the speed of the data capture technology (quicker than writing), its ease of use, accuracy and novelty; and the fact that it had produced tangible benefits in their conditions and ability to deliver care. A number of criticisms of the project were also raised, including a requirement for more training prior to data collection; more feedback during the course of the study; more discussion with a wider range of staff; and a shorter recording period.

Discussion and conclusions

The project provided managers with an enhanced patient flow model: not only did it illustrate what happened to each individual patient as they entered the hospital, but it identified who carried out the tasks, when, how often, where and at what cost. The method delivered individual patient-based resource profiles which could be analysed by patient, by staff group and by cost.

The approach enabled building blocks of data to be identified and costed which could then be aggregated according to the nature of the management problem, whether it be skillmix or contract pricing. Each variable could, in turn, be aggregated to a finished consultant episode (FCE), presented cumulatively over a patient stay or analysed on a daily basis. The directorate now knows the direct care costs of treating patients with different conditions and has used these data to inform the development of revised HRGs. These HRGs will be more homogeneous in terms of resources actually used (by grouping together similar care profiles) and will better reflect marginal increases within each episode of care. Using these, contract prices can now be cost-weighted according to operative procedure or diagnosis, length of stay, and patient dependency (using nursing dependency scores).

The directorate can now be considerably more responsive to shifts in casemix and internal resource use – for example the cost of each extra bed-day, the cost of a cancelled operation, the impact of six instead of three emergency admissions for craniotomy or the effect of a 30 per cent agency staffing level. Judgements can be made about routine admissions within the context of available resources and facilities and with greater understanding of how a change in, say, casemix, affects the nursing load on any particular day. The directorate also now has a much better chance of managing risk, whether or not by negotiating a risk factor into contracts: although based on an anticipated mix of activities, the contract can be partly 'insured' against significant shifts in demand to more complex and costly cases.

It also means that decisions about changing roles and nursing practice are directly linked to data about costs. Senior nurses have used the data to examine how the different grades work across a range of activities. Many nursing issues were to do with changing the attitudes or habits of other professional colleagues or about basic facilities or functions. Importantly also many of them were about lack of information or time or both to react to changing circumstances: this perpetual crisis management meant any available nurse was performing any necessary task, diluting the effectiveness of the more-highly trained. A shortage of skilled nurses was compounded by the fact that those few nurses available were carrying out a whole range of tasks that should have been done by someone else – leading ultimately to low morale, stress and sickness. What the data have provided is a way of reassessing and reasserting roles and boundaries – agency staff can be better targeted at specific tasks or functions rather than added to a pooled resource; physiotherapy and nursing staff can work more closely or interchange certain roles; and planned admissions can now take into account the burden on nursing staff in relation to patients already in the WNC. Traditionally, bed numbers were used as a measure of capacity; however, these do not take into account the varying nursing needs of the patients occupying those beds. Admissions can now be planned around the available facilities (theatre/ITU beds), available staff (in terms of the patients' expected dependency and care profile) and the cost – each of these factors can be evaluated before a patient is admitted.

Building an operational decision support system – the final step

The project could be described more accurately as a decision support 'database' that feeds a number of different information systems. It is not a physical entity but a process that enables the description, in readily accessible terms, of the core mechanisms, costs and relationships within the organization.

The database can be enhanced and updated for any number of purposes. Currently, work is continuing with the University of Southampton to develop a flow model to simulate changes in throughput and casemix against given capacity, using the decision support database. This will be useful for matching care profiles (what the patients need to have done and when) against variations in the availability of staff and facilities; operationally this will help managers, nurses and doctors to plan non-urgent admissions around available resources, minimize the risk of having to turn away emergency admissions and provide a more predictable working environment for nursing staff. Strategically, it will enable 'what if' modelling and scenario planning in light of changing population needs, purchasing plans, new technology and changes in the way staff work. This approach could also be employed in other specialty areas (see, for example, Millard and McClean 1994 for a resource planning DSS for geriatric care services).

The system will generate – for any given admission (diagnosis) – an 'expected' care profile for inpatient treatment with attached daily resource implications for nursing staff (on wards, in theatres and in ITU) and for facilities such as beds, theatre time and diagnostic equipment over a length of stay. This would provide faster access to information about patients currently occupying a bed, their likely length of stay and care requirements, especially when planning elective admissions. It would also indicate potential overcommitment or undercapacity which could at least be anticipated if not averted.

Technically the method provides a straightforward, affordable means of developing a local decision support system based on continuous observations. The barcode technology has now also been applied in other specialties, departments and sites for reviewing junior doctors' hours, evaluating administrative tasks in medical records and outpatients, and profiling consultant activity. It is also currently being used in an extensive primary care project.

It can be as simple or complex as needed, as comprehensive as the questions demand and as reliable as data capture can be – collected by the people who will use it and make judgements about it. The technology is simple, the data easy to interpret and value is added to existing directorate information systems. The DSS in this project is only in its infancy but has already been used to inform operational as well as strategic decisions and has provided a solid platform on which to base more sophisticated models.

Acknowledgements

This project could not have taken place without the enthusiastic support of a number of sponsors including the National Casemix Office, the Resource Management Team at the Department of Health and Secta Group Ltd. It was also a collaborative venture between Southampton University Hospitals Trust, the University of Southampton Department of Accounting and Management Science and the Wessex Institute of Public Health Medicine.

In particular thanks go to June Farrah, Lorraine Clapham and all the nursing and physiotherapy staff who carried out the barcoding; Doris Lees and Katie Smith who set up and ran the project; Hannah Searle and Peter Benton for analysing the HRGs and performing the clustering exercise; and Nicky Chapman and Bridget Carpenter for analysing the nursing skillmix data and organizing the workshops.

References

Carpenter, B. (1995) Profiling patient-care activity, *British Journal of Healthcare & Information Management*, 12: 25–7.

Foster, I. (1994) *The Resource Analyser*. Ower, Secta Consulting.
Millard, P. H. and McClean, S. T. (1994) *Bed Occupancy Modelling and Planning*. London, Royal Society of Medicine.
National Casemix Office (1994) *Healthcare Resource Groups Version 2: Definitions Manual*. Leeds, NHS Executive Information Management Group.
National Steering Group on Costing (1994) *Guidance on Costing for Contracting*. Leeds, NHS Executive.
Neil-Dwyer, G., Lees, P. D., Claxton, M. and Lewis, J. (1992) Beware shifts in casemix under the block contract, *British Medical Journal*, 304: 1383–4.
Packwood, T., Keen, J. and Buxton, M. (1991) *Hospitals in Transition: the Resource Management Experiment*. Milton Keynes, Open University Press.
Schmaus, D. (1991a) The basics of barcode technology, *Association of Operating Room Nurses Journal*, 53: 1542–8.
Schmaus, D. (1991b) Implementing barcode technology in the operating room, *Association of Operating Room Nurses Journal*, 54: 346–51.
Weilert, M. and Tilzer, L. (1991) Putting barcodes to work for improved patient care, *Clinics in Laboratory Medicine*, 11: 227–38.

Part 4
Policy and organizational learning

Introduction

In the accounts of DSS in earlier Parts of this book, there has been a significant play made of the 'learning' that results from efforts to structure and explore options for service change. This results from the attempt to specify and apply the planning models contained within the systems: this is a learning that comes from 'simplification' of complex problems. More significantly, it is held to result from the process of simulating 'what if' this option or that option were chosen. Learning results from the ability to see the consequences of implementing a choice; it results, too, from the greater range of imagination that is possible. Options do not have to be closed off before they have been allowed to develop or settle. The DSS acts as a means of steadying and ordering thinking and deliberation and, in this way, enables greater complexity to be handled.

The majority of DSS seen in Parts 2 and 3 are essentially predictive models which also result in learning. The two illustrated in this fourth Part are specifically designed to promote learning by providing techniques of representation and processes of use which aim to elicit managers' mental models of policy and organizational issues. These are not necessarily data-driven, as many of the previous DSS have been – they do not purport to model the 'real world', but rather to explore the ways in which planners and managers understand the world as it affects and defines their (and others') scope for intervention and their intention to act. Both use qualitative modelling methods to build representations of thinking. Each offers means of identifying important features of thinking – beliefs about chains of consequences which feed back on themselves, delays, dilemmas, policies and goals – which have implications for how managers might decide to act. Each is a means of representing significant facets of organization and for learning about the organizational context of action.

Changes to the health care system of delivery often have unexpected – and sometimes unfortunate – consequences. Chapter 12, by Eric Wolstenholme and John Crook (a DSS developer, and a policy maker and manager, respectively) describes the use of systems dynamics methodology to represent and explore complex chains and loops of consequences in patterns of service delivery. Systems thinking focuses attention on the relationships between the component parts of services and can be used to examine the effects of interventions to change particular components of systems on other components and on the performance of the system as a whole. The process of developing an appropriate system representation, the process of analysis and the processes of learning from the modelling effort are discussed using specialist simulation software as a basis. The case study seeks to understand the effects of the transfer of community care budget and planning responsibility to social services.

Chapter 13, by Steve Cropper, gives an account of a system which captures, structures and allows for analysis and retrieval of qualitative data. Used for drawing together arguments about the nature of problems and possible responses, the system can also be used to develop and review sets of linked objectives including strategic direction, business plans and IPR (individual performance review). Three case studies are used to illustrate the method: work with a single manager on an organizationally difficult set of issues; work with a Trust Strategy Steering Group to clarify the purpose and method of review of its strategic direction; and a DSS developed to help a Trust director to manage IPR objectives setting, monitoring and review.

12 A management flight simulator for community care

Eric Wolstenholme and John Crook

Introduction

This chapter describes the use of system dynamics modelling to aid understanding of the effects on service delivery of community care for the elderly, resulting from a major shift in central government legislation in 1993 to budget cap this service and to transfer responsibility for it to social services directorates (SSD) in local authorities. The system dynamics approach provides a means of sharing mental models and improving communication and dialogue, thus assisting in breaking down barriers involving culture, attitudes and beliefs (Senge 1990, 1994; Wolstenholme 1990, 1993b).

The chapter starts by outlining the anticipated benefits, problems and issues generated by the community care policy changes. Then it introduces the underlying philosophy and methodology of system dynamics, a mapping and simulation modelling approach which uses modelling as a learning medium to help managers understand and test change agendas. The case study describes the stages of development of two system dynamics models as they were created in practice. These models are distinct in character and purpose and together demonstrate the full scope of the method.

Model 1 is a strategic representation of the process flow of elderly people from NHS hospitals into community care: it focuses on issues at the NHS–SSD interface. This model emphasizes the contribution of the system dynamics approach to *qualitative* thinking about the links between processes and strategies in organizations. Its purpose was to tease out any unintended and time-delayed consequences of the community care reforms and to suggest ways of minimizing these effects. Although powerful in its own right, the model is relatively simple and transparent and provides a platform for explaining the general approach and technicalities of applying system dynamics.

Model 2 is more complex and comprehensive in its representation of services for the elderly by a social services directorate. The purpose of the model was to enable managers to address a range of issues arising in the implementation of community care services for the elderly under the new arrangements. It subsumes some of the ideas of Model 1 and is presented as a management 'flight simulator'. The aim has been to develop a decision support system which allows and encourages managers to work with the model using a 'control panel'. This concept can help to accelerate the learning process and to test alternative strategies and structures for service delivery in much the same way, and for much the same reasons, as a new pilot might train or a new aircraft might be tested using simulation. This model emphasizes the contribution of the approach to analysing *quantitatively* what might happen over time as a result of the interconnection of processes and strategies in organizations.

Community care – the management task

Community care for the elderly is a complex area which embraces residential, nursing and domiciliary care services. Many organizations, both public and private, contribute to the delivery of these services: a brief description and recent history of changes is presented here in order to indicate the importance of the area and the difficulty of the management task.

Prior to April 1993, funding for community care services for the elderly was provided by the Department of Social Security. In 1980 the cost to the Department was around £80 million, largely in respect of residential and nursing homes. As a result of legislation in the early 1980s, which gave people a right to have their fees paid, residential capacity (particularly private) expanded quickly. The cost of the service grew to £2.4 billion within 12 years, with the Government unable to restrain expenditure.

Equally importantly, the growth in residential and nursing home care was contrary to a widespread political and professional consensus which placed more importance on the provision of domiciliary care for elderly people, in the form of home helps, day centres and respite care. A further problem in developing this sector was the existence of expenditure restrictions on local authorities.

There was, therefore, a perverse incentive to allow residential care to grow; the Government was committing very significant resource only to achieve the exact opposite of the policy intention.

In view of this and a number of audit reports in the late 1980s, the Griffiths Report (Department of Health and Social Security 1988) recommended that the Department of Social Security budget be transferred to local authorities and that they become responsible for all residential and nursing placements after an assessment of service needs on an individual client basis. This had the double effect of rationalizing the policy and, because of the limits on local authority expenditure, setting a cap on the Government's financial commitment. The Griffiths Report was implemented from April 1993 after a year of preparatory action: these changes, coming on top of the earlier NHS reforms, set an enormous challenge for management in the NHS and SSD, not least of which was the task of creating improved joint working between service contributors at all levels (Raynes 1993; Sargent 1993; Smith 1993; Lewis and Glennerster 1996).

System dynamics modelling – the rationale

The situation described above is typical of change management in many large organizations. Change is often made for well-intended reasons at a high level without sufficient testing of plans and ideas and with scant regard for their wider consequences: organizations have to adjust in the best way they can.

One reason why little effort is placed on testing of plans is a lack of time and motivation at the end of the planning process. The services must continue to be provided while new procedures are devised and implemented. The result is stress on both the people and the organization and a focus on the detail of what is currently happening. Another reason is the inherent difficulty of testing. The human ability to think through consequences over time is severely limited and interestingly at odds with the strength of their ability to envisage and conceive plans. The outcome of the simplest of changes in organizations is difficult to predict, even ignoring the fact that there are always elements, both within and outside the organization, which will act to counter any changes made. The result is that well-intended actions often fail to meet up to their expectations and can often make matters worse.

The features of change most usually ignored at the planning stage are:

- *Feedback and interconnections* – there is a tendency to treat everyone and everything as disconnected. Yet policy, organizational structure and process are inextricably linked via information and delays, forming a management 'ecology', where changes to any one of the elements have repercussions for all. A balanced view between them is needed to design and implement appropriate change. For example, how might changes in community care funding affect GP referral rates to hospital?
- *Delays* – there is an inherent assumption in most plans that delays in information flows and operational processes do not exist and that all aspects of a plan will happen at the same time. For example, that all SSD and NHS assessment procedures for the elderly will be revised at the same time when, in fact, these are composed of hundreds of individual

actions based on many different interpretations of guidelines. Implementation of plans is inevitably accompanied by surprise when events deviate from expectations. The problem with surprises is that they usually result in reactive 'fixes' and panic measures which can cause the situation to deteriorate further. What is required is an understanding of the phasing by which different parts of plans will unfold over different time horizons, and that often things need to get worse before they get better.

- *Organizational boundaries* – processes and information flowing across organizational boundaries are disrupted by those boundaries. Different organizations, even different sectors within organizations have different cultures, budgets, stakeholders and objectives, which are often defended to the detriment of the provision of the whole service. For example, the local democratic process is very significant in the interpretation and management of events in social services and of lesser influence in the NHS. Further, the same words, such as community care, often are taken to mean different things with major effects on change implementation.
- *Non-linearities* – not only are components of plans often delayed, but they may be implemented in different ways over time in different locations. Some parts of the organization may make progressive changes while others will do nothing at first and make large changes very quickly at the last minute.

System dynamics modelling adds an extra stage to change management analysis: the exploration of change management agendas at the strategic or aggregate level before their implementation. Its use encourages managers to reflect on and share a systems viewpoint of change in

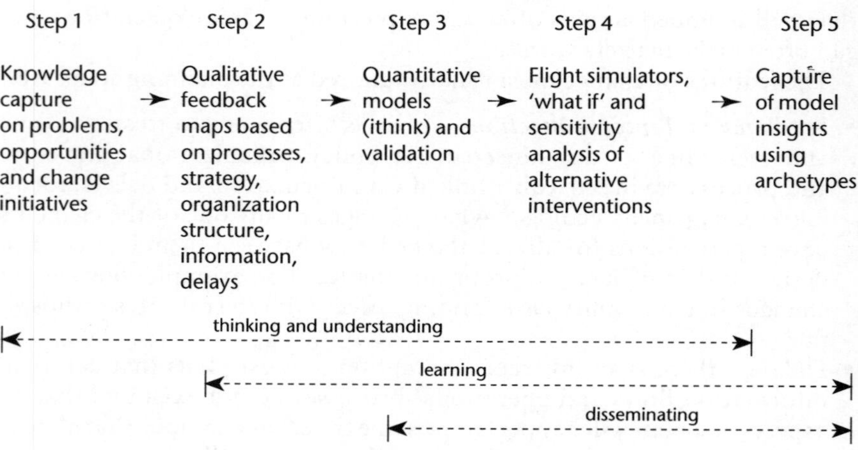

Figure 12.1 The steps of applying system dynamics

order to learn about possibly (self-defeating or unforeseen) consequences of otherwise well-intended change. The purpose of system dynamics is to improve and accelerate managerial learning about the realities of change. This may be achieved using a *transitional object*, as De Geus's (1988) discussion of 'planning as learning' argues. As children, toys serve this purpose: in system dynamics, maps and models are used. The steps shown in Figure 12.1 reflect a doctrine of 'modelling as learning' (Lane 1994). Many iterations through the steps may be undertaken to achieve the requisite learning. This approach contrasts strongly with many other decision support modelling techniques which are often concerned more with 'modelling for prediction' – for example, spreadsheets or discrete simulations which are more detailed and operational in focus and concerned with providing specific answers to specific problems. (See also the chapters by Meldrum, Forte and Bowen, or Worthington in this book.)

System dynamics – the method

In this section, important concepts relating to each step of the system dynamics method are described. Some of the subtleties with respect to learning are brought out, below, in the case studies.

Step 1: knowledge capture

The first step concerns knowledge capture or 'externalization' of the mental models of individual or groups of managers. It involves facilitation methods perhaps more commonly associated with such disciplines as strategic management and human resource management (Wolstenholme 1990; Vennix 1996). The outcome of this stage is a shared, qualitative, strategic map of the issue of interest to the organization, which is developed in step 2.

Step 1 has much in common with other systems and issue structuring methods (see, for example, Eden *et al.* 1979; Checkland 1981; Flood and Jackson 1991): comprehensive summaries of these methods are available (for example, Rosenhead 1989; Wolstenholme *et al.* 1994). Applications of Eden's methods of structuring problems using cognitive mapping are reported in Chapter 13 by Cropper. These, too, provide a means of making qualitative knowledge explicit in order that it can be subjected to analysis and to debate.

Step 2: mapping system structures

The maps developed at this second step can take two forms: influence (or causal loop) maps; and stock/flow maps. Influence diagrams link variables as causes and effects and are particularly good as a means of conceptualizing feedback structures and identifying alternative intervention points in organizations. Stock/flow maps are more rigorous and logical, separating processes from information links. It is this type of map which is used by purpose-built simulation software in system dynamics.

Whichever type is used, the aim is to enable managers to stand back from an organization and to develop maps made up of processes, strategies, organizational boundaries, information links, delays and non-linear relationships. The link between strategy and process is of prime importance in developing systemic understanding. All too often these two aspects of management are treated in isolation, with strategy being formulated without reference to operational reality and vice versa.

The key to producing well-balanced maps and models is to represent process at a level of aggregation commensurate with linking it to policy and organizational structure and responsibility. A process in system dynamics is defined as a set of aggregate activities or events organized for a purpose and represented as a chain of these activities and their intermediate accumulations or stocks. Since processes are aggregated, flows within them can effectively be treated as continuous (like water), rather than discrete (like molecules or people); this orientation differentiates system dynamics from detailed process mapping techniques such as Business Process Re-engineering (Hammer and Champney 1993) and discrete simulation in general.

Choosing an appropriate level of aggregation is more of an art than a science, but guidance is found in the aim to be strategic. For example, strategic NHS change would be more concerned with hospital discharges per month than activities like administering blood in millilitres per minute. Observing a process can be thought of as using a telescopic zoom lens. Zooming too far back generates a field of view which loses touch with the day-to-day operating reality of the process and views activities over an excessively long time horizon. Conversely, zooming in too close means becoming a prisoner of events and focusing only on reactive change. The ultimate close-up of an activity within a process would reveal only procedures and tasks rather than activities within a process.

The process and value of creating a system dynamics map is in understanding the current reality of organizations and quickly finding intervention points where effective and appropriate change can be introduced. Such 'high leverage' intervention points are often well removed in both time and space from the symptoms of problems and their use is often counter-intuitive.

Step 3: from qualitative map to quantitative simulation model

The qualitative maps produced at step 2 can be powerful in their own right. However, they are primarily a hypothesis of a situation, and its behaviour over time can only be the subject of speculation. Step 3 of the method adds considerable value to step 2 by converting the map of the organization into a simulation model capable of generating its behaviour over time (Wolstenholme *et al.* 1993; Coyle 1996). A quantitative model adds to the analysis by forcing rigorous thinking about the relationships between mapped variables and their parameter values. Data are only introduced at this stage in the development of the DSS, thus differentiating system dynamics from many other DSS which focus purely on statistical analysis and pay little attention to the structural perceptions which form an important part of managers' mental pictures of organizations.

Very sophisticated, but easy to use, purpose-built software now exists to convert maps into simulation models without programming, using graphical computer interfaces such as ithink (Richmond 1994; Stevenson 1994). Validation in system dynamics is similar to that in most decision support methods. The output 'predictions' of a quantitative model can be compared with trends in actual, historic data, and the model itself should be tested for its validity in terms of its relationships and dimensions. However, modelling as learning plays a part here. Models must be owned by their creators and be a true representation and extension of the mental models of the people who create them. Step 3 provides a powerful combination of human ability to create concepts and computer simulation to convert these ideas into visions of their practical consequences.

Step 4: using the model for policy analysis

The challenge in modelling is to keep models simple enough to assist policy analysis, but complex enough to add real value and insight. The latter requirement means that models often become sufficiently complex to require a means by which people can interact with them. Step 4 of the method provides a flight simulator or control panel interface with a model which simplifies input and output changes and so supports sensitivity and 'what if' analyses.

An important aspect of the contribution of system dynamics to change management is that insights from modelling must be disseminated to a wide range of people. Simply informing people of outcomes is neither effective nor convincing. Much work in the psychology of learning suggests that learning is not transferable: people need to learn lessons for themselves. Using the flight simulator approach at step 4 provides a means of enabling others to learn in the same way the model creators have done.

Step 5: identifying patterns and archetypes

Increased complexity means that it is useful to try to condense a model into its basic feedback loop structure and to classify its structure and behaviour by its basic form or pattern. Such patterns in system dynamics are known as archetypes (Senge 1990, 1994; Wolstenholme 1993b). Pattern recognition is fundamental to developing dialogue and communication and can be introduced after either steps 2 or 3.

System dynamics and community care

The reform of community care policy placed an immediate requirement on health and social service managers to make sense of the reforms and what their implementation might mean in practice, and not just in the short term. System dynamics was used to assist in this process of inquiry.

First, a simple model was created to clarify what senior managers in both the NHS and SSD believed to be the consequences of this change in legislation for the planning and provision of elderly care services at the NHS–SSD interface. This model will be described in terms of the sequence of steps given in Figure 12.1. Then, in the second phase a more comprehensive model was produced from a SSD perspective, to represent community care both qualitatively and quantitatively. This model was also developed into a training model and flight simulator by which insights could be disseminated.

Model 1

Conceptualization of the map

The first stage of any model creation involves a set of discussions between managers familiar with the domain to be modelled. In this case, the model was conceived by representatives of Yorkshire Regional Health and the management executive of the NHS. This model created was of a 'typical' health district and centred on the NHS–SSD interface. In particular, it sought to examine the effect of the 1993 legislation on the capacity of acute hospitals, hospital waiting lists and primary care referrals to the acute sector. This model has been reported elsewhere in detail (Wolstenholme 1993a).

Figure 12.2 shows a map of Model 1 in stock/flow form. This represents a strategic view of the process by which elderly people 'flow' from hospital into community care and is aggregated over all forms of community care. At this stage the flow of people into community care *directly* from the community was not taken into account because the focus of interest was primarily on the NHS. The story told by the loop in Figure 12.2 is as follows. Elderly people enter community care from hospital and costs are incurred which accumulate over the year. As the cumulative costs approach the budget available fewer people are allowed to enter community care up to the point in time when funds are no longer available and new entries are prohibited completely.

Understanding the map

The double-lined pipe across the bottom of Figure 12.2 represents the route by which people move from an infinitely large source (represented by a cloud) of elderly people in hospital to an infinitely large sink. The box represent the stock or accumulation of people in community care at a particular point in time. The circles (known as convertors) represent the rates of flow of people in units per month.

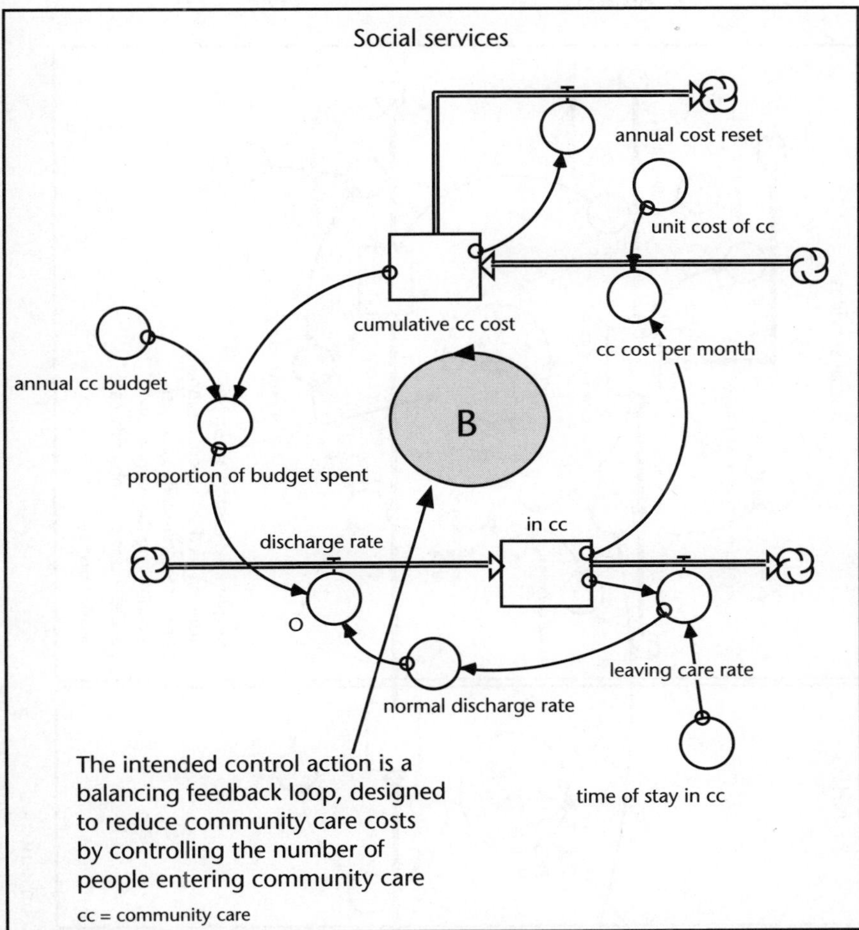

Figure 12.2 Model 1 – the intended consequence

Any resource flow can be represented by this set of stock and flow icons. The ithink software allows such concepts to be drawn directly onto the computer screen. A second resource flow of money again consists of one state (costs accrued in the year to date from community care) and two convertors. The cumulative cost of community care is increased each month and then decreases to zero at the end of the financial year ready for the next year.

Single-line arrows represent the information flows and logic in the organization which make the rates, and hence resource flows, operate over time. Information about the numbers of people in community care multiplied by the unit cost per month per person creates the cost incurred per month. Likewise, the cumulative-to-date spend on community care

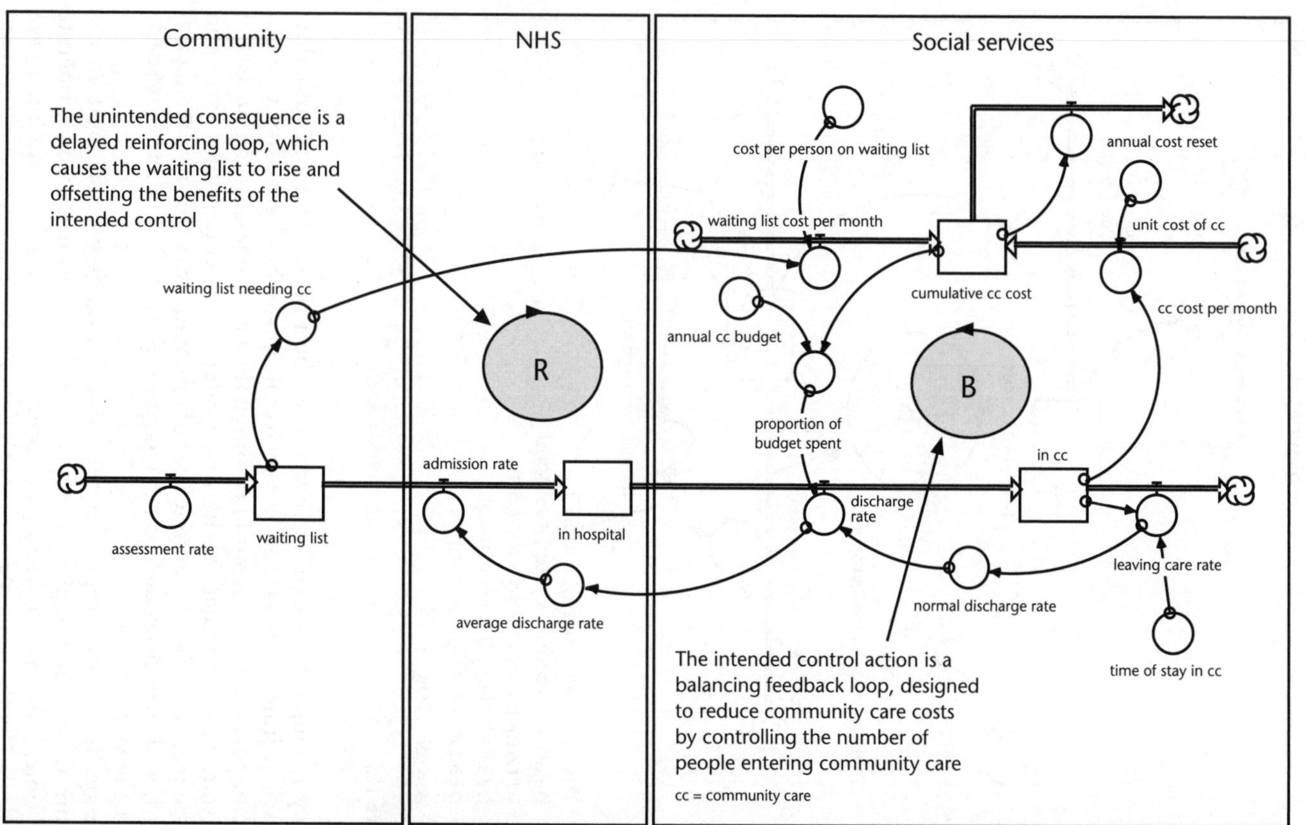
Community
NHS
Social services
The unintended consequence is a delayed reinforcing loop, which causes the waiting list to rise and offsetting the benefits of the intended control
cost per person on waiting list
annual cost reset
unit cost of cc
waiting list cost per month
cumulative cc cost
waiting list needing cc
cc cost per month
annual cc budget
R
B
proportion of budget spent
in cc
admission rate
discharge rate
assessment rate
waiting list
in hospital
leaving care rate
normal discharge rate
average discharge rate
time of stay in cc
The intended control action is a balancing feedback loop, designed to reduce community care costs by controlling the number of people entering community care
cc = community care

Figure 12.3 Model 1 – the unintended consequence

can be compared with budget to determine whether funds are available to allow further admissions.

A balancing feedback loop

The right hand side of the map captures a set of linkages made up of both resources and information. In system dynamics terms these constitute a negative, control or balancing (B) feedback loop. Such a loop is characterized by having a control variable and a policy variable. The control variable has an actual and a desired state and the purpose of the loop is to keep the control variable at or within the target state by regulating the policy variable.

In this model, the control variable is community care cost and the hospital discharge rate is the policy variable. The actual state of the control variable at any time is the cumulative cost; the target state is the budget. Cumulative costs are controlled within this target by regulating the hospital discharge rate.

The loop in Figure 12.2 is recognized technically as a balancing loop, since it has one link which acts to balance or oppose two of its variables. Apart from the link marked with a letter 'O', all other links reinforce one another. Cycling round the feedback loop and moving forward through time at the end of each cycle is what simulation is and does: it can be thought of as the unfolding of a story and is mapped out as time graphs.

Using the map to identify unintended consequences

'To every intended managerial action there is an opposing and unintended reaction or consequence, often occurring after a time delay and in a sector of the organization remote from the action' (Wolstenholme's first law of system dynamics).

Figure 12.3 shows how simple maps can be extended to trace out unintended consequences. It maps out a much longer resource flow of people than considered in Figure 12.1, extending back though the primary health and secondary health sectors. One 'unintended consequences' story might be as follows. As community care spending approaches the budget available, a reduction in hospital discharge rates is likely to contribute to bottlenecks and bed blocking within hospitals. This might also happen at a time when hospitals are trying to increase discharge rates to meet other objectives such as increased throughput targets, thus inevitably leading to cross-boundary blame.

One response from hospitals might be to reduce their admission rates, although other factors outside their control, such as a high level of emergency admissions, might confound such a policy. In any case, such a change will not take place immediately as it will take some time for all hospitals to take up any slack or switch beds between specialties, to recognize there is a discharge problem and to act. When they do there will be, in turn, an increase in hospital waiting lists. Likewise, the only way to prevent an increase of waiting lists is to introduce more stringent referral criteria, and this requires recognition of the problem and coordinated action (more delays) by a significant number of GPs.

There is an interesting paradox in Figure 12.3 between GP professional policy and resource management policies. GPs might argue that their referral criteria are based on trying to provide the best service for each individual person, whereas the reality is that the capacity of the organization they are referring to is being governed by resource policies further downstream. Unintended consequences are often associated with the way in which organizations respond to eliminate the effects of paradox. The unintended consequence shown in Figure 12.3 is that as the numbers of elderly people on hospital waiting lists for acute cases (e.g. hip replacement) increase, more are likely to need community care facilities at home. This situation will affect SSDs and further deplete community care funds. However, the delays involved may well distort the true cause of the problem. It is likely that the additional demands for funds will not occur until late in the budget cycle (or perhaps not until the next budget cycle) and the delayed timing may well cause managers to explain and react to the cost increases in terms of other causes which are closer to the current point in time. Their reaction may then be to force other cost savings, for example by reducing capacity, and make further reductions in hospital discharge rates – which will only worsen the effects described.

The consequences of these actions inevitably appear at a time and place well removed from their cause and will undoubtedly be complicated by other issues. Unless the total picture of the system and its dynamics is appreciated, much time and effort can be wasted on solving the wrong problems.

A reinforcing feedback loop

The linkages around the left hand side of Figure 12.3 captures the second form of feedback loop encountered in system dynamics, the positive feedback loop. This is also known as a reinforcing loop, because each variable in the loop reinforces the behaviour of the others resulting, over time, in exponential growth or decay. As hospital discharges are reduced the effect comes into play, countering the effects of the intended control. Over time, pressure on hospital discharges causes a reduction in admissions, hospital waiting lists rise and community care resources are used up in supporting elderly people *on the waiting list* rather than those waiting to leave hospital. This type of unintended consequence appears straightforward and inevitable when described in this way. However, it is far from easy at the detailed level in any of the organizations involved to see this sort of 'big picture' interaction, and the situation is doubly hidden by the distorting effects of time delays.

Figure 12.4 captures this in an influence diagram which helps to clarify the feedback loop structure. This map emphasizes the fact that a number of the links making up the reinforcing loop are policy links (p1–p3). They are not inevitable relationships, but are created by management:

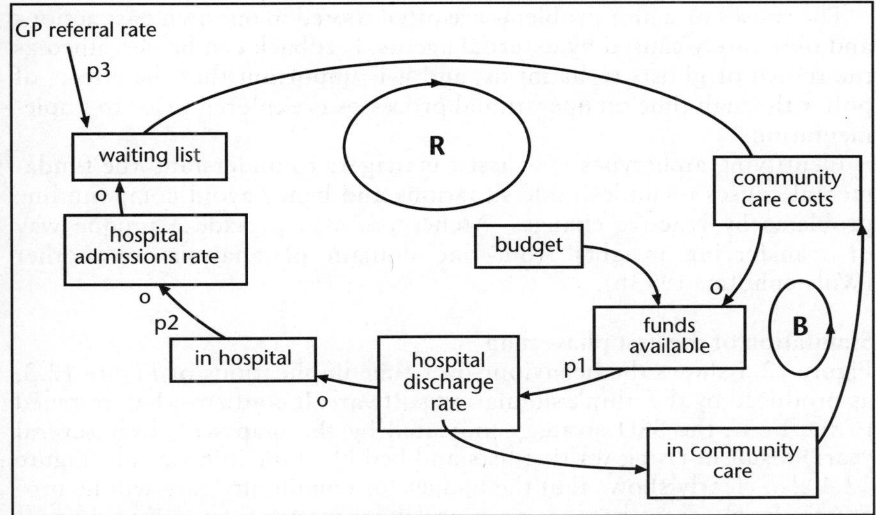

Figure 12.4 Influence diagram of the community care model

alternative policies might be possible. Link p1 is the community care policy. Link p2 is the hospital's response to reduce admissions and p3 is the effect of GP referral policy on waiting lists. Clearly, many other potential unintended consequences and feedback effects could be traced out from these maps (Wolstenholme 1993a).

Generic insights

A powerful attribute of systems modelling is the ability to condense a complex map into a basic feedback loop structure or generic pattern known as a system archetype. Figures 12.3 and 12.4 show an archetype commonly found in systems modelling studies, known as 'fixes that fail'. A well-intentioned policy results in a chain of reaction which eventually feeds back on itself to undermine the intention of the original policy. Archetypes have important characteristics:

- They can often be condensed into two feedback loops, and it is important to recognize the sequence of appearance of these loops. In Figures 12.3 and 12.4, the balancing loop comes first and the reinforcing loop is the consequence which appears after a delay. The managerial implication is that if a balancing loop is created it makes sense to start a search for the reinforcing consequence, and vice versa.
- Understanding archetypes is the key to improving communication. If a team of managers can recognize that a suggested change is effectively a specific case of a 'fix that fails' then they have the potential to tease out the likely consequences and perhaps rethink a more appropriate policy change.

The causes of major problems are often rooted in our own past actions and only rarely caused by external agents. Feedback can be described as the return of ghosts to haunt us, and it is important that the effects of policy through time on operational processes is explored prior to implementation.

Identifying archetypes may assist managers to understand the fundamental causes of undesirable situations and hence avoid compounding problems by reactive changes. Archetypes also provide a unique way of transferring insights from one domain of analysis to another (Wolstenholme 1993b).

Simulation of the first phase map

Figure 12.5 shows the behaviour-over-time implications of Figure 12.3, as produced by the ithink simulation software. It confirms that, pursued to the limit, the SSD strategy indicated by the map will (over several years) result in rising waiting lists and bed blocking in hospitals. Figure 12.4 also clearly shows that the budget for community care will be progressively overspent because more and more money is needed to support the community care needs of elderly people on hospital waiting lists rather than elderly people *leaving* hospital. This outcome is in line with early experience in the NHS of the community care reforms; it indicates that alternative strategies will need to be found.

Alternative interventions

The purpose of the first phase model was more to do with sharing mental models than with identifying solutions to the consequences of policy implementation. Indeed, no solutions to the problems arising from community care funding were prescribed. However, the model has been used for a whole range of experiments including: interventions associated with increasing the community care budget; rationing the domiciliary element of community care; varying the assumptions concerning future increases in the anticipated rate of presenting and referral; changing funding arrangements (the mix of direct budget and means-tested funding); and providing alternative community care facilities within the NHS sector for some categories of continuing care. Such use of the model continues.

Managerial learning associated with Model 1

Managerial learning associated with Model 1 included:

- The map can act as a repository for the thinking and knowledge generated by different people using it at different times.
- The map can serve as a picture that generates alternative intervention points; many existing links related to a policy choice and these were open to challenge and rethinking. Use of a map created a way of developing non-threatening challenges to plans.
- Services for elderly people were based on processes that crossed many organizational boundaries and that to create the best service for the

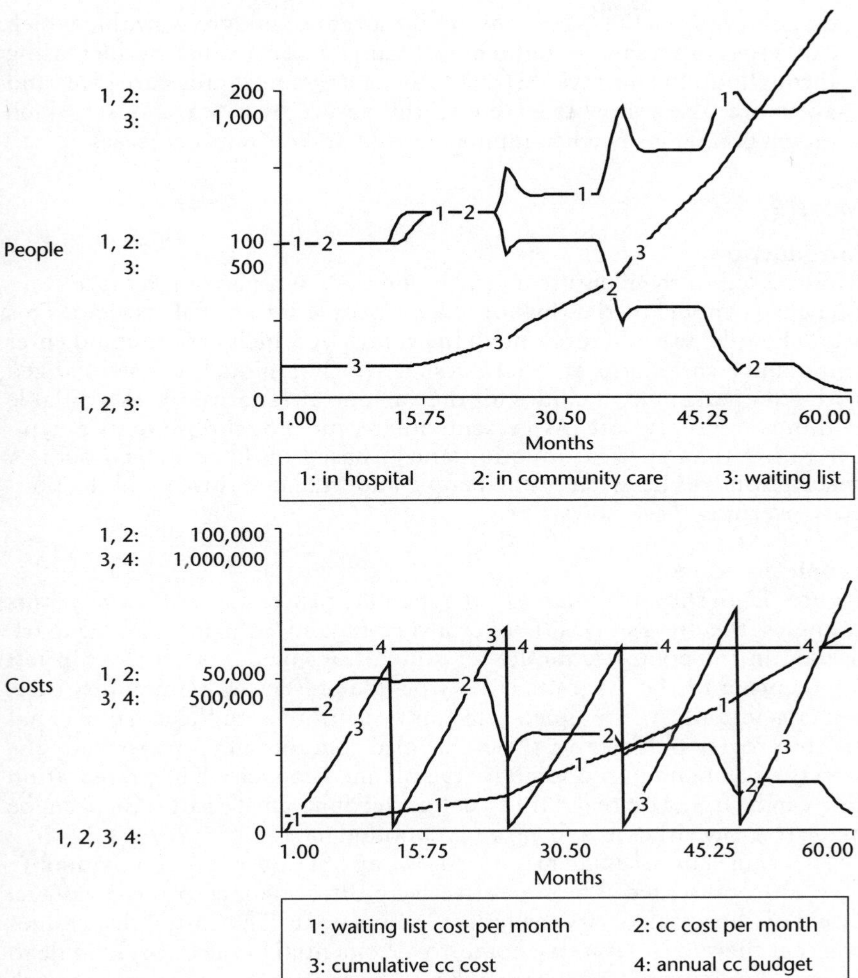

Figure 12.5 Behaviour over time generated by SSD strategy

most people required better ways of joint working and communication across boundaries.

- The changes to community care for elderly people had far-reaching consequences affecting all sectors of health provision (primary, secondary and tertiary).
- There was a need to bridge the gap between professional thinking about the individual, and management thinking about resource constraints.
- It was important to improve understanding of the different natures (and hence responses) of the NHS and SSDs to the elderly. In system

dynamics terms the NHS is more like a rate or activity variable which can solve problems of tightening financial constraints by increasing throughput. In contrast SSDs have to act as a continuing care giver and are more like a stock variable in the nature of a 'warehouse' which incurs greater costs when inputs increase and outputs decrease.

Model 2

Introduction

Model 2 led to the identification, by one SSD, of a need for a more comprehensive model of the flow of elderly people into social services. This second model was to represent all the routes by which people could enter community care from an SSD perspective. The model, conceptualized with SSD personnel, includes all the various alternative states available within community care. As presented here, the model represents a 'typical' rather than specific situation and is based on hypothetical data. A description will be given of the people and financial flows, and the policies governing these flows.

People processes

Figure 12.6 shows a map of the people processes. For clarity, this excludes the infrastructure of convertors and information feedback needed in the complete model for simulation purposes. At the top left hand corner of the diagram, elderly people present for community care, perhaps initially at a planned rate commensurate with the existing capacity of provision. However, the model also contains a facility to study the effects of demand over and above the planned capacity. The presentation rate can be based on real data or defined around a base rate which can be made to grow either in a linear or compound mode.

Two stages of assessment carried out by SSD for entry to community care are represented. The first effectively filters people into two routes: direct to hospital or to secondary assessment. The latter determines whether they go to a nursing home, to a residential home or back home to receive domiciliary-based care. The proportions of people taking each route can be adjusted within the model, which also allows for people to be assessed as 'not currently in need of any category of provision'. A proportion of these people are assumed never to re-present and the rest are assumed to make a deferred return to the first stage of assessment. The model also specifies an average time of stay in each category of community care, assuming that most people will die in community care and leave by this route.

Additionally, routes are provided by which people can enter the three states of community care direct from hospital (with or without priority over those arriving by non-hospital routes), and for people to return direct to hospital from community care. An additional exit is provided from day care which allows for people to cease receiving this provision and either not to re-present, or to re-present after a period of time.

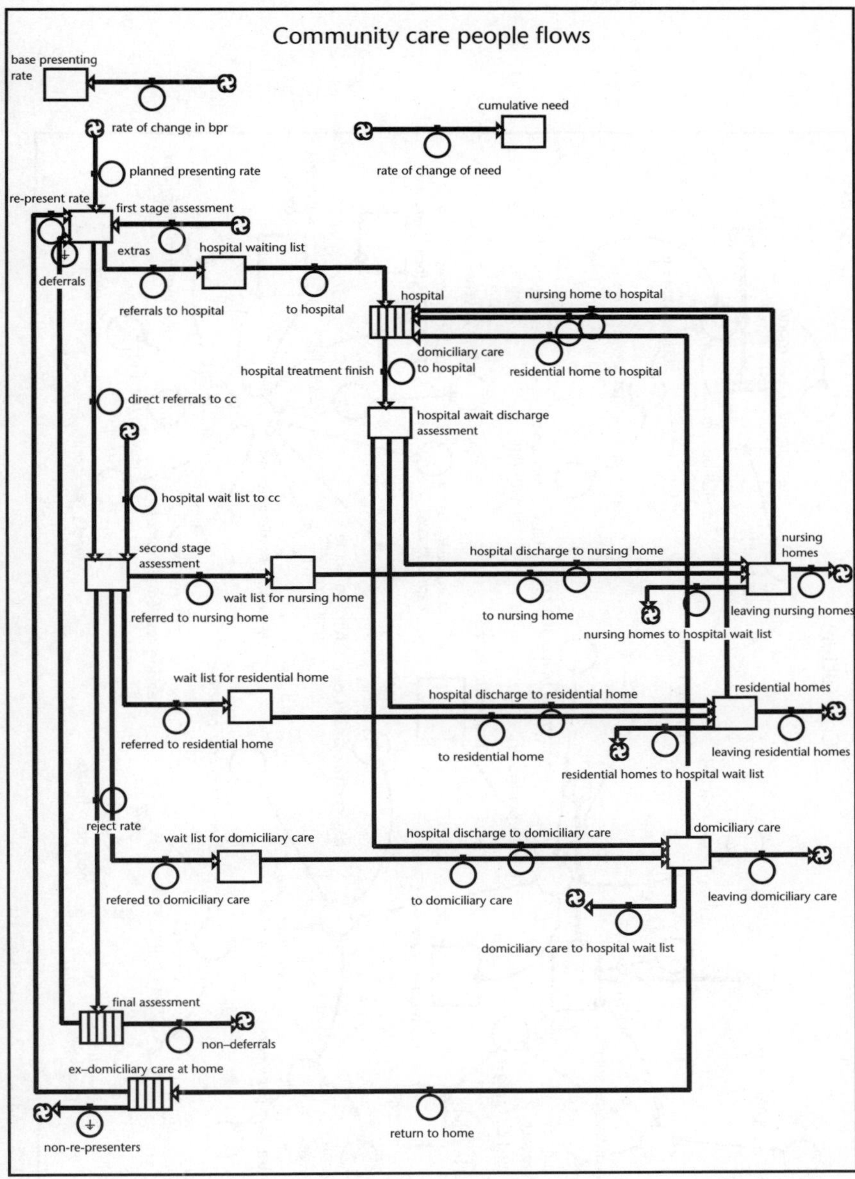

Figure 12.6 Model 2 – people flows

Finally, people on the waiting list for hospital can also enter second stage assessment and receive community care. When admission to hospital occurs these people exit from each state of community care to prevent double counting.

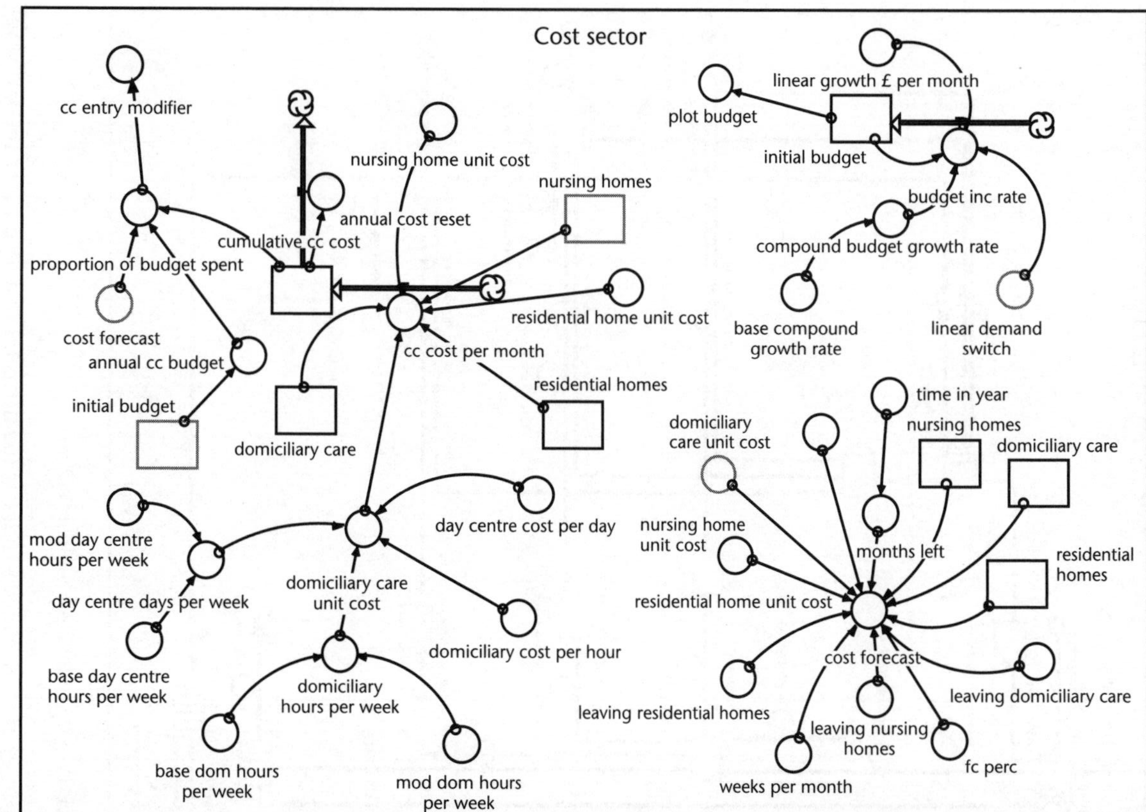

Figure 12.7 Model 2 – cost sector

Financial processes

Figure 12.7 shows the financial processes of the model. These are much simpler than the people processes and hence the convertor and information infrastructure is included.

As in Model 1, the costs associated with all states of community care are accrued over each year and compared with the social services budget. When the budget is reached all further entries in community care are suspended for the year. This is achieved via the variable referred to as the 'community care [cc] entry modifier' in Figure 12.7, which is 'ghosted' back to the people flows sector in Figure 12.6 to affect each route of entry into community care.

One of the problems of budgetary control is that it is too late to prevent a budget overspend if entry to community care is only restricted when the cumulative costs reach the budget. This is because there are stocks of people in each state of community care who will continue to create costs for the remainder of the year. What is required, as in practice, is a procedure to forecast the costs of each category of community care throughout the year, based on the numbers of people in community care and their rates of leaving. To keep within budget, entry to community care must be closed at the point at which the *forecast* cumulative costs, rather than actual cumulative costs, exceed the budget. An algorithm which does this is included in the model: its components are shown in the bottom right hand corner of Figure 12.7.

The flight simulator control panel

Use of the second model can be simplified by a 'control panel'. Such panels can be built with slider bars and other devices to aid the manipulation of selected input and output parameters and policies. The flight simulator control panel for the community care model is shown in Figure 12.8 comprising six groups of slider bars: each bar controls the setting of, and presents the base value of, a parameter in the model.

The first two groups facilitate experimentation with the demand for community care and with the budget. The third allows for changes to be made to the times of stay in each category of community care. The fourth allows for changes to the costs of community care and, in the case of domiciliary care, changes to the time allocated to each person. The fifth group allows modification to the proportion of people sent to each category of community care to be made. Finally, a policy switch is provided to change the priority of entry to community care between people out of hospital and those direct from the community.

Demonstration experiments with the model and outputs from the model

In general, experiments involve studying a group of performance measures for the model under different external scenarios and different

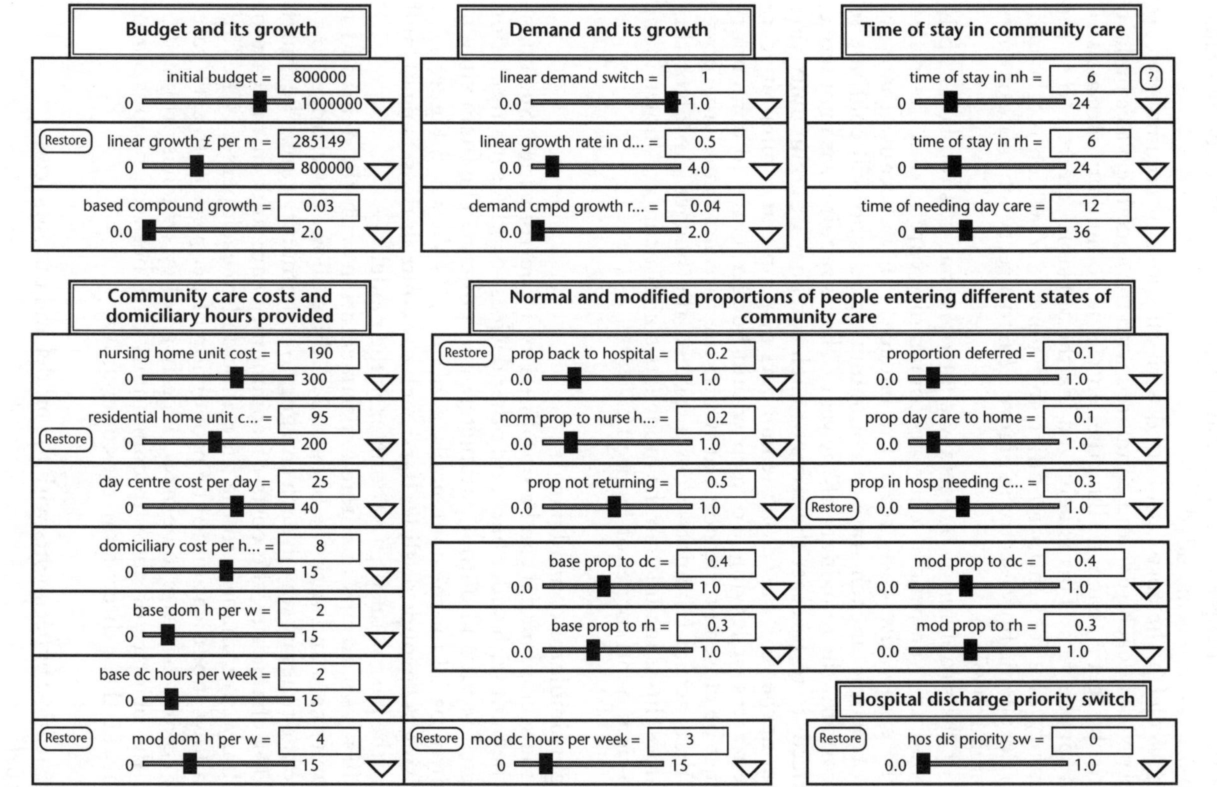

Figure 12.8 Model 2 – flight control panel

internal structures and policies. Scenario variables are usually the ones over which there is little control by the organization.

Each of the experiments reported here has the same base scenario. This makes the following assumptions:

- a linear growth in demand for community care over a 12-year period;
- a priority entry to community care for ex-hospital patients;
- a 3 per cent monthly compound budget growth rate applied at each year end from month 24 onwards;
- of the people presenting, 10 per cent are referred to hospital;
- of the remaining, 20 per cent are referred to nursing homes, 30 per cent to residential homes, 40 per cent provided with some form of domiciliary care and 10 per cent are assessed as not needing any care at all;
- people do not return to hospital from community care.

Figures 12.9 to 12.12 each show output from the model in the form of three graphs. The first graph (a) shows the numbers of people in each state of community care. The second (b) shows the presentation rate to (and the total people treated in) community care together with the budget and actual cumulative community care cost. The third (c) shows the waiting lists for each category of community care. Each figure also shows the total number of people treated in community care over the 12-year period.

Results from the experiments

Figure 12.9 shows the results of the base experiment. The numbers of people in each category of community care increases steadily until 'year 3' when insufficient money is available and entry to community care is restricted. At this point, waiting lists (except hospital) increase and the number of people in community care falls. Eventually, the rate of increase of the budget catches up with the growth in demand (the budget is not all used from year 6 onwards) and waiting lists disappear.

Figure 12.10 shows the results from using the model under the same assumptions as Figure 12.9 except that 10 per cent of people in community care are assumed to require hospital treatment. This creates a reinforcing element of demand for community care and, although the assumed budget allows demand to be satisfied and waiting lists to disappear, this recovery takes considerably longer. However, the total number of people treated over the 12 years simulated rises from 5,800 to 8,750.

Figure 12.11 shows the results of using the model under the same assumptions as Figure 12.10 except that, to reflect increased dependency, domiciliary costs are assumed to rise after three years as a result of an increase in demand for both day care hours per person per week and for day centre hours per person per week, from two to four. This effect has a dramatic effect on community care with all entry, including that from hospital, being restricted. All waiting lists and the numbers in hospital rise. It is eight years before there is a noticeable reduction in the rate of

(a) Numbers of people in each state of community care

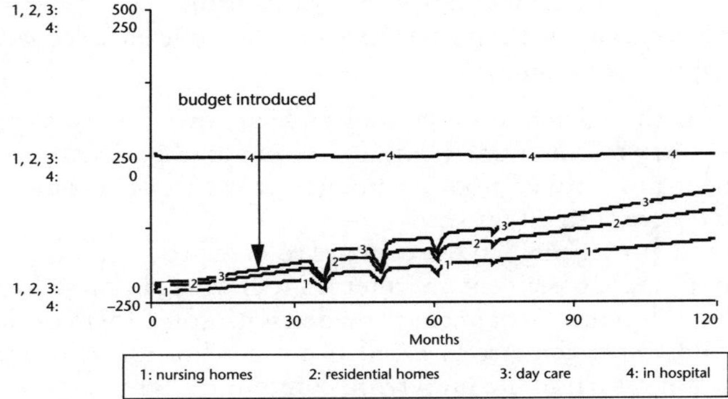

(b) Rate at which people present and total costs vs. budget

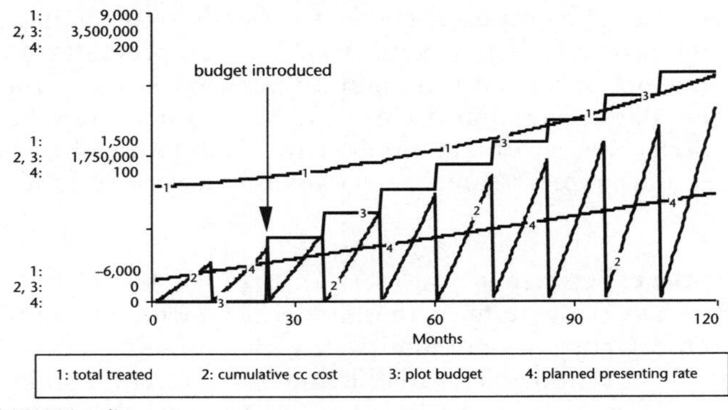

(c) Waiting lists

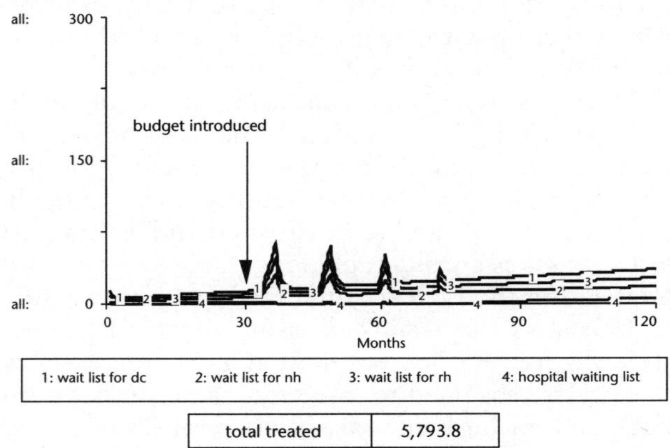

total treated	5,793.8

This scenario shows no recycling from community care to hospital and a budget introduced at month 24.

Figure 12.9 Community care model – scenario 1

(a) Numbers of people in each state of community care

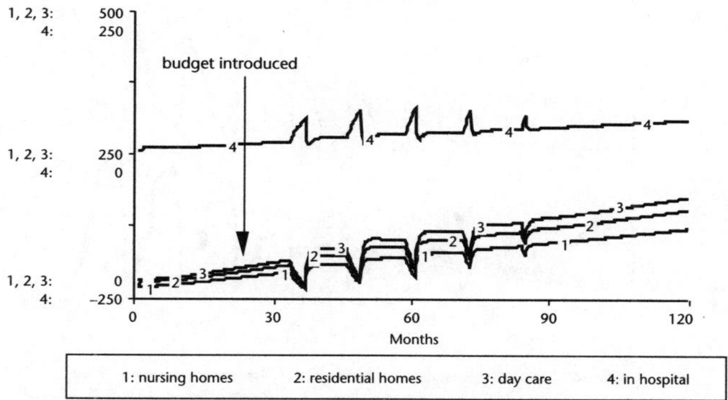

(b) Rate at which people present and total costs vs. budget

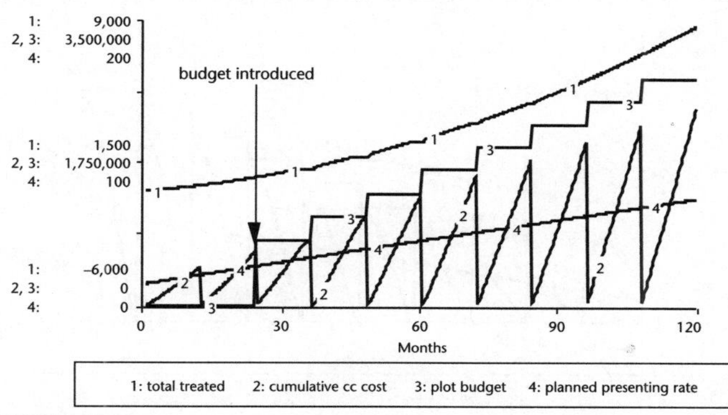

(c) Waiting lists

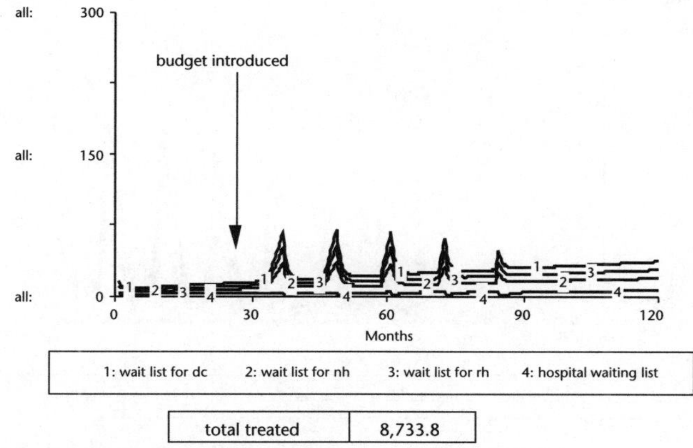

total treated	8,733.8

This scenario shows a budget introduced at month 24 and 10% per month recycling between community care and hospital.

Figure 12.10 Community care model – scenario 2

(a) Numbers of people in each state of community care

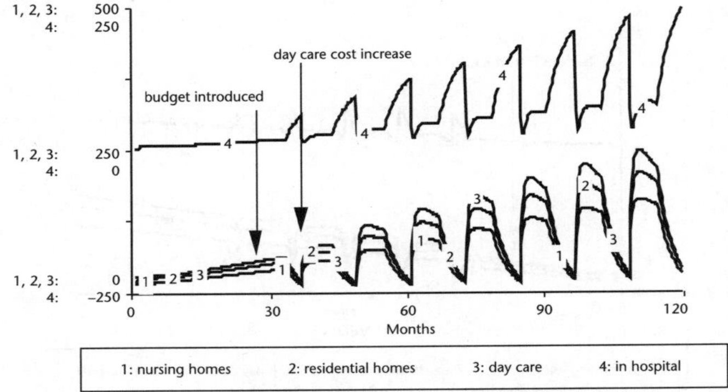

(b) Rate at which people present and total costs vs. budget

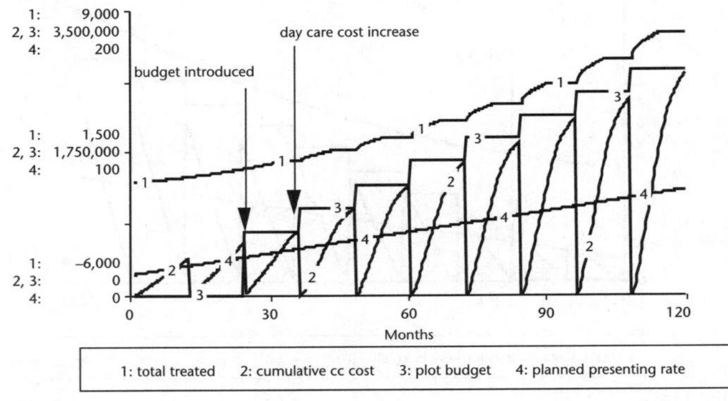

(c) Waiting lists

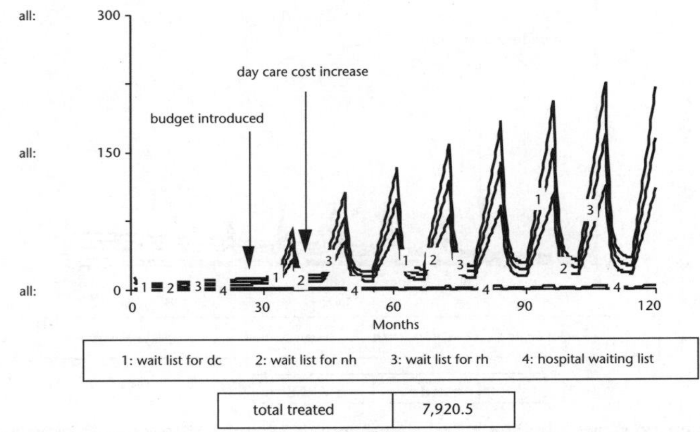

total treated	7,920.5

This scenario is as Figure 12.10 but with a day care cost increase at month 36.

Figure 12.11 Community care model – scenario 3

(a) Numbers of people in each state of community care

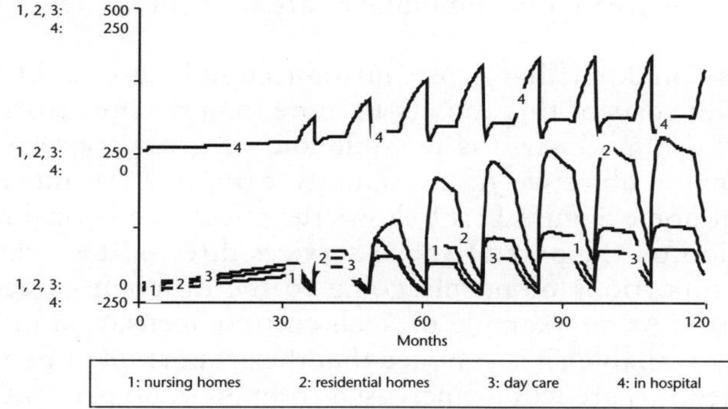

(b) Rate at which people present and total costs vs. budget

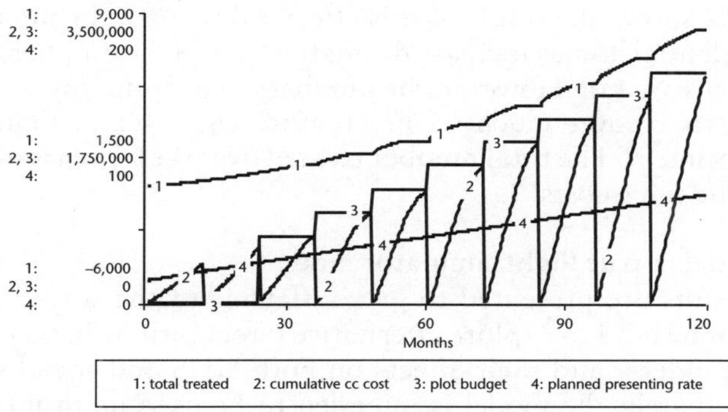

(c) Waiting lists

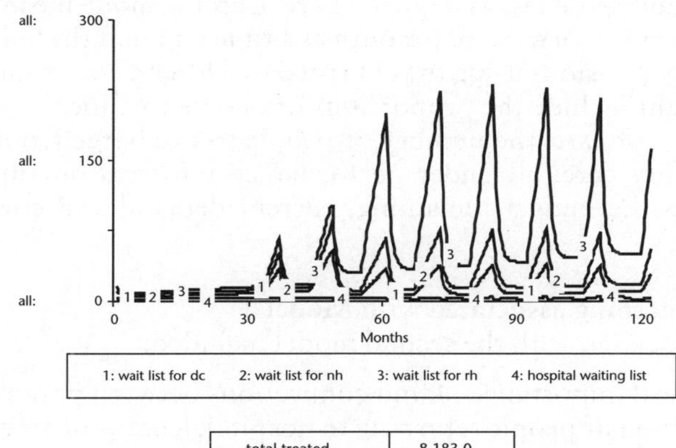

total treated	8,183.0

This scenario is as Figure 12.11, but with a switch in the proportion of people from domiciliary to residential care at month 48.

Figure 12.12 Community care model – scenario 4

increase in waiting lists and ten years before they start to fall. The total number of people treated in community care over the 12 years is about 8,000.

The increases in domiciliary costs introduced in Figure 12.11 increase the average unit costs of this activity to more than the unit costs of residential care. Such a scenario is possible and of great concern since it defeats the major objective of community care, to have more people receive help at home. Figure 12.11 shows the effect of a logical response to this situation on the part of social services directorates, which is to change the proportions of people going to the different categories of community care. As an example of such cost compensation (and given that places are available), it is assumed that the proportion of people allocated to residential care will be increased from 30 to 60 per cent and the proportion of people allocated to domiciliary care will be reduced from 40 to 10 per cent after four years.

Figure 12.12 shows the result of this effect. Obviously, the numbers of people in residential homes increase dramatically and the numbers receiving domiciliary care fall. However, the numbers in hospital fall and, overall, waiting lists recover much sooner (before eight years) than in the previous experiment. The total number treated over the 12 years increases to 8,200 for the same costs.

Using the model in true flight simulator mode

The above results are presented to give a flavour of the ways in which Model 2 might be used to explore alternative interventions in service provision for the elderly and their effects on both NHS and social services activities. Ultimately, the model is intended to be used in an interactive gaming mode by individual managers rather than in continuous mode based on in-built policies, as depicted here. Gaming mode means that the model would move forward one month at a time and that the 'pilot' would enter monthly decisions using the control panel levers. For example, these decisions might include the proportions of people to allocate to alternative categories of care, the number of people to discharge from hospital and community care, all under performance information supplied on such items as the budget remaining, current demand and current care leaving rates.

Managerial learning associated with Model 2

Learning associated with the second model included:

- the numerical importance of and connections between parameters like the proportion of people returning to hospital, lengths of stay in different sectors of community care, the unit costs of care and the rate of increase in demand;
- the difficulties of keeping SSD costs within budgets, given the rising demand for services and the 'stock' nature of community care;

- the difficulty and importance of balancing priorities between accepting referrals to community care from hospitals and from the community.

Conclusions

System dynamics is demonstrating itself in a number of industries to be an important framework for improving understanding of complex organizations. Its use of 'models as learning' – involving descriptions of organizations in terms of aggregate processes, policies, organizational boundaries, information links and delays – can lead to improved communication and sharing of mental models and, ultimately to breaking down barriers involving culture, attitudes and beliefs.

In the cases described here the work is at an early stage, but the two complementary models have the potential to assist in identifying the consequences of, and developing improved understanding of, the new world created by recent changes.

Dedication

This chapter is dedicated to the memory of John Crook who died shortly after its completion. John's thinking was always ahead of its time and his contribution to the provision of social services will be sadly missed.

References

Checkland, P. B. (1981) *Systems Thinking, Systems Practice*. Chichester, Wiley.

Coyle, R. G. (1996) *System Dynamics Modelling*. London, Chapman Hall.

De Geus, A. P. (1988) Planning as learning, *Harvard Business Review*, 66: 70–5.

Department of Health and Social Security (1988) *Community Care: an Agenda for Action* [The Griffiths Report]. London, HMSO.

Eden, C., Jones, S. and Sims, D. (1979) *Thinking in Organisations*. London, Macmillan.

Flood, R. L. and Jackson, M. C. (1991) *Creative Problem Solving – Total System Intervention*. Chichester, Wiley.

Hammer, M. and Champney, J. (1993) *Re-engineering the Corporation – a Manifesto for Business Revolution*. New York, Nicholas Brearly.

Lane, D. C. (1994) Modelling as learning: creating models to enhance learning amongst management decision makers, in J. D. W. Morecroft and J. D. Sterman (eds) *Modelling as Learning*. Portland, OR, Productivity Press.

Lewis, J. and Glennerster, H. (1996) *Implementing the New Community Care*. Buckingham, Open University Press.

Raynes, N. (1993) The SSDs' management challenge, *Health Services Management*, March: 10–12.

Richmond, B. (1994) *ithink Version 3 User Manual*. Hanover, NH, High Performance Systems.

Rosenhead, J. (ed.) (1989) *Rational Analysis for a Problematic World: Problem Structuring Methods for Complexity, Uncertainty and Conflict*. Chichester, Wiley.

Sargent, J. (1993) Mountains to climb, *Health Service Journal*, January: 24–6.
Senge, P. (1990) *The Fifth Discipline*. New York, Doubleday.
Senge, P. (1994) *The Fifth Discipline Fieldbook*. New York, Doubleday.
Stevenson, R. W. (1994) Strategic business process engineering: a systems thinking approach using ithink, in K. Spurr, P. Layzell, L. Jennison and N. Richards (eds) *Software Assistance for Business Re-engineering*. Chichester, Wiley.
Smith, J. (1993) Countdown to community care, *British Medical Journal*, 306: 566–8.
Vennix, J. A. M. (1996) *Group Model Building – Facilitated Team Learning Using System Dynamics*. Chichester, Wiley.
Wolstenholme, E. F. (1990) *System Enquiry – a System Dynamics Approach*. Chichester, Wiley.
Wolstenholme, E. F. (1993a) A case study in community care using system thinking, *Journal of the Operational Research Society*, 44: 925–34.
Wolstenholme, E. F. (1993b) 'Towards a core set of archetypal structures in system dynamics', Proceedings International System Dynamics Conference, Cancun, Mexico.
Wolstenholme, E. F. with Henderson, S. and Gavine, A. (1993) *Evaluating Management Information Systems*. Chichester, Wiley.
Wolstenholme, E. F., with Richardson, G. P. and Morecroft, J. D. W. (eds) (1994) Systems thinking, systems thinkers, *System Dynamics Review*, 10: 1–3.

Software availability

The systems dynamics software 'ithink' is available in Macintosh and Microsoft Windows formats in the UK from COGNITUS Systems Ltd, 1 Park View, Harrogate, North Yorks, HG1 5LY.

13 Decision support in objective-setting, monitoring and review

Steve Cropper

Introduction

A fundamental task of management is to establish a sense of purpose or direction, and to set the conditions in which that direction can be translated into more specific objectives, actions and behaviour. This much was proposed 30 years ago by Selznick (1957) in his discussion of institutional leadership. The two sides to this task – the search for a sense of direction and for ways of giving practical significance and meaning to it – are intimately connected.

Setting direction is not a one-off task. Purpose which makes good sense at one time and in one set of circumstances starts to make less sense as the operating environment of the organization changes, the needs, expectations and values of its members change, and technologies and the organization itself change in structure, character and behaviour. Because of this flux, there is unlikely to be a single, unequivocal response to such questions as What are we aiming for? What do we need to do to achieve it? Is what we are doing, right? Responses to these questions are likely to be fragmentary: areas of clarity will be matched by others where it is difficult to be confident about direction.

Clarity may come in two ways. First, it may be helpful to look for connections between broad intentions and the more detailed objectives and actions which elaborate the meaning of the broader goals. Talk about 'improved quality' might be elaborated by examples of more specific objectives such as 'increased responsiveness to service users' or 'developing evidence-based health care'; and these may, in turn, be elaborated further to explain what 'improved quality' means. This type of connection works both ways. Where a set of concrete actions are required, the issue of direction is related to setting those actions in context – why these actions rather than others? Where the broad goal is defined, the issue is more salient – how to get there, what to do first or next and what to do later, how to mobilize the necessary resources? Thus Eden (1990: 35) argues that 'a problem cannot be defined without reference to possible courses of action . . . encouraging people to define their world in an "idealized form" is unnatural and unhelpful.'

Second, even where there is a well-elaborated set of ideas about action and its relationship to future identity and performance, there will often be a number of different objectives which influence management decisions and actions. It can be difficult to be confident about the relationship between development activities and objectives because there are competing objectives, each with roughly equivalent status, which suggest different types of action.

That there will be contradictions in the objectives of health service organizations is hardly new. Nor is uncertainty a new theme. The issue is how to organize thinking about objectives, purposes and actions so that 'what to do and why' is at least the subject of debate.

For health service managers, the question is the extent to which it is useful to take the creation, communication and maintenance of a coherent system of objectives as a critical task. Management practice often gives a lesser priority to forms of words than to engaging with people at the sharp end or responding to the situation, but there is still a need for direction, consistency and coherence in action and behaviour. This process of acting thoughtfully needs careful attention. For individuals, reference to purpose is an important part of making sense of problematic situations and of charting an appropriate way through them. At a group or team level, the issue is one of negotiating, agreeing and coordinating action that makes sense collectively. At the organizational level, there are more complex issues of signal and symbol, steerage and control. In each case, the formal setting of objectives, and related processes of monitoring and review, interacts with informal undeclared motives, objectives and intent. The development of a general and business management ethos in the health services has brought with it a strong emphasis on setting explicit, formal objectives. This is matched in clinical practice with such developments as protocols, care pathways and individual care plans. These extend the preoccupation with purposeful action in organizational settings and bring negotiation, steerage and control of organizations into the domain of explicit, accountable work.

This chapter explores how a computer-based decision support system (DSS) can help both in the search for practical coherence in systems of objectives and in support for managers' efforts to articulate and use these objectives in their work, whether publicly or as part of a private struggle. Three cases are used to illustrate how the DSS is adaptable to different circumstances and requirements.

The first case concerns personal decision support for a project officer charged by a joint health and social services planning team with developing new 'locality forums' for consultation on community care plans. The DSS was used to help her to think and talk through what the principles behind the new arrangements might mean in practice and how the development work might be best taken forward. This case introduces the basic 'means–ends' modelling discipline which is used in each of the three cases. The second case reports on the early stages of work to steer revision of an acute Trust's statement of strategic direction: it illustrates certain analytical features of the DSS which help to identify what may be critical aspects of the task. The third case illustrates how the Individual Performance Review (IPR) process, another formalized process of setting objectives, was enhanced by a DSS approach.

A DSS approach to objective-setting, monitoring and review

Few decision support systems have focused specifically on working with language as the primary data. Yet, especially in setting objectives at the strategic level, the basic task is to find meaningful language to describe and communicate intentions. Facts and figures may be part of the raw material used in setting objectives, but these are embedded in interpretations of their significance for direction and action.

While word processors and spreadsheets can be used to capture and structure non-quantitative data, they lack any means of analysing or structuring them so as to express objectives. In short, they offer no prompts about method. The DSS described here uses Microsoft Windows-based software called Graphics COPE and is based on the modelling technique of *cognitive mapping*. This has been developed and used in supporting problem solving and strategy development by individuals, teams and organizations (Eden 1988, 1989; Cropper *et al.* 1992). The modelling technique allows the representation and analysis of problems, issues, objectives and possible actions in the terms they are described by individuals with some responsibility for them.

The basic form of the model is a network of *linked phrases*. Each phrase captures and directly reflects the way an individual has expressed an idea or *construct*. Constructs may be expressed as statements of fact, problems, opportunities, needs, impositions; or they may be considered in an action-orientated way – for example, as an objective. Each construct may be linked to one or more others in such a way that explanations are linked to consequences and means to ends. The resulting map represents a system of beliefs – that doing x will lead to the consequences y and z – and so ties objectives together with the actions that will bring them about and the goals to which objectives contribute. The general form of the model is shown in Figure 13.1.

Mapping can be used as a pen-and-paper technique (Eden 1989). However, the computer software becomes useful, and then increasingly essential, as the description of a situation becomes more extensive. With more than 50 interrelated constructs, it is more difficult to understand

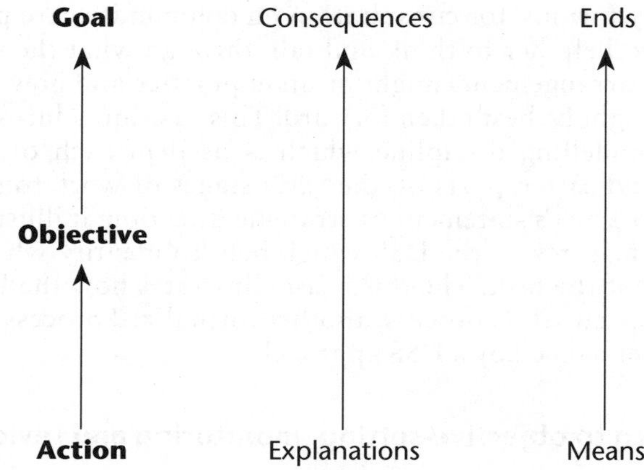

Figure 13.1 The general form of cognitive maps

the shape and character of the map without the help of the analytical and presentational tools in the software. Most importantly, where there is a continuing process of exploration and elaboration, the computer provides flexibility in retrieval, input, exploration and analysis.

Direct data entry is extremely easy and intuitive. Double-clicking the mouse on the screen prompts the appearance of a concept reference number; text can be typed in a 'block' centred on that point on the screen. Linking concepts is equally easy: use of a 'drag and drop' facility produces an arrow linking any pair of concepts. This unit of two linked concepts is the building block of a (cognitive) map. A number of such units link together to form a system of intent: this is often structured as a hierarchy with broad goals and consequences at the top and more-specific concerns and objectives lower down.

The software is neither 'intelligent', nor active; it enables users to enter, retrieve and view the constructs as lists or as maps and, for the latter, to zoom in or out from overview to detail and back out again. Parts of the model can be abstracted and displayed. More importantly, software contains analytical routines which help to identify important characteristics of the system of beliefs and objectives (Eden 1991; Eden *et al.* 1992). These include analyses which will rapidly:

- identify and report constructs which may describe goals or significant consequences;
- identify and focus on 'vicious and virtuous circles' which may suggest points for management intervention;
- suggest points in the map which might capture the essence of strategic issues;

- suggest how the map might usefully break down into different areas or clusters of concern around such issues;
- draw out of the model potential programmes of action related to goals and objectives; and
- trace through the model to identify implications, positive and negative, of implementing a proposed action.

These analyses are often used 'in the backroom', and the results used to tidy up a model to gain insight into its structure and key characteristics, and to test whether those insights match and help to clarify the user's own sense of the issues in hand. The software is eminently capable of use by managers, but it is often used by facilitators, working with managers on problem solving or strategy development.

As with other uses of cognitive mapping in health planning and management (e.g. Blackham and Corless 1992; Telford *et al.* 1992; Roginski 1995), the applications reported here have been integrally linked to decision making processes. Each helps to build up an overall account of the method and, together, they illustrate different forms of DSS to which they can lead. The ways in which the approach can be used in practice are almost infinitely variable. Choices depend, perhaps most crucially, on: how many people are to be involved in developing and using the DSS; the point or points in the process at which the computer-based software can appropriately be used; the outcomes or products required (the purpose of use); and, where use is facilitated, the role the facilitator is able to secure in relation to the design and management of the decision making process.

A personal DSS for project management

Projects are commonly used to facilitate change and innovation, and to offer a challenging management task. Projects involving more than one organization provide perhaps the most complex setting of all. Managers of inter-agency projects meet forms and levels of resistance (and support) which are more difficult to understand than those found within a single organization. The project manager is often left exposed: building commitment, finding 'champions', securing resources and establishing management protection can be difficult. Goals and terms of reference are usually vague: it takes action on the ground to test and find what are the appropriate balances and emphases.

The problem is one of making sense of the task and developing a strategy – at least in part, for this is not intended to belittle what is required to make it happen. Project planning methods have increasingly been used in the NHS, especially for large projects such as information systems development and implementation. Techniques and software are available which suggest how to structure sequences of related tasks in a logical way, and which use them as a basis for monitoring and control. The methods

Issues

1 Making the groups work
2 Maximizing user/carer involvement
3 Identifying needs – not meeting needs
4 Prioritizing – lack of resources
5 Effective ways of identifying/prioritizing needs – participatory
6 Project worker support!

Figure 13.2 Judith's agenda

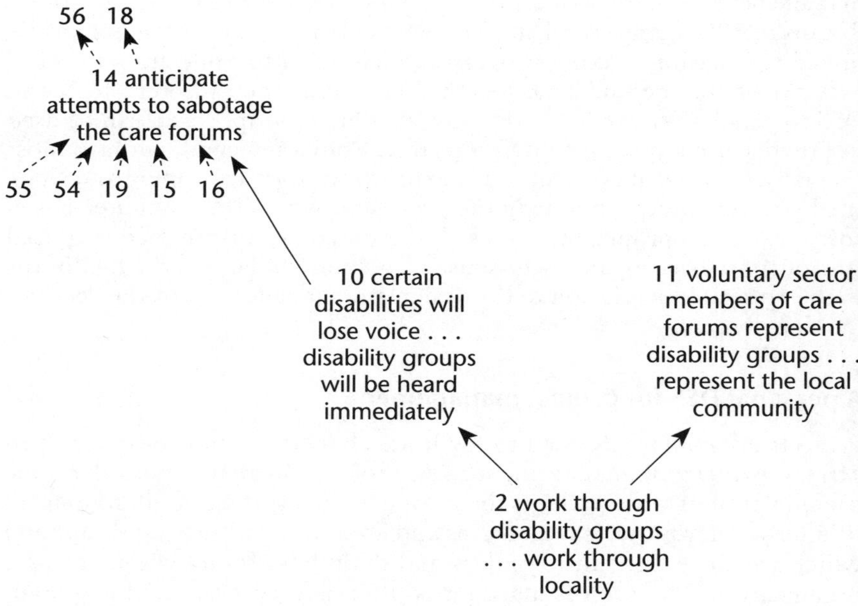

Figure 13.3 Segment of Judith's map

Note: The representation of arguments uses a particular convention which in some cases distinguishes contrasting possibilities by the use of three dots: these dots should be read as 'rather than'. For example, the construct 10 should be read as 'certain disabilities will lose voice rather than disability groups will be heard immediately'. Relations between constructs are indicated by arrows. Thus Figure 13.3 captures an argument suggesting that if certain disabilities will lose voice then one should anticipate attempts to sabotage the care forums. Some arrows have a negative sign beside them indicating that the arrow switches the influence from the first side of one construct to the second side of the other to which it is connected. Thus the 'loss of voice' is a consequence of 'work through locality rather than work through disability groups' whereas 'work through disability groups' would mean that 'disability groups will be heard immediately'.

may also provide a way of thinking about and creating organizational mechanisms – steering groups, working groups, core teams, specifications of roles and responsibilities, etc. – which bring appropriate clarity, expertise and advice to the project arrangements (Bentley 1992). Yet, these provide little help to the project manager in making sense of the *politics* of change.

Case study

In the summer of 1995, a project officer working to a Joint Strategic Purchasing Team – consisting of health authority and social services senior managers jointly responsible for preparation and oversight of the Community Care Plan – met the author to discuss what seemed to be a specific 'technical' task – defining the kind of information that new consultation arrangements with users and carers should bring to the planning process.

At this initial meeting, much of the discussion was about means of designing effective and meaningful forms of user group participation or consultation – points 1, 2 and 5 on a personal six-point agenda which the project officer (Judith) had sketched out beforehand (see Figure 13.2).

Each of these issues was clearly connected to the others and – even with a focus on issues 1, 2 and 5 – there were references to other aspects of what is often called a 'messy problem' (Ackoff 1981). In listening to Judith talk, I made notes in 'map' form, using, as closely as possible, her own words. I showed this to Judith to illustrate how we might work on the problem, but, when we next met, this pen-and-paper model was on the computer and tidied up. A snippet from this first meeting is shown in Figure 13.3 as two small groups of linked constructs.

The numbering of the constructs reflects the order in which they were recorded on the computer. The three dots which separate words in the text of each construct signify a contrast and should be interpreted as meaning 'rather than'. For example, Construct 11 suggests that 'voluntary sector members of care forums represent particular disability groups *rather than* the whole community within their locality'. Identifying such contrasts (these may be drawn, for example, between 'circumstances here and circumstances elsewhere', between 'past, present and future', or between 'alternative futures') is an important way of understanding the nature of a concern, a principle or an idea for action.

A second way of elaborating the significance of an idea is to ask what its implications would be or to ask how it might be brought about. The new consultative arrangements which Judith was to see into effect involved a shift for the health and social services agencies away from structuring consultations through disability groups to working with new locality forums (Construct 2). User and carer groups were unclear how these would work, but 'winners and losers' were clearly anticipated (Construct 10) and this had given rise to concerns that the care forums

1 care forums identify local needs . . . care forums take responsibility for consultation processes
2 work through disability groups . . . work through locality
3 feed in information
4 groups around mental health concerned that care forums will be required to act as screening mechanism
5 care forums take responsibility for consultation process . . . care forums monitor community care planning process
6 monitor effectiveness of action
7 care forums take watchdog role
8 JK identify responsibilities of care forums
9 let JSPT know
10 certain disabilities will lose voice . . . disability groups will be heard immediately
11 voluntary sector members of care forums represent disability groups . . . represent the local community
12 set ourselves up so people don't have those feelings
13 tell people to come on board or get left behind
14 anticipate attempts to sabotage the care forums
15 respond to challenge through User care forum in east of county
16 respond to challenge through JSPT
17 get voluntary sector care forums to reassert the formal procedure of care forums
18 pull everybody back into the model
19 understand power bases and dynamics . . . events take me by surprise
20 keep ear to the ground
21 colleagues in statutory bodies keep me informed
22 JK as focal point for all forums
23 people want the process and structure to work
24 statutory authorities have investment in the care forums working . . . no consequence if care forums don't work
25 flak transferred from statutory authorities to JK about the change in structure
26 believe new structure is a better way . . . no one believes new structures are better way
27 care forums created by JSPT . . . right people involved (purchasers, providers, etc.)
28 voluntary sector wants to see action
29 voluntary sector want actions clearly set and to get on with it . . . feel swamped by the politics and lack of clear direction
30 JSPT sets clear direction for JK . . . JSPT unclear

Figure 13.4 List of concepts 1–30

would be 'sabotaged' (Construct 14). This was a vulnerable time: the roles and functions of these forums were not strongly specified and a process of negotiation which would find roles acceptable to all was required. This turned out to be the crux of the matter for Judith, as the list of the first 30 constructs in the model started to suggest (Figure 13.4).

Because the software is easy to use, it is possible to use it simply to brainstorm and doodle with ideas (Procter 1991) as well as to use it in a more structured manner. Our use fell halfway between the two. Over a series of seven meetings, held more or less monthly, we used a computer running the COPE software to build a model of Judith's concerns, putting some order on them and starting to identify ways in which she could start to address her task. Much of the value of this lay in 'seeing the overall pattern of the problem' and in the 'reflecting back' as I tried to understand and clarify what Judith was trying to achieve and what the constraints were.

Cognitive mapping uses people's words as closely as possible so that the resulting model is likely to be seen as their own. However, the technique suggests that some change be made in the way problems are described. In particular, the technique is *action-orientated*: part of the value of using the technique comes in converting descriptive accounts of worries into accounts which are suggestive of action. This is a key part of the intervention and one which demands careful attention to points where negotiation over words may be useful and constructive. As Eden (1989: 29) argues: 'Changing the language used by the client, so that it becomes orientated to action rather than problem description, without the client losing "ownership" of the model, is not a trivial exercise.'

At the end of each meeting, Judith left with a print-out of the new material as it was linked to the old. These 'on-line minutes' were not very tidy: however, they contained reminders of what had been striking about the discussion, which Judith could take back and consider in the 'cold light of day'. Figure 13.5 shows a part of such a print-out. The reminders appear as different 'styles' in the text of the constructs which can be defined by the user. Figure 13.6 shows the styles created with Judith.

The meetings seemed to offer Judith a valuable opportunity to talk things out aloud: at points of greatest stress, it provided catharsis. That there was another person involved, listening and reflecting back, suggesting where clarification or, more importantly, elaboration and connection might help, added a discipline which it is difficult to sustain alone. At other times, it was more like a form of rehearsal: trying out a script gives some confidence that arguments to be used in defending or promoting the project can be marshalled and that they stand up, at least in front of a disinterested party. Such help can be found in many organizations, or among friends outside, but what is not usually found is attention to argument which comes from a command of the 'means–ends' modelling technique. Nor can the role of 'the screen' and associated computer functions be easily replicated. For Judith, seeing her words – captured and linked in front of her, available for use in emphasizing a point or to focus on while pondering a question or a thought – made a difference. As she said, 'It shows you are not imagining it – it's there in front of you. You can break the problem down . . . You can see how one thing affects another and what you need to deal with first.'

The ability of the system to recall past material, the rapid input and the flexibility of the representation are all virtues here, while the analytical functions of the software were little used. When they were, Judith found them of less value than the maps and lists which captured her own analysis of the task and its associated political sensitivities. Systematic validation of the model was not an issue of importance either: the model was

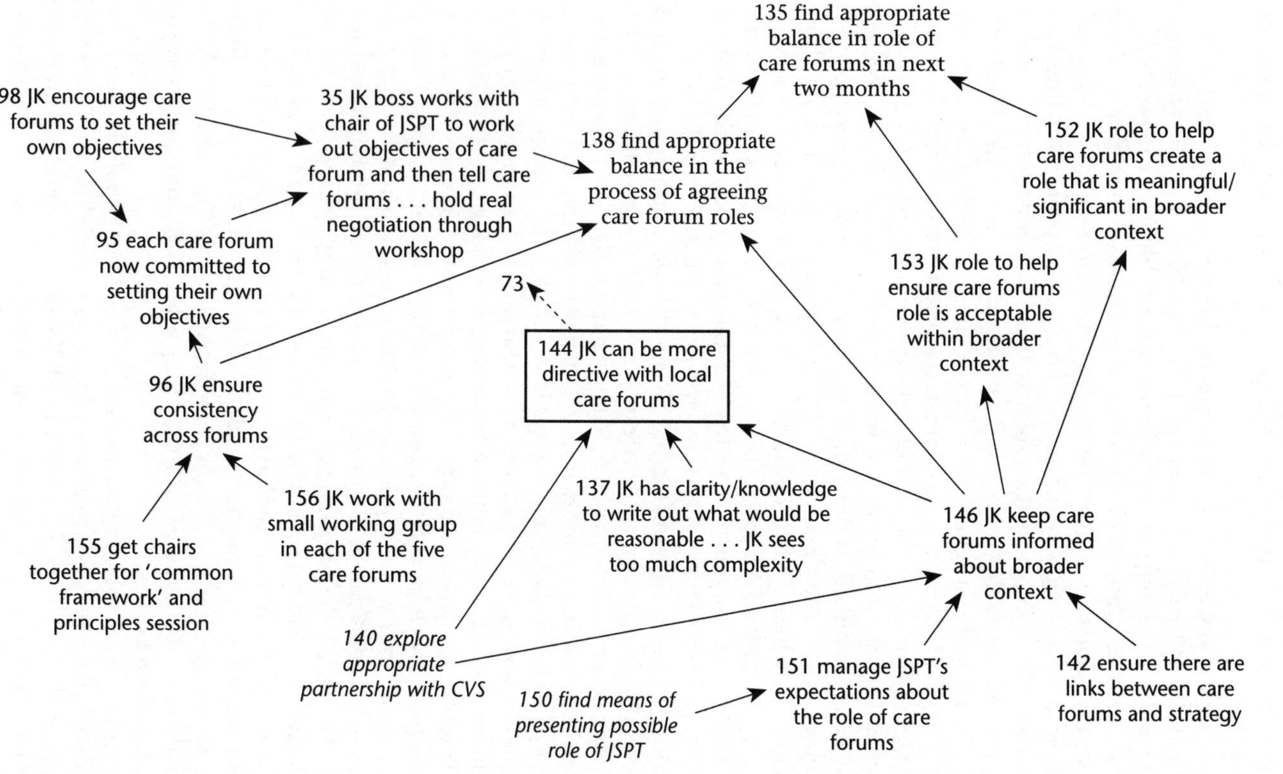

Figure 13.5 Extract of a record of discussion about care forum roles

251 principles to guide development work

250 objectives

249 standard – thinking and talking

248 actions decided or to consider

252 procedures to adopt in development work

253 now questions

254 April questions

255 purpose of questions

Figure 13.6 List of styles (Judith's model)

ephemeral, a device to assist in the process of articulating and pulling together the reasons to act in one way or another. In one meeting, for example, Judith became preoccupied by the power and behaviour of another key member of staff who, she felt, intended to sabotage her attempts to make progress on the care forums. As she talked about this person and how she, Judith, might manage this situation, several strategies seemed possible, but one emerged as the one to which Judith would commit: a call to cooperative working on one issue of common concern. This would 'test' directly what the other person's stance was, and Judith could also imagine ways of testing her concerns indirectly. The decision to do it this way was not taken *explicitly* at the meeting, but it was clear from the way Judith 'relaxed' that the commitment was made. Formal analysis of the model was largely irrelevant, even as it became more extensive and more amorphous. This was a *personal* decision support system: there was no need to ensure a tidiness or 'coherence' in the model which would mean any other person could understand its implications for action: rather, it had to be judged in relation to its function as a means of connecting and helping to explore the issues and dilemmas which Judith needed to address as she arrived at each meeting. Eden's (1986) account of the process of 'problem finishing' perfectly captures this process of piecing together fragments of data to make sense of a messy problem and to determine how to act in relation to them: it is a description which works both at the individual level and at the level of the group, to which the next section turns.

A group DSS: preparing for a review of Trust strategic direction

As a part of effective management and, in part, to discharge public accountability, NHS Trusts are obliged to prepare and publish a summary of their annual business plans and, less frequently, statements of five-year strategic direction (NHS ME 1992). The review of strategic direction comes approximately once every three years, so many Trusts have now prepared such a statement of strategic direction twice. On the first occasion, Trusts usually drew heavily on their applications for Trust status. The second round has perhaps been more meaningful but, as a result, more difficult to circumscribe. Not only has the very idea of an 'internal market' been tested and adjusted, but health policy has developed, inevitably affecting the role of Trust services.

Case study

In 1995, Mid-Cheshire Hospitals, a first-wave acute NHS Trust, took the view that its first review of strategic direction should be a substantial development exercise which would deliver a Trust-wide working strategy and not just a public relations document. A Strategy Steering Group (comprising the Chief Executive, other executive directors and a non-executive director, the Head of Continuing Medical Education, and representatives of the CHC, the health authority and GPs) was established. I was invited to work with the Steering Group as 'facilitator' (Huxham and Cropper 1994).

This role was defined in the first stage of work with the group to start the process of building a shared sense of what the review exercise should be aiming to achieve; that is, 'agree a plan for the plan' (Bryson 1988). While the Chief Executive had prepared a briefing document including terms of reference for the review of strategic direction, some time had lapsed since they had been considered, and several members of the Steering Group had not been a party to the previous discussions. It seemed worth revisiting the purpose of the exercise. The 'means–ends' modelling technique was used as part of a method for supporting group decision making known as Strategic Options Development and Analysis (SODA) (Eden 1989).

Over a period of one week, I interviewed each member of the Steering Group and noted their views about the purpose of this planning effort in map form using pencil and paper. Between the last interview and the first meeting of the Steering Group some necessary 'backroom work' was completed; sorting and refining the data, weaving together complementary arguments and juxtaposing any conflicting views. A single integrated model of 180 constructs and 220 links resulted, which captured many significant arguments about the review of strategic direction.

Use of analytical procedures in the software had helped to reveal important characteristics of the model. Two analyses were particularly striking. First, the strategy task could be summarized (more neatly than is often the case) by nine interrelated propositions (Figure 13.7), shown as a hierarchy – 'making strategy more meaningful' is taken as the outcome which encompasses all the others. On the left hand side are three constructs reflecting concerns to relate the Trust's work to the context of health strategy and the notion of a primary-care-led NHS. On the right hand side are three constructs which suggest concern to ensure that the form of strategy and the process of development are such that strategy is a meaningful currency of management within the Trust. Finally, the two central constructs reflect a concern about the balance of activity and services within the Trust.

Each of these constructs was surrounded by a mass of more detailed issues and proposals as to how they might have come about, or might be achieved. For example, the statement, 'address issues of resourcing/activity (im)balance' at the base of the hierarchy summarized a complex of factors. Analysis of the model identified a vicious circle, fuelled by events and trends at various points in its structure – what Wolstenholme in Chapter 12 terms a reinforcing feedback loop (Figure 13.8). The basic loop relates consultant staffing levels, junior medical staffing and hospital activity. Fuelling factors include pressure on resourcing, loss of consultant staff (and posts) from the Trust, national requirements and standards affecting junior doctors, and the challenge of establishing appropriate continuing medical education.

At the first meeting of the Steering Group, a portable computer and a means of projecting its images through an overhead projector were used to take the group through the map (Figures 13.7 and 13.8 were two such images). As members of the group responded to the screens, their comments were added to the model, appearing immediately on the display and sparking discussion around areas of critical concern to the group. The following day, a print-out of the revised map was circulated as a record of the meeting.

The aim of this work was to ensure that the preparation of the framework for review and development of strategic direction was a well-considered process. A number of members of the SSG subsequently made a point of saying that the seven meetings that followed this intervention were different – opportunities to 'talk about ideas'. In part, this must be because strategy can be an excuse to stand back: but to do so also requires a process which enables an appropriate form of productivity. The major concern in the NHS has been with the cost of meetings (e.g. Knibbs and Sellick 1991) and with improving their efficiency rather than their effectiveness. This intervention represented a response to a call for a process which would ensure that the views of the various interests in the SSG were recognized and aired, in an organized and productive manner. This effort was informed by principles of group decision support (Eden and Radford 1990; Huxham and Cropper 1994), with the DSS as a means of drawing together initially diverse views, identifying important points for the group

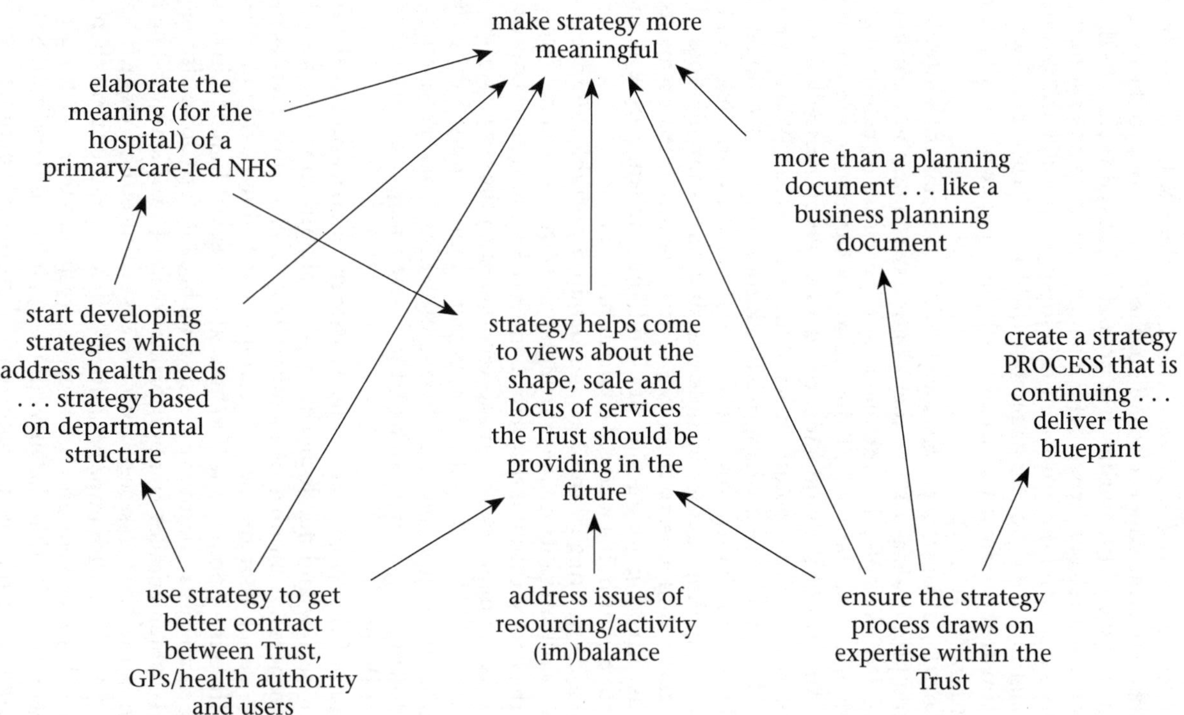

Figure 13.7 Overview hierarchy: steering the development of Trust strategic direction

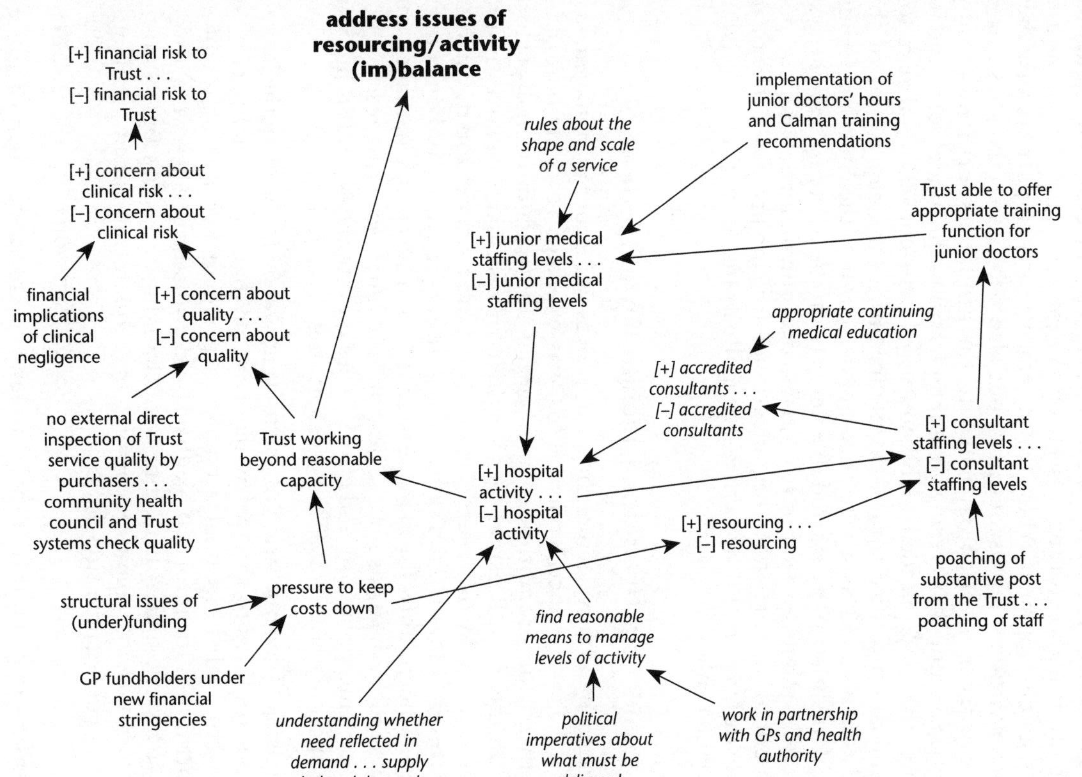

Figure 13.8 Vicious circle: balancing resources and activity

as a whole to recognize and consider, and enabling constructive negotiation about the purpose of the review of strategic direction.

The original intention was to continue with use of the DSS during subsequent meetings. After the first two meetings, however, attention was focused on converting the agreements reached by the group into guidance for the clinical directorates – seen by the group as the 'engine house' of strategy development. Maps travel rather poorly, in part because they are unconventional representations, but also because the language used in the constructs is often particular to the group; a shorthand rapidly develops. So while the Steering Group understood the model form and its contents, the maps needed to be converted into conventional text for communication to directorates. In the meantime, the paper copy of the map clusters served as a reference point to which the Steering Group returned as the strategy started to emerge from the directorates. The system served a purpose in supporting group decision making, but it had not broken out to support wider, organizational decision processes. The third example of DSS for IPR objective-setting illustrates how it can be used in such a wider role.

A DSS for IPR objective-setting, monitoring and review

Introduced in 1986 to strengthen the process of general management, Individual Performance Review (IPR) was expected to contribute substantially to the promotion of managerial and organizational performance. In theory, IPR establishes a system of task-like objectives in the form of a hierarchy or 'cascade' which, working from the top down, disaggregates the organization's objectives into targets, tasks and objectives and development aims for managers across each successive management tier. These form the basis for a review of individual performance.

Despite widespread use, and efforts to adapt it to the NHS, IPR has not been without its problems. Thus a recent study concluded:

> Criticisms of the operation of the present system focused on the lack of opportunities to the review team rather than individual performance, to relate individual to corporate performance and to provide opportunities for informal feedback and evaluation. They were also seen to lack flexibility in dealing with changing objectives and to suffer from lack of commitment and inadequate implementation in some [NHS organizations].
>
> (Dawson *et al.* 1995: 156)

Notwithstanding the difficulty of judging performance against objectives in a fair and consistent way, the process of setting objectives can become an annual 'raindance' rather than a meaningful discussion of purposeful action. Nor do the resulting lists reflect the complexity of linkage both between IPR objectives and between these and other organizational processes (Dawson *et al.* 1995; Flanagan and Spurgeon 1996).

Case study

At the time of wholesale mergers between provider units seeking Trust status, the newly appointed Director of Operations in an acute unit, newly formed from two hospital groups, saw the negotiation of IPR objectives as an opportunity to establish a shared set of expectations about the way the directorate would be managed. The directorate management team included eight heads of departments including Human Resources, Estates, Hotel Services and clinical support services. About half of the managers came from each of the two merged Trusts. In the post-merger uncertainty and anxiety, there were few clear signals about the direction the unit would take other than an intention to achieve Trust status in the next round: indeed, the implications for management work in the short- to mid-term were not defined and so there was little clear context for the IPR discussions. The issue was whether it would be possible to develop and impart a persuasive, motivating first sense of direction for this rather disparate directorate using the IPR process as a vehicle.

The Director had used the mapping and issue analysis approach on a previous occasion for development of a quality assurance strategy and had found it to be a means of combining a task focus with team and organizational development. Telford *et al.* (1992) report this organizational process and Ackermann *et al.* (1993) describe how a rudimentary DSS resulted: this recorded responsibilities for short-term actions in the context of the overall strategy. On that occasion, however, the more powerful output had been a series of written strategy documents. In this new, rapidly changing context, a computer-based DSS in which IPR objectives could be recorded – together with any other tasks, objectives and goals – seemed more appropriate. The content could be updated as discussion of strategy and purpose led to a clearer sense of direction: indeed, it might help achieve that clarity.

Discussions held between the Director of Operations and each member of the directorate management team produced a set of IPR objectives which met both individual and directorate needs. Sitting in on these meetings, however, it was clear that the discussions also contained broader statements about values and purpose and some emerging ideas about 'what was needed for the new Trust to move forward' (the Director's opening question to each of the heads of department): these statements were used in shaping, negotiating, testing and agreeing the IPR objectives. Quite often, they were reused and amplified by the Director of Operations as the series of interviews progressed and confidence developed that there was at least a basic shared agenda. For example, messages which the Director found a way of weaving into each discussion concerned 'skill mix', 'development of mechanisms for business management' and 'training for quality'. Such statements were added to the IPR model and used as ways of clustering the more specific objectives by type.

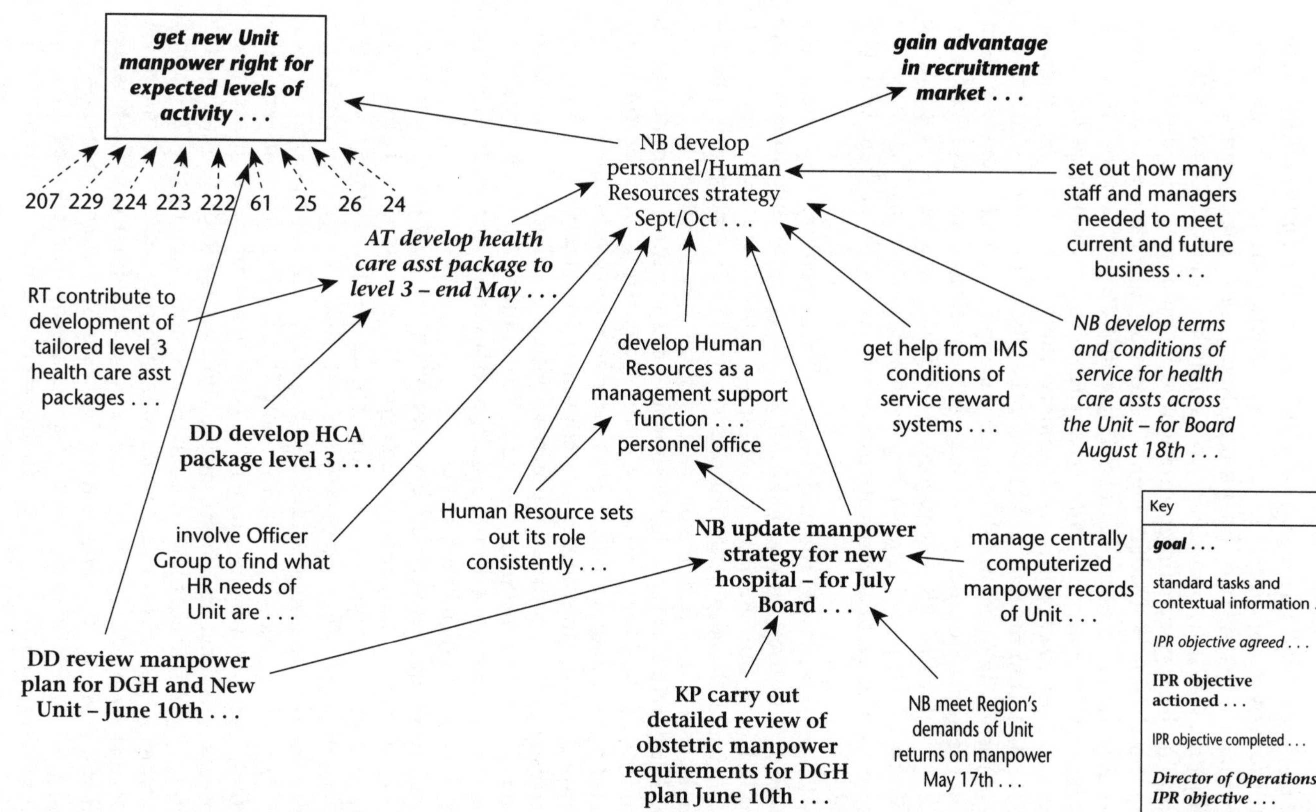

Figure 13.9 Fragment of the IPR DSS

All objectives concerned with promoting business management in the Trust, or a more entrepreneurial style of management were grouped together simply by linking them to the construct representing the theme. A third source of raw material for the DSS was found in emerging statements of strategy and direction for the Unit drawn from documents, texts of recent presentations by the Chief Executive, and elsewhere. These, too, were used as an anchor for the more fragmentary material, where appropriate.

The result was a preliminary model of the IPR objectives linked to fragments of a direction which represented the rationale and context to the objectives. To ensure that the source and status of each entry was clear, constructs were given particular styles so that, on screen and in print-outs, IPR objectives could easily be differentiated from other tasks, 'elements of strategy' and other statements of Trust-wide purpose. Where the IPR objectives related to each another directly – for example, where one member of the team had to deliver before another could make a start – this was clearly indicated by attaching their initials to their agreed IPR objectives. Where appropriate, a date for completion of the task was recorded. Figure 13.9 illustrates the nature of the DSS and shows, in particular, a cascade of objectives where one manager relied on another to complete an IPR objective.

As more material was added, including the Director's own IPR objectives and further contextual material from the first heads of departments meeting, it was possible to refine and elaborate the emerging direction. In working through this, the facilitator asked the Director of Operations about the way in which he kept track of progress on IPR and other objectives. Much of this monitoring and control activity was informal, although there was an existing computer-based system which automatically generated IPR 'reminders' and 'report forms' at different stages. This was most effective as the target date for completion approached. What the emerging DSS offered the Director of Operations was a means of anticipatory or 'forward control' (Ansoff and McDonnell 1990) in which his preferred style of management – more concerned with anticipating potential future problems than with identifying and correcting failures in performance – could be given some powerful support.

A simple convention for tracking and recording progress was agreed. IPR objectives were initially coloured red on the screen. When the manager responsible confirmed that a start had been made, it could be recoloured green (for 'go'). As the task was tackled and then completed, the style would be changed to purple and dark blue respectively. Using simple sorting and retrieval commands, it was then possible to see at a glance how each individual was doing against the six or so IPR objectives each had agreed. Other substantial development tasks allocated to the managers were also recorded in the system and helped the Director assess workload. Lists of IPR objectives at the different stages could be generated and compared against the overall set, enabling the Director to check whether there were any developments which were moving too slowly. The map displays also helped to show whether there were any tasks which were likely to cause a hold-up on other IPR objectives.

However, for the computer-based system to be sustainable and useful, some further steps were required. In particular, the Director of Operations needed to be confident he could update and use it independently and that the system would not 'fall apart' as a result. He wanted to be able to use the system as an integral part of the management process, rather than as backroom support and to be able to sit with the managers in his directorate using the system as necessary to define new objectives and tasks and to review progress on existing tasks. This would, in effect, help juggle and balance the absolute and relative demands on each individual and assess how priorities should be reinforced or shifted in relation to wider strategic direction. Ultimately, he wanted to be able to use the system as a way of keeping track of strategy at Trust and directorate levels, as it emerged, and to map the relationships between them.

Two training courses were held, involving the Director of Operations, the Head of Training and a clinical manager. Further visits to the Trust to work with them led to the preparation of a DSS manual, with instructions for use tailored to the types of use the Director typically made of the system. A habit of ten minutes use of the system each morning and increasingly frequent use with managers both led to a gradual development of in-house ability. Eventually the Director reached the stage where the system was used in both formal and informal meetings and reviews, and was regularly maintained by the Director of Operations and/or supporting staff. The system promoted strategic thinking across the directorate management team, and formed a *usable* part of the organizational memory (Walsh and Ungson 1991).

This DSS was tightly linked to the managerial style of a particular individual and to that individual's good experience of computer-based decision support systems. The relationship between manager and system developer was crucial here, for the development effort required something of an act of faith. On the basis of past experience, the manager could understand broadly what the development effort might produce and, just as importantly, that it would be genuinely committed to meeting his needs. The system developer, too, contributed not just technical expertise, but also suggested and rapidly tried out with the Director possible managerial uses of the system as it developed; this seemed to bring about a more appropriate and effective outcome. The investment resulted in a DSS which contributed both to the Director's managerial competence and to that of the directorate management team.

The use of a DSS results from an intense understanding of its origins and potential and a close fit between system and managerial style. With the retirement of the Director, the system has not survived as an organizational process – the commitment to it (despite efforts to broaden involvement and use) was, in the end, too closely vested in one person.

Conclusions

Objective-setting, monitoring and review is a pervasive managerial activity. Where management tasks are complex, circumstances are uncertain or emotionally charged, it can be helpful to work intensively on finding an appropriate direction and actions which are consistent with that direction. Quinn (1980) has suggested that analytical and planning processes:

- encourage vigorous communication about goals, issues and resources;
- make possible the creation of a network of information and understanding;
- enable managers to extend time horizons and to broaden their view;
- link anticipation of the future back to short-term decision making;
- offer a greater sense of comfort about the future in the face of anxiety; and
- allow preparation for specific strategic decisions.

None of these will be achieved without an appropriately designed and managed process of strategic thinking. In finding such a process and then in holding the results of thinking and deliberation for future reference, a flexible, approachable and non-prescriptive means of support can be valuable. The cases described have been used to illustrate a means–ends modelling technique and computer-based tool which have provided support to managers seeking to make sense of difficult, complex tasks related to setting and addressing a future direction.

The qualitative modelling and DSS which COPE and its underlying methodology offer can help in articulating systems of objectives which are directly related to the issues and problems which are most powerfully felt by managers: the need to find a practical, plausible and coherent way forward, in the face of intense uncertainty and complexity.

Acknowledgements

The ideas of my colleagues Colin Eden, Fran Ackermann and Chris Huxham endure and are plain to see. Thanks are due to Judith, Mid-Cheshire Hospitals NHS Trust and its Strategy Steering Group, and especially, the Director of Ops for valuable insight into their ways of thinking. None, of course, are required to agree with the translation.

References

Ackermann, F., Cropper, S. and Eden, C. (1993) The role of decision support in Individual Performance Review, in P. W. G Bots, H. G. Sol and R. Traunmuller (eds) *Decision Support in Public Administration* (A-26). North Holland, Elsevier.

Ackoff, R. L. (1981) The art and science of mess management, *Interfaces*, 11: 20–6.

Ansoff, I. and McDonnell, E. (1990) *Implanting Strategic Management*. London, Prentice Hall.

Bentley, D. (1992) *Practical PRINCE – a Guide to Structured Project Management*. Oxford, Blackwell/NCC.

Blackham, R. B. and Corless, R. (1992) The potential of cognitive mapping in planning health provision, *Journal of Management in Medicine*, 6: 13–22.

Bryson, J. (1988) *Strategic Planning for Public and Non-Profit Organisations*. San Francisco, Jossey-Bass.

Cropper, S., Ackermann, F. and Eden, C. (1992) Exploring and negotiating collective action through computer-aided cognitive mapping, *The Environmental Professional*, 15: 176–85.

Dawson, S., Winstanley, D., Mole, V. and Sherval, J. (1995) *Managing in the NHS: a Study of Senior Executives*. London, HMSO.

Eden, C. (1986) Problem solving or problem finishing, in M. Jackson and P. Keys (eds) *New Directions in Management Science*. Aldershot, Gower.

Eden, C. (1988) Cognitive mapping: a review, *European Journal of Operational Research*, 36: 1–13.

Eden, C. (1989) Using cognitive mapping for strategic options development and analysis (SODA), in J. Rosenhead (ed.) *Rational Analysis for a Problematic World: Problem Structuring Methods for Complexity, Uncertainty and Conflict*. Chichester, Wiley.

Eden, C. (1990) Strategic thinking with computers, *Long Range Planning*, 23: 35–43.

Eden, C. (1991) Working on problems using cognitive mapping, in S. C. Littlechild and M. Shutler (eds) *Operational Research for Managers*. Oxford, Prentice Hall.

Eden, C. and Radford, J. (eds) (1990) *Tackling Strategic Problems: The Role of Group Decision Support*. London, Sage.

Eden, C., Ackermann, F. and Cropper, S. (1992) The analysis of cause maps, *Journal of Management Studies*, 29: 309–24.

Flanagan, H. and Spurgeon, P. (1996) *Public Sector Managerial Effectiveness: Theory and Practice in the National Health Service*. Buckingham, Open University Press.

Huxham, C. S. and Cropper, S. A. (1994) From many to one: an exploration of some issues in facilitation. *Omega, International Journal of Management Science*, 22: 1–11.

Knibbs, J. and Sellick, R. (1991) Tell them I'm in a meeting, *Health Service Journal*, 101: 18–19.

NHS Management Executive (1992) *Business Planning Guidance*. London, Department of Health.

Procter, R. A. (1991) The importance of creativity in the management field, *British Journal of Management*, 2: 223–30.

Quinn, J. B. (1980) *Strategies for Change: Logical Incrementalism*. Homewood, IL, Richard D. Irwin.

Roginski, C. (1995) Applying SODA in the NHS: a facilitator's story, *OR Insight*, 8: 28–32.

Selznick, P. (1957) *Leadership in Administration*. New York, Harper and Row.

Telford, W. A., Cropper, S. A. and Ackermann, F. (1992) Quality assurance: the role of strategy building, *International Journal of Health Care Quality Assurance*, 5: 5–11.

Walsh, J. P. and Ungson, G. R. (1991) Organizational memory, *Academy of Management Review*, 16: 57–91.

Software availability

Graphics COPE, now marketed as Decision Explorer, is available from Banxia Software Ltd, 141 St James Road, Glasgow G4 0LT. Tel: (+44) 0141 552 3082, fax: (+44) 0141 552 5765.

Part 5
Future prospects

Introduction

The chapter by David Clayden and Martyn Croft examines future prospects for computer-based decision support systems both in terms of potential changes already taking place on the technological side, and in terms of potential applications that will be required by users. It is also likely that new technologies may create new demands hitherto not considered. There are limiting factors, however. While advances in technology proceed, consideration needs to be given to the training and skills base of those people who will use such systems. There are also likely to be major implications for hierarchical management structures as information – at least potentially – becomes more widely available. Decision processes will also have to change as more explicit bases for resource decisions develop. Time previously taken in merely assembling raw data can be used instead for deliberation and analysis and, specifically, in considering a wider range of options.

Future prospects: issues, informatics and methodologies

David Clayden and Martyn Croft

Introduction

The DSS described in this book cover a wide range of management scenarios in health service settings. A number of factors influencing their adoption and effective use have been noted, including:

1 Intellectual considerations, driving the need for 'better' *use of information* for decision making, are fundamental to the requirement for, and effective utilization of, DSS. All information-based interventions rely on the belief that more appropriate, timely, and accurate information leads to better decision making.

2 Technological innovations or limitations also set boundaries or open new frontiers in the field of information; changes in the *use of technology* offer new ways of supporting (and sometimes hindering) decision making process in health services management.

3 DSS solutions need to be incorporated into business processes and to respond to – and help shape – changes in the socio-organizational environment. The issues and methodologies of *implementing information support* need to be better understood in order to resolve and avoid some of the difficulties identified in this book and elsewhere. The importance of this understanding cannot be underestimated as it will shape the future role and success of DSS.

An analysis of the history of information-related activities in the NHS is needed before passing any judgement on likely future changes in these areas. This chapter briefly reviews ways in which information has been used, ways in which information technology (IT) is changing, and lessons which have been learned in implementing DSS in health service management. This establishes the basis for the form and direction of DSS in the future, and the chapter concludes with some thoughts and speculations as to its potential nature.

The use of information

Information assists in the formation of ideas (our own, or shared and communicated with others), and also in the confirmation or refutation of notions which have been previously formed. It can lead directly to a decision or, more commonly in a strategic timeframe, it can address questions along the lines of 'What would happen if . . .?' It is here that decision support is particularly relevant, as the case studies earlier have argued. Information simply presented as 'facts' may not be readily appreciated by the user; it may possibly require skilled interpretation to make it comprehensive, or salient, or both. Managers' attitude or receptiveness to information is vital. There is evidence, for example, that clinicians who read the results of clinical trials in medical journals are less likely to change their practice in line with the published findings than their peers directly involved in the clinical trial or other scientific research. Thus the influence of information seems to reduce with the remoteness of involvement and with the strength of other contextual factors which impinge on the relationship between communication of guidance and change in a doctor's behaviour (Harrison 1994). Advice gained simply through access to information is in constant danger of becoming just a 'background noise'. This, in turn, has important implications for establishing shared professional or organizational views and procedures.

The growing use of electronic mail (e-mail) in organizations suggests that 'the written word', is readily transferable from paper to an electronic medium, and can be processed more efficiently (Rudy 1996). However, providing managers with tables of data or graphs to guide business decisions can be more difficult, because the same understanding, skills and attitudes are not always present to the same extent as they are with natural language, nor is the context and type of activity quite so familiar.

Kinston (1985) proposes that measurement can be represented at five levels:

1 identifying and *labelling* an entity, representing it as an object of interest or value (e.g. 'This is a hospital bed');
2 *observing* entities, in other words defining them in practical terms and counting them (e.g. 'Do we agree how a daycase is defined?');
3 *comparing* the value of different entities against a standard (e.g. ranking them according to criteria such as usage or cost);
4 *measuring* entities, and thus quantifying them (e.g. how many patients can occupy a bed in a period of time under defined circumstances);
5 *making a relation* between entities to provide meaning in a specific context (e.g. the occupancy of the beds can be seen to change the patients' lengths of stay and the efficiency with which patients are discharged and admitted).

Much of the measurement work in the NHS has focused on the first two levels, which gives rise to a 'data rich' organization. The impact of the reforms has been to place more emphasis on levels three and four, while the fifth level has become increasingly significant as organizations seek to become more accountable, efficient and effective in their use of resources – or, in other words, 'better managed'.

There is an important distinction to make between activities in the first four levels, which are primarily concerned with *handling* data (including the practical tasks of defining, creating, collecting, storing and retrieving it), and the fifth level where establishing the *value* of information is the principal characteristic. Those who have most to gain through having appropriate access to information are generally in the position of defining the tasks which lead to the definition, observation, comparison and measuring of information, and are required to interpret the results from the fifth level. Between the levels, information (and decision) support may be required, and the extent of this support varies between individuals and between roles.

Bensaou and Venkatraman (1996) describe the performance of an organization as a balance between information processing *needs* and information processing *capabilities*. Focus on the former can be seen as ways of reducing uncertainty: in an organization's environment (e.g. the continued process of change in the political and operating environment); on internal and inter-organizational uncertainties (e.g. changes in organizational boundaries and responsibilities); and on uncertainty surrounding tasks which have to be carried out. Three sources of this 'task uncertainty' are described: the ability to define the actions required for each task; the frequency of unanticipated events; and interdependencies between tasks.

The information processing capabilities of an organization are expressed in terms of their coordinating mechanisms. To improve structure and clarity in processes, there has been much organizational restructuring and 'business process re-engineering' work to provide IT support. These IT-mediated mechanisms are considered to have important characteristics positively related to information processing capability, including their intensity of use, their degree of access, their integration and their scope. While mostly grounded in 'technology', their effective application relies on appropriate human involvement; that is, a willingness – as well as an ability – to share knowledge.

While in recent years the capacity to manipulate, transform and compare data has been put within the reach of all managers by the proliferation of the desktop PC, it can also be argued that there has not been a concomitant expansion in the appropriate and effective use of this technology or in training for it. Current information management and technology (IMT) training tends to concentrate on 'hands on' skills training – the ability to use software rather than establishing what to do with it or how to assess information critically for its appropriateness in addressing a particular management issue.

Take, for example, a modern spreadsheet – a basic yet powerful decision support tool aimed at non-expert users and available on every computer. It might contain up to 20 specific data analysis functions in addition to more than 300 general-purpose programmable functions. For most average users this is a positively overwhelming capability for information analysis. Spreadsheets make it simple to collate, compare, summarize and present information, but 'making sense' of what it means is still the prerogative of the manager. While differing interpretations of the same dataset can offer a richness of management choice, it is also possible that well-presented, seemingly comparable analyses may actually have been based on different assumptions, measurements and even different datasets, thus confounding the issues at stake.

A recent series of IMT courses delivered to senior clinicians (Clayden 1995) provided participants from one regional health authority with methods, techniques and information to enable them to structure and analyse their own research, clinical and resource-related situations in the context of national and local IT actions and possibilities. A pre-course questionnaire completed by the participants showed that almost all had access to a PC, often available at both home and work, and that the majority of them used a PC for more than half an hour every day. However, much of this work was wordprocessing, with few of the participants familiar with even the basic principles of manipulating data in a spreadsheet. Many of them felt helpless working with data from the information systems in their hospitals and, where they did act to structure their information gathering, they tended to do so in isolation from other information systems.

DSS are usually designed in support of a particular management task, often integrating and using data obtained from the standard reports of a number of information systems. However, their frequent development as 'stand-alone' software applications means that these data often require re-entering into the DSS rather than automatically feeding into it. The overall scope of corporate data requirements includes:

- business planning and operational management of hospital processes;
- the administration of patients;
- clinical care information, and review of its quality;
- access to data from a variety of sources to a variety of users;
- provision of clinical support.

These data tend to be held in many disparate systems; this, in turn, poses problems for users requiring reconciliation and summaries of cross-functional data. This situation seems unlikely to be quickly remedied in the future since the perceived benefits and ease of implementation suggest that insular, departmental information systems will continue to be developed (although perhaps under the guise of being described as 'modular' solutions where, in theory, they can be linked). In these circumstances the information user will continue to be faced with the collation of multiple datasets which have similar values for the same items, but rarely contain the same data. Experience shows that decision making in the presence of conflicting information is often worse than having no information at all.

In establishing a data-rich environment we should consider whether the computer-literate, data-aware health care manager and clinician will become a reality, or whether management by information will still require numerate intermediaries. Maybe it will remain an unattainable goal. In the meantime there will be a continuing reliance on 'specialists' not only to design and construct information systems, but also to operate them and, often, interpret their output. These factors limit the way in which DSS can be effective – through problems in the availability of appropriate data, and through difficulties users have in making valid and effective use of information to instigate change in work practice.

The use of technology

Over the past 10 to 15 years many NHS Trusts bought 'off-the-shelf' computer systems in order to minimize risk, and to enable a speedy delivery of the system and its benefits. Some of these systems have proved to have a short shelf life as technical limitations related to storage or processing capacity became evident, or changes in functionality were required before, during and after their implementation, making system specifications become rapidly out of date. More adventurous Trusts invested in partly developed systems, or even had systems developed to meet their own specifications to try and get around some of these problems.

With continuing pressure to implement new (and update existing) information systems, it is likely that data derived from planning and delivering health care will become increasingly available (Department of Health 1990). These 'transaction' data (typically held in patient administration systems such as PAS) are beginning to be made available alongside data concerned with the functioning of laboratory services or operating theatres, to inform decisions that cross functional boundaries (see Morgan 1996). This is becoming possible through a move towards the use of relational database management systems (RDBMS) for data storage in preference to more traditional file-based data management (Date 1986). Although the tendency has been to stick with well-differentiated, process-based systems (which are also tried and tested) and which collect mainly transaction-based data, the need to provide support for health care functions in totality rather than isolation has encouraged the growth of the 'corporate database' and the migration towards an RDBMS system. The design aspects and performance constraints of current database systems suggest that multiple database, and indeed multiple vendor, sites will continue to be the norm, confounding a view that NHS datasets can potentially be standardized.

In a market as volatile and dynamic as health care computing, the only predictable feature is that there will be an increase, rather than decrease in the variability of approach, as technological advances provide short-term business benefits to one company or another. However, the trend towards RDBMS-based systems is likely to benefit the DSS practitioner. While developments are awaited in technical areas, such as parallel processing, to deliver respite from the problems of maintaining both 'real time' transaction processing and analytical processing queries across the corporate database, post-processing of archive data into a 'data warehouse' can provide an important source for DSS datasets.

The NHS Data Model (NHS Corporate Data Administration 1986) and the Common Basic Specification (Frandji *et al.* 1994) together define a generalized model of all health care data items. As an example of an integrated information system, the Hospital Information Support System (HISS) initiative (discussed later) sought to encompass all data in a single whole hospital information system, consisting of IT support for:

- an integrated patient-based environment (corporate and functional applications for the administration and the direct clinical care of patients);
- a data communication network (allowing the integration of data from, and enabling access by users to, all applications);
- an order communications system (providing clinical support services);
- external links (to other external organizations, such as purchasers, GPs, etc.).

Hospitals also require business, clinical review and resource management systems. These are not part of the core functionality of a HISS, although data from the core functions are integral to its operation. Data from HISS can also provide a valuable source for use in decision support systems.

When available, an RDBMS can provide a useful platform for DSS as, with data specification and system design work already in place, DSS developers can concentrate on the application, and not its data feeds. However, DSS to date do not seem to have been a priority at the limited number of hospital sites which have a HISS. The focus of obtaining data for contracting, lack of DSS skills in-house, and lack of awareness of DSS or their potential among managers and clinicians has tended to keep the number of implementations small. Instead, more 'reactive' information systems have focused on addressing the development of executive or management information systems (EIS/MIS) able to take advantage of the RDBMS to present the data in the most applicable and appealing way to the information user. Add to this popular spreadsheets, such as Microsoft Excel and Lotus 123, which can also access RDBMS, and it seems clear at first sight that there is immense scope for delivering DSS directly to the user's desktop without the involvement of any DSS professionals. However, as these systems proliferate and become easier for the end-user to implement, the likely risks of seeing nonsense information (such as a 'mean ward of admission'!) will increase, and the previously made points about the need for appropriate education in the critical use of information, as well as the development of technical skills, will become vitally important.

The inclusion of metadata (data about the data) in the database – and the mechanisms to do so in future RDBMS – will also help managers obtain more meaningful data. The task facing such applications in the short term, however, is to ensure that if the user does not understand the constraints of the data, then the application itself does; perhaps through forms of automatic checking procedures.

Implementing information support

Over the last 20 years, there have been massive changes in health and health care provision, impacting on the support that managers require for decision making – the discussion in Chapter 1 has highlighted the consequences. Developments in information and medical technology have shown the potential to identify needs and support health care – encouraged by, and requiring, a dramatic growth in clinical and managerial knowledge.

However, the health service has a poor record of implementing the sorts of information systems required to collect the 'nuts-and-bolts' data about its day-to-day management. With little data of adequate quality, the type of support traditionally provided to managers by backroom data analysts in other types of organizations has rarely been seen in anything but the higher echelons of the NHS. Responses to situations requiring management intervention at an operational level have often been made with summary information arising from intuition, precedent, and disregard of up-to-the-minute data, while solutions requiring a broader view of the corporate situation have been difficult to support technically.

During the 1990s there were a number of Government-sponsored information initiatives associated with the NHS reforms. Two key initiatives of relevance to the use and future of DSS were the Resource Management Initiative (RMI) and the HISS programme. The focus of both initiatives was on acute hospital care but, since then, more attention has been paid to primary and community care, and their interface with acute care.

The Resource Management Initiative

The aims of the RMI, established by the Department of Health in 1990, were to enable acute hospitals to assess and improve their data and data processing resources, and to provide management information with appropriate and timely data to support the running of services and the contracting process (Health Economics Research Group 1991). These implementations were of *information systems* rather than *decision support systems*.

In some hospitals, the functionality of the information systems extended to provide medical or clinical audit, and improved laboratory results reporting. Clinicians were involved to differing extents, but with a clear 'steer' towards the definition and adoption of more efficient ways of managing resources to provide health care. Overall conclusions (see Packwood *et al.* 1991) from the RMI intervention were that there were:

- key technological shortcomings in hospital information systems;
- inadequate databases and interfaces;
- insufficient appropriate IT skills in NHS staff;
- inappropriate implementations of systems.

The HISS programme

The HISS programme has had variable success in the UK. Since the early 1980s, a number of 'big bang' procurements and implementations have been followed by a larger number of 'incremental' implementations. There are 24 suppliers listed in the HISS Catalogue as providing complete HISS, or HISS elements (NHS Executive Information Management Group 1994). Working systems to be found on hospital sites have tended to be difficult to apply directly to others, in business, technology and implementation terms. The 'roll-out' of major hospital information systems is now seen to be as much a 'people and implementation' exercise as a technology project.

The effects of these initiatives have been to create a major increase in IT infrastructure and to have improved the validity of data and efficiencies in resource use, but they have also put some strain on the manager–clinician and clinician–clinician relationship. The lack of an integrated approach to examining and changing multidisciplinary working practices in parallel with IT investment has restricted the benefits from that investment. However, recent moves towards evidence-based medicine and the establishment of treatment protocols have followed medical and clinical audit initiatives, and work on the adoption of common clinical terms (NHS Executive Information Management Group 1995) may improve the potential for DSS based on the new IT infrastructure.

Above all, however, the information systems of a health care organization need to be based on the philosophy and the objectives of the organization, and the policies and procedures which are applied in delivering its services. The successful operation of the organization will be limited by the extent to which the business objectives, policies and processes, the staff abilities, motivation and mode of work as well as the IT strategy, design, implementation and support are all in harmony (Scott-Morton 1991). There have been a number of DSS implementations in health services in recent years. However, often the work is only known within the organization or department where the application is carried out.

DSS currently working depend largely on their own local or departmental information systems, and not on any coherent organization-wide dataset. This has been a defining constraint in that the hard data to support an analysis of problem areas may be lacking. Simulation-based systems may address this issue to some extent by synthesizing data. Recent information developments, referred to in this section, will improve the current situation but still require some educated model of the various business processes on which to base their functions. With a focus on the likely trend for an increase in data quantity and an improvement of data quality the following section addresses some of the areas that may underpin the future of decision support systems.

Future prospects

The previous sections have described the current environment and have suggested how it may change in the immediate future. Recall the intellectual, technological and socio-organizational influences described in Chapter 1. These drive the short-term future requirements, in terms of users and their requirements, technological direction, and the implementation of the health care information agenda, and DSS developers need to take these into account. The final part of the chapter, however, goes on to consider some longer-term prospects.

How will our use of information develop?

Several points can be made with confidence. The increased availability of high powered software, together with universal access within organizations to data about the organization, is likely to lead to a *greater utilization of data in decision making*. The current use of on-line services to identify and obtain relevant research papers, journals, books, etc. is likely to expand, and more extensive use will be made of the World Wide Web on the Internet to access simulations, video clips, and sound to communicate the context of the results as well as the results themselves.

With the increased use of PCs as a device for presenting information from sources beyond those controlled by the staff of an organization, there will be an increased reliance on *access to evidence* from observations – and interpretations – of others rather than from personal experience.

From here, the forward view becomes more exploratory. *Experience* will increasingly be gained through information systems and DSS, rather than as a direct 'hands-on' event. A combination of simulation and virtual reality will enable experience to be gained by junior managers and clinicians. Already there are developments in this field; one example is the use of virtual reality in simulating patient flow through an outpatient clinic (Ferreira de Oliveiro 1995). Here the user sees the rooms and people on a screen and can view the simulation from 'within', adopting the perspectives of different participants – patient, receptionist, nurse, doctor – as required.

Developments like this may encourage more *risk-taking behaviour* by decision makers. They will have some justification for their actions because these are underpinned by the assumptions used by others skilled in creating the virtual world. Indeed, this development will be a logical extension of the current vogue for 'evidence-based practice'. It is just that the 'evidence' will be in a different form, with the intellectual work in creating these virtual environments being as much the responsibility of the system developers as the 'clinical technicians' doing the face-to-face work. Or, decision makers will find that decisions are increasingly arbitrary, the decision basis insufficiently varied to enable effective recognition of patterns and differences and discriminate between problems and background noise (Weick 1985).

Application of *knowledge-based approaches* and software to managerial problems will become commonplace. In operation such systems will analyse the available data for rules. Algorithms for inference of rules from example data are well understood and can generate production type rules of an 'if *x*, then *y*' style. Application of rules of this type, both derived and factual, by an expert system could offer an essential variation to the more traditional management indicators, enabling automatic interrogation of databases. Reporting 'by exception' will become the norm as volumes of data rise, and processes become more defined. Information will be on a 'need to know' basis. With the removal of layers of coordinating management from health organizations, and their functions being undertaken by technology operating defined processes, specialists and 'troubleshooters' will be required, able to respond to situations that cannot be coped with automatically.

Educational requirements will change, with the criteria for accepting medical and nursing students for training, for example, changing towards flexibility and imagination, rather than memory and stamina. The clinical curriculum will need to focus more on rational, experiential, decision-supported exercises rather than mass repetitive storage of known 'clinical facts' (which change with knowledge over time so that recently qualified clinicians have out-of-date knowledge). The pressure to be continually up to date will result in an increased demand for both facts and understanding. Here the role of clinical DSS in meeting the need for rapid access to medical knowledge, using combinations of concise and focused local 'expert systems', and making extensive use of on-line access to remote, encyclopaedic databases (as noted by Bradley in Chapter 7) is already being explored. The management training agenda will also have to adapt and develop, with greater training being given to understanding and appreciating modelling.

What changes in technology are likely?

In meeting these changing demands, technology has a crucial role. Advances are significant here, both in functionality and speed.

General hardware and software developments

The adoption of modern hardware platforms and RDBMS for applications software will enable greater future *integration* of corporate data. The definition and widespread adoption of a variety of international *data standards* will also provide better 'goalposts' for companies to aim at when designing computer systems or system components. Cheaper and more powerful hardware will, in turn, support modern software development and enable very *rapid application development*. This is likely to provide the flexibility for change that is required by users to the extent that system development will also fulfil user demands for a more complex, but friendly, human–computer interface to be realized.

Mass storage and rapid access to *image data* is expected to revolutionize the potential for accessing up-to-date clinical data, as well as handling *multimedia data* (sound, voice, video, image, text). This will provide a greatly expanded role for the *clinical workstation*.

Knowledge-based systems will become more prevalent, driven by the availability of both the technology and formalized clinical and business knowledge. To date, the merger of EIS and DSS has been slow; however, an information robot or 'infobot' capable of keeping a watching brief and delivering advice on particular areas of concern may prove an interesting prospect.

The rapid expansion of networking and associated communications technologies will provide opportunities for access to *external information sources* (see Sheaff 1995) such as the World Wide Web (WWW) or to marketing or clinical effectiveness databases, in addition to existing internal networks which the current generation hospital information systems have concentrated on. Such services may become obligatory clinical and medical education requirements for major hospitals, and will certainly be valuable in attracting high calibre staff. More sophisticated and automated searching procedures with global access will enable 'up to date' to mean 'instant'.

Patient-focused technological developments

The *geographical* constraint will be reduced or even removed in some cases, with patients able to 'consult' with doctors for screening, diagnosis, treatment and monitoring, without having to attend a clinic or hospital. Surgical *treatments* will be possible using robots and high speed telecommunications lines. In a similar fashion non-clinical managers will be able to consult with specialists able to screen for organizational support conditions, and to cure organizational ills, by remotely 'tuning' the 'management module' of the overall health care information system.

More will be known about individual patients from birth to death. Data on genetic susceptibilities, regular health monitoring statistics, contacts with health and other social services will enable rich evaluations of *individual risks and interventions* (as opposed to group evaluations). Each patient *will* be different, and this will enable optimum treatment when health parameters fall outside quality control confidence limits. Resource management will become based on the projection or extrapolation of individual life histories.

One system containing patient-relevant data which will remain 'noncorporate', however, is the actual patient! Historically, it is a doctor's role to extract relevant data from the patient and store them in a structured form for further processing during treatment. The patient may in future keep this information themselves, as a copy of, or substitute for, records held by the organization. With increasing levels of education, awareness of patients' rights and accepted standards of care, there is likely to be a greater degree of scrutiny of patient information: by the patient, searching for focused information via WWW-type services, and by doctors, keeping abreast of data from the latest research and about practice policy.

Future consultations are less likely to involve patients visiting their GP in the first place: advances in telecommunications should make feasible distance consultations with highly specialist doctors using decision support from video conferences. Doctors will provide greater access to their own knowledge bases while using on-screen patient-specific information. In the future a doctor's 'screenside' (rather than bedside) manner may well become more important.

What changes in implementation of DSS are likely?

With the massive organizational and business changes which have taken place there are a number of implications for the implementation of decision support systems in the future.

To support the geographical dispersal of health care provision based on patient preference and cost will require not only new technologies but also an ability to access and use information. Greater automation of processes which are currently manual will be inevitable (e.g. to collect and store relevant data, to act in an apparently intelligent manner when information is requested, and to provide advice). Processes that are currently largely information-independent will be linked to reduce waste of effort and error, and to provide benefits in better treatment through clinical and managerial collaboration.

Data and IT in health care will become much more available, enabling better corporate use of IT to support decisions and business planning.

Education in the appropriate use of information, especially how to manage it, will become more vital. Merely knowing where to get the data or use a model 'mechanically' will no longer be sufficient.

Improvements in multimedia require a greater understanding of the human–computer interface. DSS design needs to consider that technical developments take place more rapidly than the capacity for the management culture to absorb it fully.

Perhaps more important, however, will be an understanding of how to manage interactions between changing organizations, changing information systems and the knowledge they each contain. Current efforts make use of local stand-alone systems to 'repair' the previous attempts at creating integrated systems. We offer a view which sees emerging technologies, and understanding about their place in organizing and management processes, as the basis for a combination of the two previous approaches.

Ancient to modern?

Health care consists of a complex set of processes. With the future developments identified above, it will become more, not less, complicated. In ancient times, when a drama was performed which involved a complex plot, a device called a *deus ex machina* was introduced into the play, to resolve the situation being portrayed. A system is proposed, a DEcision Utopian Support (DEUS), with similar characteristics, which will help resolve future health care decision support problems.

Unquestionably these systems will be smart, providing ready access to a vast resource of data from a variety of contexts throughout the world. They will have interfaces that will make them approachable and easily used, adapting readily to the knowledge, skill level and requirements of the user. From their knowledge base they will be able to take control and make routine business decisions automatically, only asking advice or guidance from the human when events outside their knowledge domain occur, or when the implications of a decision are critical. Their decisions will be open to interrogation and modification at all times, but only to users with the right to override this support.

Those currently responsible for decision making will feel either stimulated or threatened by such systems. Education rather than training will be a necessity and will be increasingly mediated by this type of DSS. Those who fail to learn will 'do' rather than decide. Roles in management need revising to take account of the needs for valid data sources and to provide the necessary elements of human expertise.

Finally, and heroically, the holistic view taken by DEUS will make redundant any apparent benefits of short-term or crisis-style management strategies. Indeed, automatic consideration and *post hoc* review of past decisions and outcomes will ensure a consistency of approach to management through evaluation and sound advice.

Ultimately, health care and health services management are incredibly complex processes, ill-understood at this time and arguably impossible to encapsulate in rigid rules. It is the extent to which managers, clinicians and information users are prepared to work collaboratively with each other, and are prepared to be guided by *decision* support systems, rather than the available information technology, which will dictate the nature and form of that support in the future.

References

Bensaou, M. and Venkatraman, N. (1996) Inter-organizational relationships and information technology: a conceptual thesis and a research framework, *European Journal of Information Systems*, 5: 84–91.

Clayden, A. D. (1995) *Information Management and Technology Workshop*. Leeds, Nuffield Institute for Health, University of Leeds.

Date, C. J. (1986) *An Introduction to Database Systems, Vol. 1*, 4th edition. Reading, MA, Addison Wesley.

Department of Health (1990) *Working for Patients: Framework for Information Systems: Information*. HMSO, London.

Ferreira de Oliveiro, M. J. (1995) 3D visual simulation and hospital admission systems management: the flow of patients in a virtual scenario, in *Proceedings of the 21st Meeting of the European Working Group on Operational Research Applied to Health Services*. Maastricht, ORAHS.

Frandji, B., Schot, J., Joubert, M., Soady, I. and Kilsdonk, A. (1994) The RICHE reference architecture, *Journal of Medical Informatics*, 19: 1–11.

Harrison, S. (1994) Knowledge into practice: what's the problem? *Journal of Management in Medicine*, 8: 9–16.

Health Economics Research Group (1991) *Final Report of the Brunel University Evaluation of Resource Management*, Health Economics Research Group Research Report 10. Uxbridge, Brunel University.

Kinston, W. (1985) Measurement and the structure of scientific analysis, *Systems Research*, 2: 95–104.

Morgan, R. F. (1996) An intelligent decision support system for a health authority: solving information overload, *Journal of the Operational Research Society*, 47: 570–82.

NHS Corporate Data Administration (1986) *NHS Data Model Version 1*, Volume 1, Birmingham, NHS Corporate Data Administration.

NHS Executive Information Management Group (1994) *HISS Catalogue*. Leeds, Department of Health.

NHS Executive Information Management Group (1995) *Clinical Terms Development and Refinement Projects*. Leeds, Department of Health.

Packwood, T., Keen, J. and Buxton, M. (1991) *Hospitals in Transition: the Resource Management Experiment*. Buckingham, Open University Press.

Rudy, A. (1996) A critical review of research on electronic mail, *European Journal of Information Systems*, 4: 198–213.

Scott-Morton, M. S. (ed.) (1991) *The Corporation of the 1990s: Information Technology and Organisational Transformation*. Oxford, Oxford University Press.

Sheaff, R. (1995) The future of UK health informatics, in R. Sheaff and V. Peel (eds) *Managing Health Service Information Systems*. Buckingham, Open University Press.

Weick, K. E. (1985) Cosmos vs. chaos: sense and nonsense in electronic contexts, *Organizational Dynamics*, **14**: 51–64.

15 Conclusions

Paul Forte and Steve Cropper

Introduction

A definition of DSS, and the potential of such systems to inform, support analysis and promote deliberation was proposed in the second of the two introductory chapters. Ways in which the idea of DSS translates into practice have been illustrated in subsequent chapters through a series of case studies. The choice of case studies was deliberately eclectic in order to illustrate their potential application in a wide range of health management and planning circumstances. In two cases (care services for elderly people and managing maternity services), separate chapters reported how DSS have been applied to the same broad issue: these highlight how DSS can usefully differ within the same area of interest. Here we draw together and consider lessons learned from experience about how these systems might, in practice, enhance the decision making process.

Variety in DSS

Our definition of DSS sought to encapsulate what is distinctive about DSS, highlighting the combination of information, analytical method and computing power as it is focused on specific management tasks. DSS reported in subsequent chapters have shared these characteristics while varying, to differing degrees, in their emphasis. In effect, the way the component characteristics are 'blended' can vary. This adaptability is an intrinsic feature of DSS, reflecting the need to design and implement systems, with both the management task and the local resources available for the decision making process clearly in mind.

The case studies have revealed a variety of design considerations:

- fit with management task or process;
- whether they are to be used with facilitation or directly by the end-user;
- flexibility and ergonomics of the system;
- the degree of control over the system the user can exert;
- the value that can be gained during different stages of its use;
- the emphasis placed on analytical power;
- compatibility with existing ways of structuring information and information technology.

Deliberation and analysis of relevant information

All of the DSS presented analyse information relevant to management tasks, although some have a wider scope than others. In general, those DSS which are 'data rich' (such as those described by Bradley in Chapter 7, and the GIS presented by Clarke and Clarke in Chapter 3) offer a wider source of information to draw on and, therefore, a potentially wider range of tasks to be addressed. However, along with that flexibility comes more responsibility for the user in directing analyses and drawing out the relevant information. By contrast, more closely focused systems (such as those presented by Meldrum *et al.* in Chapter 8 and Beech *et al.* in Chapter 9) tend to offer 'built in' analytical capabilities targeted on the management task being addressed, and to demand and use *particular* information. The DSS described by Lees and Macfarlane (Chapter 11) lies somewhere between these: the database they describe focuses on a defined area of interest which, in turn, helps to steer management analysis, enquiry and action.

Each DSS described can be used in ways which promote discussion and debate among participants in the decision making process. Apart from paper-based reports, computer-based systems are now sufficiently fast, approachable and responsive that they can be used directly in meetings to help 'live' debate and the questioning and exploration of alternative options. Some of the systems take particular advantage of that ability, especially those where facilitation is regarded as important in the effective use of the DSS and where the subject emphasizes the development of organizational structure and processes. Thus for Cropper (Chapter 13) and Wolstenholme and Crook (Chapter 12), using the systems directly with managers is an essential part of the process. For other systems it is highly desirable at least in some stages of the application. For example, Bowen and Forte (Chapters 4 and 5) and Keenan (Chapter 6) describe systems where the immediacy of its use and ability to capture and test ideas directly with users – either singly or in groups – makes an important contribution to debate. Interestingly, some systems can thus create opportunities for participants who are less accustomed to working with more formal, written reports to engage in the process more fully. For the other systems, the manner of use is left implicit, or the system is treated quite explicitly as providing 'backroom' analytical support. For example, Worthington's work on health service queues, and the analyses by Beech *et al.* of continuity of care seem to operate more in this way.

Complexity and uncertainty

An important claim for DSS is that they enhance the decision making process in complex and ambiguous situations where it is difficult to reach a reasoned decision. The review of the changing nature of health services and health service organizations in Chapter 1 highlighted the forms of complexity and the pervasive uncertainty that managers have to deal with. The search for structure in and insight into the nature of the origins and consequences of what are often puzzling and frustrating issues, is a crucial part of the decision making process and one where DSS can make a unique contribution. Solutions – or, more precisely, frameworks helpful in identifying or exploring possible solutions – were found in several cases for specific issues where people had otherwise focused on a very narrow range of options or were unable to address the problem 'rationally' in the first place. Cropper with his objective-setting examples, Bowen and Forte with the Business Planning Model, Worthington on the waiting lists analyses, and the examples offered by Clarke and Clarke in addressing issues of equity in health care provision all emphasize this characteristic of DSS and illustrate the range of levels – from the individual to the organization – at which DSS can be applied.

The majority of DSS lead to the quantification of the relationships between variables involved. In doing so, they sharpen a sense of uncertainty about the future – or potential futures – and the implications arising from them: they also provide a means by which such uncertainty can be considered and managed. An important contribution DSS make is to help establish data and information requirements, thus making the hunt for the 'right' (i.e. useful) supporting material much simpler. The effect is to make the decision making basis more systematic and its basis more explicit. In principle, then, it becomes more accountable, as Keenan strongly argued in describing the use of DSS in capital investment appraisal. Some might regard this as anything but an 'enhancement' of decision making if, for example, conflicting views slow down, or otherwise disrupt the process. That depends on the point of view, but it is not a function of DSS *per se*, any more than it is a symptom of the political environment within which the decisions are being made. In any case, DSS in skilled hands provide one means of working through the politics (Eden 1991; Phillips and Phillips 1994).

Computer-assisted modelling methods

Some of the DSS portrayed here take advantage of database/information systems which are directly accessible by managers. Increasingly, such systems have built-in DSS functions; the case studies illustrate how they can be used in planning and management (e.g. Bradley, Lees and Macfarlane). Others are more clearly specialist tools – often 'stand-alone' systems – and are more commonly used in a facilitated management support fashion. All of them, however, profit from being computer-based. There are several reasons why DSS developers want to take advantage of the speed and power that this offers. Clearly, where there are complex underlying mathematical models – and especially coupled with handling large amounts of data – the DSS would not be possible otherwise. The spatial interaction models described by Clarke and Clarke, and the resource analysis calculations of Lees and Macfarlane are good examples. Another reason is that computers enable the DSS to be used in 'real time' to facilitate discussion where changes and their results can be recalculated and viewed instantly, and in high quality presentation formats (graphs, maps, simulations, etc.). The Balance of Care model (Forte and Bowen), the waiting list models (Worthington), and objective-setting using COPE (Cropper) are examples where this feature is particularly important.

As basic modelling platforms – spreadsheets, outliners, databases, simulation packages, etc. – become more widely used, then the technical capacity to develop *ad hoc* or 'throwaway' decision support systems will become more commonplace. However, the technical development of information systems and modelling software tends to happen more rapidly than the capacity of the managers and organizational structures to absorb and make use of the new versatility and functionality offered (as noted by Clayden and Croft, Chapter 14). This is a point also made by Eden (1991: 205), who argues that

> it is often presumed that simply using computers to support groups should increase productivity – after all they are fast processors of data, they have an immense power to conduct analyses. However, alongside these optimistic views is the experience managers have of the inadequacy of their information systems and decision support systems. [They] are concerned that computers will get in the way of conducting efficient meetings.

The introduction of computer-based support systems into management processes still remains a highly contingent process. Decisions about when and how it is appropriate to introduce systems *ad hoc* or to institutionalize computer-based support systems depend immediately on the receptiveness of the organization and managers to such devices. This depends, in turn, on two things: first, on the forms of investment – cultural, technical and intellectual – that have already been made in the decision processes; and second, on the value that can be seen to flow immediately from the DSS. This value can also be considered in terms of the mix of cultural, technical and intellectual contributions to the capacity to undertake a management task.

Exploring options for future action

The ability to generate a variety of different options and then explore their implications as possible futures is one of the most important and powerful arguments for DSS. In experiential terms, the ability to structure a variety of options and to trace through their implications (and the process of doing so) gives decision makers a greater sense of control, and, in equal measure, a sense of excitement and 'fun'. Decision makers may have a wide variety of reasons for wanting to examine options for future action. Handling uncertainty has already been mentioned, but the ability to recognize and take on board a wide range of views of different interested parties (such as in examining capital planning options or elderly care services) is also important. DSS can either be used 'reactively' to examine the potential implications of already given proposals, or more 'proactively' to set an agenda for action. As Smithin and Eden (1986) suggest,

> You should look forward to using a decision support system and not see it as a chore. When you do something you should get some response, and as you use it there should be a sense of becoming skilled with the tool in the prosecution of a task. You should not be worried if there are things that you do not understand, nor should you 'live in fear' of causing a disaster. You should be able to design and plan your own actions, and you should be able to learn about this as you go along . . . Overall, you should feel that you have some control of the system, and that when using it, you are getting some informed and relevant help with your task.
>
> (Smithin and Eden 1986: 150)

DSS enable managers to explore and learn about the future implications of their actions without having to invest large amounts of resources in building or developing new services first and awaiting the consequences later. As Keenan (Chapter 6) illustrates, increasingly there are calls for a more thorough examination of the benefits and costs associated with such projects to avoid them becoming redundant before they are even completed. Whereas one or two options might have been developed for a project in the past, DSS offer (in theory) a wider set of possibilities to be considered.

Transferability

In terms of their translation to other locations, there is also variation in the DSS reported here. The majority are available commercially – some with and some without facilitation – which immediately implies that there is potential for their application in different localities. There is a variety of geographical information systems and practice-based information systems commercially available; those systems with a more specific modelling focus (presented by Meldrum and colleagues, Keenan, and Forte and Bowen) also come with facilitation as an integral part of the package. The software employed by Cropper and by Wolstenholme and Crook is also available. These 'DSS generators' are less commonly found than, say, spreadsheets, and while they are highly accessible software, their effective use also requires an understanding of the underlying modelling method. In this sense, training or facilitation is likely to be valuable.

The book contains examples of different types of application. In all cases, DSS have provided *computer-based* support to single or several managers. However, it is worth distinguishing between the application of generic modelling platforms and task-specific models. Cropper (Chapter 13) and Wolstenholme and Crook (Chapter 12) each describe highly flexible support systems, capable of use in addressing many different types of issue. A DSS only becomes fully defined when there is a task-specific model, and the challenge for Cropper and for Wolstenholme and Crook is to build such a system together with the managers who will use it. Others come 'ready prepared' (e.g. Meldrum *et al.*, Keenan, Forte and Bowen, Beech *et al.*, Bowen and Forte) and thus immediately provide specific guidance on how to describe the management task. This is appropriate where tasks are shared by whole classes of manager: business planning, for example, is a management task shared across health service providers (and purchasers, too). The need to understand types and rates of activity, historical and future prospects, resource consumption, and so forth, is also a generic part of management, and suggests support systems which could be applicable in many settings.

Such more focused systems might serve to spread 'best practice' in conducting business planning, or to ensure that central guidance on required practice in capital investment appraisal is capable of being operationalized, for example. Wolstenholme and Crook (Chapter 12) also emphasize the value of their system dynamics model to accumulate the learning and insight of many different users. At the same time, experience of information system development and implementation suggests that local circumstances are critical in determining the success of such systems. Not all providers would use the same 'norms' of staffing to activity, for example, or be at the stage where they can include 'internal trading' between directorates in a business planning model. The ability to be able to tailor systems to such circumstances – rather than building them from scratch on each occasion – is therefore critical and a necessary feature of DSS. Apart from anything else there is the time and resources saved by not reinventing the wheel on each occasion.

The more open information systems (e.g. Bradley's primary care database, and Clarke and Clarke's GIS) are highly portable, but the more specialized models can also travel: the Balance of Care system, for example, has been used in different locations not only in the UK, but also in other European countries (the organizational circumstances might be different, but the underlying planning issue being addressed remains fundamentally the same). Some of the other DSS are only fairly recently developed (notably, the maternity models) and have not yet got an extensive track record of transferability other than that obtained from piloting. The Business Planning Model is an example where successful use in one acute unit has not yet been followed by applications elsewhere. Why this might happen to DSS is further considered below.

Who uses DSS?

Paradoxically, the flexibility of DSS to adapt from place to place or over time makes it difficult to categorize the nature of applications rigidly; a given DSS might be applied in different ways given different circumstances. Even if it appears to be very specifically designed to fulfil a particular function and with a particular end-user in mind, the chances are that in one case the manager will be perfectly happy to operate the system without outside help while, in another, the responsibility for using the system might be delegated to an external facilitator or an in-house analyst. Other DSS are designed to be used by an intermediary or facilitator in the first place. Finally, the question of who the operator is may change over time; as experience is gained with applications and the system itself develops (as reported by Keenan and by Cropper), facilitators can withdraw leaving the manager as both user and operator.

Not all of the DSS reported involved direct interaction between a manager and the computer system itself. In the case of the maternity workforce planning system reported by Meldrum *et al.* (Chapter 8), the system is designed for the manager to be the analyst: this is also the case with the systems outlined by Bowen and Forte (Chapter 5), Bradley (Chapter 7), Beech *et al.* (Chapter 9) and Lees and Macfarlane (Chapter 11). Others, such as Forte and Bowen (Chapter 4), Keenan (Chapter 6) and Worthington (Chapter 10) report on applications which involve less direct control, use or interaction between manager and computer. In the cases outlined by Worthington, for example, the analyst uses the computer; first for simple statistical analysis and then for implementation of a more specialist DSS to help understand the nature of queueing problems and to test a range of possible interventions to improve the performance of the system. Use of the computer is, if not exactly in the backroom is, at least 'somewhere in the corridor' – one stage removed from the management process.

The Business Planning Model, presented by Bowen and Forte, is in some ways similar to this, although they also report on its use as a training vehicle which the managers themselves use directly (this is not exclusive to the Business Planning Model; it is something which many DSS could be adapted to do). Then there are the more obviously facilitated systems: the account by Cropper (Chapter 13) of using a DSS in objective-setting; that of Forte and Bowen on planning long-term care for elderly people; and the system dynamics analysis of the implications of changes in community care funding by Wolstenholme and Crook (Chapter 12) all strongly emphasize the role of facilitated decision support. There are a number of reasons for adopting this approach: the inherent complexity in the modelling process; practical reasons of operating with large groups of people; or a wish to bring in someone from outside the organization who is seen as 'independent'. Such systems enter the decision making process directly and shape its form. Indeed, they provide a means of creating new types of decision making process – and experience.

The experience of using DSS

The case studies highlight a range of different types and experience of DSS applications. In applications of the Balance of Care system, for example, the facilitated workshop led to the adoption of the system and the embedding of its general principles in planning services at the operational as well as strategic level. At the general practice level, Bradley (Chapter 7) reports on its routine use in clinical decision support as well as practice management. In capital planning, Keenan reports that the DSS he presents has had a role to play in investments totalling £900 million.

If, then, there are so many apparent advantages in using DSS, why have they not been more widely embraced by NHS managers? One reason may lie in the difficulty of defining the concept; there are probably as many definitions as there are users of computer-based information so, in a broad sense, nearly everyone *is* using (or claims to be using) a 'DSS'. Many will not be using DSS as we have defined the term. The technological image of DSS remains a powerful one; and there is still a sense among managers that anything to do with computers and information is the realm of the 'information unit' rather than of direct assistance to the managers themselves; more so if it involves any sophisticated manipulation of data. In part, some of the blame lies with DSS developers who, in the past especially, focused too much on the intellectual and/or technical dimensions of systems without paying enough attention to its organizational context and the nature of a productive relationship between computer and user. This involves more than just finding out the basic issue to be addressed, but goes right through to the implementation stage of the DSS: who is likely to use it, in what contexts, and for what purposes. Smithin and Eden (1986) make the point well:

> If [users] attribute the wrong characteristics to the software then they will become dissatisfied and frustrated because the system 'will not make sense'. More importantly, they will not be able to make use of the specific advantages that are available when using a machine to aid thinking . . . This implies that in the design of any decision support system it is important to construct an appropriate role for the machine, to present the system in such a way that the user is able to

> construe it as an 'intelligent' machine rather than as an intelligent person.
>
> (Smithin and Eden 1986: 144)

No one likes to be 'shown up' by a computer-based system, particularly if it contains a clear exposition of their own particular task domain. The potential value of a DSS application might thus be played down, ignored, or rubbished (perhaps more justifiably so if it is viewed as a technology in search of an application). While many of the case studies described DSS that are familiar, at least in the way the model represents knowledge and information, others (Cropper, Worthington and Wolstenholme and Crook, in particular) introduced novel, if intuitive, modelling disciplines. Even the familiar can be threatening, however. This may be simply to do with one's sense of keyboard competence. Or it might surface when one's judgements, made under great uncertainty and taking into account many different factors, are encapsulated in a single figure entered publicly into a computer model in front of a group of peers. Working up a scenario developed for exploratory 'what if' analysis is very different from the usual experience of planning meetings where parties often come to the table with 'a worked-up position'.

Suchman argues that 'Every human tool relies upon, and reifies, some underlying conception of the activity that it is designed to support' (1987: 3). The debate in the field of decision theory between substantive and procedural rationality, outlined in Chapter 1, has been reflected in the development of modelling methods and DSS. In many early examples, they were seen as sophisticated and optimizing mathematical 'solution finders'. With hindsight this can be seen to be implausible, guaranteed to provoke a negative reaction among managers. Instead, DSS are now increasingly seen as devices for learning, reflecting a developing understanding of decision making, e.g. Mintzberg (1989). But this, too, means that expectations of the status, purpose and method of exploratory DSS must be clear.

While at one level there may be a broad, if somewhat poorly articulated, recognition of a 'need' for DSS-type instruments for management support and training, there remains the important, and non-trivial, issue of how to get DSS embedded into an organization in the first place. Clearly, this will not always be a relevant issue as not all DSS are designed or expected to be used on a continuing basis. Assuming that is not the case, though, identifying the factors is important.

The application focus of the system is one of these. The case studies are again revealing. Where a DSS addressing a specific management issue also has a clear, logical structure and prescribed process of use (e.g. Meldrum *et al.*), then guidance that explains the concept and its application potential to a non-expert user can be produced in the expectation that users will be able to use it with little or no further assistance. At the other extreme, where the system is more data-rich and less decision-focused (such as those described by Bradley, and by Lees and Macfarlane) users will get information out of the system at a level of detail and analysis they feel comfortable with – there is no prescribed method, although methods may emerge as custom and practice. In the middle ground, where systems are focused on a particular issue but nevertheless remain highly flexible in use, then it can be more difficult for non-expert users to get started. The level of commitment is crucial. If managers are actively searching for solutions to a particular problem, then, as in the examples presented by Worthington, the learning curve is not such a problem. Where there is a vested interest in the process, there will probably be an equal concern to ensure the system can be sustained, and managers may well be willing to take on 'the system' (or some version of it) as a management method under their own steam. Where there is a less pressing concern to improve management performance, then there may be more 'selling' of the concept to be done. Thus Bowen and Forte report an example where, at least initially, the principal driver behind the development of the DSS (and its training and education application) was a demand from senior management for greater business planning competency. With Balance of Care (Forte and Bowen), one difficulty which has been encountered is getting managers' attention in the first place to appreciate the potential of the application. In such circumstances, finding a 'champion' – of the system, of the process or method of implementation, or of an outcome which the system might promote – is critical to take-up of a DSS. Champions might be an individual or group within an organization, or perhaps an organization as a whole. These act essentially as a conduit for learning, a way of working out what is possible; they provide a means of demonstrating a 'real' application to other individuals or organizations. Individual champions are also very important for maintaining a momentum within an organization, especially if the DSS involves externally based facilitators.

Future agenda

The premise that 'better' information leads to 'good' decision making was a fundamental concept of NHS reforms, and much emphasis was placed on the development of data and information systems to achieve that end. The NHS R&D initiative has further strengthened the push for 'informed' decision making at all levels. However, the point has already been made in previous chapters, that technological innovation is not itself enough: people and their organizational settings must be included prominently in the equation. We believe that DSS as we have defined and described them have a role here, although they may not be destined to become part of the mainstream management decision making unless two important aspects are addressed. These are:

- organizations must develop corporate and individual competency in the use of information, and improve their understanding of how decision support systems can enhance decision making processes; and
- those who develop DSS must foster a greater appreciation of the social and organizational settings in which their systems will operate.

Progress in IT is not dependent on what happens in health service management: the issue is how the NHS can assimilate its potential in useful, productive applications – lessons from past experience of information system developments in the NHS provide cautionary tales here. While DSS will undoubtedly seek to exploit continuing developments in informatics, it is more important to emphasize the role of DSS in promoting the development of decision frameworks and a culture of decision making which is informed, thoughtful and procedurally clear.

Developing organizational and managerial competency

This theme has recurred throughout the book. Unfortunately, 'education' in practice often tends to mean basic computer skills instruction: while increasingly necessary, this is not sufficient. Many managers also need to develop skills in the appreciation of information: specifying and designing it, analysing it and applying it convincingly to their management tasks. In the past, a lack of even basic analysis could always be attributed to the impossibility of getting hold of the right data in time; increasingly this is less of an issue. The question has shifted from 'Where do you get the data?' to 'Getting data is no longer the problem, but what do you want them for?' This move towards a more critical appreciation of information for management is where the focus of basic and continuing management education should lie.

DSS can assist in this in two ways. First, involvement in a DSS application can help managers to learn about the services they are managing and understand the complexities involved – this extends their substantive knowledge. Second, DSS bring general analytical frameworks and methods which can then be applied in other circumstances – this extends managers' procedural competencies. We are not advocating that all managers must become expert modellers or computer programmers in their own right; rather that a greater understanding of the analytical approaches DSS can bring to management tasks and learning will prove beneficial.

It is in the interests of organizations as much as individuals to consider their investment policy. If it is not desirable for all managers to be expert information analysts, then neither is it healthy for expertise to reside solely in one individual. In some midpoint between the two there might be a core team with good analytical capabilities working in conjunction with other managers who have at least basic skills; specialists (with specific remits and objectives) might be brought in as required from outside the organization. This would maintain an 'organizational memory' while, at the same time, enabling fresh ideas to be imported from time to time. In the midst of this DSS could be used both to cover gaps in competencies and support education and organizational development.

Perhaps in the long term, as Clayden and Croft suggest, technological developments will themselves release managers from the need to develop their own understanding of how to use the information available. In the meantime, however, DSS are an increasingly important means of capitalizing on investments in information and of making the most of information that is available. Where DSS are facilitated, the costs will be higher, but might be recouped through improved organizational competence and through direct improvements in management of services. DSS can also help managers to use their own expertise and understanding in ensuring that the health services and organizations for which they are responsible are appropriately defined and enabled to perform. At a time when expectations of managers and decision makers in health services are increasingly great, DSS offer a means of strengthening and enhancing the decision making process.

References

Eden, C. (1991) A framework for thinking about group decision support systems (GDSS), *Group Decision Negotiation*, 1: 199–218.

Mintzberg, H. (1989) The manager's job, in H. Mintzberg, *Mintzberg on Management*. New York, Free Press.

Phillips, L. D. and Phillips, M. C. (1994) Facilitated work groups: theory and practice, *Journal of the Operational Research Society*, 44: 533–49.

Smithin, T. and Eden, C. (1986) Computer decision support for senior managers: encouraging exploration, *International Journal of Man–Machine Studies*, 25: 139–52.

Suchman, L. A. (1987) *Plans and Situated Actions: the Problem of Human Machine Communication*. Cambridge, Cambridge University Press.

Index

AAH Meditel, 130
Abel-Smith, B., 73
accountability, and decision making, 6–7
Ackermann, F., 26, 261
Ackoff, R. L., 251
active decision support, in primary care consultations, 135–8
acute hospital management, 41, 86–102
  Business Planning Model, 41, 87–8, 89–102
  GP referrals, 86
ageing population, 72, 73
AIDS (Acquired Immune Deficiency Syndrome), and spatial epidemiology, 65
Allan, K., 143
Anderson, D. R., 179
Ansoff, I., 263
Armstrong, D., 45
Audit Commission, 5, 13

Bailey, N. T. J., 184
Baines, D., 77
Balance of Care (BoC) system, 40–1, 71, 74–84, 292–3, 294, 296
  applications, 78–82
  care options model, 76, 77–8
  population model, 76–7
  and respite care, 79–80, 81, 82
  workshop programme, 80–2
balancing feedback loop, in system dynamics, 227
barcoding, and decision support systems in neurosciences, 127, 202–3, 210
Barnes, M., 77
Barrett, S., 9, 13
Belton, V., 23, 116
Bennett, A. R., 89
Bensaou, M., 274
Bensley, D. C., 20, 21, 22
Bentley, D., 251
Berkhout, F., 45
Berrington, A., 72
Bertuglia, C. S., 58
Bevan, G., 45
Bhuptani, B., 24
Birkin, M., 53, 59
Blackham, R. B., 249
'block' contracts, setting prices, 200
Boden, P., 60
Boldy, D., 25, 78–9
Bond, J., 76
Bowen, T., 75, 79
Brahimi, M., 184
Brailer, D. J., 25
British Medical Journal, 129, 137
Brown, P. J., 46

Bryson, J., 6, 256
Bullen, N., 51
Bunn, D., 26
Business Case, 103, 106–22
  option appraisal, 112, 113–18
  risk assessment methodology, 118–21
  variables
    demand, 108, 110
    departmental relationships, 109, 110
    performance, 108–9, 110
    planning currency, 108
Business Planning Model, 41, 87–8, 89–102, 289, 293
  application, 93–100
  impact on training programmes, 102
  training exercise, 100–1
business plans/planning, 216, 292
  and practice management, 138
Business Process Re-engineering, 222

Canvin, R., 75
capital investment appraisal, 41–2, 103–22, 289, 294
  and Business Case, 103, 106–22
  and the case for change, 107–13
  and CBA (cost-benefit analysis), 106
  decision support for, 105–7
  investment decision making, 103–4
  and PFI (Private Finance Initiative), 104–5, 118–21
  recent developments in, 104–5
care pathways, 246
  coronary care, 20–2, 23, 26
Carlson, E. D., 19
Carpenter, B., 202
Carstairs, V., 76
CBA (cost-benefit analysis), and capital investment appraisal, 106
CD-ROMs, reference sources for GPs on, 137
Challis, L., 74
Chalmers, I., 137
Champney, J., 222
Changing Childbirth (Department of Health), 126
Checkland, P. B., 221
'citizen juries', 6
Clarke, A., 8
Clarke, G. P., 59
Clarke, M., 59, 60
Clayden, A. D., 275
clinical directorates, resource management issues in, 200–1
clinical DSS (CDS)
  evaluating, 29–30
  vs. management DSS, 22–3, 28
  CLINIQUE (computer-based DSS), and queue management, 187–9, 193, 196
cognitive mapping, 247–9, 251–5, 257–60
Common Basic Specification, 277
community care, 7, 40, 216, 217–43
  costs, 225–7, 239, 240, 241
  financial processes in, 235
  and GPs, 129
  management 'flight simulator', 218, 235, 236, 242
  management task, 218–19
  numbers of people in, 239, 240, 241
  people processes in, 232–4
  project management, personal DSS for, 251–5
  and system dynamics modelling, 224–43
    Model 1 (NHS–SSD interface), 217–18, 224–32
    Model 2 (SSD services), 218, 232–43
  waiting lists, 227–8, 229, 230, 231, 233, 237–41
Community Care Act (1990), 73, 74
community information systems (CIS), 24
computer-assisted modelling, 20, 289–90
constructs, in cognitive mapping, 247–8, 251–2, 257, 260
contract prices, in neurosciences, 200–1, 202
Corless, R., 249
coronary care pathways model, 20–2, 23, 26
Coyle, R. G., 222
Craft, A., 53
Crail, M., 9
'crisis management', 11

Crisp, R., 9
Cropper, S., 247, 256, 257
Crosby, B. C., 6
Cross, M., 24

Date, C. J., 276
Dawson, D., 8
Dawson, S., 260
De Geus, A. P., 221
Dean, J. W., 9
decision analysis-based DSS, 23
decision making
  capital investment, 103–4
  complexity, 3–7
  greater utilization of data in, 280–1
  and information, 272
  investments in, 11–16
  knowledge-based approaches to, 281
  local, 5, 6, 39
  and organizational boundaries, 5–6
  procedural rationality in, 9–10, 295
  and risk-taking, 281
  substantive rationality in, 8–9, 10, 295
  theories, 7–11
decision support tool, Business Planning Model as, 100
delays in planning, and system dynamics, 219–20
democracy, and decision making, 6–7
Densham, P. J., 53
Department of the Environment, 58
Department of Health, 104, 126, 145, 165, 178, 182, 276
Department of Health and Social Security (DHSS), 4, 218
dependency data, elderly care services, 75
descriptive theories of decision making, 7, 10–11
DEUS (DEcision Utopian Support), 284
diabetes, active decision support in management of, 135–7
doctors
  distance consultations with, 283
  and outpatient clinics, 189, 190–1, 193–4
  see also GPs (general practitioners)
Donabedian, A., 138
Dowell, J. S., 140
Dowie, J., 23
DSS (decision support systems), 4, 10–35
  Balance of Care (BoC) system, 41, 71, 83, 292–3, 294, 296
  Business Case, 103, 106–22
  Business Planning Model, 41, 87–8, 89–102, 293, 298
  and capital investment appraisal, 41–2, 103–22, 289, 294
  case for, 125–6, 291
  changes in implementation, 283–4
  cognitive mapping, 247–9
  complexity and uncertainty, 24–5, 289
  computer-assisted modelling, 20, 289–90
  defining, 19–22, 287
  deliberation and analysis of relevant information, 288–9
  design, 30–3, 287–8
  embedding and diffusing, 29
  evaluating contribution of, 29–30
  experience of using, 294–6
  facilitated decision support, 294, 298
  generators, 292
  IPR (Individual Performance Review), 216, 247, 260–4
  management use of, 32–3, 290, 293, 294–6, 297–8
  MatS maternity staffing model, 145–64
  midwifery services, 165–70, 293
  models, 25–6
    computer-based, 26–9
    development process, 31–2
  in neurosciences, 127, 199–211
  and operational management, 126–7
  options for future action, 291
  and outpatient services, 127
  and PFI (Private Finance Initiative), 105
  predictive models, 215
  in primary care, 126, 128–44
  for project management, 249–55
  project methodology, 180–1
  qualitative modelling methods, 215
  and queue management, 177–98

for review of Trust strategic direction, 256–60
spatial, 40, 43–68, 53
stand-alone vs. integrated systems, 31
task-specific models, 292
transferability of, 291–3
users, 293–4
variety in, 287–93
and workforce planning, 126–7
see also clinical DSS; management DSS

Eden, C., 10, 24, 26, 27–8, 29, 221, 246, 247, 248, 253, 255, 256, 257, 289, 290, 291, 294–5
education and changing technology, 281–2, 284, 297
Edwards, N., 9
EIS/MIS (executive or management information systems), 277, 282
elderly care services, 40–1, 71–85
and the ageing population, 72, 73
Balance of Care (BoC) system, 40–1, 71, 74–84, 292–3, 294, 296
costs of, 72–3
dependency data, 75, 76–7
informal carers, 72, 75, 77
mentally ill patients, capital investment appraisal, 113–21
and NHS reforms, 73
respite services, 72, 79–80
strategic planning for, 73–5, 83–4
see also community care
electronic medical records (EMR), 130–1, 134–8
Ellis, B. W., 182
e-mail (electronic mail), 138, 273
emergency admissions, and the Business Planning Model, 91, 93
'environment of inquiry', 27
executive or management information systems (EIS/MIS), 277, 282

FCE (finished consultant episode), 208
Ferlie, E., 4, 5
Ferreira de Oliveiro, M. J., 281
Fienberg, S. E., 59
Finlay, P., 24, 26
Flanagan, H., 260
Flood, R. L., 221
Forte, P., 13, 75, 79
Foster, I., 203
Frandji, B., 277
Frankel, S., 182
Freemantle, N., 8
Friend, J. K., 6, 10

Gass, S. I., 25, 31
Gatrell, A. C., 53
geographical constraints, removal of, 282
geography of health care reforms, 44–6
geriatric care facilities, spatial modelling for, 60–3
GIS (geographical information systems), 40, 43, 46–53, 288, 291
data linkage, 51–2
data storage, retrieval and display, 46–51
geocoding, 52
modelling, 44, 54–65
data synthesis and integration, 58–9
data transformation, 56–8
impact analysis, 60–5
microsimulation, 54, 59
spatial interaction, 54–9, 60–5
updating and forecasting, 59–60
network analysis, 52–2
and spatial analysis, 53
and spatial modelling, 65–8
Glennerster, H., 219
Goves, J. R., 143
GPs (general practitioners)
decision support for, 126, 128–44
and electronic medical information, 137
and electronic medical records (EMR), 130–1
fundholding, 129, 131, 139
growth of computing, 129–33
New Contract for, 128–9, 130
and practice management, 133, 138–41
referrals, 86
and the Business Planning Model, 89, 90, 94, 95, 96, 97, 98

geographical variations in, 45–6
and resource management policies, 228
see also primary care
Greenhalgh and Company Ltd, 138
Griffiths report, 4–5, 219
Guardian, 108

Hale, D., 51
Ham, C., 6, 8
Hammer, M., 222
Harmon, M. M., 3
Harrison, S., 273
Haynes, R., 43
Hays, S. M., 54
Hayward, J., 8
health care reforms, geography of, 44–6
Health Economics Research Group, 279
'Health of the Nation' strategy, 7, 20
health promotion, 7
healthcare resource groups, *see* HRGs
Henwood, M., 73
Hickling, A., 10
Hirschfield, A., 51
HISS (Hospital Information Support System), 24, 277, 278, 279–80
HM Treasury, 107
HMSO, 7
Hobbs, R., 130
HOMS (head of midwifery services), 147–8, 150, 152, 153, 155
Hood, C., 5
'hospital at home' scheme, 101
Hospital Information Support System, *see* HISS
hospital outpatient services, *see* outpatient services
hospital waiting lists, *see* waiting lists
hospitalization rates, and spatial modelling, 63–5, 66–7
House of Commons Health Committee, 165
on Maternity Services, 145, 165
Howarth, F. P., 130
HRGs (healthcare resource groups), 127, 199, 201, 202, 204, 205, 208
Hundley, V. A., 146
Hunter, D., 73
Huxham, C. S., 256, 257

IM & T strategy, 14, 15
image data, 282
impact analysis, and spatial modelling, 60–5
Impallomeni, M., 72
IMT (information management and technology) training, 274–5
individual care plans, 246
individual risks and interventions, evaluation of, 283
information
developing use of, 280–2
external sources, 282
implementing information support, 272, 278–80
managers' attitude to, 273
processing needs and capabilities, 274
use of, 272, 273–6
see also technology
Information Management Group, 15, 143
information systems, and Resource Management Initiative (RMI), 279
information technology (IT), 272, 279–80, 283, 297
intellectual domain of investment, 11, 12, 14, 15–16
'intelligent GIS', 53
intensive care unit (ICUs) management, DSS for, 181–2, 195, 196
investment, domains of, 11–16
IPR (Individual Performance Review), 216, 247, 260–4
IT (information technology), 272, 279–80, 283, 297
iterative proportional fitting, 59

Jackson, M. C., 221
Jennings, D., 7
Jones, A., 52
Jung, C. G., 33

Keen, J., 14, 15, 23
Kinston, W., 273

Kirby, R., 9
Kleindorfer, P. R., 7
Knibbs, J., 257
knowledge-based systems, 281, 282
Knox, P. L., 54
Kroll, D., 166, 167

Lagergren, M., 23, 25, 26
Laing, W., 74
Lancet, *The*, 137
Lane, D. C., 221
Leopold, J., 4
Lewis, J., 219
Lilford, R. J., 23
local decision making, 5, 6, 39
Lock, C., 11, 13
Lucey, T., 139

McClean, S. T., 210
McConnell, E., 263
McGrew, A. G., 7
McKee, M., 8
McMahon, L., 9, 13
McMoran, S., 137
MacVicar, J., 146
Maguire, D. J., 46
management DSS
  evaluating, 29, 30
  vs. clinical DSS, 22–3, 28
  vs. MIS, 23–4
management training, 281–2
managers, use of DSS, 32–3, 290, 293, 294–6, 297–8
March, J. G., 7, 8
Martin, D., 54
MatS maternity staffing model, 145–64
  applying the model, 152–61
  building the model, 149–50
  tables of results, 158–61
  testing the model, 149, 150
  understanding maternity services, 148–9
Mayer, R. T., 3
Maynard, A., 8
'means–ends' modelling technique, 247, 253, 256, 265
Mechanic, D., 9
medical publications, electronic, 137
medical records
  electronic medical records (EMR), 130–1, 134–8
  traditional records, 133–4
Meldrum, P., 149
Metcalfe, L., 5
microsimulation, in spatial modelling, 54, 59
Midwifery, 164
midwifery (maternity) services, 126–9, 293
  antenatal care, 152–3, 171, 172, 174, 175
  community, 146, 151, 160, 161
  continuity of care/carer, 166, 167, 170, 171–5
  DOMINO, 147, 156, 157, 159, 160, 161, 162
  home, 146, 147, 156, 157, 159, 161
  HOMS (head of midwifery services), 147–8, 150, 152, 153, 155
  hospital, 146, 147, 151, 158–9, 161
    dependent inputs, 168–9
  intrapartum care, 155–8, 172, 173
  MatS maternity staffing model, 145–64
  modelling approach to, 147–8
  named midwife system, 126, 165, 166, 175
  non-hospital dependent inputs, 168
  planning, 145–7
    continuity of care, 165–76
  policy inputs, 169
  postnatal care, 146, 147, 171, 173, 174
  staffing costs, 158–62
  team midwifery, 126, 166–7, 170–1
  working arrangements, 167
Millard, P. H., 210
Mintzberg, H., 10, 32–3, 295
Miquest project, 142–3
MIS, vs. management DSS, 23–4
modelling for prediction, 221
Mohan, J., 43, 44
Morgan, R. F., 276
Morgan, T., 23
Morris, N., 72
multimedia data, 282, 283
Muris, N., 14, 15
Murphy, C., 28
Murphy, M., 72

Nagel, S., 22
National Casemix Office, 201
National Steering Group on Costing, 201
Neil-Dwyer, G., 200
network analysis, in GIS (geographical information systems), 52–2
neurosciences, 199–211
  contract prices, 200–1, 202
  'expected' care profile, 210
  and HRGs (healthcare resource groups), 199, 201, 202, 204, 205
  identifying costs of care, 203–4, 208
  managing nursing resources, 201–2, 205–8, 209
  methods of data collection, 201–3
New Public Management, 5
NHS Corporate Data Administration, 277
NHS Data Model, 277
NHS Executive, *Capital Investment Manual*, 104, 107
NHS Executive Information Management Group, 279
NHS Management Executive, 6, 14, 15, 87, 184, 256
NHS R & D initiative, 296
Nicholson, D., 4
Nocon, A., 40, 74
normative theories of decision making, 7, 9–10
Norris, D. F., 29
nursing resource management, in neurosciences, 201–2, 205–8, 209

objective-setting, monitoring and review, 245–65
  DSS approach to, 247–9, 293
    IPR (individual performance review), 247, 260–4
  and 'improved quality', 245
Office for Public Management, 15
Openshaw, S., 46, 53
operational management, 126–7
ophthalmology clinics, queue management, 189–94
organizational boundaries
  in community care, 230
  and decision making, 5–6
  and strategic service planning, 40–1
  and system dynamics, 220
organizational competency, developing, 297–8
outpatient services, 41, 86
  and the Business Planning Model, 90–1, 93, 94, 95, 96, 97, 98, 99
  queue management, 127, 184–95, 196
    clinic build-up model, 191–2
    CLINIQUE model, 193
    spreadsheet model, 192–3
    vicious-circle model, 190–1

Packwood, T., 15, 200, 279
passive decision support, in primary care consultations, 134–5
patient-focused technological developments, 282–3
Patient's Charter, 41, 87
  and the Business Planning Model, 92, 94, 99, 100, 101
  and outpatient services, 127
  and queue management, 178
  and waiting lists, 182, 189
Paul, R., 187
Pearson, N., 143
Peel, V., 13, 23
people processes, in system dynamics modelling, 232–4
performance indicators, spatial, 56–9, 65
performance targets, in capital investment appraisal, 109
Pettigrew, A. M., 13
PFI (Private Finance Initiative), and capital investment appraisal, 41, 104–5, 118–21
Phillips, L. D., 117, 289
Phillips, M. C., 117, 289
Phillips, D. R., 54
PHCT (primary health care teams), 129, 133
Pidd, M., 31
Pierskalla, W. P., 25
planning as learning, 221
plaster check clinics, queue management, 184–9
'policy stress', 6

polygon overlay, in GIS (geographical information systems), 51
practice management, decision support in, 133, 138–41, 291
prescribing activity, in practice management, 139–40
primary care
  decision support, 126, 128–44
    in the consultation, 133–8
    in practice management, 133, 138–41
    and wider planning of services, 133, 141–3
  and drug costs, 126
  see also GPs (general practitioners)
primary health care teams (PHCT), 129, 133
Prince, C., 137
Pringle, M., 130
Private Finance Initiative, *see* PFI (Private Finance Initiative)
private sector hospitals, and GIS (geographical information systems), 51
procedural rationality, in decision making, 9–10, 295
Procter, R. A., 252
Prodigy system, 137
project management, personal DSS for, 249–55
Promoting Better Health, 128
protocols, 246
purchaser–provider split
  and geographical factors, 44–6
  and resource management, 200
Purves, I., 137

quantitative simulation models, 222–3
queue management, 177–98, 289
  DSS approaches, 180–1
  hospital waiting lists, 182–4, 195, 196
  intensive care beds, 181–2, 195, 196
  outpatient services, 184–95, 196
  problems, 178–80
Queueing Theory, 179–80
Quinn, J. B., 265

Radford, J., 257
Ransford, J., 83
Ranson, S., 6
rationality, in decision making, 8–10
rationing health care, and decision making, 6, 9
Raynes, N., 219
RDBMS (relational database management systems), 276–8, 282
Rees, P. H., 60
reinforcing feedback loop, 229, 257
resource allocation, geography of, 44
resource management
  in a clinical directorate, 200–1
  and GP referrals, 228, 229
  using DSS for, 203–8
Resource Management Initiative (RMI), 15, 200, 278–9
Review Body on Nursing Staff, Midwives, Health Visitors and Professions Allied to Medicine, 150
Rhodes, R. A. W., 5
Richards, S., 5
Richmond, B., 223
Riley, K., 9
risk assessment metholodogy, in Business Case, 118–21
risk taking behaviour, by decision makers, 281
RMI (Resource Management Initiative), 15, 200, 278–9
Roginski, C., 249
Rosenhead, J., 221
Royston, G., 4, 23, 25, 43
Rudy, A., 273

Sager, T., 10
Sandwell Health Authority, 79
Sandwell Social Services Department, 79
Saper, R., 74
Sargent, J., 219
Schmaus, D., 202
Schuck, G., 27
Scotland, MatS maternity staffing model, 145–64
Scott-Morton, M. S., 280
Scottish Health Services Common Services Agency, 149

Scottish Needs Assessment Programme, 147
Scottish Office Home and Health Department, 145, 146
Secretary of State, 128
Secretary of State for Health, 4, 44
Secta Consulting, 75
Sellick, R., 257
Selznick, P., 245
Senge, P., 217, 223
sensitivity analysis, 26
Sharda, R., 29
Sharfman, M. P., 9
Sheaff, R., 13, 23, 282
Simon, H. A., 7, 8, 9, 10
Smith, J., 219
Smithin, T., 28, 291, 294–5
socio-organizational domain of investment, 11, 12, 13–14
SODA (Strategic Options Development and Analysis), 256, 261
spatial analysis, 53
spatial buffering, 51–2
spatial decision support systems, 53
spatial epidemiology, 65
spatial interaction modelling, 40, 54–9
  and impact analysis, 60–5
spatial queries, 52
spreadsheets, 275, 277
Spurgeon, P., 260
SSDs (social services directorates)
  and community care, 217, 224
    Model 1 (NHS–SSD interface), 217–18, 224–32
    Model 2 (SSD services), 218, 232–43
Starr, J., 72
Stevenson, R. W., 223
Stewart, J., 6
strategic direction, group DSS for NHS Trusts, 256–60
strategic service planning, 39–42
strategy–process links, and system dynamics, 222
substantive rationality, in decision making, 8–9, 10, 295
Suchman, L. A., 295
surgical treatments, technological developments in, 282
system dynamics modelling, 216, 219–23, 292, 293
  archetypes, 229–30
  balancing feedback loop, 227
  for community care, 216, 224–43
    financial processes, 235
    Model 1 (NHS–SSD interface), 217–18, 224–32
    Model 2 (SSD services), 218, 232–43
  flight simulator control panel, 218, 235, 236, 242
  identifying patterns and archetypes, 223
  ithink simulation, 230
  knowledge capture, 221
  mapping system structures, 221–2
  models as learning, 243
  people processes, 232–4
  and quantitative simulation models, 222–3
  reinforcing feedback loop, 228
  using for policy analysis, 223

Taket, A., 75
technological domain of investment, 11, 12–13, 14–15
technological innovations, 271, 272, 282–3, 290, 296
technology
  use of, 276–8
  see also information
Telford, W. A., 249, 261
Thomas, R. W., 43, 65
Thompson, L., 29
Tilzer, L., 202
Times, The, 58
'transaction' data, 276
transitional objects, in system dynamics, 221
Trusts
  and Business Case, 107
  and business planning, 87–9
  and decision making, 5, 6
  review of strategic direction, 256–60
  setting contract prices, 200–1
  and strategic service planning, 39
Turban, E., 19

Ungson, G. R., 264
unintended consequences, identifying, and system dynamics, 227–9

VAMP, 130
Venkatraman, N., 274
Vennix, J. A. M., 221
vicious circles, and objective-setting, 248, 259
Vincent, P., 53
virtual reality, 280–1

waiting lists, 41, 86, 179
 and the Business Planning Model, 90, 91, 92, 93, 94, 95, 96, 97, 98, 99
 and community care, 227–8, 228–9, 230, 231, 233, 237–41
 management of, 182–4, 195, 196
Walsh, J. P., 264
Ward, A., 52
Wattam, S., 7
Weaver, R. R., 30
Weick, K. E., 10, 281
Weilert, M., 202
West, R., 182
Wharton, F., 181
'what if' modelling, 26, 60–5, 68, 215
 and maternity services, 163, 168
 in neurosciences, 209–10
 and outpatient services, 127
 and practice management, 140–1
Whynes, D., 77
Williams, H. C. W. L., 54
Williams, J., 65
Williamson, P., 59
Wilsdon, T., 72
Wilson, A. G., 60
Wilson, M. J., 7
Wistow, G., 40, 77
Wolstenholme, E. F., 217, 221, 222, 223, 224, 227, 229, 230, 257
women on HRT, planning services for, 140–1, 142
workforce planning, and DSS (decision support systems), 126–7
Working for Patients, 44
World Health Organization, 76–7
World Wide Web (WWW), 282, 283
Worthington, D. J., 179, 182, 184
Wyatt, J., 19, 29
Wyatt, T. D., 140

Zuboff, S., 15